# Essays in
# CONTEMPORARY
# ECONOMIC
# PROBLEMS, 1986

# Essays in CONTEMPORARY ECONOMIC PROBLEMS, 1986

# The Impact of the Reagan Program

Phillip Cagan, editor
Eduardo Somensatto, associate editor

American Enterprise Institute
Washington, D.C.

The Library of Congress has cataloged this serial publication as follows:

Essays in contemporary economic problems.—1981/1982 ed.—
   Washington, D.C.: American Enterprise Institute for Public
   Policy Research, c1981.

   1 v. : ill. ; 23 cm.

   Annual.
   Vol. for 1981/82 has subtitle: Demand, productivity, and population.
   Continues: Contemporary economic problems.
   ISSN 0732-4308 = Essays in contemporary economic problems.

   1. United States—Economic policy—1981-   —Periodicals.   2. Economic policy—Periodicals.   3. Economics—Periodicals.   I. American
Enterprise Institute for Public Policy Research.

   HC106.7.A45a                330.973′005                82-642433
                                                      AACR 2 MARC-S

   ISBN 0-8447-3602-3 (cloth)
   ISBN 0-8447-3603-1 (paper)

   ISSN 0732-4308
   AEI Studies 443

*Printed in the United States of America*

# CONTENTS

# FOREWORD

When the Reagan administration took office in 1981 it promoted a new attitude toward the role of the federal government and initiated changes in the direction of public policy. This was particularly true for economic policy, for which the administration in its initial program proposed reducing the role of government regulation, containing inflation, lowering taxes, and cutting government expenditures. These changes in policy have had a major impact on the U.S. as well as the world economy.

In this latest issue of AEI's annual volume *Contemporary Economic Problems*, eleven scholars look at the economic adjustments to the Reagan program and its evolution. The studies examine the wide-ranging effects of the program, the only major omission being the development of budget deficits, a subject that was thoroughly reviewed in last year's volume.

The coverage of the studies ranges from the effects of lower business taxes on investment to the adjustments resulting from disinflation, displaced workers, foreign competition, and deregulation and to changes in the welfare, medical, and agricultural programs.

This series reaffirms AEI's commitment to clarifying important national economic issues with analysis by leading experts. Some of the past volumes have dealt not only with the economic effects of budget deficits but with disinflation and slower productivity growth. The volumes are edited by Phillip Cagan in association with Eduardo Somensatto. The American Enterprise Institute welcomes and greatly appreciates the contributions of the academic specialists who, along with our resident scholars, wrote these essays.

WILLIAM J. BAROODY, JR.
*President*
*American Enterprise Institute*

# Introduction

*Phillip Cagan*

In his first Economic Report to the Congress (February 1982), President Reagan set the domestic objectives for his administration: a cutback in the growth of government expenditures and progressive reduction of the federal deficit, a lowering of taxes, a reform and scaling back of government regulations, and the containment of inflation. These objectives reflected a concern that government had grown too big and its intervention in the private economy had gone too far, that many welfare programs were too expensive for the benefits received or were not targeted to the truly needy, and that inflation resulted from expansive monetary policies which could be reversed. Attainment of these objectives would revitalize the economy's potential for growth. The economic program was the most far-reaching in half a century.

The present volume places the Reagan program in historical perspective and assesses the results after the first five years. Eleven studies, each of which opens with a detailed summary of its topic, analyze the adjustments in the economy to administration policies and to related developments and policy initiatives in the government and the private sector. The authors discussed their work in several joint meetings and benefited from the others' perspectives.

In this introduction I give a brief overview of the topics and some of the main conclusions. The results of the Reagan program so far are mixed, and the assessments vary by area.

Federal expenditures as a fraction of Gross National Product at first continued to creep upward despite the administration's intention to cut back. A major restructuring of the budget occurred, however, with an expansion of military spending and curtailment of some nondefense programs. The cuts generated heated controversy over the government budget.

Cuts in welfare programs were criticized for endangering the "safety net" for the poor. The most widely cited measure of well-being among the lowest income groups is the poverty index. Although a rise in this index in recent years has raised concern that the cuts in welfare programs went too far, analysis of other measures of poverty indicates that most of the rise reflected the 1981–1982 recession rather than the policy changes. The budget battles left social insurance and entitlements intact, and other poverty programs subject to cuts composed only a small proportion of welfare expenditures. Since the

1

administration also succeeded in targeting benefits more to the lowest income groups, the social safety net protecting the poor was not significantly altered.

The most prominent accomplishment of the Reagan administration was the reduction in income taxes. Combined with the upward creep in expenditures, the tax reduction resulted in a large budget deficit—the focus of our 1985 volume, *The Economy in Deficit*. A major intention of the cut in income taxes was to stimulate saving and investment. Household saving did not increase, however; indeed, the saving rate declined. Investment, though it recovered sharply from the 1981–1982 recession, did not show effects from the tax cut. The initial tax reduction (ERTA in 1981) was appreciably rescinded, before it went fully into effect, by new legislation in 1982 (TEFRA). The tax effects on investment incentives vary according to the method of financing. For equity financing and disregarding the decline in inflation, the new corporate tax rates substantially reduced the user cost of structures, whereas the comparable effect for equipment was not large and, indeed, appeared to be overwhelmed by the increase in real interest rates. Yet the strong cyclical recovery in investment in 1983–1984 came mainly in equipment and thus apparently could not be attributed to the tax cut.

Though intended as a stimulus to saving and investment, the tax cut was also motivated by a second consideration: the indirect costs of taxes. Taxes discourage the most efficient use of the economy's resources and so have a sizable collection cost of lost output, estimated to be from a quarter to a half of each dollar of revenue. The administration believed that the benefits of many government programs did not exceed the tax revenue plus the collection cost of financing the expenditure and so were not justified. To be sure, cutting taxes without eliminating the corresponding expenditure did not avoid a collection cost but merely shifted its source from taxes to deficit borrowing.

Regulatory reform initially had high priority in the president's program. Besides extending the reforms begun in previous administrations, Reagan gave authority to the Office of Management and Budget to review the economic effects of new regulations, with the intention of restraining their proliferation and economic costs. Also, antitrust enforcement shifted to a different track based on new views of markets and competition and away from firm size. Yet, despite the restraint on regulations, the impetus to simplify and cut back soon faded. Reform of social regulations in particular met too many political impediments, and the administration concentrated its political capital on its other objectives.

Regulatory change only partly reflected policy initiatives, however. Financial deregulation in particular, though given importance by the appointment of a high-level task force headed by Vice President Bush, was overtaken by market developments. The long-standing barriers limiting competition among different classes of financial institutions were crumbling, creating dangers for the deposit insurance funds, and the rapidly evolving structure of the industry required new guidelines. The administration has largely left to Congress the initiative to set the legislative agenda in this area. The lack of administration leadership and congressional consensus has slowed adoption of a forward-looking agenda, leaving the market in a changing and uncertain regulatory environment.

The objectives of deregulation as well as budget control redirected government policy in the important area of health care. To constrain the exploding costs of subsidized medical programs, the administration has imposed restrictions and given incentives to patients and suppliers for a more cost-conscious use of health resources. This inevitably has limited the coverage of benefits and raised questions about ensuring the quality of care. Political pressures to expand coverage further may eventually force adjustments. Even without expansion, program costs are bound to keep rising for reasons related to demographic trends and technological advances. No radical reforms can be expected, but improved mechanisms for paying doctors, hospitals, and other health care providers will continue to evolve in both the public and private sectors.

A major achievement of the administration has been the reduction of inflation. In the 1970s the conventional wisdom insisted that reducing the inflation rate would require a costly loss of output and employment, while optimistic administration supporters claimed that credibility with the public of an announced intention to subdue inflation would elicit economic behavior that moderated the output costs. As it turned out, little of such a credibility effect could be detected. Still, the output costs were far less than the conventional wisdom had predicted, which made the extended anti-inflation policy feasible. Though inflation persists at 3 to 4 percent per year, it has not so far turned upward. This unusual failure of inflation to revive in a business recovery can be attributed to a continuing decline in inflationary expectations and to the strong dollar. Indeed, as the dollar finally began to decline in 1985, the Federal Reserve had to worry that too rapid a fall would raise the inflation rate.

While disinflation produced a smaller loss of output than had been predicted, the accompanying recession of 1981–1982 and appreciation of the dollar exacerbated the difficulties of certain sectors.

3

Lower prices for land, the strong dollar impeding exports, and high interest rates combined to put many farmers in dire straits, which stiffened the refusal of Congress to cut subsidies and eliminate acreage controls. Thus in agriculture the administration's plans to disengage have not been achieved. The costs of the farm program have actually increased.

Permanent job losses due to plant closings and the like in recent years were significant in industries already depressed by import competition. An assessment of the job displacement, however, indicates that, apart from their concentration in manufacturing, those who lost their jobs were a fairly representative cross section. Moreover, the unemployment experience of most of these workers was similar to that of other workers looking for new jobs, and their wages in new jobs compared favorably with their wages in the jobs they lost. Net reductions in jobs were also small relative to either overall employment adjustments or growth in jobs in other sectors.

It is the sting of the strong dollar reflecting the administration's large budget deficit, not the costs of the anti-inflationary policy, that has left U.S. industry reeling. Exports have stagnated, and imports have intensified foreign competition. The impact has nevertheless been selective, with some firms within depressed industries being in a position to compete effectively and even to prosper. Yet the overall effect has created political pressure for trade restrictions, which threatens to compromise further the administration's free trade position.

The clamor for protectionism runs against the trend of trade liberalism since World War II, which ushered in an unprecedented expansion of world trade and a historic period of world economic growth. An administration that stood for less intervention by government in the private sector found itself pushed into trade restrictions to fend off even stronger protectionist measures.

Thus many of the administration's failures ironically stemmed indirectly from its successes. The tax reduction without a cut in expenditures produced large deficits, and these in turn led to the strengthened dollar, import competition, and thence trade restrictions. The strong dollar combined with the reduction of inflation to create a farm crisis. The anti-inflationary monetary policy and large budget deficits brought high real interest rates, which aggravated the plight of farmers, small businesses, and the thrift institutions. The ailing thrift institutions made financial regulatory reform more imperative but, at the same time, made it more complex and difficult to accomplish. The high interest rates also so improved the financial condition of pension funds that many reduced funding, thus reducing the aggregate saving rate, contrary to administration intentions to increase it. As a final irony, domestic financial problems along with deterioration of third world debts led the Federal Reserve to follow an easy monetary policy that endangered the success in containing inflation.

Thus some of the administration's domestic objectives proved to be in conflict. Disinflation in particular made budget cutbacks more difficult. And disinflation can be consistent with large deficits only for a limited period.

It is widely believed that deficit reduction must and therefore will occur, accompanied by further cuts in expenditures. Yet government programs, once begun, build a constituency that protects them against budget cuts. If such protection again proves successful, government expenditures as a fraction of GNP are not likely to be reduced much below the present 25 percent. In the long run, expenditures, not taxes, determine the size of government. If expenditures remain at 25 percent of GNP, holding taxes at the present 20 percent level eventually becomes untenable. Given the past inexorable tendency of the expenditure fraction to rise, holding it at present levels may stand, along with disinflation, as the administration's major economic achievement.

# 1

# The Reagan Domestic Budget Cuts: Proposals, Outcomes, and Effects

*John C. Weicher*

## Summary

*The domestic policy changes of the Reagan administration have centered on programs for the poor—the "social safety net"—and grant programs to state and local governments. The rapid real growth of means-tested benefit programs over the previous two decades has almost been brought to a halt, but the level of benefits has not changed very much. Grant programs were cut much more sharply, by one-third in constant dollars between 1981 and 1982, but Congress refused to cut them further after that, and expenditures have begun to grow again. About half the increase in recent years has been for highway construction, funded from the increase in the federal gasoline tax voted in late 1982, but expenditures for other grant programs have risen as well.*

*The effect on the poor is hard to measure because the severe 1981–1982 recession coincided with the policy changes, but it seems likely that the recession was much more significant. The poverty income deficit—the amount of money needed to raise everyone in poverty up to the poverty line—increased by one-third, some $9 billion, from 1981 to 1983. The cuts in cash benefit programs were about $2 billion during this period. The deficit also increased by $7½ billion between 1980 and 1981; the policy changes cannot have contributed much to this increase. In-kind benefit programs—food stamps, nutrition programs, subsidized housing, and Medicaid—were cut more sharply, but at most they can account for less than half the increase in the income deficit, measured after counting these benefits as income. The Reagan administration also seems to have achieved one of its major goals, targeting benefits more narrowly to the poor; the share of benefits going to eliminate poverty has increased.*

*State and local governments have chosen to offset most if not all of the*

I would like to thank Leslie Lenkowsky for comments, Terry J. Hartle and Sean Sullivan for information on federal grant programs, and John Carnevale of the Treasury Department for unpublished data.

*federal grant reductions, despite the recession. In some categories the states have moved to replace the federal grants. State governments have increased their grants to local governments to operate mass transit systems; as federal operating subsidies have decreased by five percentage points as a share of transit system revenues, state subsidies have risen by the same number of percentage points. The states have also taken advantage of new flexibility in spending federal grants to shift funds away from energy assistance, which Congress did not cut, to social services, which Congress did; and they have also provided money from their own revenues for social services. The net effect is to compensate for the federal grant reduction.*

*The most severe budget cuts came in federal grants for job training and employment. Here state governments are beginning to develop their own substitute programs, such as job programs for young people, but they are spending much less than the federal government used to do. In community services, the last organizational remnant of the original "war on poverty," the states have not replaced federal funds at all, but the community service agencies are finding new, private sources of revenue.*

*The reduction in federal grants may prove to be only temporary, but it is causing some subtle changes in the role of state and local governments. They are beginning to assume some new responsibilities for some of these activities, stepping in to replace the federal government, at least in part.*

## Introduction

When President Ronald Reagan came into office in 1981, he sought major changes in domestic policy, including most notably reductions in spending on programs for the poor and in programs that provide grants to state and local governments. The changes were dramatic enough to be termed at least a counterrevolution, if not a revolution.[1] Now, five years later, seems to be an appropriate time for a preliminary evaluation of the effects of these changes.

This paper considers two kinds of effects. First is the change in the well-being of poor people—the beneficiaries of the "social safety net." The low-income benefit programs provide either cash or in-kind benefits, such as food, housing, and medical care.

Second, the paper describes the effects of the grant reductions on the fiscal position of state and local governments and their responses to the cuts. These lower levels of government receive a fairly large share of the domestic budget in the form of grants for a variety of purposes (about 11 percent in 1984, excluding interest on the federal debt from the domestic budget); they also administer many federal programs, including some of the low-income benefit programs.[2] These programs have incurred a substantial share of the budget cuts. Both aggregate fiscal effects and effects on some specific program categories are reviewed.

## Programs for the Poor

This section evaluates the changes in the safety net, or the low-income benefit programs—those that provide benefits in cash or in kind to the poor and only to the poor, with the amount inversely related to the recipient's income. These programs are Aid to Families with Dependent Children (AFDC); Supplemental Security Income (SSI); public housing, Section 8, and other subsidized housing programs; food stamps and child nutrition; Medicaid; low-income home energy assistance; and the refundable earned-income tax credit. The housing, food and nutrition, and Medicaid programs provide benefits in kind; the others provide cash. These programs constitute about half the "income security" budget category, plus Medicaid, which is included under "health." They also make up the definition of the "social safety net" adopted by the Reagan administration in its 1985 and 1986 budgets, although the term was originally given a rather different meaning, including only AFDC among the low-income benefit programs but also including social security (and perhaps Medicare), veterans' benefits, and unemployment compensation.[3]

Enough information is available to form a fairly good picture of the effects of the administration's budget cuts in cash assistance on the overall well-being of the poor. It is more difficult to assess the outcomes of the changes in the programs providing benefits in kind.

**Federal Budget and Policy Changes.** *Program growth before 1980.* When President Reagan was elected in the fall of 1980, outlays for low-income benefit programs had been growing rapidly for two decades. They were projected to continue rising, albeit much more slowly, for the next five years.

Table 1–1 shows the changes in both nominal and real dollars from 1960 to 1980 for each program category. Because inflation was so serious and rapid during the 1970s, it is more meaningful to discuss changes in real dollars; the year 1980 is a convenient base. The table also shows nominal dollars because this is the most common form of presentation. Programs are divided into cash transfers and in-kind benefits, an important distinction for the later analysis. Real outlays for all programs combined doubled during the 1960s and doubled again by 1975. From 1975 to 1980 the growth rate slowed, but outlays still rose by about 40 percent. That was faster than the growth of the U.S. economy or the rest of the federal budget.

9

TABLE 1–1
NOMINAL AND REAL LOW-INCOME BENEFIT PROGRAM OUTLAYS,
FISCAL YEARS 1960–1980
(billions of dollars)

| | 1960 | 1965 | 1970 | 1975 | 1980 |
|---|---|---|---|---|---|
| Current dollars | | | | | |
| Cash transfers | 3.5 | 4.6 | 6.0 | 9.9 | 16.8 |
| Aid to Families with Dependent | | | | | |
| Children | 2.1 | 2.8 | 4.1 | 5.1 | 7.3 |
| Supplemental Security Income | 1.4 | 1.8 | 1.9 | 4.8 | 6.4 |
| Low-income home energy assistance[a] | 0 | 0 | 0 | 0 | 1.8 |
| Earned-income tax credit | 0 | 0 | 0 | 0 | 1.3 |
| In-kind benefits | 0.3 | 0.8 | 4.2 | 15.5 | 33.3 |
| Housing assistance | 0.1 | 0.2 | 0.5 | 2.1 | 5.4 |
| Food and nutrition programs | 0.2 | 0.3 | 1.0 | 6.6 | 13.9 |
| Medicaid | 0 | 0.3 | 2.7 | 6.8 | 14.0 |
| Total | 3.8 | 5.4 | 10.1 | 25.5 | 50.1 |
| 1980 dollars | | | | | |
| Cash transfers | 9.0 | 11.0 | 11.7 | 14.1 | 16.8 |
| Aid to Families with Dependent | | | | | |
| Children | 5.3 | 6.7 | 8.1 | 7.3 | 7.3 |
| Supplemental Security Income | 3.7 | 4.3 | 3.6 | 6.8 | 6.4 |
| Low-income home energy assistance[a] | 0 | 0 | 0 | 0 | 1.8 |
| Earned-income tax credit | 0 | 0 | 0 | 0 | 1.3 |
| In-kind benefits | 1.0 | 1.9 | 8.1 | 22.1 | 33.3 |
| Housing assistance | 0.4 | 0.5 | 0.9 | 3.0 | 5.4 |
| Food and nutrition programs | 0.6 | 0.7 | 1.9 | 9.4 | 13.9 |
| Medicaid | 0 | 0.7 | 5.3 | 9.7 | 14.0 |
| Total | 10.0 | 12.9 | 19.8 | 36.1 | 50.1 |

NOTE: Current dollar outlays have been converted to 1980 dollars using the GNP deflator for the calendar year.

a. Energy assistance was given either in cash or in kind, at the option of the states.

SOURCE: Office of Management and Budget, *Budget of the United States Government*, various years.

Most of these programs were created or substantially expanded during the 1960s or early 1970s; AFDC is the only one that was large in 1960 and that retained basically the same form during the whole period. The new, rapidly growing programs usually took the form of in-kind benefits. In 1965, before the "Great Society" was established, cash transfers amounted to about 85 percent of federal benefits for the poor. By 1970, after Medicaid was created, cash transfers were down to about 60 percent. Five years later the share was down to 40 percent; in this period the food stamp program was dramatically restructured and expanded, and the Section 235 and Section 236 housing programs grew sharply and then were abruptly terminated. After 1975 the new earned income tax credit was more than offset by the Section 8 housing program, enacted in 1974, and the continued growth of the nutrition programs and Medicaid. Cash transfers were only about one-third of the total by 1980.[4]

*Policy after 1980.* Further growth was anticipated in President Jimmy Carter's last budget, submitted as he was leaving office in January 1981. As table 1–2 shows, he proposed a nominal increase of more than 50 percent from 1980 through 1984. Most of this, however,

TABLE 1–2

PROJECTED AND ACTUAL LOW-INCOME BENEFIT PROGRAM OUTLAYS,
FISCAL YEARS 1980–1984

(billions of dollars)

| | 1980[a] | 1981 | 1982 | 1983 | 1984 |
|---|---|---|---|---|---|
| Current dollars | | | | | |
| Carter FY1982 budget (January 1981) | 50.1 | 57.5 | 62.8 | 71.2 | 77.1 |
| Carter reestimate (March 1981) | 50.1 | 57.4 | 63.0 | 70.0 | 74.3 |
| Reagan revision (March 1981) | 50.1 | 56.9 | 56.5 | 60.7 | 62.2 |
| Omnibus Budget Reconciliation Act | | | | | |
| (August 1981) | 50.1 | NA | 58.0 | 63.8 | 67.7 |
| Actual outlays | 50.1 | 58.9 | 59.6 | 66.8 | 70.0 |
| 1980 dollars | | | | | |
| Carter FY1982 budget (January 1981) | 50.1 | 52.1 | 52.0 | 54.4 | 54.6 |
| Carter reestimate (March 1981) | 50.1 | 52.2 | 52.9 | 55.0 | 55.1 |
| Reagan revision (March 1981) | 50.1 | 51.8 | 47.5 | 47.6 | 46.1 |
| Omnibus Budget Reconciliation Act | | | | | |
| (August 1981) | 50.1 | NA | 48.7 | 50.1 | 50.1 |
| Actual outlays | 50.1 | 53.8 | 51.4 | 55.3 | 55.4 |

NA = not applicable.

NOTE: Current dollar outlays have been converted to 1980 dollars using the GNP deflator for the calendar year.

a. 1980 outlays are actual in all cases.

SOURCES: Office of Management and Budget, *Budget of the United States Government,* various years; *Congressional Quarterly,* August 15, 1981; Office of Management and Budget, *Additional Details on Budget Savings,* March 1981; and G. William Hoagland, "Perception and Reality in Nutrition Programs," in John C. Weicher, ed., *Maintaining the Safety Net: Income Redistribution Programs in the Reagan Administration* (Washington, D.C.: American Enterprise Institute, 1984).

was inflation; in real terms, the budget called for only a 9 percent increase, with a further increase to 14 percent by 1985 (not shown in the table).[5]

President Reagan's revised budget proposal was quite different. It called for only a 25 percent nominal increase and an 8 percent real decrease by 1984. Nearly all the difference in real outlays was accounted for by changes in the programs; differences in economic assumptions had little effect.

Congress essentially split the difference between the two presidents in the Omnibus Budget Reconciliation Act (OBRA), passed in August 1981. Real outlays were budgeted to remain constant from 1980 to 1984. It is interesting to note that Congress gave the president a decreasing share of his proposals for later years. It approved nearly everything the president requested for fiscal year 1982, about two-thirds for fiscal year 1983, and slightly more than half for fiscal year 1984.[6]

The differences between President Carter, President Reagan, and OBRA were not very large; President Reagan asked for $21.8 billion less (in 1980 dollars) than President Carter over the three-year period, and Congress approved $15.0 billion less. President Reagan sought about $7.3 billion less per year, and Congress approved about $5.0 billion less. But the differences appear relatively small because President Carter's budget itself proposed a sharp deceleration in the growth of the low-income benefit programs, from 40 percent to 14 percent over five years. Since his budget is the baseline for the others, the change in policy that it proposed serves to minimize the differences from the later proposals. It is problematic whether President Carter could have achieved such a substantial departure from the long-established trend of previous policy, including his own. What is certain is that President Reagan and Congress did in fact enact an even more substantial departure, almost bringing the *growth* of the safety net to a halt. They did not, however, propose any very significant changes in the existing *level* of benefits going to the poor.

*The effect of the recession.* Actual outlays turned out to be rather different from those projected, because of the 1981–1982 recession. Neither president anticipated this recession in his budget proposals. In this they were not alone; the Congressional Budget Office (CBO) did not foresee it in early 1981, nor did most private forecasters. The economic assumptions underlying OBRA and used by the CBO to calculate its budgetary effects were very similar to those used by President Reagan five months earlier. In fact, however, the recession was just beginning as the budget was approved.

The recession drove up actual nominal and real outlays in 1982 by about 4 percent above the OBRA projections for the year and by successively smaller amounts in 1983 and 1984. Thus real outlays proved to be close to President Carter's original budget. Had the policy changes not been enacted, however, real outlays would have been still higher. Table 1–3 compares actual outlays for 1982 and 1983, the years of highest unemployment, with those that would have occurred under the Carter and Reagan budgets. The Carter budget would have resulted in additional outlays of about $5.5 billion each year: the Reagan proposals would have saved $1.7 billion in 1982 and $7.6 billion in 1983. The Reagan proposals shown in table 1–3 are not fully comparable with those in table 1–2, because they include the effects of changes proposed in the fiscal year 1983 budget.

The major increases were for food stamps and AFDC, which are most sensitive to changes in business activity. Congress approved a reduction of $1.7 billion for food stamps for 1982, for example, but the rise in unemployment pushed outlays up by $1.2 billion. Moreover, the recession had lingering effects on outlays. Although it was well in the past by 1984, the unemployment rate was still about a full percentage point above both presidents' 1981 projections, causing outlays to be automatically about $600 million higher.[7]

The recession had some positive side effects for the poor. Outlays are fixed in nominal terms for several programs: AFDC, energy as-

---

TABLE 1–3

ACTUAL LOW-INCOME BENEFIT PROGRAM OUTLAY CHANGES
RESULTING FROM POLICY CHANGES, FISCAL YEARS 1982–1983
(billions of current dollars)

|  | 1982 | 1983 |
|---|---|---|
| Carter FY1982 budget (January 1981) | 65.0 | 72.4 |
| Actual policy | 59.6 | 66.8 |
| Reagan proposals (March 1981 and February 1982) | 57.9 | 59.2 |

NOTE: Reagan proposals differ from March 1981 budget revision, including further changes proposed in FY1983 budget.

SOURCES: For Carter proposal and actual policy, Congressional Budget Office, "Major Legislative Changes in Human Resources Programs since January 1981," staff memorandum, August 1983; omitted programs (earned-income tax credit, nutrition program administration, Section 32, food donations, and special milk program) and differences between current policy in January 1981 and Carter budget estimated by the author. For Reagan proposals, Office of Management and Budget, *Additional Details on Budget Savings*, April 1981; *Budget of the United States Government, Fiscal Year 1983*, February 1982; and "Sensitivity of Federal Expenditures to Unemployment," unpublished technical staff memorandum, April 18, 1980.

sistance, and the earned-income tax credit. The recession and the Federal Reserve's monetary policy resulted in a much lower inflation rate than anyone anticipated; by 1984 the GNP deflator was 10 percent lower than President Carter's projection and 6 percent lower than President Reagan's. The real value of benefits under these programs continued to decline, but more slowly than anticipated and much more slowly than in the 1970s.

*Changes by program.* Table 1–4 shows the composition of the budget cuts contained in OBRA. Reductions were particularly large in the food and nutrition programs. Congress approved cuts of 16 percent (larger than the president requested) in the food stamp program and 29 percent in the child nutrition programs over the three years. About a quarter, however, occurred simply because Congress made permanent certain temporary changes that it had enacted in 1980.

Other large reductions were approved for AFDC and the earned-income tax credit. The former was cut by about one-sixth for the three-year period. The latter was cut still more, by about one-quarter; but this was a "cut" from a Carter proposal to increase the credit, beginning in 1983. The Reagan administration simply withdrew the proposal.

In other areas the administration was less successful. OBRA reduced Medicaid outlays by less than 5 percent, and Congress did not

TABLE 1–4

BUDGET CUTS APPROVED IN OMNIBUS BUDGET RECONCILIATION ACT OF 1981, FISCAL YEARS 1982–1984

(billions of current dollars)

|  | 1982 | 1983 | 1984 |
|---|---|---|---|
| Cash transfers | 1.2 | 2.0 | 1.9 |
| Aid to Families with Dependent Children | 1.2 | 1.4 | 1.4 |
| Supplemental Security Income | 0 | 0 | 0 |
| Low-income home energy assistance[a] | 0 | 0 | 0 |
| Earned-income tax credit | 0 | 0.6 | 0.5 |
| In-kind benefits | 4.2 | 5.0 | 5.6 |
| Housing assistance | 0.1 | 0.3 | 0.5 |
| Food and nutrition programs | 3.1 | 3.7 | 4.1 |
| Medicaid | 1.0 | 1.0 | 1.0 |
| Total | 5.4 | 7.0 | 7.5 |

a. Energy assistance was given either in cash or in kind, at the option of the states.

SOURCES: *Congressional Quarterly*, August 15, 1981; Hoagland, "Perception and Reality"; and Office of Management and Budget, *Additional Details*.

approve any cuts in most other programs. The administration sought to cut energy assistance by about a quarter, converting the program to a block grant, and it asked for a cut of about 1 percent in SSI.

Housing is a special case. In 1982 the administration was able to stop almost all subsidized construction for the poor. Section 8, the largest program, was terminated, and public housing construction was halted, although the program remained in existence. This was a fundamental change, reversing the housing policy of half a century. Ultimately it will save the federal government hundreds of billions of dollars. But it has saved almost nothing so far and has had almost no effect on the budget, because subsidized housing projects are funded on a long-term basis, over thirty years or more into the future. Outlays in any one year are primarily payments for units built in the past; they are either mortgage interest payments, interest payments for bonds to finance public housing, or rental payments for low-income residents of private housing. The administration had mixed success in reducing current outlays. It persuaded Congress to increase the share of income that tenants must contribute toward their rent, from 25 to 30 percent over a five-year period; but it could not achieve a reduction in public housing operating subsidies.

To summarize, Congress approved virtually all the president's requests in AFDC, about 85 percent in food stamps and child nutrition programs, and about 40 percent in Medicaid; and it accepted his decision to withdraw the Carter proposal to increase the earned-income tax credit. It approved none in the other three programs, but the only proposed large change in these was in energy assistance.

These budgetary changes were accomplished through systematic and generally consistent structural changes across the programs. Four basic themes can be identified:

1. Benefits were targeted more narrowly to individuals with the lowest incomes. In food stamps, child nutrition, and subsidized housing, the administration proposed to lower the income limit closer to the poverty line but still above it, and it won congressional approval for food stamps and subsidized housing.

2. The administration sought to target benefits to the "deserving poor" or the "truly needy"—a phrase from the 1981 budget revision that quickly became a cliché. In practice, this meant terminating AFDC and therefore automatically Medicaid benefits for the working poor. This goal interacted with the first, since the working poor typically have higher incomes than the nonworking poor.

3. Benefits were reduced to some extent for those below the poverty line. The largest reductions occurred in subsidized housing, already mentioned, and in Medicaid, where the administration asked

for a 5 percent ceiling on the growth in Medicaid outlays, which was transformed by Congress into a reduction in the rate at which the federal government would match state outlays. These changes each saved about $500 million annually. A number of small changes were made in most programs—tightening eligibility rules, changing the base period for determining benefits, and deferring cost-of-living benefit adjustments.

4. In accordance with President Reagan's long-expressed concern, the administration sought to curtail fraud, waste, and abuse by giving state and local governments new incentives for reducing errors in the programs they administer and imposing new penalties if they do not.

**The Budget Cuts and the Poor.** The effect of all these changes on the well-being of the poor has been the subject of some controversy. It was one important aspect of the "fairness issue" during the 1984 presidential campaign.

It is clear that the poor were worse off in the early 1980s than they had been before, but it is less clear why, or how important the policy changes were. This is partly because there has not yet been enough time for much systematic research but mostly because of the severe 1981–1982 recession. Just as the recession complicates the process of measuring the changes in safety net programs, it complicates the process of measuring their outcome. It is necessary to separate the effects of the policy changes from the effects of the recession and to measure their relative importance. This is difficult but not impossible. This section offers a preliminary analysis, from which I conclude that the recession was probably much more important than the program changes.

*The poverty rate.* The most widely discussed measure of the well-being of the poor is the poverty rate—the fraction of the population living in households with incomes below the poverty level. The concept of a poverty-level income was introduced in 1964; it was originally based on the cost of a minimally adequate diet, multiplied by three to reflect the fact that poor families typically spent about one-third of their incomes for food. Since 1968 it has been adjusted annually by the consumer price index rather than by the cost of food. It is also adjusted for the number of people and the number of children in the household and the age of the household head; before 1982 it was adjusted for the sex of the household head and whether the household lived on a farm.

Table 1–5 reports the poverty rate annually since 1970 and for

TABLE 1–5
INCIDENCE OF POVERTY, 1959–1984
(percentage of all persons in the United States)

| | Official Incidence (net of cash transfers) | | Official Incidence (net of cash transfers) |
|---|---|---|---|
| 1959 | 22.4 | 1976 | 11.8 |
| 1960 | 22.2 | 1977 | 11.6 |
| 1965 | 17.3 | 1978 | 11.4 |
| 1970 | 12.6 | 1979 | 11.7 |
| 1971 | 12.5 | 1980 | 13.0 |
| 1972 | 11.9 | 1981 | 14.0 |
| 1973 | 11.1 | 1982 | 15.0 |
| 1974 | 11.2 | 1983 | 15.2 |
| 1975 | 12.3 | 1984 | 14.4 |

SOURCE: U.S. Bureau of the Census, Current Population Reports, Series P-60, no. 149, *Characteristics of the Population below the Poverty Level: 1984*, table 1.

selected earlier years. The rate declined sharply during the 1960s and early 1970s, both before and after the establishment of the Great Society. By 1973 it reached what has so far proved to be its lowest level. It fluctuated within a narrow range for the rest of the decade and then rose sharply during the early 1980s, through the two recessions; it kept rising, slightly, during the first year of the recovery and then declined by almost a full percentage point in 1984. The second recession and recovery coincide with the Reagan administration's program changes.[8]

Several economists have analyzed the changes in the poverty rate in an effort to separate economic influences from program changes. Two papers predicted the 1984 rate before it was published in August 1985, thereby permitting a test of their analyses. Sheldon Danziger and Peter Gottschalk came very close to the actual level, projecting a decline to 14.5 percent. They argued that rising unemployment and the administration's budget reductions were about equally responsible for the rise in poverty through 1983.[9] Rebecca Blank and Alan Blinder, who concluded that unemployment has much more effect on poverty than federal programs, proved to be optimistic; they predicted that the poverty rate would decline to 13.5 percent in 1984, twice as much as it actually fell.[10]

Other factors probably have a smaller effect on poverty. Blank and Blinder estimate that a one-percentage-point increase in the inflation rate raises the incidence of poverty by just under 0.1 percentage point. This occurs primarily because AFDC program benefits are fixed

17

in current dollars and decline in value in the absence of legislated changes. The inflation of the 1970s may therefore have contributed to the upward secular trend in the incidence of poverty after 1973, and the disinflation of the early 1980s may have offset to a minor extent—perhaps about a quarter—the effects of rising unemployment during the recession.

Demographic changes, particularly the growth in families headed by women and other household types for which the incidence of poverty is high, also help to account for the upward trend in poverty since 1973; Danziger and Gottschalk have estimated that poverty has risen by about 0.1 percent of the population per year since 1973 because of such changes. This implies that the continuing increase in households headed by women is responsible for about a quarter of the rise in the poverty rate since 1980. The growing "feminization" of poverty is sometimes viewed as reducing the effectiveness of economic growth in reducing poverty and increasing both the importance of transfer programs and the negative consequences of the budget cuts, but this argument has been questioned.[11]

*The income deficit.* The poverty level is a useful concept with some logical underpinning, but it is probably not the best available measure of the well-being of the poor. A family with an income $100 below the poverty line is not fundamentally worse off than a family with an income $100 above the line; a family with an income $5,000 below the line is clearly much worse off than a family just below the line, but both are counted equally. It is more useful to look at the amount of income required to bring all of the poor up to the poverty line. In addition, it is possible to say more about the effect of the budget cuts on this measure of well-being than on the incidence of poverty.

Table 1–6 reports this income deficit, or "poverty gap," in both nominal and real dollars. It seems clear that not much of the increase in the income deficit since 1980 can be attributed to the program cuts enacted in 1981. The income deficit in the table includes cash transfers but not in-kind benefits. Cash transfers were cut by $1.2 billion for 1982 and $2.0 billion for 1983, as reported in table 1–4. From 1981 to 1983 the income deficit increased by $9 billion. In addition, the deficit increased by $7½ billion from 1980 to 1981; almost none of that can possibly be attributed to President Reagan's program. Nearly all the increase in the income deficit over the three years is due to the severe 1981–1982 recession. The budget cuts accounted for at most about 15 percent of it. This would still have been true if Congress had approved the president's proposed cuts in SSI and energy assistance, which amounted to about $0.6 billion annually.

TABLE 1–6
INCOME DEFICIT FOR PERSONS BELOW THE POVERTY LINE, 1959–1984
(billions of dollars)

|  | Current Dollars | 1980 Dollars |
|---|---|---|
| 1959 | 13.7 | 38.6 |
| 1960 | 13.9 | 38.6 |
| 1965 | 11.6 | 30.3 |
| 1970 | 11.6 | 24.5 |
| 1971 | 12.0 | 24.5 |
| 1972 | 11.4 | 23.7 |
| 1973 | 12.0 | 22.2 |
| 1974 | 13.3 | 22.2 |
| 1975 | 16.1 | 24.6 |
| 1976 | 16.7 | 24.2 |
| 1977 | 17.8 | 24.1 |
| 1978 | 19.5 | 24.6 |
| 1979 | 23.3 | 26.5 |
| 1980 | 29.7 | 29.7 |
| 1981 | 37.1 | 33.5 |
| 1982 | 42.9 | 36.6 |
| 1983 | 46.0 | 38.0 |
| 1984 | 45.2 | 35.8 |

NOTE: Current dollars are converted to 1980 dollars using the consumer price index.

SOURCE: U.S. Bureau of the Census, Current Population Reports, Series P-60, nos. 133, 149, *Characteristics of the Population below the Poverty Level: 1980* and *1984*, table 6 and table A-1.

*Targeting benefits.* The effect of the budget cuts may be overstated because some of the AFDC benefits may lift families above the poverty line. It is not possible to categorize AFDC benefits on this basis and determine the amount that actually fills the poverty gap. It is possible, however, to estimate the extent to which cash transfers as a whole serve to reduce the income deficit. Estimates can be constructed for the past few years, from 1979 to 1984; they suggest that the administration has had some success in its efforts to target benefits more narrowly to the poor.

Table 1–7 reports two measures of the income deficit for these years, the first without including means-tested cash benefits in the household's income and the second when these benefits are included. The latter is the income deficit corresponding to the official poverty rate. The difference is the share of means-tested benefits that reduces

19

TABLE 1–7

CASH BENEFITS AND THE POVERTY INCOME DEFICIT, 1979–1984

(billions of current dollars)

| | Excluding Means-tested Cash Benefits | Including Means-tested Cash Benefits | Difference | Total Means-tested Cash Benefits | Share of Cash Benefits Reducing Poverty (percent) |
|------|------|------|------|------|------|
| 1979 | 33.5 | 23.3 | 10.2 | 23.2 | 44.0 |
| 1980 | 41.8 | 29.7 | 12.1 | 25.5 | 47.4 |
| 1981 | 50.4 · | 37.0 | 13.4 | 26.9 | 49.9 |
| 1982 | 57.2 | 42.9 | 14.3 | 27.2 | 52.4 |
| 1983 | 61.6 | 46.0 | 15.6 | 27.6 | 56.6 |
| 1984 | 61.7 | 45.2 | 16.5 | 28.8 | 57.2 |

SOURCE: U.S. Bureau of the Census, Technical Papers, nos. 51, 52, 55, *Estimates of Poverty Including the Value of Noncash Benefits: 1979–1982, 1983, 1984.*

poverty by bringing households up to the poverty line. The table also shows the total amount of these benefits.

The share of benefits serving to reduce the poverty income deficit grew substantially after 1979. The increase coincided with the administration's attempt to target benefits more narrowly to the poor and reduce or eliminate benefits to those above the poverty line. The table thus provides some support for the administration's program and some evidence that it was able to accomplish one of its goals. Total benefits did not rise in nominal terms and certainly fell in real terms, but the share and the amount of benefits going to eliminate poverty increased. Part of the increase may have been a result of the recessions; there were more poor people to receive benefits. But the data suggest that the program changes were primarily responsible: the share kept increasing after 1982 despite the recovery.[12]

The low-income benefit programs were not the only ones cut in 1981, and some of the other cuts probably increased the income deficit as well. In particular, unemployment compensation was cut by $1.0 billion for 1982 (but increased for 1983). This is not large enough to affect the basic conclusion, however; even if it is assumed that all the money would have gone to those below the poverty line, the largest share by far of the increase in the income deficit would still be a result of the recession.

*In-kind benefits and poverty.* Tables 1–6 and 1–7 omit in-kind benefits, which bore the largest share of the administration's budget cuts and program changes. When these benefits are counted, both the incidence of poverty and the size of the income deficit are substantially reduced. The poverty rate net of in-kind benefits has generally changed in the same direction as the official incidence, with the significant exception that the former fell after the 1973–1975 recession while the latter increased.[13] Since 1979 the Census Bureau has annually published three measures of poverty net of in-kind benefits, each using a different technique for valuing benefits. All have risen and fallen in almost exactly the same way as the official rate from year to year. This suggests, but certainly does not prove, that the recession and the welfare program changes may have contributed about equally to the increase in the poverty rate net of in-kind benefits, as well as in the official rate, during the early 1980s.

The census data can also be used to measure the effectiveness of the in-kind benefit programs in reducing the income deficits and further to get some sense of the effect of the 1981 program changes. Table 1–8 shows both the income deficit corresponding to the official poverty rate and the deficit when in-kind benefits are counted as income. From 1980 to 1983 the latter deficit increased by $10.5 billion. Over the same period all low-income benefit programs combined were cut by $7.0 billion. These numbers are not directly comparable, however. They come from different sources. Benefits are underreported in the Current Population Survey (the source of the income deficit), so the reduction comparable to the change in the deficit is smaller than $7.0 billion, by about 20 percent. In addition, a substantial share of the in-kind benefits went to people above the poverty line, and many changes were intended to reduce that share. Between 1980 and 1982, the proportion of beneficiaries below the poverty line rose markedly in the programs where the administration was able to improve targeting. Part of the change was undoubtedly caused by the recession, but only part. There was a lesser increase in programs that were not changed in 1981.

Changes in beneficiaries do not necessarily imply similar changes in the distribution of benefits, but they serve as a rough guide, in the absence of better data. The best available information concerns housing. Over 60 percent of the rent increase ($190 million in 1983) was borne by tenants above the poverty line.[14] The largest cuts came in the nutrition programs. Former Food and Nutrition Service administrator William Hoagland has estimated that "The bulk of the savings was achieved from income groups above the safety net level."[15] This amounted to over $800 million in 1983. Similar calculations cannot be made for the other programs, but it seems likely that the burden of the cuts fell more on those below the poverty line, except perhaps for food stamps. The most reasonable conclusion may be that the

## TABLE 1-8
### NONCASH BENEFITS AND POVERTY INCOME AND DEFICIT, 1979–1984
(billions of current dollars)

| | Income Deficit Excluding In-Kind Benefits | Income Deficit Including In-Kind Benefits | Difference | In-Kind Benefits Going to the Poor | Share of Benefits to Poor That Reduce Poverty | Total In-Kind Benefits | Share of Total Benefits That Reduce Poverty |
|---|---|---|---|---|---|---|---|
| | | Including Benefits to the Elderly | | | | | |
| 1979 | 23.3 | 13.5 | 9.8 | 18.8 | 52.1 | 54.5 | 17.9 |
| 1980 | 29.7 | 17.3 | 12.4 | 23.2 | 53.6 | 62.0 | 20.1 |
| 1981 | 37.0 | 22.4 | 14.7 | 26.0 | 56.5 | 71.3 | 20.6 |
| 1982 | 42.9 | 25.9 | 17.0 | 29.8 | 57.0 | 79.5 | 21.4 |
| 1983 | 46.0 | 27.8 | 18.2 | 31.8 | 57.3 | 83.6 | 20.4 |
| 1984 | 45.2 | 26.8 | 18.4 | 32.9 | 55.9 | 89.8 | 20.4 |
| | | Excluding Benefits to the Elderly | | | | | |
| 1979 | 20.3 | 12.7 | 7.6 | 13.1 | 58.5 | 29.5 | 25.9 |
| 1980 | 26.4 | 16.4 | 10.0 | 16.1 | 61.9 | 33.4 | 29.9 |
| 1981 | 33.3 | 21.5 | 11.8 | 17.9 | 66.1 | 36.8 | 32.1 |
| 1982 | 38.8 | 24.7 | 14.1 | 20.9 | 67.1 | 40.3 | 34.8 |
| 1983 | 42.0 | 26.7 | 15.3 | 22.3 | 68.7 | 41.9 | 36.4 |
| 1984 | 41.7 | 26.1 | 15.7 | 23.5 | 66.7 | 44.8 | 35.0 |

SOURCES: U.S. Bureau of the Census, Technical Papers, nos. 51, 52, 55, *Estimates of Poverty Including the Value of Noncash Benefits: 1979–1982, 1983, 1984.*

budget cuts are responsible for a much larger share of the increase in the deficit net of in-kind benefits than for the official deficit, but still less than half.

*Targeting in-kind benefits.* Table 1–8 also shows the changes in the extent to which in-kind benefits actually reduced poverty. The published data, unfortunately, include Medicare, which is not limited to the poor; it is larger than all the means-tested programs combined, and fully a quarter of the poor participate in it. The closest approximation that can be constructed from the published data is to exclude all benefits to the elderly. Very little Medicare goes to those under the age of sixty-five, and Medicare accounts for about 90 percent annually of all in-kind benefits to the elderly poor. The data for the nonelderly poor are shown in the lower panel of table 1–8.[16]

The share of in-kind benefits going to the poor increased during the early 1980s, but by less than the share for cash transfers. This seems to hold whether the elderly are included or excluded. The increase appears to be largely a result of the policy changes; most of the improvement in targeting during the recession was maintained in 1984.

To summarize, while it is still early to make a definitive judgment about the effects of the Reagan budget cuts on the well-being of the poor, it seems clear that the 1981–1982 recession had a much greater influence on their well-being than the policy changes. Insofar as there was a safety net in 1980, it has remained essentially intact.

## Federal Grants to State and Local Governments

Federal grant programs incurred substantial budget cuts during the first years of the Reagan administration; but then expenditures leveled out, and they have begun to grow again. This pattern has some features in common with that for the low-income benefit programs but is much more pronounced.

**The Growth of Federal Expenditures.** *Expenditures before 1980.* Table 1–9 shows the growth in federal grants to state and local governments since 1960, in both current and constant (1980) dollars. Like the safety net programs, these grants grew rapidly in the two decades before 1980: annual real expenditures quadrupled from 1960 to 1978 while nominal expenditures increased twelvefold.

The growth and change in federal grants reflect the changes in domestic policy during the period. The pattern of gradual growth is punctuated by years when important new programs were created and outlays rose abruptly. Before 1966 highway programs accounted for over two-thirds of federal grants, and most of the remainder was aid to education, primarily impact aid for school districts with large concentrations of federal, and therefore tax-exempt, property. During 1966 and 1967 expenditures quadrupled in the budget category "education, training and employment, and social services," from $1 billion to over $4 billion; this category contained most of President Lyndon Johnson's Great Society programs, including the war on poverty. General revenue sharing is responsible for the next big jump, in 1973, accounting for $6.6 of the $7.6 billion increase from 1972. During the mid-1970s there were new programs in environmental protection, particularly construction grants for waste treatment plants, and in urban mass transit. The last large increase occurred in 1978, with a $3.8 billion increase in training and employment outlays as an "antirecession" measure, although the previous recession had actually

TABLE 1–9

FEDERAL GRANTS TO STATE AND LOCAL GOVERNMENTS,
FISCAL YEARS 1960–1985

(billions of dollars)

|  | Nominal Dollars | 1980 Dollars |
|---|---|---|
| 1960 | 4.5 | 15.4 |
| 1965 | 7.2 | 21.3 |
| 1970 | 15.5 | 33.4 |
| 1971 | 17.7 | 35.8 |
| 1972 | 20.6 | 39.4 |
| 1973 | 28.2 | 50.4 |
| 1974 | 28.8 | 46.7 |
| 1975 | 33.3 | 49.3 |
| 1976[a] | 40.3 | 55.8 |
| 1977 | 46.2 | 59.7 |
| 1978 | 53.7 | 64.4 |
| 1979 | 56.0 | 61.7 |
| 1980 | 59.5 | 59.5 |
| 1981 | 57.8 | 53.2 |
| 1982 | 50.3 | 43.3 |
| 1983 | 50.9 | 41.1 |
| 1984 | 53.3 | 40.6 |
| 1985 | 57.8 | 44.4 |

NOTE: Excludes payments for individuals; 1980 dollar figures calculated by deflating nominal dollars using the GNP deflator for state and local purchases.

a. 1976 includes transition quarter; figures in the table are prorated to an annual basis.

SOURCE: U.S. Office of Management and Budget, *Historical Tables, Budget of the United States Government, Fiscal Year 1986*, table 12.1.

ended in early 1975. This has turned out to be the peak year to date in real terms; outlays declined by almost 10 percent in the next two years. In retrospect the years from 1966 to 1978 stand out as a period of exceptional growth; annual nominal outlays quintupled, and real outlays tripled.

*President Reagan's 1981–1982 changes.* The newly-elected president proposed dramatic reductions in federal grant programs, and most of his recommendations were approved by Congress. The results are manifest in table 1–9. After 1980 there is a sharp break from the previous pattern: nominal expenditures declined by almost one-sixth ($9 billion) from 1980 to 1983, while real expenditures fell by nearly one-third ($19 billion) through 1984. Even after a $3 billion increase in 1985, real outlays have been cut back nearly to their level in 1972, before revenue sharing was enacted.

Table 1–10 emphasizes the change in policy by comparing President Carter's final budget with President Reagan's revision and with congressional actions. The table includes both budget authority and outlays. In several programs, most notably transportation, budget authority to spend money is approved well before the outlays actually occur, so that authority is a good leading indicator of future outlay trends. Whereas President Carter proposed about a 12 percent nominal increase in budget authority for 1982, President Reagan immediately proposed a 6 percent cut during the current 1981 fiscal year and a one-third reduction for 1982.

The president's proposed cuts were concentrated in a few programs, but nearly all programs were affected to a minor extent. Virtually half the reduction in budget authority for 1982—$9.8 billion—was in the budget category of education, training and employment, and social services; within this category the proposed cuts amounted to 40 percent of the Carter proposals. The largest share of these cuts was in the job training subcategory, where the president proposed to eliminate the $4.6 billion Public Service Employment component of the Comprehensive Employment and Training Act (CETA). Another $4.2 billion was to be cut in natural resources and environment, where the administration withdrew the entire 1982 budget request of $3.7 billion for construction of waste treatment plants. This would have cut the budget category by almost 90 percent. In transportation the administration proposed to save $5.0 billion, or about 20 percent, largely by stretching out the construction of "lower-priority highway projects" and by halting new mass transit projects; funds would be spent only for subway projects currently under construction. These three categories accounted for over 90 percent of the proposed cuts.

TABLE 1–10
PROJECTED AND ACTUAL FEDERAL GRANTS TO STATE AND LOCAL
GOVERNMENTS, FISCAL YEARS 1980–1983
(billions of current dollars)

| | Budget Authority | Outlays |
|---|---|---|
| 1980 | | |
| Actual | 56.4 | 58.4 |
| 1981 | | |
| Carter budget (January 1981) | 55.8 | 57.0 |
| Reagan revision (March 1981) | 52.8 | 56.6 |
| Actual | 51.6 | 56.1 |
| 1982 | | |
| Carter budget (January 1981) | 62.3 | 58.6 |
| Reagan revision (March 1981) | 42.3 | 48.9 |
| Actual | 45.7 | 48.9 |
| 1983 | | |
| Carter budget | NA | 63.7 |
| Reagan budget (February 1982) | 39.6 | 43.8 |
| Actual | 56.7 | 49.9 |

NA = not available.

SOURCES: Office of Management and Budget, *Budget of the United States Government*, Special Analysis H, various years; and Office of Management and Budget, *Fiscal Year 1982 Budget Revisions*, March 1981.

In the smaller category of community and economic development, the Urban Development Action Grant (UDAG) program, created in the Carter administration, was to be folded back into the Community Development Block Grant (CDBG, the successor to urban renewal), and both the Economic Development Administration and the Appalachian Regional Commission (except for highway construction) were to be eliminated. The president also wanted to end most grant programs for energy.

In effect, President Reagan was proposing to cut back or eliminate most of the major grant programs enacted under the administrations of his four predecessors, back to and including the days of the Great Society. The only large recent program to escape unscathed was general revenue sharing. (But in 1985 this program was eliminated by Congress at the request of the president—the only major program to be terminated as part of the 1986 budget.)

While the president was trying to reduce the amount of aid to state and local governments, he was simultaneously offering to increase their power to spend the remaining funds as they saw fit. He proposed a large number of block grants to replace categorical programs, particularly in the categories of health, education, and social services. In health he proposed block grants for primary health care, maternal and child health services, preventive health and health services, and alcohol, drug abuse, and mental health. In education he proposed to replace Titles I and II of the Elementary and Secondary Education Act with block grants. He also proposed block grants for social services and community services. Most of these consolidated several categorical programs into a single grant. The most extensive was the block grant replacing Title II; the administration proposed to consolidate thirty-eight programs into this grant and succeeded in persuading Congress to include twenty-nine. The block grant was not a new idea; several were created during the Nixon and Ford administrations. But the Reagan administration went much further.

One reason for block grants was the belief that programs can be administered more effectively and less expensively by state or local governments if there is less federal regulation. The administration therefore proposed to reduce funding for the new block grants, in the expectation that administrative savings would allow the same level of services to program beneficiaries. But reducing federal regulation was more than just a budget ploy; the administration also proposed regulatory changes in areas where few if any savings were involved, among them bilingual education and community development.

Congress gave the president over four-fifths of the budget cuts he requested for 1982 and approved seven new block grants. It reduced outlays for education and social services and voted to eliminate the Public Service Employment program. It eliminated the parent CETA program as well and replaced it with a new program emphasizing training rather than employment. It did not, however, terminate many of the other programs, although it did cut them back sharply. This was commonly true in those programs that supported construction of local infrastructure and public works, such as the waste treatment plant construction program, new urban mass transit systems, economic development, and UDAG. These cuts added up to $17 billion below President Carter's 1982 request and $6 billion below actual 1981 budget authority.

*Policy since 1982.* Fiscal year 1983 was a different story. As table 1–10 shows, the president proposed a further reduction in budget authority by 13 percent from the 1982 level. Congress instead voted a substantial increase, about a quarter, bringing budget authority back to the 1980 level, measured in current dollars. The primary reason for

27

this abrupt change was probably the continuing recession, through the end of 1982. More than a third of the increase came from the rise in the federal gasoline tax from four to nine cents per gallon, voted by the lame duck session of Congress in December 1982. Most of this was earmarked for highway construction, but one cent was set aside for mass transit.

In addition, Congress increased funds for a wide variety of programs in the course of the normal budget and appropriations process, particularly for education and training and employment. The appropriations bill, enacted during the lame duck session, added $1.6 billion for job training above the president's proposal. In education Congress added substantial sums for the two largest programs, education for the disadvantaged (Title I) and for the handicapped; in both cases the increases restored budget authority to about the 1980 level in current dollars, rather than continuing to cut the programs as the administration proposed.[17] Congress also rejected further reductions in social service outlays and would not let the administration close out the Community Services Administration, the last of the war on poverty agencies.

Finally, in March 1983, the new Congress passed the Emergency Jobs Act (although the recession had ended several months earlier), which provided additional funding for a wide range of grant programs, with the largest share going for community and regional development. Half the community development funds could be used by local governments for "public services," which came close to providing for additional local government employment in the same manner as the Public Service Employment component of CETA that was repealed in 1981. The Emergency Jobs Act thus included a partial temporary reversal of one of the administration's major achievements in 1981. The funds provided, however, were much smaller than the original program. The details of these acts are shown in table 1–11.

Since 1983 the administration has continued to request more modest reductions in budget authority, with modest success. Its fiscal year 1984 budget would have cut authority by about $3 billion; Congress instead voted for an increase of about $4 billion, to $61 billion. For 1985 the administration proposed to cut $5 billion, back below the 1983 level; instead, Congress held budget authority roughly constant. The 1986 budget again proposed substantial cuts of about $7 billion as part of the effort to control the deficit, reducing grants to about $52 billion. This time it met with more success. Congress approved about $3 billion in reductions for fiscal year 1986 in the course of the budget process. In addition, it approved the termination of the general revenue-sharing program, effective in fiscal year 1987. This will save

# TABLE 1-11

## REAGAN PROPOSALS AND ACTUAL BUDGET AUTHORITY, BY FUNCTION, FISCAL YEAR 1983

(billions of dollars)

| Budget Category | Proposed | Actual | Difference | Surface Transportation Act | Emergency Jobs Act | Other 1983 Legislation |
|---|---|---|---|---|---|---|
| Natural resources and environment | 3.0 | 3.6 | 0.6 | 0 | 0.4 | 0.3 |
| Agriculture | 0.4 | 1.9 | 1.4 | 0 | 0 | 1.4 |
| Transportation | | | | | | |
| Highway trust fund | 7.6 | 12.4 | 4.8 | 4.8 | 0 | 0 |
| Mass transit | 3.1 | 4.4 | 1.3 | 0.8 | 0.1 | 0.4 |
| Other | 0.9 | 1.6 | 0.8 | 0 | a | 0.7 |
| Community and regional development | 4.4 | 5.7 | 1.3 | 0 | 1.1 | 0.2 |
| Education | 4.2 | 7.5 | 3.3 | 0 | 0.1 | 3.2 |
| Training and employment | 2.3 | 4.4 | 2.2 | 0 | 0.2 | 2.0 |
| Social services | 4.7 | 5.3 | 0.6 | 0 | 0.3 | 0.3 |
| Health and income security | 2.2 | 2.7 | 0.5 | 0 | 0.2 | 0.3 |
| General fiscal assistance | 6.5 | 6.3 | -0.3 | 0 | 0 | -0.3 |
| Other[b] | 0.3 | 0.8 | 0.5 | 0 | 0.1 | 0.4 |
| Total | 39.6 | 56.7 | 17.1 | 5.6 | 2.5 | 8.9 |

a. Less than $50 million.

b. Includes national defense, energy, commerce and housing credit, veterans' benefits, administration of justice, and general government.

SOURCES: U.S. Office of Management and Budget, *Budget of the United States Government, Fiscal Years 1983, 1985*, Special Analysis H; and Richard P. Nathan and Fred C. Doolittle, "Overview: Effects of the Reagan Domestic Program on States and Localities," unpublished paper, June 7, 1984.

about $4.6 billion annually. For 1987, the administration is proposing to meet the Gramm-Rudman-Hollings targets partly by a very deep cut in grants, about $10 billion. This if enacted would bring budget authority below the 1982 level, to about $43 billion.

As budget authority has increased, outlays have begun rising again, with a lag; 1985 outlays were $58 billion. By 1985 nominal budget authority and outlays were very close to the 1980 level; in effect, real outlays are now being cut simply by the rate of inflation, although earlier in the administration they were being cut much more severely.

Table 1–12 shows the pattern of outlays by budget category during the Reagan administration. In most programs as well as in the aggregate, expenditures have recovered to about their 1981 level in nominal terms, after declining during 1982 and 1983. Only training and employment remains at its 1982 level, slightly more than half the 1981 outlays. Here the administration has apparently made a permanent difference, despite the increases in 1983. Expenditures are also down for construction of waste treatment plants, contained in the category of natural resources and environment, and for social services; they are up sharply for highways and to a lesser extent for mass transit, thanks to the 1982 gas tax increase. Under the 1986 budget resolution highway outlays will continue to rise, but mass transit will level off. Since the administration has not yet persuaded Congress to cut out grants for new subway systems, however, funding may increase again in the future.

**The State and Local Government Response.** The recessions of the early 1980s complicate the analysis of the effects of these reductions on state and local governments, as well as the effects of the changes in welfare programs on the well-being of the poor. In general, however, state and local governments have apparently taken action to offset most of the cuts. It is certainly difficult to ascertain any significant effect of the federal budget cuts on aggregate state and local expenditures, although there have been some effects in specific program areas.

*Aggregate expenditures.* Over the postwar period total state and local expenditures have generally risen in response to population and income growth and to increases in federal aid. During the early 1980s this pattern seems to have changed: expenditures continued to rise with population and to rise and fall with the economy, but they did not fall very much as federal aid was reduced. The departure from the previous pattern was quite pronounced. During the preceding two decades, as federal aid increased, state and local expenditures rose on about a dollar-for-dollar basis in response to the aid.[18] But

## TABLE 1-12
### REAGAN PROPOSALS AND ACTUAL OUTLAYS, BY FUNCTION, FISCAL YEARS 1981–1985
(billions of current dollars)

| Budget Category | 1981 Proposed | 1981 Actual | 1982 Proposed | 1982 Actual | 1983 Proposed | 1983 Actual | 1984 Proposed | 1984 Actual | 1985 Proposed | 1985 Actual |
|---|---|---|---|---|---|---|---|---|---|---|
| Natural resources and environment | 5.2 | 4.9 | 4.7 | 4.9 | 4.2 | 4.0 | 3.6 | 3.8 | 3.4 | 4.1 |
| Transportation | | | | | | | | | | |
| Highways | 8.8 | 9.2 | 8.0 | 8.0 | 8.3 | 8.9 | 8.3 | 10.6 | 8.6 | 12.8 |
| Mass transit | 3.9 | 3.8 | 3.5 | 3.8 | 3.1 | 3.7 | 2.9 | 3.7 | 2.8 | 3.4 |
| Other | 0.5 | 0.5 | 0.5 | 0.4 | 0.5 | 0.7 | 0.5 | 0.7 | 0.5 | 0.9 |
| Community and regional development | 6.2 | 6.1 | 6.0 | 5.4 | 5.0 | 5.0 | 4.4 | 5.2 | 4.6 | 5.2 |
| Education | 7.0 | 6.9 | 5.9 | 6.6 | 5.4 | 6.1 | 4.5 | 6.2 | 3.8 | 7.4 |
| Training and employment | 8.0 | 8.0 | 5.2 | 4.3 | 2.0 | 4.3 | 2.6 | 3.6 | 2.2 | 4.0 |
| Social services | 6.0 | 6.2 | 5.3 | 5.7 | 4.8 | 5.8 | 4.7 | 5.6 | 4.7 | 6.4 |
| General-purpose fiscal assistance | 6.8 | 6.7 | 6.3 | 6.3 | 6.5 | 6.3 | 6.8 | 6.7 | 7.1 | 6.7 |
| Other[a] | 4.2 | 3.9 | 3.5 | 3.6 | 4.0 | 5.2 | 3.7 | 5.9 | 2.5 | 7.1 |
| Total | 56.6 | 56.1 | 48.9 | 49.0 | 43.8 | 49.9 | 41.9 | 53.3 | 40.2 | 57.8 |

a. Includes national defense, energy, agriculture, commerce and housing credit, income security, veterans' benefits, administration of justice, and general government.

SOURCES: Same as table 1–10; 1983 and later Reagan proposals calculated from Special Analysis H of the fiscal year 1983 budget.

TABLE 1–13

NOMINAL AND REAL STATE AND LOCAL GENERAL EXPENDITURES,
FISCAL YEARS 1960–1984

| | Current Dollars (billions) | 1980 Dollars (billions) | 1980 Dollars Per Capita |
|---|---|---|---|
| 1960 | 52.0 | 134.7 | 746 |
| 1965 | 74.6 | 178.9 | 921 |
| 1970 | 131.3 | 256.2 | 1,249 |
| 1971 | 150.7 | 280.0 | 1,348 |
| 1972 | 166.9 | 297.7 | 1,418 |
| 1973 | 181.1 | 305.5 | 1,442 |
| 1974 | 198.6 | 307.9 | 1,442 |
| 1975 | 229.5 | 325.5 | 1,507 |
| 1976 | 255.6 | 344.5 | 1,580 |
| 1977 | 273.0 | 347.8 | 1,579 |
| 1978 | 295.5 | 350.5 | 1,575 |
| 1979 | 326.0 | 355.9 | 1,581 |
| 1980 | 367.3 | 367.3 | 1,614 |
| 1981 | 407.4 | 371.7 | 1,616 |
| 1982 | 435.3 | 374.5 | 1,612 |
| 1983 | 466.4 | 386.5 | 1,648 |
| 1984 | 505.0 | 403.4 | 1,705 |

NOTE: Current dollars are deflated by the GNP deflator to calculate 1980 dollars.

SOURCES: U.S. Advisory Commission on Intergovernmental Relations, *Significant Features of Fiscal Federalism*, 1984 edition, table 15; and U.S. Bureau of the Census, *Government Finances in 1983–1984*, table 3.

during the early 1980s, as aid was reduced, expenditures seem to have fallen by only about a third of the cut; the rest was made up by increased expenditures from state and local revenues.

Table 1–13 shows general expenditures since 1960 in nominal and real dollars and real dollars per capita.[19] The table illustrates both the long-term trend of increased expenditures and the influence of economic cycles, which shows up most clearly in the real per capita figures, as in the recession of 1973–1975.

In the early 1980s aggregate nominal state and local outlays kept rising while federal grants were basically constant. Between 1980 and 1983 federal grants fluctuated within a $6 billion range while state and local expenditures increased by about $30 billion per year. In real per capita terms, outlays were virtually unchanged from 1980 to 1982 while federal aid declined by $74; in 1983 expenditures rose by about 2 percent, or $36, while aid did not change.[20]

It seems clear that the dominant factor affecting state and local expenditures during the early 1980s was the state of the economy. This can be seen by examining the behavior of state and local governments during this period in more detail.[21]

The best measure of the fiscal condition of state and local governments is the accumulated balance, rather than the annual surplus or deficit. Unlike the federal government, nearly all state and local governments are required to balance their budgets, usually annually. To avoid unexpected deficits—requiring tax increases, borrowing, or expenditure cuts on short notice, all painful options—they typically try to accumulate surpluses during prosperous years, which can be spent if needed during recessions. A common rule of thumb is that these accumulated balances should amount to 5 percent of projected expenditures for the next fiscal year.

The decade of the 1980s began with state and local governments running a current operating surplus of about $6 billion on an annual rate; they had been running surpluses as large or larger since the 1973–1975 recession. But the years from 1980 through 1982 saw two recessions with a weak recovery in between. The first recession did not have a significant effect on state and local governments; their surpluses declined sharply in mid-1980 but then rose quickly back to the $6 billion level. The second was more serious; the budget surplus vanished by the end of 1981, and the sector ran a deficit during all of calendar year 1982. This recession was particularly painful because it lasted longer than anticipated; most state and local governments formulated their budgets for fiscal year 1983 on the expectation that the recession would end by the middle of 1982. Instead, it continued for another six months. By the end of fiscal year 1983 in June, eight states, including California, New York, and Pennsylvania, had exhausted their accumulated balances, and another fourteen had balances amounting to less than 1 percent of outlays.

State and local governments met this problem to a large extent by raising taxes. From the beginning of 1981 to the end of fiscal year 1983, tax increases may have amounted to about $18 billion annually. This enabled them to avoid any real reductions in outlays. The growth rate was certainly much smaller than it had been during the 1970s. Real expenditures increased by less than 1 percent in both 1981 and 1982. For the first time in many years, state and local government employment declined, by 2 percent, from 1980 to 1982. Given the cuts in aid, however, it is surprising that expenditures rose at all and that employment did not decline further.

The tax increases were not enough to enable state and local governments to balance their current operating budgets during the recession; they continued to draw down their accumulated balances. But the new taxes contributed to the large surpluses that developed during the economic recovery in 1983 and 1984. By the second quarter of 1983, six months after the trough of the recession, the fiscal problems were easing. Although many governments had exhausted their accumulated balances, they had started to run current account surpluses. In the second quarter state and local governments ran a $7 billion surplus on an annual basis; through early 1985 the surplus averaged about $10 billion. This enabled them to begin expanding outlays again; by the end of 1985 the surplus was dwindling.

*Changes by program.* The responses to the federal budget cuts have varied widely among the individual program categories. Some general trends can be discerned, although counterexamples can easily be found. State and local governments have provided money from their own tax revenues to replace part or all of the reductions in federal funds for most of the individual grant programs, but in a few categories expenditures have declined. The governments have also tended to follow the same expenditure patterns in the new block grants as in the former categorical programs, rather than take advantage of the increased flexibility that the block grants offer.

*Mass transit.* Operating subsidies for mass transit offer a particularly clear example of the substitution of state and local government funds for federal. The federal government first provided operating subsidies in 1975, at $300 million nationally. They had reached $1.1 billion by 1980 and remained at that level in 1981. The Reagan administration has tried to eliminate them altogether, without success, but it was able to cut them by about 25 percent ($268 million) between 1981 and 1983. During the same two years state and local operating subsidies increased by almost $1 billion. In several instances, including Los Angeles and Seattle, the additional subsidies were provided through new tax levies specifically earmarked for mass transit; in others increased state or local aid was justified explicitly as a substitute for the federal subsidy. Measured as a share of total transit revenues, increased state and local aid has almost exactly offset the federal cutback; federal subsidies have declined by 5.2 percentage points while state and local funds have increased by 5.4 points.[22]

Rather surprisingly, apparently few transit authorities have resorted to fare increases, preferring to meet higher costs out of taxes, even though the federal aid cuts occurred during a severe recession. Operating revenues increased by almost $500 million but remained at about 37 percent of total revenue. Operating revenues per trip and per mile have both increased, and the average fare rose by 7.6 cents, or 16 percent, but similar increases occurred in the late 1970s, before federal subsidies were cut. Richard Nathan and Fred Doolittle, who have been studying state and local responses to the reductions in federal grants, report that only one of fourteen cities surveyed (Cleveland) raised fares in response to the change in federal policy.[23] Actual ridership was apparently unaffected; it declined in 1982 but rose in 1983. This is consistent with what has happened in previous recessions.

*Elementary and secondary education.* The most sweeping of the block grants is Chapter II of the Elementary and Secondary Education Act. This grant replaced twenty-nine programs previously funded under Title II of the act and reduced federal aid by about one-third, or almost $250 million, from 1980 to 1983. In this instance it is very difficult to measure the extent to which state and local governments made up the difference; Chapter II is a very small share of total education expenditures, and the categorical grant funds were spent for a wide variety of purposes. Nevertheless, some interesting information on the actual spending of the block grant funds, from several studies of individual states, suggests that school districts did change their behavior.[24]

The new block grant required individual states to develop their own formulas for allocating funds to local school districts. This proved to be a complicated and controversial political process. States were required to take enrollment and cost factors into account but had great latitude in choosing the cost factors to be included and determining the weights. State education agencies were also allowed to spend up to 20 percent of the funds at their own discretion, and most chose to spend the full amount.

Total state and local expenditures on elementary and secondary education rose steadily during the 1980s, from $101 billion in 1980 to $122 billion in 1983, and have continued to rise. Total federal aid to elementary and secondary schools decreased at the same time from $5.2 to $4.3 billion; thus Chapter II and its predecessors are almost insignificant in the aggregate and not very important even in the context of federal aid to education.

When Congress approved the administration's consolidation and funding cutback for Title II programs in 1981, many state education authorities and local school districts were concerned that this was only the first step; they feared further aid reductions. This has proved to be unfounded; Congress refused to approve further cuts, and aid has stabilized at around $500 million per year. But initially school districts tended to devote most of their Chapter II funds to capital expenditures that would not require continuing future outlays. The General Accounting Office (GAO) surveyed thirteen states and reported that about 55 percent of the funds in the 1982–1983 school year were spent on instructional materials. Microcomputers accounted for 24 percent, books 21 percent, and audiovisual equipment 10 percent. The GAO did not attempt to compare this pattern in any detail with expenditures under Title II, although it quoted state education officials as saying that they were funding similar activities in both cases. But other analysts have felt that the block grant was a departure from previous experience and have predicted that expenditures will shift toward teacher salaries and other continuing outlays as school districts come to expect and rely on a steady funding level.[25]

There is some evidence that expenditures in one sensitive area have been reduced. A few large states used Title II to support school desegregation activities, such as magnet schools. Most of the local school districts in the GAO survey conducting such activities reported a decrease in their outlays under the new block grant. But at least four states allocated funds from their 20 percent set-aside to help local school districts continue desegregation programs. The net effect is uncertain.[26]

*Social services.* The social services block grant, like Chapter II, consolidated a large number of programs into a single grant, but the legislative change by itself was not particularly important. Title XX of the Social Security Act, which authorized the categorical programs, already functioned much like a block grant.

Title XX was funded at about $3 billion in fiscal year 1981. The block grant cut social services funding by about $600 million, or 20 percent, in 1982; half of the cut, however, was restored in the Emergency Jobs Bill of 1983, and funding has been maintained at about $2.7 million since.

State governments have chosen to offset most of the cut, partly by shifting funds among block grants and partly by providing funds from their own revenues. In New York and Pennsylvania, state funds alone more than compensated for the loss of federal money.

The shifts among block grants are especially interesting, as an example of the states' use of their new powers. When Congress created the seven new block grants in 1981, it allowed states to reallocate up to 10 percent of the funds among the various block grants. The states have chosen to use this authority almost entirely to increase social service funding. The GAO survey of thirteen states found that over $100 million was transferred to social services during 1982 and 1983 from the new low-income home energy assistance block grant. The energy grant was the only one funded at a higher level than the programs it replaced.[27] These states received almost half the total block grant funds. If that sample represents the nation, then states cut energy assistance in absolute dollars while Congress was voting to increase it, and this policy alone offset about a quarter of the total social service reductions in those two years.

Other funds came from local governments, private donations, and user fees for services. In all, total social services spending increased by $288 million from 1981 to 1983 while federal funding was declining by $50 million.

Several states also shifted certain activities from social services to other programs, most often choosing to transfer home health care to the Medicaid program or day-care expenses for welfare recipients to AFDC. Both changes permit a state to receive federal matching funds.

There are no obvious national trends in the funding of particular activities. States are continuing to support the same activities that were funded directly by the federal government. There have been some changes in administrative procedures, the most common being tighter eligibility standards for day care.

*Community services.* The community services block grant replaced the Community Services Administration, which was itself the successor to the Office of Economic Opportunity and the last of the war on poverty agencies created during the Johnson administration. The block grant, like the eight previous categorical programs, has the purpose of fighting poverty. Funds are spent for many of the same goods and services provided by other federal programs, such as housing, food assistance, and job training. They can even be spent to administer other federal programs. But community services are often provided by a different kind of entity, a local community group such as a private nonprofit organization, operating outside the normal government channels and, in the earlier years, sometimes in opposition to the local government. (Some community action agencies are part of local governments.) And the agencies often provide goods and services in a different way from other federal programs: instead of food stamps, for example, they offer emergency food assistance.

Under the block grant, funds have been cut by more than 25 percent, from $525 million in fiscal year 1981 to an average of about $370 million since, and are likely to remain at the current level. Except for $25 million in the Emergency Jobs Bill of 1983, the cuts have not been even partially restored.

State governments have done less than nothing to replace the federal funding reductions. Of the thirteen states in the GAO study, ten originally spent nothing on community services and have not begun to; all three of the states that did spend some of their own money to start with cut their outlays at the same time that the federal government did.[28] Nathan and Doolittle report that none of the states in their sample replaced federal funds from their own revenues.[29] A few states transferred funds from other block grants to community services, but other states reversed the process.

Nonetheless, community services agencies were able to find ways to mitigate the effects of the block grant reductions. Some received money from other federal programs, such as Operation Head Start for disadvantaged preschool children. In part this simply involved a change in the administrative responsibility for a federal program; the community services agency replaced another unit of local government, as happened with low-income home energy in some places. This may have been important for the agency, but it does not reflect increased federal funding for the specific purpose.

There were more important changes from a broader social standpoint. Many community services agencies were able to get more money from private organizations. Some began to charge fees for their services; some started business activities. Many reduced the size of their paid staff and relied more heavily on volunteers.

As a result of these and other efforts, a number of agencies were able to offset the reduction in federal funding completely. Although twenty-four of forty-four agencies surveyed by the GAO reported a decline in total funds between 1981 and 1983, this was fewer than the thirty-three that received less from the federal community services programs. In general these agencies did not rely heavily on the community services programs to begin with; in 1981 they received 28 percent of their funds through the categorical programs, and in 1983 they received 21 percent from the new block grant.

The federal cuts did result in some operational changes. General trends are hard to discern among the welter of local responses to local situations, but there seems to have been a shift away from long-term strategies to ameliorate poverty toward direct immediate help for people with pressing problems, although the recession might have contributed to this trend as well. Some agencies eliminated some services; at least one turned away from providing aid itself toward becoming a referral service to other organizations.

The most fundamental organizational change was to bring the states into the process of distributing the block grant funds. Under the prior categorical programs, funds went directly from the federal government to local governments or private agencies, on a competitive or discretionary basis. The law required the states to continue funding the same agencies the federal government had funded in 1981, but they could choose how to distribute funds to the agencies and how much to give to each one. They have generally spread funds more evenly through their states, so that more money has gone to small cities and rural areas. Several states have chosen to establish allocation formulas that give substantial weight to the incidence of poverty; in at least one state, Michigan, this formula shifted funds away from Detroit to rural outstate areas. In some western states funding cuts were particularly severe for Indian tribes and other Indian organizations.

Federal administrative costs for the new block grant are much below those for the former programs; they were cut from about $40 million in 1981 to about $2 million in 1985. State administrative costs have increased, but there is very little information on how much.

*Job training.* By far the biggest change, in both program structure and budget, came in job training and employment programs. The termination of Public Service Employment and the replacement of CETA by the Job Training Partnership Act (JTPA) effectively cut federal funding by half within a single year, and outlays have remained around $4 billion annually. Since the JTPA was enacted, however, a dozen states have voted to spend more of their own money on job training, as a direct response to the federal government's action.[30] In most states the funds simply come from state appropriations, but Delaware has enacted an earmarked tax on business, and Vermont is issuing bonds specifically to finance public service jobs; Oregon is setting up a state lottery for job creation and economic development. State spending on these programs is small so far; initial appropriations amounted to about $100 million, far less than the reduction of about $4 billion in federal outlays. It is nonetheless interesting that states are willing to provide some support even for these much-criticized programs.

Some states have taken action to replace federal programs to train youth. In 1977 several youth programs were added to CETA. Some were directed to out-of-school youth and offered academic credit as well as work experience; others were open to all unemployed youth regardless of family income. President Carter's last budget proposed to consolidate these programs into a Youth Initiative, funded at $2 billion annually. President Reagan withdrew the proposal, and most of the federal youth programs were terminated in the process of replacing CETA by the JTPA. In response, however, eleven states have chosen to establish their own youth corps programs. Most are not means-tested but are open to all unemployed youth. It is too early to form any impression of how well the states are doing with these programs, but it is an example of their moving into an area as the federal government moves out.[31]

**Implications for the Federal Government and Federalism.** Viewed in the light of the federal budget, the Reagan administration had a stunning initial success but has not been able to repeat it and may not prove able to sustain it. It imposed severe funding cuts for grants to state and local governments in 1981, but Congress partly reversed the cuts in later years, and the early 1980s may yet prove to be only a temporary downward blip in the growth of federal grants.

Viewed in the light of the responses of state and local governments, however, the administration may have some subtle but important accomplishments. State and local governments have generally increased their own expenditures to make up for the federal cuts. In the process they have taken increased responsibility for certain governmental functions. In at least one case they have not tried to fill the gap, but the grant recipients have themselves been able partly to offset the cuts by turning to the private sector.

These outcomes may well be what the administration wanted or would settle for. Mass transit, a service with local rather than national benefits, is now being provided to a much greater extent by local governments; the federal share of operating costs is dwindling. In education, traditionally a local responsibility although it confers benefits on the nation as a whole, local and especially state governments have become more important as federal aid has diminished. In community services an administration that favors private sector initiatives to meet social problems can hardly be unhappy if community action agencies have found private support.

These changes have led some observers to see an emerging trend toward a stronger role for the states and perhaps a significant change in the structure of American government.[32] In 1983 President Reagan proposed a New Federalism, redistributing responsibilities between the states and the federal government. His specific proposals have vanished from the political arena, but he may be achieving a new federalism nonetheless.

Viewed in the light of providing goods and services to the people, it is not yet clear if these intergovernmental changes really matter. Many of these functions have not been performed very effectively by the federal government, which is one reason why Congress has been willing to give the president the block grants and the budget cuts that he asked for. But for some, such as education, part of the original impetus for federal aid was the widespread view that state and local governments were not doing the job adequately. Whether they are now able to do it any more efficiently remains to be seen.

# Notes

1. The term "counterrevolution" is used in John L. Palmer and Isabel V. Sawhill, eds., *The Reagan Experiment* (Washington, D.C.: Urban Institute Press, 1982), p. 28.

2. "Payments to individuals" that initially take the form of federal grants to state and local governments amount to another 9 percent of the domestic budget. Most low-income benefit programs fall into this category.

3. For a more extended discussion of the evolution of the "social safety net" concept during President Reagan's first term, see John C. Weicher, "The Safety Net after Three Years," in John C. Weicher, ed., *Maintaining the Safety Net: Income Redistribution Programs in the Reagan Administration* (Washington, D.C.: American Enterprise Institute, 1984), p. 2.

4. The low-income energy assistance program is included in the table as a cash benefit, but the states, which actually administer the program, have the option of providing aid either in cash or in kind, as payments to vendors.

5. Budget projections for 1982 to 1984 were published in detail in the fiscal year 1982 budget prepared by President Carter. Revisions and reestimates for those years and also for 1985 and 1986 were published in President Reagan's revised budget (U.S. Office of Management and Budget, *Additional Details on Budget Savings*, March 1981). The figures published in the revision as the "Carter budget" differ slightly from those in President Carter's budget. The Omnibus Budget Reconciliation Act of 1981 established budget totals for 1982 to 1984 only. Detailed and generally consistent data are thus available for 1982 through 1984 but not for later years. For data on 1985 see Weicher, "Safety Net."

6. The most comparable estimates are the Carter reestimate, the Reagan revision, and OBRA; the economic assumptions are nearly identical. OBRA estimates are taken from *Congressional Quarterly*, August 15, 1981, except for child nutrition programs, which are taken from G. William Hoagland, "Perception and Reality in Nutrition Programs," in Weicher, *Maintaining the Safety Net*. Thus there is some possible small inconsistency in the totals.

7. The effect of the recession on actual outlays is calculated by the author from an OMB Technical Staff Memorandum, "Sensitivity of Federal Expenditures to Unemployment," unpublished paper, April 18, 1980.

8. Elsewhere I have shown that the official poverty rate has overstated the incidence of poverty since 1967, because the CPI measured the cost of homeownership incorrectly (John C. Weicher, "Mismeasuring Poverty and Progress," paper presented at the American Enterprise Institute Public Policy Week, December 5, 1985). By my calculations, the lowest poverty rate was reached in 1978 and 1979, not 1973, and the increase during the early 1980s has been smaller by about one percentage point of the population. Correcting the poverty rate thus changes the specific numbers contained in this sub-

section, but it does not affect the qualitative analysis or the general conclusions.

9. Peter Gottschalk and Sheldon Danziger, "Macroeconomic Conditions, Income Transfers, and the Trend in Poverty," in D. Lee Bawden, ed., *The Social Contract Revisited* (Washington, D.C.: Urban Institute Press, 1984). The estimate for 1984 appears in Sheldon Danziger and Peter Gottschalk, "The Impact of Budget Cuts and Economic Conditions on Poverty" (Paper presented at hearings before the U.S. House of Representatives, Committee on Education and Labor, February 21, 1985).

10. Rebecca M. Blank and Alan S. Blinder, "Macroeconomics, Income Distribution, and Poverty," unpublished paper, April 1985. The 1984 estimate appears in footnote 35.

11. Gottschalk and Danziger, "Trend in Poverty," p. 207; see also Timothy M. Smeeding, "The Anti-Poverty Effect of In-Kind Transfers: A 'Good Idea' Gone Too Far?" *Policy Studies Journal*, vol. 10 (March 1982), pp. 499–522, esp. p. 515. A more optimistic view of the effect of economic growth on poverty among female-headed households is offered by June O'Neill, "Comment," in Bawden, *Social Contract Revisited*, pp. 218–19.

12. The programs included are not precisely the same as the social safety net; the table includes means-tested veterans' pensions and state general assistance programs, as well as AFDC and SSI, but excludes energy assistance and the earned-income tax credit. The targeting percentages are so low because the data for total means-tested cash benefits are more inclusive than the poverty income deficit estimates. The latter, based on the Current Population Survey, underreport cash benefits. The CPS estimates of reported benefits have been published for some but not all years since 1979 and for some but not all of the means-tested programs (means-tested veterans' benefits are not reported separately from service disability pensions). These estimates show a similar pattern of an increase in targeting since 1979, with much higher targeting percentages.

13. There have been several estimates of the poverty rate net of in-kind benefits and some controversy over the estimates and the methods used to construct them, but all the estimates show a similar trend. See, for example, Morton Paglin, *Poverty and Transfers In-Kind* (Palo Alto, Calif.: Hoover Institution Press, 1979); Congressional Budget Office, "Poverty Status of Families under Alternative Definitions of Income," Background Paper no. 17, 1977; G. William Hoagland, "The Effectiveness of Current Transfer Programs in Reducing Poverty" (Paper presented at the Middlebury College Conference on Economic Issues, April 19, 1980); and Timothy M. Smeeding, "What the Official Estimates Fail to Show," in Sheldon Danziger et al., *Recent Increases in Poverty: Testimony before the House Ways and Means Committee* (Madison, Wis.: Institute for Research on Poverty, Discussion Paper no. 740-83, November 1983).

14. This figure has been calculated by the author from U.S. Department of Housing and Urban Development, *Alternative Operating Systems for the Public Housing Program*, May 1982, table 2.

15. Hoagland, "Nutrition Programs" p. 64.

16. Not all elderly individuals can be excluded, because the published data identify only those living alone and those who head two-person households. These categories include at least 78 percent of all elderly each year. Depending on the age of the second household member, the data may include up to 95 percent of all elderly each year.

17. For an extensive discussion of education programs, see Denis P. Doyle and Terry W. Hartle, "Ideology, Pragmatic Politics, and the Education Budget," in Weicher, *Maintaining the Safety Net*, pp. 119–53.

18. See Peter Mieszkowski and Robert N. Stein, "Trends and Prospects in State and Local Finance," *Journal of Urban Economics*, vol. 14 (September 1983), pp. 224–41, for a discussion of the economic literature on the relationship of federal grants to state and local government expenditures.

19. General expenditures exclude utilities and liquor stores, operated by some state and local governments, and insurance and trust expenditures. The figures are for state and local fiscal years ending during the calendar year; typically these fiscal years end in June, and the federal fiscal year ends in September. This difference, however, does not affect the trends in the tables.

20. The figures for federal grants cited in the text include payments to individuals made through state and local governments (primarily in income security programs and Medicaid) and are thus more inclusive than the figures in table 1–11. For this reason, the figures in the text cannot be derived from the table.

21. For a more detailed description of the state and local fiscal situations during the 1980s, see John C. Weicher, "The State and Local Government Sector and the Federal Deficit," in Phillip Cagan, ed., *Essays in Contemporary Economic Problems: The Economy in Deficit* (Washington, D.C.: American Enterprise Institute, 1985), pp. 59–79.

22. Information on aggregate expenditures is taken from American Public Transit Association, *Transit Fact Book*, Washington, D.C., 1985.

23. Richard P. Nathan and Fred C. Doolittle, "Overview: Effects of the Reagan Domestic Program on States and Localities," unpublished paper, June 7, 1984.

24. The three studies are ibid.; U.S. General Accounting Office, "Education Block Grant Alters State Role and Provides Greater Local Discretion," Report no. HRD-85-18, November 19, 1984; and Education Policy Research Institute, "The Interactions of Federal and Related State Education Programs," Washington, D.C., February 1983. Among them the three studies report on twenty-six states, including the ten largest.

25. Doyle and Hartle, "Education Budget," pp. 136–37.

26. Nathan and Doolittle, "Effects on States and Localities," conclude that "the combination of federal aid cuts and the new state distribution formulas for federal aid appears to have reduced the geographic and social targeting of this type of federal aid for education" (p. 29).

27. U.S. General Accounting Office, "States Use Several Strategies to Cope with Funding Reductions under Social Services Block Grant," Report no. GAO/HRD-84-68, August 9, 1984, pp. 9–15. Nathan and Doolittle report sim-

ilar findings but do not report that total funding increased in individual states ("Effects on States and Localities," p. 31).

28. U.S. General Accounting Office, "Community Services Block Grant Program: New State Role Brings Program and Administrative Changes," Report no. GAO/HRD-84-76, September 28, 1984.

29. Nathan and Doolittle, "Effects on States and Localities," p. 30.

30. National Conference of State Legislatures, "Directory of State Legislative Involvement with the Job Training Partnership Act," Washington, D.C., Spring 1985.

31. For further discussion of federal youth training programs, see Sean Sullivan, "Youth Employment," in Jack A. Meyer, ed., *Meeting Human Needs: Toward a New Public Philosophy* (Washington, D.C.: American Enterprise Institute, 1982), pp. 215–57.

32. Nathan and Doolittle, "Effects on States and Localities," p. 48; and Denis P. Doyle and Terry W. Hartle, *Excellence in Education: The States Take Charge* (Washington, D.C.: American Enterprise Institute, 1985).

# 2
# Taxation and Business Investment

*Joel Slemrod*

## Summary

*This chapter is divided into two parts. The first part offers a brief review of the modern theory of how the tax system affects business investment. The second part examines the behavior of business investment following the tax legislation of 1981 to see what can be learned from the recent experience.*

*Tax policy can directly affect business investment by altering the benefits and costs to a firm making additional capital investment. In the approach pioneered by Robert Hall and Dale Jorgenson, the entire effect of the tax code on the incentive to purchase investment is summarized in a single measure known as the user cost of capital. The user cost depends on the rate of interest, the corporate tax rate, the schedule of cost recovery allowances, and the rate of investment tax credit. Knowing the statutory corporate tax rate is not sufficient to understand the net impact of the tax system. When, for example, capital investment can be immediately written off (expensed), the tax system provides no disincentive to an equity-financed investment regardless of the tax rate.*

*The user cost, along with the price of other inputs and the firm's output target, determines the firm's desired capital stock at any point. The response of the desired capital stock to changes in the user cost depends on the ability to substitute capital for other inputs and the effect on desired output. The response of current investment to a change in the desired stock of capital depends on the adjustment costs attendant to installing new fixed investment.*

*Tax policy may also affect the incentive to invest through its effect on interest rates, its interaction with corporate financial policy, its effect on the riskiness of investment, and its effect on expectations concerning the future course of tax policy. Much recent research has focused on these issues, although no resolution concerning their importance has been reached. The simple user-cost approach, although useful as a guide to the influence of tax policy, by no means represents a consensus view of the net effect of the tax system.*

*A modern alternative to the user-cost approach, known as Tobin's q theory, is based on the simple idea that if the increase in a firm's market value due to the investment exceeds the net cost of the asset it should be undertaken. The principal potential empirical advantage of this approach is that it is based on an observable value, the ratio of the market value of capital to its replacement cost, and does not require arbitrary assumptions about expectations and other factors. Its potential has remained unfulfilled because of both theoretical difficulties and the poor performance of empirical models.*

*One of the principal objectives of the Reagan administration's tax policy initiatives was to increase the incentives for business investment. To that end, the Economic Recovery Tax Act of 1981 (ERTA) included several provisions designed to reduce the effective tax rate on new investment, including a system of more rapid capital cost recovery allowances and an expanded investment tax credit. However, in response to concern over the rising deficits and to a feeling that ERTA had "gone too far," the Tax Equity and Fiscal Responsibility Act of 1982 (TEFRA) cancelled some further investment incentives scheduled to be phased in under ERTA and cut back on others.*

*The passage of ERTA approximately coincided with the peak of the short-lived recovery that began in 1980:III. The decline in investment during the subsequent recession was severe, though not much more severe than in other postwar recessions. The rebound in investment was particularly strong, averaging a 13.7 percent annual rate of growth compared with a typical rate of growth over the nine quarters following a cyclical trough of 6.6 percent. Over the entire course of the business cycle, investment grew at an annual rate of 5.6 percent, nearly double the average rate of growth during comparable recent cycles. Over the cycle the capital-GNP ratio increased by 1.5 percent.*

*The strong performance of equipment investment cannot, however, be directly attributed to the changes in business taxation. Calculations show that ERTA, as modified by TEFRA, had a negligibly small effect on the user cost of equipment. (ERTA in its fully phased-in version, unmodified by TEFRA, would have caused a large reduction.) Furthermore, changes in the expected rate of inflation and the real rate of interest certainly outweighed the effect of tax policy on the user cost. For these reasons, it is concluded that the recent performance of investment in equipment can tell us very little about the effectiveness of tax incentives for investment. On the other hand, the strong performance of investment in structures is consistent with the reduction in the effective corporate rate provided by ERTA, even as modified by TEFRA.*

## Introduction

Tax changes designed to increase the rate of business investment have been a major component of fiscal policy under the Reagan administration. In part, these policies represented a response to the widely held perception that net capital formation as a share of GNP had fallen substantially since the late 1960s and was proceeding at a much slower rate than that of many of our major trading partners. The relatively poor performance of net investment was held to be at least partly responsible for the decline in productivity growth and international competitiveness.

The Economic Recovery Tax Act of 1981 (ERTA) included several provisions designed to reduce the effective tax rate on new investment, including a system of more rapid capital cost recovery allowances, an expanded investment tax credit, and a provision called "safe-harbor leasing" designed to allow firms without current taxable income to immediately benefit from the investment incentives. However, in response to concern over the rising deficit and a feeling that ERTA had "gone too far," the Tax Equity and Fiscal Responsibility Act of 1982 (TEFRA) cancelled some further investment incentives scheduled to be phased in under ERTA, cut back on others, and curtailed safe-harbor leasing.

ERTA's passage approximately coincided with the beginning of a steep recession, in which investment (as well as GNP) fell sharply. The recovery that began in the fourth quarter of 1982 was, however, significantly stronger than the typical recovery and, in particular, the recovery of investment was significantly greater than in previous recoveries. Over the entire cycle, the growth in the real net capital stock has slightly exceeded the growth in real GNP.

The purpose of this chapter is to assess the effectiveness of tax incentives for investment. It proceeds in two steps. First it reviews the economic theory of how the tax system influences investment. Special attention is paid to recent developments in the theory, and the areas where disagreement remains are noted. The second part of the paper discusses, using the insights gained from the theory, the investment incentives enacted in ERTA and TEFRA and their effect on the subsequent performance of investment in the United States.

## The Theory of Taxation and Business Investment

Most theories of business investment begin with the presumption that firm managers make investment decisions in the best interests of the shareholders. In the neoclassical framework introduced by Hall and Jorgenson in 1967, an investment is in the best interests of the shareholders if the present value of the additional revenues generated by the additional capital exceeds the cost of the investment.[1] According to Tobin's $q$ theory of investment, an investment is in the best interests of the shareholders if it increases the value of the firm's outstanding shares. As discussed later, these two criteria boil down to essentially the same thing.

Taxation can affect business investment because it influences the path of GNP. If tax policy stimulates overall growth of the economy,

47

then business investment will also be stimulated. In this respect, tax policy is no different from other forms of fiscal policy, monetary policy, or microeconomic policies aimed at improving economic performance. Tax policy can also directly affect business investment by altering, for any given path of GNP, the benefits and costs to a firm of making additional investment. It is this latter mechanism that this chapter focuses on.

**User Cost of Capital.** In the approach pioneered by Hall and Jorgenson, all of the effects of the tax code on the benefits and the costs of making a new investment are summarized into a single measure known as the user cost of capital. The analysis begins with the observation that a profit-maximizing firm will purchase a new capital asset as long as the present discounted value of the stream of returns generated by the asset exceeds the cost of acquiring the asset. Imagine that a firm proceeds with all capital investment projects that meet this criterion. It will invest until, for the marginal project, the present discounted value of its returns just equals the acquisition cost. In order to simplify the calculations it is assumed that the productivity of the capital asset depreciates exponentially (that is, its output falls by a constant fraction each year). Then it can be shown that the following condition applies to the marginal investment:

$$f = q\,(r+d) \tag{1}$$

Here $f$ stands for the annual return to one unit of capital at the time of acquisition, $q$ is the unit cost of acquisition, $r$ is the firm's annual rate of discount, and $d$ is the rate of economic depreciation (that is, the output declines $100d$ percent per year). The right-hand side of expression (1) is called the user cost of capital, or the rental price of capital. It is the annual cost to the firm of using one unit of capital. Part of the cost, $qd$, is due to the loss in value of the capital asset because of wear and tear or obsolescence.[2] The other part of the user cost, $qr$, is the opportunity cost of tying up funds in the capital good. If not used for capital investment, the funds could earn a rate of return equal to $r$.

Holding $q$ and $r$ constant, equation (1) apparently implies that the user cost of capital for shorter-lived assets is higher than the user cost for longer-lived assets, because of their more rapid depreciation (a higher value of $d$). This does not, though, imply that it is less costly for a firm to use longer-lived capital goods when possible. The unit price of a capital good, $q$, will reflect its rate of depreciation, so that an asset that, for example, initially produces the same flow of services as another but wears out more quickly will have a lower acquisition price per unit of initial output.

Introducing corporation taxes into the model does not change the fundamental equilibrium condition that firms will purchase capital goods as long as the present discounted value exceeds the acquisition cost, nor the condition that for the marginal investment the two will be equal. Under a corporation tax the revenue generated by the capital is taxed at the corporate tax rate, denoted $u$, and the acquisition price is reduced by any applicable investment tax credit, denoted $k$. In addition, purchasing a capital asset entitles the owner to a stream of subtractions from taxable income which are now known as cost recovery allowances, and which were known as depreciation allowances in the years preceding ERTA. It is useful to think of the present discounted value stream of tax reductions generated by the cost recovery allowances as a reduction in the acquisition cost of the asset. It is standard to use $z$ to represent the present value per dollar of acquisition cost of the cost recovery allowances that can be deducted from taxable income. Then $uz$ is the tax reduction resulting from the cost recovery allowances due to one dollar of investment. With these adjustments for the presence of corporation taxes, equation (1) can be rewritten as follows:

$$(1-u)f = q(1-k-uz)(r+d) \qquad (2)$$

In (2), the effective acquisition cost of the asset is no longer $q$, but is reduced by the investment tax credit and the cost recovery allowances to $q(1-k-uz)$.

If equation (2) is rearranged to read

$$f = q\left(\frac{1-k-uz}{1-u}\right)(r+d) \equiv c, \qquad (3)$$

then the right-hand side is the user cost of capital ($c$), also known as the rental price. If $f$ exceeds this expression, an investment is worth doing. As long as $(1-k-uz)/(1-u)$ is greater than one, the net effect of corporate-level taxation is to increase the user cost, which implies that some projects that would be worth doing in the absence of taxation are no longer worth doing.

A look at two special cases of corporation tax policy is revealing. First consider "expensing," under which all investment expenditures are deductible from taxable income in the year incurred, and there is no investment tax credit. In this case, the present value of the cost recovery allowances, $z$, is simply equal to one. Because $k$ (the investment tax credit) equals zero, the expression $(1-k-uz)/(1-u)$ reduces to exactly one. Thus expression (3) is identical to expression (1), the no-tax case—the tax system called expensing has no effect on the marginal investment decision. In essence, the government contributes the fraction $u$ of all investment expenses and recovers the same fraction $u$ of all gross revenues generated. Any project that was worthwhile in the absence of this "silent partnership" role of the government will still be worthwhile in its presence.

A second instructive special case occurs when the cost recovery allowances exactly mirror the decline in value of the asset (its "economic" depreciation). This is the case of a pure income tax. Under these circumstances (and exponential depreciation) it can be shown that $z$, the present value of future cost recovery allowances, equals $d/(r+d)$. If $d/(r+d)$ is substituted for $z$ in expression (3) and $k$ is set to zero, (3) reduces to

$$f = q \left( \frac{r}{1-u} + d \right) \equiv c \tag{4}$$

A comparison of (4) with the no-tax case of (1) reveals that the income tax increases the user cost by multiplying the required rate of return, net of depreciation, by the factor $1/(1-u)$.

In general, the effect of the corporation tax system on the incentive to invest depends on both the statutory tax rate and the system of cost recovery allowances as well as the investment tax credit. Even a system with an apparently high statutory rate can have little or no disincentive effect on new investment and may even provide a subsidy to new investment.

Before continuing this story, it is valuable to point out several assumptions implicit in this calculation of the user cost of capital. First, the calculation assumes that the price of capital goods $q$, the tax rate $u$, the investment tax credit $k$, and the system of depreciation allowances will not change over the life of the asset, or that no such changes are anticipated. It is also assumed that the corporation will in every year have enough taxable income that any investment tax credits and cost recovery allowances reduce tax liability immediately and need not be carried forward to future tax years. Furthermore, the potential effect of the tax system on the discount rate of the corporation has been ignored. It may be argued, for example, that because of interest deductibility, the corporate tax reduces the net cost of funds to the corporation. Finally, the model ignores the uncertainty of the return to capital and how taxation affects the desirability of a risky investment. These issues are taken up later in the chapter.

The user cost of capital is the price per year to firms of using a unit of capital. This price, along with the price of other inputs and the firm's output target, determines the firm's desired stock of capital at any point. If the system of taxation changes so as to reduce the user cost of capital, then the cost-minimizing response of firms is to substitute capital for other inputs, such as labor. The precise response of the desired capital intensity of production to a change in the relative price of inputs obviously varies depending on the production process. Empirical estimates of the substitutability of capital for labor for the economy as a whole have yielded mixed results. Cross-section estimates have generally found that a 1 percent decrease in the relative cost of capital will induce a 1 percent increase in the desired capital-labor ratio. Time-series estimates, however, have found a much lower-responsiveness. The cross-section estimate corresponds to a production technology known as Cobb-Douglas, where the desired capital stock is proportional to desired output and inversely proportional to the user cost of capital as follows:

$$K^* = \frac{\alpha y^{*\prime}}{c} \tag{5}$$

where $K^*$ is the desired capital stock, $y^*$ is desired output, $c$ is the user cost of capital, and $\alpha$ is a constant factor that reflects the technology of production.

One simplification that the Cobb-Douglas formulation allows is that demand for a particular type of capital good depends on, in addition to output, its own user cost and not on the user cost of other inputs, including other capital goods. For other production technologies this simplification is not valid. It is conceivable for example, that equipment and structures are complementary inputs, implying that changes in their relative price do not induce much substitution of one type of capital for the other. In this case the demand for equipment may depend almost as much on the user cost of structures as on the user cost of equipment; similarly, the demand for structures may depend on the user cost of equipment.

Demand for investment arises either to replace existing capital or to expand the existing capital stock. If the capital stock could be instantaneously and costlessly adjusted to the desired level, the actual capital stock would always equal the desired capital stock. In this case small variations in $y^*$ or $c$ could imply large swings in investment as the capital stock is adjusted to achieve its new desired level. That such large swings in investment are usually not observed is probably due to the cost of quickly installing new capital and to the fact that changes in $y^*$ or $c$ may be perceived as temporary. When installation costs are important, current investment depends not only on the current desired capital stock but also on the desired levels of the recent past that were not immediately attained. If, once chosen, the technique of production (factor proportions) cannot be altered, then the response of investment to changes in the user cost of capital should be slower than the response of investment to changes in desired output. This is so because the capital intensity of production can be altered only as new capital is installed.

As may be obvious by now, tracing the effect of a change in the tax law on investment entails a rather complicated series of steps. One step is to calculate the effect of the tax policy change on the user cost of capital. How a tax reform affects $u$ and $k$ is a matter of record, and the calculation of $z$, the present value of cost recovery allowances, is a fairly straightforward matter. An analysis of the full effect on $c$, however, requires information on how the relative price of capital goods, $q$, will change, and how the firm's discount rate, $r$, will change. Furthermore, although it is not explicit in expression (3), the firm's beliefs about the permanence of the tax change are critical, as are its beliefs about the future course of $q$ and $r$. More will be said about each of these considerations later.

Assuming that the effect on $c$ can be discerned, the effect on the desired capital stock depends on the elasticity of the capital-output ratio and the effect on desired output. Finally, and of critical importance, the response of current investment to a change in the desired stock of capital depends on the adjustment costs attendant to installing new fixed investment.

**Effective Tax Rates and Neutrality.** A convenient measure that summarizes the effect of the tax system on the user cost of capital is the effective tax rate on new investment, denoted here by $t$. It is designed to measure the difference between the real social return earned on a real asset and the rate of return received by the investor (before any personal taxes). Although there are alternative ways to express the effective tax rate, it is usually defined as the difference between the user cost net of depreciation and the rate of discount, expressed as a fraction of the user cost net of depreciation, or

$$t \equiv \frac{(c-d)-r}{c-d} = \frac{(f-d)-r}{f-d} , \tag{6}$$

where $c$ is the gross user cost.[3] It is a measure of the additional return (in excess of $r$) that an investment must earn because of taxation in order to provide a return of $r$ to the investor. If the tax system actually subsidizes investment, then $t$ will be negative. In this case, an investment needs to earn a return before taxes of less than $r$ in order to return $r$ to the investor after taxes.

In a pure income tax system with economic depreciation, the effective tax rate is equal to the statutory corporate tax rate. Under an expensing system, the effective tax rate is zero. In general it depends on the statutory tax rate, the system of cost recovery allowances, the investment tax credit, the real rate of discount, and the expected rate of inflation. It is important to note that equal changes in the effective tax rate have differential effects on the user cost for different rates of capital. In particular, an equal change in the effective tax rate will have a proportionately greater effect on the user cost of long-lived assets than it will have on short-lived assets. This is discussed in more detail later in the chapter.

Only when effective tax rates are equal for all types of capital assets will the capital stock be allocated efficiently. Otherwise, the marginal productivity of the preferred assets will be lower than the marginal productivity of the nonpreferred assets. Under the current tax system effective tax rates vary widely depending on the type of assets. In fact, a recent study estimated that the resource cost of misallocation of capital caused by differing effective tax rates within the corporate sector in 1981 was equivalent to wasting $65 billion of capital every year.[4] Although the focus of this chapter is the effect of taxation on the overall level of investment and the capital stock, the tax system also clearly has important effects on the mix of investment and the capital stock.

**Taxation and the Rate of Discount.** The preceding analysis has skirted the problem of determining the appropriate rate of discount and how it is itself affected by the tax system. This turns out to be a difficult question, and this section endeavors only to convey a sense of the issues involved.

Because the rate of interest equilibrates the supply of saving and the demand for investment, any tax policy that increases the demand for investment will in general increase the equilibrium rate of interest and to some degree offset the increased incentive to invest. How much the interest rate will rise depends, in a closed economy, on how responsive national saving is to changes in the interest rate. If there is no responsiveness at all, investment incentives will result in higher interest rates and no increase in investment. The more elastic the saving response, the less interest rates will rise and the greater will be the influence on investment.

In an open economy how much the rate of interest changes depends on the responsiveness of both total world saving and non-U.S. business investment to changes in the rate of interest. If total saving is fixed, then changes in the demand for U.S. business investment will not affect total world investment. The fraction of total investment allocated to U.S. business investment will change, though, depending on the sensitivity of other investments to the rate of interest. If other investments are not interest sensitive, then tax incentives to U.S. business investment simply drive up the rate of interest until U.S. business investment is no higher than in the absence of the incentives, which in both cases is the difference between world saving and non-U.S. business investment. If, on the other hand, alternative investments are highly interest-sensitive, investment will be attracted to the U.S. business sector from other sectors and the interest rate will rise only slightly. To the extent that world saving is interest-responsive, increases in the interest rate caused by greater investment demand will generate more saving. In this case, U.S. business investment can expand without an equal crowding out of other investments in the rest of the world.

**Financial Policy.** Because the tax treatment of business income depends on how the firm is financed, the task of understanding the influence of taxes on investment is greatly complicated. There has been a voluminous literature on this subject over the past decade. This section sketches the important issues related to this topic.

The fundamental problem in this field arises because the total tax on corporate-source capital income (paid both at the corporate level and at the personal level) apparently differs depending on the method of finance. Payments to debtholders are deductible from taxable income for the corporate borrower, but interest is fully taxable to the lender (unless the lender is a tax-exempt entity such as a pension fund). Thus the total effective tax burden on debt-financed capital is simply the personal income tax. Payments to stockholders are not deductible from taxable income (so are subject to corporation income tax), although after-tax earnings retained within the corporation generate capital gains that are preferentially taxed at the personal level. Earnings paid out as dividends are fully taxed.[5]

Assuming for the moment that there is no risk differential between holding corporate debt or holding corporate equity, the after-tax rate of return will have to be the same on both kinds of assets—otherwise, no one would hold the lower-yielding asset. If, as is likely given the current tax structure, the total tax burden on debt is less than the total tax burden on equity, then it will be cheaper for the corporation to back its capital with debt.

Joseph Stiglitz picked up on this point by constructing a model where all corporate investment is financed, at the margin, by debt.[6] This implies that the corporation tax rate has no effect whatsoever on investment decisions, although it may affect the incentive of entrepreneurs to incorporate. It is instructive to integrate this insight into the user cost of capital expression derived earlier. If the corporation borrows to obtain its financing, then its discount rate $r$ should be equal to $i(1-u)$, where $i$ is the rate of interest. Then the user cost of capital is

$$q \left( \frac{1-k-uz}{1-u} \right)(i(1-u)+d) \tag{7}$$

Note that in this case when the cost recovery schedule exactly replicates economic depreciation (so that $k=0$ and $z = d/(i(1-u)+d)$), the user cost of capital reduces to $q(i+d)$. Thus, a tax system with economic depreciation provides no disincentive to debt-financed investment. If cost recovery allowances are more generous than economic depreciation, then a debt-financed investment is actually subsidized relative to a no-tax world.

If it were true that all new investment were financed by debt issue, then (7) would be the appropriate user cost of capital. What complicates matters is that corporations utilize equity finance of capital as well as debt finance. A separate user cost of capital can be calculated for equity-financed investments, but the existence of two distinct expressions for the cost of capital is troubling. If one method of finance is cheaper than the other, why is it not used exclusively?

Several theories have been advanced to resolve this apparent inconsistency. According to one prominent theory, increased debt in a corporate financial structure increases the probability that the firm will either go bankrupt, which has real costs, or approach bankruptcy, which tends to exacerbate conflicts between the interests of bondholders and shareholders and lead to suboptimal investment decisions. Although debt is apparently a cheaper source of funds for small amounts of debt, firms use debt only until the marginal increase in expected bankruptcy costs due to greater leverage equals the cost differential.

Another theory relies on the graduated nature of the personal income tax.[7] By continually issuing the cheaper security, firms are assumed to force the cost of debt finance to be equal to the cost of equity finance. Depending on their marginal tax rate, some lenders find that the after-tax return to debt is higher than equity (those with relatively low marginal tax rates) and some lenders find the after-tax return to equity to be higher (those with relatively high marginal tax rates). Lenders are therefore specialized, owning either all debt or all equity. Any given firm is indifferent between issuing debt and equity, and the aggregate debt/equity ratio is determined by the tax structure and the distribution of lenders among marginal tax rate categories.

**Risk and Taxation.** The analysis up to this point has maintained the implicit assumption that the returns to any prospective investment are known to the firm with complete certainty. Introducing risk into the story can have profound effects on the impact of taxes on investment, although the precise resolution of the issue remains controversial.

Roger Gordon recently challenged the view that the corporation income tax, by raising the user cost of capital, reduces the incentive to invest.[8] He suggests that in the presence of uncertainty about the return to capital the tax reduces the risk attendant to owning corporate equity, and the expected value of tax payments is approximately equal to the premium a corporation would willingly pay to be rid of the amount of risk that the government absorbs.

To assess Gordon's argument, it is useful to embed the user-cost approach into the standard capital asset pricing model, which is a simple description of behavior under uncertainty and market equilibrium that presumes perfect market conditions prevail and that uncertainty can be summarized by a mean-variance approach. Individuals are compensated by additional expected return only for the systematic (undiversifiable) risk they bear, since diversifiable risk is costlessly eliminated.

In this model, without taxes, a firm will purchase capital until, at the margin,

$$\bar{f} = r + d + a \tag{8}$$

where $\bar{f}$ is the expected marginal product of capital, $r$ and $d$ are as above, and $a$ is a measure of the undiversifiable risk of the investment (the covariance between the marginal product and the excess rate of return on the market portfolio over a riskless investment multiplied by the expected excess return on the market portfolio). Expression (8) illustrates that an investment with higher undiversifiable risk must have a higher expected return in order to be accepted.

Under a pure income tax with perfect loss offset,[9] equilibrium requires that

$$(1-u)\,(\bar{f}-d) = r + a(1-u), \tag{9}$$

$$\text{or } \bar{f} = \frac{r}{1-u} + d + a$$

Expression (9) indicates that the government bears $100u$ percent of the risk of the investment and taxes away $100u$ percent of the net of depreciation return. Thus the after-tax undiversifiable risk becomes

$a(1-u)$ instead of simply $a$. In this framework, the corporate income tax may have a very small effect on the user cost if $r$, the riskless real interest rate, is very low. This is true although the expected revenue yield per unit of capital, $u(r+a)/(1-u)$, may be quite high.

Jeremy Bulow and Lawrence Summers stood Gordon's argument on its head by stressing that most of the risk in investment takes the form of changes in capital value, which are not shared by the government through the tax system, since depreciation allowances are fixed in advance and do not reflect the actual changes in value of particular assets.[10] In this case the equilibrium condition is

$$(1-u)(\bar{f}-\bar{d}) = r+a \tag{10}$$

$$\text{or } \bar{f} = \frac{r+a}{1-u}+\bar{d}$$

The effect of the corporate tax rate depends on the riskless interest rate, $r$, plus the risk premium, $a$. The disincentive to investment caused by the corporate income tax system is greater in this case because the tax system reduces the return premium earned by risky assets but does not share in the risk that a firm's capital stock may suffer a decline in value.

**Expectations.** Another critical assumption made in the construction of the user cost of capital measure is that all tax variables are assumed to remain constant throughout the life of the asset. Experience tells us, though, that this would be an exceedingly naive assumption on which to base decisions. If, though, firms have particular beliefs about the course of future tax law, then the user cost of capital changes dramatically. As an example, consider the case in which a firm believes that, at the start of the next tax year, the investment tax credit will be substantially increased. Given this expectation, the user cost of capital purchased now is considerably higher than is indicated by the right-hand side of expression (3) calculated using the current value of $k$. The correct expression would also include the capital loss that will be sustained once identical capital goods become cheaper to purchase in the new tax year. Especially for short-lived assets, this capital loss can be very large compared with the standard user cost computed above.

Expectations regarding future inflation are also critical. The expected net cost of funds depends on the nominal interest rate minus the expected rate of increase of prices. Different firms undoubtedly have different expectations about future inflation, and certainly even the mean expectation of firms is not known to economists trying to estimate the course of investment.

**Tobin's *q*.** A modern alternative to the user-cost approach that does not require an estimate of expectations is Tobin's *q*. It is based on the simple idea that if the increase in a firm's market value due to an investment exceeds the net cost of the asset, the investment will increase the wealth of the stockholders and should therefore be undertaken. In his original formulation of this approach, Tobin assumed that the market value of an additional unit of investment (marginal *q*) would be approximately equal to the market value of a unit of the existing capital stock (average *q*).[11] In this case, a potentially observable value, the ratio of the market value of capital to its replacement cost, known as the *q* ratio or Tobin's *q*, would be an indicator of the incentive to invest. In order to gauge the effect of tax policy, one needs to understand its likely effect on *q* and the effect of *q* on investment. Presumably this latter relationship can be discerned from historical experience.

Fumio Hayashi later showed that the marginal *q* will be equal to average *q* only under a set of rather restrictive conditions, including the homogeneity of capital.[12] In cases where the average *q* diverges from the marginal *q*, it is always the latter that is relevant for investment, and there will be no readily observable value.

Summers discussed how Tobin's *q* must be adjusted in the presence of taxes in order to reflect the incentive to invest.[13] One adjustment is for the difference between the outstanding depreciation allowances per dollar of existing capital and the allowances (and investment tax credit, if applicable) available for newly installed capital. The other important adjustment concerns the taxation of corporate capital income at the personal level. If all new equity is financed by retained earnings, and the debt-capital ratio is a constant, then at the margin the firm is faced with a choice between retaining and investing a dollar or paying it out as dividends. Because the rate of dividend taxation exceeds the rate of capital gains taxation, firms will invest past the point at which a dollar of retained earnings raises market value by a dollar. Thus, where in the absence of personal taxation a *q*-ratio of one would make a firm indifferent to investment, in the presence of personal taxation the *q* ratio leading to indifference for an all-equity firm is $(1 - m)/(1 - g)$, where *m* is the marginal rate of tax on dividends and *g* is the effective accrual-equivalent rate of tax on capital gains.

Because the *q* approach to investment is based on the same intertemporal optimization framework as the user-cost approach, it is not surprising that the two approaches' analyses of permanent changes in the tax code are essentially similar. Andrew Abel showed in 1982 that the equilibrium value of $q$ is proportional to $(1-u)/(1-k-uz)$, so that $q$, which is what determines investment, is affected (inversely) by exactly the same term that multiplies $(r+d)$ in the user cost of capital in expression (3) above.[14] One theoretical advantage of the $q$ approach over the user-cost approach is that it permits a rigorous analysis of the path of response to temporary as well as permanent tax changes or anticipated but not yet effective tax changes. The principal potential empirical advantage of the $q$ approach is that it is based on an observable value and does not require arbitrary simplifying assumptions about expectations, financial policy, government risk absorption, and the like. This advantage remains only a potential one, however, because the relationship between constructed $q$-ratios and the conceptually appropriate marginal $q$ is not perfect and itself depends on a number of arbitrary assumptions about such issues as valuing existing capital and the nature of technological change.

The ultimate test of the value of the $q$ approach is whether it is more successful than the user-cost approach in explaining the actual behavior of investment. On that score, its performance to date has been mixed. Studies based on aggregate data for the United States, the United Kingdom, and Japan have not demonstrated that $q$ models are superior to user-cost models. Studies using cross-industry and cross-firm data have also generated mixed results. Peter Clark's 1979 study of alternative investment models using aggregate U.S. data concluded that relative to alternative investment equations, the $q$ model does not perform adequately in terms of either within-sample or out-of-sample statistics.[15] Andrew Abel and Olivier Blanchard concluded that the empirical performance of models based on average $q$ has "not been that impressive," and their analysis of a marginal $q$ model led them to observe that "the data are not sympathetic to the basic restrictions imposed by the $q$ theory."[16]

## Review of Theory and Evidence

The bottom line in this area for most policy makers is how much a given change in the tax law will affect investment and, ultimately, the capital stock. This review of the issues should suggest that the path from the simple economic theory predicting an increase in investment demand after a decline in the price of capital to a quantitative prediction is a long and winding one.

How much demand for capital would respond to a fully perceived, certain, and permanent decline in its price depends on the substitutability of capital for other productive inputs. Evidence on the extent of that substitutability is mixed. How quickly investment responds to a change in the desired stock of capital depends on delivery lags and construction lags.

The principal problem is how a particular tax change ultimately translates into the relative price of capital goods. This depends on the elasticity of the supply of funds to the business sector, the flexibility of financial policy, the degree that taxes reflect government risk sharing, and the expectation of future tax changes. On each of these issues, our understanding remains incomplete. In the absence of one universally accepted analytical framework, it is useful to look at the empirical research on the historical relationship between tax policy and investment.

There is a voluminous literature on estimating the determinants of investment, some of which has investigated the role of taxation. Many of these studies assume rather than estimate the degree of substitutability between desired capital and its user cost and then estimate the path of adjustment, which determines investment behavior. As the 1983 survey by Robert Chirinko elaborates, econometric estimates of the effects of tax policy on investment have varied widely.[17] Chirinko and Robert Eisner analyzed the investment equations in six quarterly macroeconometric models and found that a doubling of the investment tax credit for equipment and the institution of a 10 percent credit for structures led to a mean increase in investment, after five years, of $9.3 billion, with the estimates varying from $1.4 to $15.8 billion.[18] The increase of $9.3 billion amounts to 7.1 percent of the actual investment in that period. These results did not consider the feedback effects on investment of induced changes in prices and interest rates, although Chirinko and Eisner found that, for the six macroeconometric models, incorporating these feedback effects reduced the projected investment stimulus by only about one-fourth.[19]

Summers (1981) used his econometric estimates of a tax-adjusted $q$-theory model of investment to simulate the effect of a doubling of the average level of the investment tax credit. He found that this policy change would increase investment by 5.5 percent in the first year, by 7.4 percent after five years, and eventually by 17.3 percent. Summers's exercise, however, assumes that the elasticity of substitution between capital and labor is one, so essentially the only parameter to be estimated is the speed of adjustment of the capital stock to its new desired level, which he finds to be exceedingly slow (a half-life of close to twenty years). Other assumptions include a constant debt-capital ratio and a constant real rate of interest. This latter assumption rules out the possibility that investment will be "crowded out" by rising costs of capital.

**The Reagan Experiment.** One of the principal objectives of the Reagan administration's tax policy changes was to increase the incentives for business investment. To that end, ERTA included several provisions designed to reduce the effective tax rate on new business investment. With the hindsight of four years of post-ERTA experience, it is worthwhile to see if the tax changes that were enacted had any discernible impact on actual investment behavior. Of course, no policy change is a controlled experiment, so one must contend with the fact that during this time many other determinants of investment were changing, including large (possibly policy-induced) changes in interest rates. Furthermore, 1981 does not begin the historical record on the relationship between the level of investment and its determinants; the recent evidence should be evaluated along with the earlier data.

These caveats notwithstanding, it is altogether too tempting a period to resist focusing on. After a brief review of the recent history of investment performance, the remainder of this chapter first discusses the business tax changes instituted beginning in 1981 and their likely influence, according to the user-cost model discussed above, on investment. Then the actual performance of investment since 1981 is examined in order to see what can be learned about the effectiveness of the tax incentives. The treatment here is impressionistic and does not purport to be a rigorous empirical analysis. Nevertheless, a few valuable insights do emerge.

**Pre-ERTA Investment Performance.** It is valuable to view recent investment behavior in the context of postwar experience. In 1984 the share of real GNP represented by real gross business fixed investment reached its highest point since 1948. This ratio shows a gradual upward trend since 1949, averaging about 9 percent in the 1950s and early 1960s, then about 10 percent until 1975, and most recently about 11 percent. In 1980 the gross investment share stood at 11.2 percent.

However the behavior of real *net* fixed investment as a share of real GNP is a very different story. Since 1949 this measure shows substantial fluctuation and no discernible trend, averaging about 3 percent. The ratio in 1980 came to 3.0 percent.

For the purpose of understanding capital accumulation, it is net, and not gross, investment that is of interest. Net investment is the addition to the capital stock provided by the flow of new investment. The divergence between the recent performance of net investment and gross investment is due to the shift in the composition of investment toward shorter-lived capital goods, which increases the average rate of depreciation of the existing capital stock. An increase in gross, but not net, investment merely reflects increased replacement of assets that wear out (or become obsolete) more quickly, and does not reflect an increase in productive capacity.

The composition of investment has been undergoing a secular shift from structures to equipment since about 1955. In that year, real net investment in structures comprised 62 percent of total real net fixed investment. By 1965 real net equipment investment was about equal to real net structures investment. By 1984 the fraction consisting of structures had fallen to 30 percent. A large part of the compositional shift since 1965 reflects a roughly constant share of nominal spending but a declining price of equipment versus structures. The implicit price deflator for investment in equipment was 1.21 times higher than that of structures investment in 1965, but only 0.70 as high in 1984, a decline in relative price of 42 percent in that period.

**Recent Changes in Business Taxation.** As of 1980, the investment tax credit was 10 percent for all equipment with a tax lifetime of at least seven years and for public utility structures, $6\frac{2}{3}$ percent for equipment with a tax lifetime of between five and seven years, and $3\frac{1}{3}$ percent for equipment with a tax lifetime of less than five years. Structures other than public utility structures were not eligible for an investment tax credit. Under ERTA the investment tax credit system changed to 6 percent for three-year property (mainly automobiles and light trucks) and 10 percent for all other equipment and public utility property. TEFRA retained ERTA's investment tax credit rate structure, but reduced the basis for depreciation by one-half of the applicable credit.

In 1980 depreciation for tax purposes was based on guideline lifetimes introduced in 1962. The pattern of depreciation allowances varied by asset type. For equipment, public utility structures, and residential structures, both double-declining balance and sum-of-the-years'-digits methods could be used. In most cases, it was more advantageous to begin with double-declining balance depreciation and at some point in the asset's lifetime to switch over to the sum-of-the-years'-digits method. For nonresidential structures, firms could use a 150 percent declining balance depreciation pattern with a switch to straight-line depreciation at the point the latter became more favorable.

ERTA greatly simplified the depreciation system by assigning all assets to one of four categories. All automobiles, light trucks, research and development equipment, and personal property with a tax lifetime of four years or less was assigned a lifetime of three years. All other equipment was assigned a five-year lifetime. Public utility structures and other assets with an accelerated depreciation recovery lifetime between eighteen and twenty-five years were assigned a ten-year lifetime. All other structures were given a fifteen-year lifetime.

ERTA specified year-by-year depreciation schedules which initially replicated 150-percent declining balance for new equipment and 175-percent declining balance for both residential and nonresidential structures. The method of depreciation for new equipment, however, was scheduled to gradually accelerate, first to 175-percent declining balance and, after 1985, to double-declining balance with a switchover to sum of the years' digits when that became advantageous. TEFRA, though, cancelled the scheduled acceleration of cost recovery allowances for new equipment, leaving equipment with a 150-percent declining balance with a switchover to straight-line depreciation.

**Effect on the Cost of Capital Goods.** This section utilizes the simple version of the user-cost approach to establish reasonable bounds for the quantitative effect of the ERTA and TEFRA tax changes on investment. The qualifications to the basic user-cost framework discussed above are not pursued here. These calculations are then compared with the evidence on investment performance since 1981.

Attention is focused on three particular categories of asset: office and computing machinery, general industrial equipment, and commercial buildings. This concentration brings out the inter-asset differences in tax treatment and at the same time keeps the amount of detail required to a minimum. In order to apply the user-cost approach quantitatively, certain assumptions are required. First, it is assumed that the real after-tax rate of discount of business investors is 4 percent, and the expected rate of inflation is 6 percent. In addition, it is assumed that the geometric rate of economic depreciation for each asset is known and in fact corresponds to the estimates of Charles Hulten and Frank Wykoff.[20] Finally, for notational simplicity, the unit of investment is normalized so that the price of each kind of investment is one.

The first column of table 2–1 gives the user cost of capital for each type of capital, given these assumptions, in the absence of taxation. The second column gives the user cost and effective tax rate under pre-ERTA tax law, and the third column under fully phased-in ERTA. The last column shows the user cost and effective tax rate under ERTA as modified by TEFRA.

Several results in table 2–1 are of interest. First, note that the net effect of either the 1980 tax system or ERTA/TEFRA on the user cost of capital for both kinds of equipment is very small, although the relative impact of the tax systems on the user cost for structures is quite large. The net effect of ERTA/TEFRA on the user cost compared with 1980 law is a decline of .006, or about 4 percent, for general industrial equipment and an *increase* of .006, or about 2 percent, for office and computing equipment. Although different assumptions would alter these quantitative conclusions somewhat, the basic message is fairly clear—ERTA/TEFRA did not substantially reduce the user cost of capital for equipment for a given real discount rate and expected rate of inflation.

This conclusion would not have applied had ERTA's fully phased-in version taken effect and had TEFRA not reduced the depreciable basis of assets eligible for the investment tax credit. As table 2–1 shows, this set of tax rules would have reduced the user cost of office and computing machinery by .029, or nearly 10 percent, and the user cost of general industrial equipment by .017, also about 10 percent of its user cost under 1980 law.[21]

The effect of ERTA/TEFRA on the user cost for commercial buildings is substantial, in contrast to the case for equipment. The user cost falls from .106 under 1980 law to .090, a decline of about 15 percent. Note that TEFRA did not rescind much of the tax reduction originally scheduled for structures under ERTA.

Even uniform changes in the effective tax rate on new investment will cause a higher proportional change in the user cost of capital for structures. This is so because depreciation comprises a higher fraction of the total user cost for short-lived assets. For short-lived assets, the forgone interest and tax payments are small relative to the cost of

TABLE 2–1

USER COST OF CAPITAL AND EFFECTIVE TAX RATES FOR SELECTED
ASSETS UNDER ALTERNATIVE TAX LAWS

| | Tax Law | | | |
|---|---|---|---|---|
| Asset Type | No taxes | 1980 law | Fully phased-in ERTA | ERTA as modified by TEFRA |
| Office and computing machinery | | | | |
| User cost | .313 | .308 | .277 | .314 |
| Effective tax rate | 0 | − .158 | − 10.3 | .016 |
| General industrial equipment | | | | |
| User cost | .163 | .169 | .152 | .163 |
| Effective tax rate | 0 | .139 | − .376 | .008 |
| Commercial buildings | | | | |
| User cost | .065 | .106 | .088 | .090 |
| Effective tax rate | 0 | .508 | .370 | .388 |

SOURCE: Author's calculations.

continually replacing worn-out or obsolete equipment. Even large increases in the effective rate of taxation of capital income cause small proportionate changes in the total cost of using the capital. The limiting case of a short-lived asset is a noncapital input such as electricity, which is used up immediately upon purchase. The effective tax rate on capital income has no effect at all on the total price of using electricity in the production process.

One conclusion suggested by table 2–1 is that unless there is a substantial effect on demand for equipment of the user cost of structures, the recent performance of investment in equipment is likely to tell us very little about the effectiveness of tax incentives for investment. In the absence of such a cross effect, the net effect on the tax-related incentive to invest in equipment was small and, as will be discussed next, was likely overshadowed by the course of other determinants of investment.

During this period other influences on the user cost fluctuated widely. The long-term real interest rate, which was about 2 percent at the end of 1979, increased in 1980 and hovered around 7 percent between mid-1981 and mid-1982, then fell to about 5 percent until the end of 1983, and climbed to above 6 percent in 1984.[22] Changes in the real discount rate of corporations directly enter the user cost of capital and indirectly enter through the calculation of the present value of the cost recovery allowances. Table 2–2 illustrates how variations in

TABLE 2–2

USER COST OF CAPITAL AND EFFECTIVE TAX RATES FOR SELECTED ASSETS UNDER ALTERNATIVE REAL DISCOUNT RATES AND THE ERTA/TEFRA TAX RULES

| | Real Discount Rate | | |
|---|---|---|---|
| Asset Type | .02 | .04 | .06 |
| Office and computing machinery | | | |
| User cost | .286 | .314 | .342 |
| Effective tax rate | −.528 | .016 | .125 |
| General industrial equipment | | | |
| User cost | .140 | .163 | .188 |
| Effective tax rate | −.202 | .008 | .073 |
| Commercial buildings | | | |
| User cost | .060 | .090 | .122 |
| Effective tax rate | .433 | .388 | .379 |

SOURCE: Author's calculations.

the real discount rate can affect the user cost and effective tax rate calculations. A swing of .02 in either direction from the baseline assumption of .04 changes the user cost of either type of equipment much more than did the introduction of ERTA/TEFRA, for any given real discount rate in that range; the variation also exceeds the reduction in user cost for commercial buildings. Note that in all cases the user cost changes by more than the given change in the real discount rate. This occurs because the effective tax rate changes in the same direction as the real discount rate, enhancing the total effect on the user cost. Note also that the measure of the effective tax rate can change substantially when the real discount rate changes. For example, the effective tax rate on investment in office and computing machinery falls from .016 to −.528 when the real discount rate goes from .04 to .02 and all the tax rules are unchanged. This change reflects the fact that the required social rate of return falls from .041, implying a slight positive tax, to .013, which implies a substantial subsidy.[23]

Changes in the expected rate of inflation affect the user cost and effective tax rate calculations, holding constant the real discount rate, because the real value of the nominally-fixed cost recovery allowances falls when inflation rises. Between 1981 and 1984 inflation declined rapidly, falling from 9.0 percent (as measured by the change in the GNP deflator) in 1981 to 4.3 percent in 1982, 3.8 percent in 1983, and 3.5 percent in 1984. Presumably expectations of future inflation also fell during this period, though perhaps not as abruptly.

Table 2–3 shows how changes in the expected rate of inflation affect user cost and effective tax rates. A decline in the expected inflation rate from 8 percent to 4 percent would reduce the user cost of capital for office and computing machinery by .015, for general industrial equipment by .008, and for commercial buildings by .006.

This discussion highlights the fact that the post-ERTA period featured sharp changes in important nontax determinants of investment. The increase in real interest rates may have been partially a result of the tax changes. Because the nontax determinants changed so much, no simple comparison of investment performance and changes in the tax treatment of business investment will be very instructive.[24]

**Post-ERTA Investment Performance.** The focus now shifts to the recent behavior of investment, specifically on real gross private fixed nonresidential investment. Net investment figures are not available on a quarterly basis, so gross figures must suffice. Because depreciation does not have a significant cyclical component, this is not a critical problem for present purposes.

ERTA became law in early August of 1981, and its changes in

business taxation applied to property placed in service after December 31, 1980. Its passage approximately coincided with the peak in 1981:III of the short-lived recovery that began in 1980:III. The decline in investment during the subsequent recession was severe, though not much more severe than in other postwar recessions. By the cyclical trough in 1982:IV, real business fixed investment had fallen by 9.3 percent from the previous cycle's peak, compared with an average peak-to-trough drop of 8.8 percent in the four previous recessions.[25]

The rebound in investment from the recession was, however, particularly strong. The annual rate of growth in investment over the first nine quarters after the trough (1982:IV to 1985:I) was 13.7 percent, compared with a typical rate of growth over the nine quarters following a cyclical trough of 6.6 percent. Growth was especially strong in commercial buildings, which experienced a 20.2 percent annual real growth rate in this period, compared to a 5.4 percent average real rate of growth in recent recoveries. For broad categories of investment, producers' durable equipment was stronger (16.3 percent annual real rate of growth) than structures (8.0 percent real rate of growth). The growth in equipment was spread among most categories, with the exception of mining and oil field equipment, aircraft, and ships and boats. Particularly strong growth in investment came in transportation equipment, trucks, and autos, which all tend to be exceptionally strong

TABLE 2–3

USER COST OF CAPITAL AND EFFECTIVE TAX RATES FOR SELECTED ASSETS UNDER ALTERNATIVE EXPECTED INFLATION RATES AND THE ERTA/TEFRA TAX RULES

| | Expected Inflation Rate | | |
|---|---|---|---|
| Asset Type | .04 | .06 | .08 |
| Office and computing machinery | | | |
| User cost | .306 | .314 | .321 |
| Effective tax rate | −.220 | .016 | .166 |
| General industrial equipment | | | |
| User cost | .159 | .163 | .167 |
| Effective tax rate | −.103 | .008 | .094 |
| Commercial buildings | | | |
| User cost | .087 | .090 | .093 |
| Effective tax rate | .356 | .388 | .412 |

SOURCE: Author's calculations.

in cyclical upturns.[26] Investment in office equipment, mainly computers, was also especially strong.

Because the period since ERTA includes a decline in investment during the recession and an increase in investment during the recovery, it is natural to assess the performance of investment over the entire course of the cycle. This is not a straightforward exercise, since the future path of the recovery is not known and since, for comparative purposes, past recessions and recoveries have varying duration. One reasonable benchmark for comparison is the growth over the fourteen quarters after the peak of the previous cycle. For the current cycle, this corresponds to the period 1981:III to 1985:I. Over this period, the annual growth rate in investment was 5.6 percent, higher than the average of 2.9 percent growth in three recent comparable cycles. (Note that real GNP growth over this period was below that of the average fourteen-quarter post-peak growth, 2.6 percent compared with 3.4 percent.) Both structures and equipment experienced higher growth than usual. The same sectors that grew exceptionally fast during the recovery show strong performance over the cycle as a whole.

An alternative measure of the performance of investment is the change in the capital-output ratio. After all, the primary reason that increased investment is deemed desirable is that it increases the capital intensity of production. Over the period 1981:III to 1984:IV, the real net stock of equipment increased by 11.2 percent, or at an annual rate of 3.6 percent, while the real net stock of structures rose by 7.7 percent, or 2.3 percent per year. The overall growth in the net stock of fixed capital was 10.7 percent, or 3.0 percent at an annual rate. This compared to a growth in GNP of 9.2 percent, or 2.8 percent annually. Thus, there was a slight (1.5 percent) increase in the capital-GNP ratio over these thirteen quarters and a slight shift from structures toward equipment, a continuation of a twenty-year trend.

The stylized facts about the behavior of business fixed investment can be summarized as follows. ERTA was enacted amid signs that the economy was weakening. The recession was not averted, and investment declined precipitously to a level, relative to its peak, not unlike earlier downturns. The recovery from the trough of both investment and GNP has been very strong, leaving the ratio of net investment to GNP at about the same level in 1980, and the capital-output ratio at a slightly higher level.

### Conclusions

What conclusions can be drawn from this review?[27]

1. Considerable controversy remains about the relationship be-

tween the tax system and the incentive to invest. The roles of corporate financial policy, uncertainty, and expectations are all potentially important and warrant further study. The simple user-cost approach is useful as a guide to the effect of tax policy, but by no means does it represent a consensus view of the net effect of the tax system.

2. ERTA, as modified by TEFRA, did not provide a substantial decrease in the user cost of capital for equipment. Thus, unless there is a substantial effect on demand for equipment of the user cost of structures, which did decline because of ERTA/TEFRA, the recent performance of equipment investment does not provide any information on the effectiveness of tax incentives for investment. The experience of 1981 to 1984 does not provide a natural experiment for assessing the influence of taxes on investment because the effective tax rate did not ultimately change much for equipment. The strong performance of investment in structures is consistent with the reduction in its effective corporate tax rate.

3. The performance of investment in the recent expansion has been particularly strong. Over the entire cycle, the ratio of net capital stock to GNP has risen by approximately 1.5 percent. Over this period not only did the tax treatment of business investment change but so also did other potential determinants of investment such as real interest rates, inflation, output, the deficit, and the individual income tax system. It is the task of future research to try to identify the role of tax policy in recent economic performance.[28]

# Notes

1. Robert E. Hall and Dale Jorgenson, "Tax Policy and Investment Behavior," *American Economic Review*, vol. 57 (June 1967), pp. 391–414.

2. The assumption of exponential depreciation implies that the proportional decline in value is equal to the proportional decline in the current productivity of the asset.

3. Alternatively, the effective tax rate can be defined as a ratio to the return to the investor (rather than the social return), so that $t = ((c-d)-r)/r$. See David Bradford and Don Fullerton, "Pitfalls in the Construction and Use of Effective Tax Rates," in Charles Hulten, ed., *Depreciation, Inflation, and the Taxation of Income from Capital* (Washington, D.C.: Urban Institute, 1981).

4. Alan J. Auerbach, "Corporate Taxation in the United States," *Brookings Papers on Economic Activity* (2: 1983), pp. 451–505.

5. One exception to this statement is the dividend exclusion provision, which applies at the margin to a small fraction of equity ownership.

6. Joseph E. Stiglitz, "Taxation, Corporate Financial Policy, and the Cost of Capital," *Journal of Public Economics* 2 (February 1973), pp. 1–34.

7. Merton H. Miller, "Debt and Taxes," *Journal of Finance* 32 (May 1977), pp. 261–75.

8. Roger H. Gordon, "Taxation of Corporate Capital Income: Tax Revenues versus Tax Distortions," *Quarterly Journal of Economics* 100 (February 1985), pp. 1–27.

9. Under perfect loss offset the tax treatment of losses is symmetric to the treatment of gains. This implies that a loss reduces the present value of tax liability, and is violated by the limitations on loss refundability and a progressive tax system.

10. Jeremy Bulow and Lawrence Summers, "The Taxation of Risky Assets," *Journal of Political Economy* 92 (February 1984), pp. 20–39.

11. James Tobin, "A General Equilibrium Approach to Monetary Theory," *Journal of Money, Credit, and Banking* 1 (February 1969), pp. 15–29.

12. Fumio Hayashi, "Tobin's Marginal $q$ and Average $q$," *Econometrica* 50 (January 1982), pp. 213–24.

13. Lawrence Summers, "Taxation and Corporate Investment: A $q$-theory Approach," *Brookings Papers on Economic Activity* (1:1981), pp. 67–127.

14. Andrew Abel, "Dynamic Effects of Permanent and Temporary Tax Policies in a $q$ Model of Investment," *Journal of Monetary Economics* 9 (1982), pp. 353–73.

15. Peter K. Clark, "Investment in the 1970s: Theory, Performance, and Prediction," *Brookings Papers on Economic Activity* (1:1979), pp. 73–113.

16. Andrew Abel and Olivier Blanchard, "The Present Value of Profits and Cyclical Movements in Investment," mimeo, Massachusetts Institute of Technology, undated.

17. Robert Chirinko, "Investment and Tax Policy: A Survey of Existing Models and Empirical Results: With Applications to the High-Technology Sector," A Report to the National Science Foundation Division of Policy Research and Analysis, 1983.

18. Robert Chirinko and Robert Eisner, "The Effect of Tax Parameters in the Investment Equations in Macroeconomic Econometric Models," in Marshall E. Blume, Jean Crockett, and Paul Taubman, eds., *Economic Activity and Finance* (Cambridge, Mass.: Ballinger, 1982).

19. Robert Chirinko and Robert Eisner, "Tax Policy and Investment in Major U.S. Macroeconomic Econometric Models," *Journal of Public Economics* 12 (1983), pp. 139–66.

20. Charles Hulten and Frank Wykoff, "The Measurement of Economic Depreciation," in Charles Hulten, ed., *Depreciation, Inflation, and the Taxation of Income from Capital.*

21. According to table 2–1, the effective tax rate on office and computing machinery under fully phased-in ERTA is $-10.3$ or $-1030$ percent. This astronomical figure is obtained because the denominator of the expression for effective tax rate $(c - d)$ approaches zero. It implies that the investment is subsidized by the tax system to the extent that, in order to return 4 percent after corporation tax to the investor, the investment needs to earn a return only slightly greater than zero. Note that if the effective tax rate is defined, as suggested in footnote 3, with the required rate of return in the denominator, it will have a value approaching $-1$, or $-100$ percent.

These calculations are similar to those presented in the 1982 Economic

Report of the President. Its table 5–6 (p. 124) indicates an effective tax rate of −.481 (calculated as the listed real before-tax rate of return, 2.7, minus the real discount rate of 4.0 percent divided by 2.7) on general industrial equipment and a tax rate of .344 on commercial buildings, assuming an inflation rate of 5 percent. If table 2–1's inflation rate assumption of 6 percent were used, the effective tax rate calculations would increase to be very close to the −.376 and .370, respectively, presented in table 2–1. Note that the calculations in table 5–6 of the Economic Report refer to the fully phased-in version of ERTA, without the basis adjustment mandated in TEFRA.

Hulten and Robertson (1984) calculated the average effective tax rate on all equipment to be −.394 under fully phased-in ERTA and .035 for ERTA as modified by TEFRA, assuming 6-percent inflation and a 4-percent real discount rate. These figures are similar to those presented in table 2–1 for general industrial equipment. For investment in plant, they calculate the effective tax rate to be .350 under fully phased-in ERTA and .363 under ERTA as modified by TEFRA, again quite similar to table 2–1's estimates for commercial buildings.

Hulten and Robertson state that nearly 60 percent of the original tax cut mandated by ERTA was rescinded by TEFRA. In fact, the percentage should be higher since they include the decline in expected inflation, an assumed 8.83 percent in 1980 to 6 percent thereafter, to be part of the tax reduction ascribed to ERTA. When the alternative tax laws are all compared using a 6-percent expected rate of inflation, Hulten and Robertson's figures imply that TEFRA rescinded over 70 percent of the original tax cut, and rescinded more than 80 percent of the tax cut for equipment. Calculations are available from the author.

22. Calculations of the real interest rate depend on the expected rate of inflation, which cannot be precisely measured. This recent history draws on chart 1–1 from the 1985 Economic Report of the President, p. 34.

23. For a more detailed discussion of the effect of discount rate changes on effective tax rates and related issues, see David Bradford and Don Fullerton, "Pitfalls in the Construction and Use of Effective Tax Rates," in Charles Hulten, ed., *Depreciation, Inflation, and the Taxation of Income from Capital*, pp. 251–315.

24. For a review of studies that attempt to incorporate all the recent influences on the cost of capital, see Barry P. Bosworth, "Taxes and the Investment Recovery," *Brookings Papers on Economic Activity* (1:1985), pp. 1–38.

25. This average does not include the short-lived downturn that ended in 1980:III.

26. Some measurement issues are important here. For example, some of the boom in automobile investment reflects the trend from individual ownership, which is not classified as business investment, to leasing, which is classified as business investment. Also, the price deflator for computers has not been changed for several years, leading to an understatement of real purchases of computers.

27. This has necessarily been a somewhat cursory look at the issues involved. For a more complete treatment of the theoretical issues, the reader

should consult Alan Auerbach, "Corporate Taxation in the United States," *Brookings Papers on Economic Activity* (2:1983), pp. 451–505. Calculations on the effect of ERTA/TEFRA on the user cost of capital are discussed in depth by Don Fullerton and Yolanda Kodrzycki in "Incentive Effects of Taxes on Income from Capital: Alternative Policies in the 1980s," in Charles R. Hulten and Isabel V. Sawhill, eds., *The Legacy of Reaganomics* (Washington, D.C.: Urban Institute), and by Charles Hulten and James W. Robertson, "Corporate Tax Policy and Economic Growth: An Analysis of the 1981 and 1982 Tax Acts," in Ali Dogramici and Nabil R. Adam, eds., *Managerial Issues in Productivity Analysis* (Boston: Kluwer-Nijoff, 1984).

28. Several recent papers have begun this task. See, for example, Bosworth, "Taxes and the Investment Recovery."

# 3
# The Marginal Cost of Raising Tax Revenue

*Edgar K. Browning*

## Summary

*Do we get a dollar in benefits for every dollar in taxes we send to Washington? This chapter does not attempt to answer this question fully but instead explains why the question itself is posed incorrectly. If we wish government budgetary policy to benefit the public, every dollar in government spending must produce benefits worth substantially more than a dollar, because the taxes that finance government outlays impose costs on the public that are greater than the revenues collected. When taxes shift resources from taxpayers to government, they also distort decisions regarding the use of resources remaining in the private sector. For every dollar of tax revenue collected, the public loses that dollar, a direct cost, but also bears a cost in the form of a less efficiently functioning economy. In effect, the distortions, or welfare costs, due to taxes are a form of hidden cost associated with the expenditure of tax dollars. When the cost of raising a dollar in tax revenue is greater than one dollar, the benefits of spending tax revenue must be correspondingly greater if the overall tax-expenditure operation is to be worthwhile.*

*The relevant measure of this hidden cost of raising tax revenue is the marginal welfare cost of taxation. The marginal welfare cost is the additional loss in welfare from the distorting effects of changing tax rates by a small amount; it is expressed as a percentage of the additional revenue generated. If the marginal welfare cost is 20 percent, for example, raising an additional dollar in tax revenue imposes a total marginal cost of \$1.20 on the public, a \$1.00 direct cost as measured by the revenues themselves and a hidden cost of \$0.20 from the distortions in economic decisions induced by the tax.*

*How large is the marginal welfare cost of taxation? This depends on the interaction of a number of factors, some of which we can measure only with significant margins for error. For example, the marginal welfare cost depends on how much labor supply is affected by higher tax rates, exactly what type of tax is used to produce changes in revenue, and the initial level of taxpayers' combined marginal tax rates from all taxes in the system. Since we cannot estimate exactly the magnitudes of these factors that determine marginal welfare cost, we cannot estimate that cost precisely. We can, however, establish a range of plausible values (based on empirical evidence) for the contributing factors and estimate a range within which marginal welfare cost is likely to fall.*

*This chapter concentrates on the marginal welfare cost of raising revenue through taxes that fall on labor earnings and therefore distort labor supply decisions. (Since these taxes produce other kinds of distortions that are ignored here, the estimates developed probably understate the overall marginal welfare cost.) The estimates of marginal welfare cost developed here range from just under 10 percent to over 300 percent. Extreme (but not impossible) combinations of assumptions about contributory factors are required to generate these polar estimates. My preferred estimates lie in the range of 20 to 50 percent. Several other recent studies have also developed estimates that lie approximately in this range.*

*If the marginal welfare cost of raising tax revenue is as large as these estimates suggest, government expenditure policies financed by taxes must pass a much stiffer test than is usually recognized to be efficient. Most analyses of government spending programs, including formal cost-benefit analyses, have implicitly assumed that it costs society only a dollar for each dollar the government spends. These estimates of marginal welfare cost imply that this procedure substantially understates the true cost and therefore overstates the attractiveness of spending programs.*

*The marginal welfare cost of taxation is also relevant in deciding whether to reduce the government budget deficit by raising taxes or by reducing expenditures. Expenditures should be reduced unless they produce benefits greater than their budgetary cost by a percentage at least as large as the marginal welfare cost.*

## Introduction

Do we get a dollar in benefits for every dollar in taxes we send to Washington? Although opinions about the answer to this question vary, most discussions of government expenditure policies take it for granted that the question itself is properly posed. The Congressional Budget Office (CBO), for example, suggests the same comparison between benefits of government spending and costs of taxation by observing that "it is necessary to decide whether an additional dollar spent by government can be put to better use than an additional dollar spent by the taxpayer."[1]

Balancing the benefits of government spending against the costs of taxation as the CBO suggests, however, it is not correct if we wish government budgetary policy to promote the well-being of the public. When the government collects a dollar in tax revenue, the cost to taxpayers is actually greater than one dollar: when taxes shift resources from taxpayers to government, they also distort decisions about the use of resources remaining in the private sector. For every dollar of tax revenue collected, the public loses that dollar, a direct cost, and also bears a cost in the form of a less efficiently functioning economy. In effect, the distortions due to taxes, which are generally referred to as welfare costs, are a kind of hidden cost associated with the expenditure of tax dollars. For a government expenditure to be beneficial on balance, its benefits must be large enough to cover both the direct cost of the tax revenue raised and the hidden welfare cost produced by the tax. In short, because the cost of raising a dollar in tax revenue is greater than one dollar, the benefits of spending tax revenue must be correspondingly greater if the overall tax-expenditure operation is to be worthwhile.

In discussing the cost of raising tax revenue, the 1985 *Economic Report of the President* explains the significance of this cost in this way: "The primary policy implication is that government services and transfer payments are desirable only if their value is substantially higher than their budget cost. Government activities that fail this test should be eliminated or cut back."[2] It may therefore be reasonable to interpret attempts to reduce the deficit by cutting expenditures rather than by raising taxes as a judgment that the marginal value of the expenditures is less than the marginal cost of raising taxes. Whether this is in fact true is not clear, but recent economic research suggests that the marginal cost of raising tax revenue is substantially larger than had previously been thought. For instance it may well cost $1.40 to raise an additional dollar in tax revenue. This chapter examines the nature and determinants of this hidden cost of taxation and explains how the concept of welfare cost is relevant to a number of important policy issues.

## The Total Welfare Cost of Taxation

Taxes generally impose two kinds of costs on taxpayers, a direct cost reflected in the tax funds collected and a welfare cost reflected in a misallocation of resources remaining in the private sector. Although most taxes impose both kinds of costs, it is easiest to understand the nature of the welfare cost by taking an extreme example, where there is no tax revenue collected by the tax and the only burden on the public is the welfare cost. Consider an excise tax on vacuum cleaners that is set so high that the industry vanishes and no vacuum cleaners are produced. In this case, although there is no direct cost from the tax because no tax revenue is raised, there is still a burden on the community: the pattern of output no longer satisfies consumer demands as fully as before. The result of the tax is that fewer vacuum cleaners are produced and, as the resources formerly employed in producing vacuum cleaners shift elsewhere, more of other things. We know that consumers would prefer to have more than zero vacuum cleaners and less of other goods because they chose that pattern of production through their purchases in the absence of the tax. Thus the tax makes consumers worse off even though it collects no revenue.

Most real-world taxes produce both a direct cost and a welfare cost: they generate revenue and also distort resource allocation. The particular misallocation of resources produced varies from tax to tax. In this chapter I emphasize the welfare costs of taxes that fall on labor income because nearly three-fourths of all tax revenue derives from taxes that fall directly or indirectly on labor incomes and because the empirical evidence regarding the economic effects is better for this kind of tax.

Taxes on labor income produce welfare costs by distorting workers' decisions about how much income to earn. Consider a worker who can work any number of hours desired at a wage rate of $10 an hour. If a tax of 40 percent is applied to his labor earnings, the tax effectively reduces his net rate of pay to $6 an hour. Assuming that the worker's decisions will be guided by the after-tax, or net, wage rate, he will supply labor services up to the point where $6 just compensates him for the last (marginal) hour of work. In other words, he will choose to work an amount where the marginal cost of providing labor services is equal to $6 since $6 reflects all the benefit he received per hour of work. At this level of effort, however, his market wage rate is still $10, and the marginal benefit of his labor services to society is $10. The tax, therefore, leads him to work too little since the value to society of additional hours of work beyond the level he chooses is $10 while the cost to him is only $6. In effect, the tax introduces a "tax wedge" between his before-tax and after-tax rates of pay. The lower after-tax rate of pay will guide workers' decisions, but it is the higher before-tax rate that measures the value of their services to society.

In general, taxes on labor income lead workers to earn less than the efficient level of income given the real costs and benefits. In practice, this distortion can take many forms: workers' working too few hours, working less intensively on the job, turning down offers of better-paying jobs, taking early retirement, and so on.[3] In all cases, however, the distortion, or welfare cost, reflects the fact that taxes lower the net rate of pay that guides the decisions of workers about how much of an effort it is worth making to earn income.

In assessing the likely size of the welfare cost due to this distortion of labor supply decisions, we must also distinguish between the average tax rate and the marginal tax rate. It is the marginal rate that is responsible for the welfare cost, and it may differ significantly from the average rate. Suppose, for example, that an income tax exempts $20,000 in earnings and applies a tax rate of 40 percent to all earnings over $20,000. A person earning $25,000 then pays $2,000 in taxes, and his average tax rate is 8 percent ($2,000/$25,000). His marginal tax rate, however, is 40 percent, and it is this rate that will most influence how much he chooses to earn. In deciding whether to increase or reduce earnings, the worker will consider whether earning an extra $1,000 is worth the effort when he gets to keep only $600 or whether earning $1,000 is less desirable since his disposable income falls by only $600. At the level of earnings actually chosen, the marginal tax rate is what reduces the cost of earning less and reduces the return from earning more by introducing a wedge between before-tax and after-tax rates of pay.

The marginal tax rate produces the welfare cost, while the average tax rate determines how much tax revenue is produced. If the marginal tax rate is high in relation to the average rate, the welfare cost will be large compared with the tax revenue collected; conversely, if the marginal tax rate is low in relation to the average rate, the welfare cost will be small compared with the tax revenue collected. Consider two extreme examples that illustrate this point. Suppose the tax exempts the first $20,000 in earnings and applies a tax rate of 90 percent (this is the marginal rate) to earnings greater than this amount. In all likelihood a person initially earning $25,000 would cut back sharply, perhaps reducing earnings to $20,000, since he could take one-fifth of the year off and lose only $500 after taxes. The government would collect no revenue in this event (the average rate would be zero); yet the tax would have caused a large distortion in labor supply. Here the high marginal tax rate produces a large welfare cost and little or no revenue.

At the other extreme, suppose the tax is levied at a 10 percent rate on the first $20,000 of earnings and at a zero rate above $20,000 (much like the social security payroll tax with its ceiling on taxable earnings). As long as the worker chooses to earn more than $20,000, this tax produces no welfare cost. For example, at $25,000, the decision whether to earn $1,000 more or less is not influenced by tax considerations since there will be no change in the amount of tax paid when more or less is earned. In this case, the marginal tax rate is zero, and there is no welfare cost; yet the tax raises $2,000 in revenue.

Keeping marginal tax rates low in relation to average tax rates is the key to minimizing the distortions produced by any tax. Considerations of equity, however, operate in the opposite direction. A head tax of $5,000 per person, for example, would have a zero marginal tax rate for everyone and hence produce no distorting effect on labor supply but would impose heavy tax burdens on those with low incomes. A highly progressive income tax would shift the burden to upper-income persons but produce a substantial welfare cost, since a progressive tax uses marginal rates that are high in relation to average rates. Identifying the "best" tax system in these circumstances is understandably controversial and involves trading off equity against efficiency.

Having discussed the nature of the welfare cost, let us turn to a consideration of the determinants of its magnitude. The marginal tax rate is an important determinant, as we have already seen, but the welfare cost also depends on how responsive people are to changes in net wage rates produced by the tax system. If people continued to work the same amount, with the same intensity, and in the same jobs regardless of how heavily their earnings were taxed at the margin, the tax would produce no welfare cost since it would not cause any change in economic behavior. The more responsive labor supply decisions are to tax-induced changes in wage rates, the greater the distorting effect of any given tax will be.

Let us work through a hypothetical example to see how the marginal tax rate and the responsiveness of workers to changes in net wage rates interact to determine the size of the welfare cost. Suppose a worker confronts a 40 percent marginal tax rate and earns $20,000 a year; his market wage rate is $10 an hour, and he works 2,000 hours a year. Since the marginal tax rate is 40 percent, his after-tax wage rate is $6 per hour, and we assume that 2,000 hours is his desired level of work effort given that he gets to keep $6 per hour for the 2,000th hour supplied.

To see intuitively how much the tax has distorted his labor supply decision, imagine removing the tax wedge by allowing the worker to keep all of any earnings above $20,000 he makes without paying any tax on them. In other words, assume that the marginal tax rate is reduced to zero for any additional earnings but that the worker will keep paying whatever taxes he already pays on the first $20,000. Reducing the marginal tax rate to zero thus affects the worker much like an opportunity to work overtime (beyond 2,000 hours a year) at a wage rate of $10, or a wage one and two-thirds of his current after-tax wage of $6. Suppose under these circumstances the worker chose to earn $4,000 more by working 400 extra hours per year. If he made such a choice, we would say that the marginal tax rate of 40 percent had distorted his decision and led him to work 400 hours less than is efficient.

Because of the tax, our hypothetical worker has chosen to work 400 fewer hours. At a market wage of $10, the economy has lost $4,000 in earnings that go unproduced. This, however, is not a measure of the welfare cost since the welfare cost is intended to measure the net loss. When the worker chooses not to earn the $4,000, he gains 400 hours in free time to spend on nonwork activities, and that time has some value to him. The net loss—the welfare cost—is the difference between the $4,000 and the value of the 400 extra hours to the worker. A value can be placed on those hours in the following way. Since the worker chooses to work 2,000 hours when the after-tax wage rate is $6, that can be taken as a measure of the marginal value he places on his time when he works 2,000 hours. At a wage rate of $10, the worker would choose to work 2,400 hours; so $10 can be taken as the marginal value of his time when he works 2,400 hours. Over this range of 400 hours, the value of his time rises from $6 to $10, making the average value $8; thus we can estimate the total value of those 400 hours at $3,200. Therefore, when the worker earns $4,000 less because of the tax, society loses $4,000 in output, but the worker gains $3,200 worth of free time; the net loss is $800. The $800 is the monetary value of the distortion of his labor supply decision, that is, the welfare cost. The size of the welfare cost thus depends mainly on the marginal tax rate, which determines how much the net wage rate is reduced, and on how responsive labor supply is to reductions in the returns to work.

Economists use the wage elasticity of labor supply to measure how responsive workers are to tax-induced changes in wage rates.[4] It is defined as the percentage change in labor supply divided by the percentage change in the net wage rate that induces the change in labor supply. For example, if a 10 percent reduction in the net wage rate produced a 10 percent decrease in labor supply, the elasticity would be one. In the numerical example above, a two-thirds increase in the net wage rate (from $6 to $10) was assumed to increase labor supply by 20 percent (from 2,000 to 2,400 hours), an elasticity of 0.3 (0.2/0.67). A higher value for the elasticity thus means that a given change in the net wage rate brought about by changing the tax wedge (in a manner that keeps total tax payments unchanged, as in the example above) will produce a larger effect on the amount of labor supplied and hence on the amount of income earned.

Using η to indicate the labor supply elasticity, a convenient formula for calculating the welfare cost due to the labor supply effect of a tax on labor income is as follows:

$$W = \frac{1}{2}\eta \frac{m^2}{1-m} wL$$

(A derivation of this formula is given in the appendix.) In this formula $W$ is the total welfare cost, $m$ is the marginal tax rate, and $wL$ is total (before-tax) labor income (the market wage rate times the quantity of labor supplied). With the values assumed in the numerical example, the welfare cost calculated by this formula is

$$W = \frac{1}{2}(0.3) \frac{(0.4)^2}{1-0.4} (\$20,000) = 0.15 \frac{0.16}{0.6} (\$20,000) = \$800$$

which is the same figure arrived at in the discussion. Note in particular that the welfare cost varies more than proportionately to the square of the marginal tax rate; that is, doubling the marginal tax rate more than doubles the welfare cost. A higher marginal tax rate not only produces a larger reduction in labor supply but also reduces the average value of time gained when labor supply is reduced and consequently affects the welfare cost in a multiplicative fashion.

Ideally, equation 1 should be applied to each worker or household separately and the results summed to determine the magnitude of the welfare cost due to the effect on labor supply of a tax on labor income. In practice, we lack sufficiently detailed information to do this at all accurately. Fortunately, the results are not very much distorted by using total labor income for all workers together in equation 1, along with average values (appropriately weighted) for labor supply elasticities and marginal tax rates. Although this procedure tends to understate the welfare cost slightly, the understatement is not large enough to affect the conclusions drawn here.

To estimate the welfare cost using equation 1 requires three pieces of information: total labor income; the weighted-average marginal tax rate that applies to labor income; and the weighted-average elasticity of labor supply. A reasonably accurate estimate of total labor income is readily available, but the other two values are harder to pin down precisely.

Marginal tax rates differ among households, and the appropriate value to use in equation 1 is the average value (weighted by labor incomes). More important, the relevant value is the combined marginal tax rate that results from all taxes and other policies that reduce net wage rates below market rates. Among the obvious taxes that affect labor supply are the federal individual income tax, state income taxes, and the social security payroll tax. Sales and excise taxes also reduce net wage rates by reducing the purchasing power of a given income. Government transfer programs also often incorporate marginal tax rates on earnings through the way they reduce benefits when earnings rise. The combined effect of all these policies produces a sizable marginal tax rate for most households. One recent study estimated the combined marginal tax rates by quintiles of households in 1976; the weighted average of these rates is 43 percent.[5]

It is not clear whether combined marginal tax rates are higher or lower than in 1976. Federal income tax rates were rising between 1976 and 1981 because of bracket creep but were reduced between 1981 and 1984 by the Reagan tax cut. Available estimates suggest that for most households marginal federal income tax rates are now about the same as in 1976 or slightly lower. In addition, however, the social security payroll tax rate was increased from 11.7 percent to 14.1 percent over this period, and state income taxes also tended to rise. Overall, it appears likely that combined marginal tax rates today are not greatly different from those in 1976. Given the difficulties associated with estimating them accurately, however, it appears prudent to consider the possibility that the weighted-average marginal tax rate is somewhat greater or smaller than 43 percent. Consequently, I use a range of values from 38 percent to 48 percent that seems likely to enclose the true value.

Probably the most difficult value to estimate accurately is the appropriate labor supply elasticity. Numerous studies in the field of labor economics have estimated labor supply elasticities, but unfortunately there is no consensus on the exact magnitude. There is a consensus that elasticities vary among different demographic groups, with married women apparently more responsive to tax-induced changes in net wage rates than men, but the variations in the estimates for each group remain quite large. My survey of this literature leads me to believe that the average value is likely to fall in the range 0.2 to 0.4, 0.3 being my preferred estimate.[6]

Given the importance of labor supply elasticity in determining the welfare cost, it may be worthwhile to indicate exactly what these magnitudes indicate. Coupled with the marginal tax rate, the labor supply elasticity identifies by what percentage labor supply and earnings will rise if the marginal tax rate on any additional earnings is reduced. For example, a 40 percent tax rate and an elasticity of 0.2 imply that labor supply would rise by 13.3 percent if workers could keep all additional income they earned. (This can be calculated from $(\eta m)/(1-m)$, since $m/(1-m)$ is the percentage increase in the wage rate if the marginal tax rate is reduced to zero.) For the same marginal tax rate and an elasticity of 0.4, the implied increase in labor supply is 26.7 percent. I find it hard to believe that labor supply would rise by more than 26.7 percent under these circumstances, but several studies have estimated labor supply elasticities greater than 0.4.

Using these ranges of values for the labor supply elasticity and marginal tax rate along with the approximately $2,400 billion in before-tax labor income in 1984 in equation 1, we can easily calculate the total welfare cost of taxes that distort labor supply decisions. The results are reported in table 3–1. The sensitivity of the result to the elasticity and marginal tax rate is apparent. The welfare cost is estimated to be 7.5 percent of tax revenue when $\eta = 0.2$ and $m = 38$ percent and 28.5 percent when the highest values for these factors are used. My preferred estimate is based on the intermediate values of $\eta = 0.3$ and $m = 43$ percent, in which case the welfare cost is $116.8 billion, or 15.7 percent of revenue. Although future research is likely to narrow the range of uncertainty regarding $m$ and $\eta$ somewhat, we are unlikely ever to be able to estimate this hidden cost of taxes on labor income exactly. Nonetheless, the estimates in table 3–1 suggest that these taxes probably impose a sizable cost on the economy.

What makes these results more impressive is that they do not take into account all the ways these taxes interfere with the efficient functioning of the economy. In other words, taxes that fall on labor income often produce other kinds of welfare costs in addition to the distortion of labor supply decisions, and only the labor supply effects are evaluated in table 3–1. For instance, "loopholes" in income taxes give taxpayers an uneconomic incentive to channel part of their incomes into nontaxable forms, such as fringe benefits. Sales and excise taxes may also adversely affect the composition of output in addition to whatever effect they have on labor supply. All taxes also entail administrative, collection, and compliance costs, all of which constitute costs in addition to the revenue raised; that is, they too are forms of welfare costs. These last costs alone have recently been estimated at 5 to 7 percent of tax revenue for income taxes.[7] If all the other forms of welfare costs could be evaluated, there is little doubt that the total welfare cost of taxes falling on labor income would be greater than is suggested by the estimates in table 3–1.

## The Marginal Welfare Cost of Taxation

The welfare cost of taxation is a kind of hidden cost associated with government spending of tax revenues, but the estimates of welfare cost reported in the last section do not measure that cost in a manner

## TABLE 3–1
### Total and Average Welfare Costs, 1984
(billions of dollars)

| | $\eta$ | | |
| --- | --- | --- | --- |
| $m$ | 0.2 | 0.3 | 0.4 |
| 0.38 | 55.9 | 83.8 | 111.8 |
| | (7.5) | (11.2) | (15.0) |
| 0.43 | 77.9 | 116.8 | 155.7 |
| | (10.5) | (15.7) | (20.9) |
| 0.48 | 106.3 | 159.5 | 212.6 |
| | (14.3) | (21.4) | (28.5) |

NOTE: Figures in parentheses are welfare costs as a percentage of tax revenues from these taxes; $\eta$ = labor supply elasticity; $m$ = marginal tax rate.
SOURCE: Edgar K. Browning, "On The Marginal Welfare Cost of Taxation," Texas A&M University Working Paper, 1985, table 1.

that is relevant for the evaluation of expenditure policies. Table 3–1 gives estimates of the average welfare cost of taxes on labor income, but it is the marginal welfare cost associated with raising tax revenue that is important in comparing the costs and benefits of expenditure policies. For the government to spend $1 billion on some project, for example, it must increase tax revenues by raising tax rates above their current level (or engage in debt financing, which is discussed below). To evaluate the cost of carrying out this project, the *additional* distorting effect of the increase in tax rates is what is relevant, not the average distorting effect of all taxes in the system.

The marginal welfare cost of taxation is the additional welfare cost per dollar of revenue when tax rates are increased by a small amount. (Alternatively, it is the reduction in welfare cost per dollar of revenue when tax rates are reduced by a small amount. For small changes in tax rates, the two measures will be approximately equal.) In the next section I consider in greater detail what determines the size of the marginal welfare cost, but two brief remarks are appropriate here. First, marginal welfare cost will generally be larger than average welfare cost. This follows from the relation between total, average, and marginal welfare costs. As shown by equation 1, the total welfare cost increases more than proportionately to tax rates; the average welfare cost is thus greater, the higher the marginal tax rate. (This is also illustrated by the estimates in table 3–1.) If the average welfare cost of raising revenue increases with the amount of revenue (and marginal rates), the marginal welfare cost of raising revenue must be greater than the average welfare cost.

Second, the marginal welfare cost of raising revenue will be larger the higher the current level of marginal tax rates (that is, the higher the weighted-average marginal tax rate). Recall that the marginal welfare cost is the ratio of the additional welfare cost produced by an increase in tax rates to the increase in tax revenues produced. The additional welfare cost (the numerator in this ratio) produced when the marginal tax rate is increased from 40 to 41 percent, for example, will be larger than when the rate is increased from 10 to 11 percent. An initial rate of 40 percent causes a larger initial distortion in labor supply decisions than a rate of 10 percent; and the larger the initial distortion, the more harmful any further adverse effect will be.[8] In addition, the increase in tax revenue from an increase in tax rates (the denominator in the ratio) is likely to be smaller the higher the initial marginal tax rates. Therefore, the marginal welfare cost per dollar of additional tax revenue will increase with the level of marginal tax rates.

Figure 3–1 illustrates how the marginal welfare cost is related to the marginal cost of raising tax revenue. The horizontal axis measures the weighted-average marginal tax rate, the vertical axis the marginal cost of raising an additional dollar of revenue. The direct marginal cost of raising revenue, shown as the line $MC_D$, is drawn horizontal at $1.00 to show the direct tax burden when one dollar is taken from taxpayers. If taxes produced no distortions in the economy, that curve would also be the total marginal cost of raising revenue. When taxes distort economic activities, however, the marginal welfare cost of raising tax revenue must be added to the direct marginal cost to give the total marginal cost, shown as $MC_T$. For example, when the marginal tax rate is 45 percent, the marginal welfare cost of raising another dollar is $0.40, and the combined marginal cost of raising revenue is $1.40. (The figures used here, though intended to illustrate general relationships, are representative of the estimates presented below.)

Note that the marginal cost rises sharply with the marginal tax rate. When the marginal tax rate is 25 percent, the marginal cost of raising an additional dollar in revenue is $1.14 (the marginal welfare cost is 14 percent of additional revenues); when the marginal tax rate is 35 percent, the marginal cost is $1.25. In short, the higher the marginal tax rate, the more expensive it is to raise additional revenue by raising rates further. Other factors, such as the labor supply elasticity, also affect the shape of the $MC_T$ curve. For example, the higher the labor supply elasticity, the more steeply rising the $MC_T$ curve will be. These factors are discussed further in the next section.

FIGURE 3–1

RELATION OF MARGINAL WELFARE COST TO
MARGINAL COST OF RAISING REVENUE

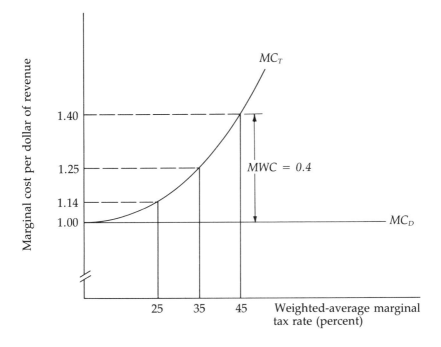

Although the numbers used in figure 3–1 are hypothetical, they do illustrate the general relationship involved. To illustrate how this measure is relevant for the analysis of government policies, assume for the moment that the weighted-average marginal tax rate is 45 percent and the marginal cost of raising revenue is $1.40. In the analysis of any government expenditure policy, a central question is how the benefits of the policy compare with the costs borne by taxpayers in financing the policy (assuming that taxes are used to finance it). What the discussion here shows is that the cost of financing an expenditure program is greater than the budgetary outlays involved. Consequently, the benefits of the expenditure policy must be larger than the marginal cost of raising the revenue if the policy is to benefit taxpayers on balance. For the $1.40 figure, any government outlay that does not produce benefits of at least $1.40 per dollar spent will be counterproductive.

This conclusion should be understood to hold for moderate changes in government spending that are not large enough to change marginal tax rates significantly (and hence the size of the marginal welfare cost itself). For instance, a $10 billion change in government spending on any program would probably require a change in the weighted-average marginal tax rate of less than one percentage point. For that small change the marginal welfare cost is approximately constant. Thus the $1.40 figure can be taken as the relevant cost of providing the revenue that finances any moderate change in government spending. The question that should be asked is, Would $1 billion more spent on Medicare or cancer research, for example, provide benefits of more than $1.4 billion? If not, the spending increase does not pass the test of providing benefits at least as large as the costs involved when we take into account the distorting effect of the higher tax rates on the economy. Similarly, reducing educational subsidies by $1 billion is actually beneficial as long as those subsidies provide benefits valued at less than $1.4 billion.

It is difficult and lies beyond the scope of this chapter to determine how large the benefits of government spending in different areas are, but it should be mentioned that it is possible for the benefits to exceed one dollar per dollar spent. In situations where private markets do not operate efficiently, government spending policies can improve resource allocation and thereby confer benefits of greater value than the outlays made. Obvious examples include national defense, medical research, and pollution abatement. Left to themselves, private markets would not provide as much of these activities as people would be willing to pay for, because of the difficulties of getting people to pay voluntarily for a service they will receive once it is produced regardless of whether they pay for it. In cases like this, government spending can be worth more to the public than the outlays involved. What the analysis here shows, however, is that the existence of imperfectly functioning private markets is not by itself sufficient evidence that government can improve matters with appropriately designed subsidies. That a market is operating inefficiently implies only that appropriate spending policies are capable of producing benefits somewhat greater than one dollar per dollar spent. For the spending policy to be worthwhile, however, the benefits must exceed $1.40 per dollar spent to offset the added inefficiency produced by higher tax rates.

Although evaluating the benefits and costs of spending programs is extremely difficult, cost-benefit analysis has been used to make such evaluations. Cost-benefit studies attempt to place monetary values on the benefits and costs of government spending (and other) programs; when the benefits are estimated to exceed the costs, it is concluded that the program is worthwhile on efficiency grounds. If all benefits and costs are correctly valued, this is a sensible approach to the evaluation of policies. In practice, however, these studies usually measure the cost only as the required government outlay, which understates the true cost because it ignores the marginal welfare cost of taxation. On the basis of our illustrative value, the costs in such studies are underestimated by a factor of 1.4. By neglecting an important part of the costs of government spending programs, many cost-benefit studies have concluded that benefits exceeded costs when in fact costs would have been estimated to exceed benefits if the marginal welfare cost of taxation had been taken into account. Cost-benefit analysis is a concrete example of the general point that marginal welfare cost is relevant in evaluating government spending programs.

Another important use for the concept of marginal welfare cost is in deciding how to deal with the government budget deficit. Assume that it has been decided to eliminate the deficit. Should this be done by increasing taxes or by reducing expenditures? The relevant issue is whether the expenditures provide benefits greater than the cost of raising tax revenue, including the marginal welfare cost. To the extent that some expenditures confer benefits of less than $1.40 per dollar of outlay, the well-being of taxpayers would be served by reducing expenditures. A special consideration in this case, however, is that the tax increase required to close the deficit is quite large and would probably require the weighted-average marginal tax rate to rise by eight or ten points. For such a large change the marginal cost of raising revenue should not be assumed to be constant. If taxes were raised to close the deficit entirely, the marginal cost of raising the last dollars necessary to eliminate the deficit might be, say, $1.60. Thus the deficit should not be eliminated in this way unless all government spending provides benefits at least this large.

A related question is, If we are not going to reduce expenditures to reduce the deficit, is it better to raise taxes or simply do nothing and live with the deficit? The marginal cost of raising taxes is also relevant here, but it should be emphasized that the alternative—borrowing to continue to finance expenditures—has welfare costs of its own. Deficit finance is likely to reduce the rate of investment and capital accumulation with adverse effects much like reductions in labor supply. In addition, borrowing today carries with it the responsibility of financing higher government outlays on interest payments on the national debt in the future, and the higher future taxes required to finance these outlays will also have distorting effects on the economy. Thus the high marginal cost of raising tax revenue does not necessarily imply that deficit finance is any better. One recent study concluded that the welfare costs of deficit finance are likely to be higher than the marginal welfare costs of raising taxes.[9] If that is correct and if expenditures are not reduced, efficiency calls for raising taxes to close the deficit.

A final important issue showing the relevance of the marginal welfare cost of taxes pertains to the evaluation of redistributional programs. I have so far deliberately neglected to emphasize the importance of who receives the benefits of expenditure programs and who bears the costs (direct and welfare) of providing the revenues. The intention of redistributional policies is to place the costs on one group of households and provide the benefits to an entirely different group. The marginal distorting effects of policies used to effect redistributions of income are still important to consider, but the marginal welfare cost of raising taxes that I have discussed does not identify the effects in the relevant way. The framework has to be modified somewhat to apply this concept to redistributional programs, and I defer an explanation of how this may be done to a later section.

In contrast, the concept of marginal welfare cost as described here and estimated in the next section is most directly applicable in situations where redistribution is not an important consequence or intention of the policies evaluated. For example, raising taxes to provide services that will accrue to all taxpayers without major redistribution among groups is the kind of setting where it is reasonable to stress the efficiency aspects of the fiscal operation by emphasizing the marginal cost of raising taxes.

### Estimates of the Marginal Welfare Cost of Taxation

To estimate the marginal welfare cost of taxation, we must determine how much a small increase in marginal tax rates increases the total welfare cost of the tax system and relate the increase to the increment in tax revenue that is produced, since we want to estimate the marginal welfare cost per dollar of revenue.[10] As suggested by the discussion of the total welfare cost, the magnitude of marginal welfare cost cannot be estimated exactly since its size depends on several factors that cannot be precisely specified. In fact, the margin of error is even wider when dealing with the marginal welfare cost since it depends on two new factors in addition to marginal tax rates and labor supply elasticities.

Four factors are critically important in determining the magnitude of the marginal welfare cost of taxation. The first two can be explained briefly since they have already been discussed in connection with the estimation of the total welfare cost.

1. The initial weighted-average marginal tax rate. The higher the current marginal tax rates, the more distorted the initial situation is, and therefore the larger is the additional welfare cost produced when marginal rates are increased.

2. Labor supply elasticity. The more sensitive are workers' decisions to tax-induced changes in their net rates of pay (that is, the greater the elasticity), the larger will be the additional welfare cost produced when marginal tax rates rise. (Recall that a higher elasticity means that a given increase in marginal tax rates has a larger adverse effect on labor supply.)

3. How much marginal tax rates rise in relation to average tax rates. Although the additional distorting effect of a change in taxes depends only on what happens to the marginal tax rate, the amount of revenue produced also depends on how much the average tax rate changes. Therefore, the marginal welfare cost per dollar of revenue will be greater the larger the increase in the marginal tax rate in relation to the increase in the average tax rate. Consider, for example, an initial tax of 40 percent on income in excess of $20,000. For a worker earning $25,000, the marginal tax rate is 40 percent, and the average rate is 8 percent. Raising the tax rate to 41 percent would raise the marginal rate by one full percentage point, but the average rate would increase only to 8.2 percent (assuming the worker continued to earn $25,000). The added labor supply distortion (due to the one-point increase in the marginal tax rate) would bulk large in comparison with the small additional revenue generated; that is, the marginal welfare cost would be large.

4. How much labor supply (and hence earnings) fall in response to the higher tax rates. This is not exactly the same as point 2 since the compensated labor supply elasticity that is relevant for evaluating the additional welfare cost of a higher marginal tax rate does not necessarily tell us by how much actual labor supply and earnings are affected. A tax on labor income may not cause labor supply to fall if the disincentive to work due to the marginal tax rate is offset by the incentive to work due to the tax when it leaves the worker poorer and for that reason encourages greater effort. Nonetheless, the tax would have a welfare cost because the unchanged labor supply would be less than the labor supply would be if the tax had not produced any disincentive to work through its marginal tax rate. In relation to the efficient response, the labor supply has fallen, and this "compensated" reduction in labor supply indicates the distortion of the tax. Whatever the effect on the compensated supply of labor (measured by the elasticity referred to in point 2), if actual labor supply

falls, there is an additional effect on the marginal welfare cost, because tax revenue will not rise as much. Since marginal welfare cost is the additional welfare cost divided by the extra tax revenue, a reduction in actual labor earnings will reduce the denominator of this ratio and therefore raise the marginal welfare cost per dollar of revenue.

Marginal welfare cost can be estimated by adapting the approach discussed in the first section to the measurement of the effects of a small change in tax rates. The estimate, however, will depend on the values assumed for each of the four factors discussed above. Appropriate values for the first two have been considered in the first section, and now we need only consider the other two.

How much the marginal tax rate rises in relation to the average tax rate when additional revenue is to be raised depends on which taxes are used to generate additional revenue and exactly how their rate structures are varied. At one extreme, if additional revenue is generated by raising the social security payroll tax rate while leaving the ceiling on taxable earnings unchanged, the average tax rate would rise by more than the weighted-average marginal tax rate. (The increase in the average and marginal tax rates would be equal for those earning under the ceiling, but those earning above it would find their average rate increased while their marginal rate remained unchanged at zero.) I will assume that the average rate rises by about 1.25 times the increase in the marginal rate in this case. At the other extreme, increasing revenues through the federal individual income tax with a proportionate increase in all bracket rates would imply a larger increase in the weighted-average marginal tax rate than in the overall average tax rate. Table 3–2 provides data that suggest the magnitudes involved. It shows, at various levels of income and for selected years, the marginal federal income tax rate and the average tax rate. In most years and at most income levels, the marginal tax rate is about twice the average tax rate. Thus, for revenue produced from the income tax, it may be reasonable to assume that the average tax rate rises by only half as much as the marginal tax rate.

Between these two extreme cases, a convenient intermediate assumption is a proportionate increase in the rates of all taxes that fall on labor income. Since the overall average tax rate on labor income is about 31 percent and the weighted-average marginal tax rate is 43 percent in our intermediate case, this suggests that the average tax rate would increase by 72 percent as much in this case.

Two possibilities seem to span the most likely effects of an increase in tax rates on actual labor supply and earnings. First, labor supply might remain unchanged. This could occur if taxpayers received little

TABLE 3–2
AVERAGE AND MARGINAL INDIVIDUAL INCOME TAX RATES, 1965–1984

| Year | 25 Percent of Median Income | 50 Percent of Median Income | Median Income | Twice Median Income | Five Times Median Income |
|------|------|------|------|------|------|
| | | Average Rates | | | |
| 1965 | 0.0 | 2.8 | 7.4 | 12.2 | 20.5 |
| 1978 | − 7.3 | 3.4 | 11.6 | 17.3 | 30.9 |
| 1981 | − 8.4 | 5.7 | 13.3 | 18.5 | 31.7 |
| 1984 | − 5.4 | 5.9 | 11.9 | 16.0 | 26.1 |
| | | Marginal Rates | | | |
| 1965 | 0.0 | 14.0 | 17.0 | 22.0 | 39.0 |
| 1978 | 10.0 | 16.0 | 22.0 | 36.0 | 55.0 |
| 1981 | 12.5 | 18.0 | 24.0 | 43.0 | 59.0 |
| 1984 | 12.5 | 14.0 | 22.0 | 33.0 | 45.0 |

NOTE: Computed for families of four with typical standard or itemized deductions. The negative average rates for lower-income families reflect the refundable earned income tax credit.

SOURCE: Congressional Budget Office, *Reducing the Deficit: Spending and Revenue Options*, February 1984, table VI–3.

or no benefits from the expenditure of the additional taxes they paid and so were left with lower real incomes that stimulated enough greater effort to offset the disincentive effect of the higher marginal tax rate. Second, labor supply might fall by an amount measured by the compensated labor supply elasticity. This could occur if taxpayers received benefits from the expenditure that fully compensated for the additional taxes they paid. In this case, there would be no loss of real income and thus no incentive to work more because of a loss of income, but there would still be a disincentive to work due to the higher marginal tax rate.

To sum up, the range of values for the four key factors that affect the size of marginal welfare cost that I use are as follows:

- Marginal tax rate: 38, 43, and 48 percent
- (Compensated) labor supply elasticity: 0.2, 0.3, and 0.4
- Change in average tax rate: 1.25, 0.72, and 0.5 times the change in the marginal tax rate
- Effect on actual labor supply: unchanged and declines by the compensated effect

There are fifty-four possible combinations of circumstances to con-

91

sider. For each combination, I have adapted the approach used in the first section to calculate the marginal welfare cost under the assumption that the weighted-average marginal tax rate is increased by one percentage point. Table 3–3 displays the results, with marginal welfare cost measured as a percentage of additional tax revenue. The average welfare cost is also shown.

What stands out clearly from these estimates is that the marginal welfare cost of raising tax revenue is very sensitive to the particular combination of contributing factors that is used. Marginal welfare cost may be as low as 9.9 percent if the most conservative assumption in each case is used or as high as 303.4 percent if the upper-bound assumptions are used. Although I find the intermediate assumptions more congenial, it must be stressed that our empirical knowledge does not allow us to rule out the more extreme estimates. In fact, given the difficulty of determining the appropriate magnitudes of the contributing factors exactly, we are unlikely ever to be able to estimate marginal welfare cost precisely.

In addition to the inevitable margin for error that surrounds any estimate, table 3–3 suggests that for most combinations of the assumptions marginal welfare cost is of substantial magnitude. For my preferred combination ($m$ = 43 percent, $\eta$ = 0.3, and a proportionate increase in all tax rates), it is 31.8 percent even if labor supply does not fall and 46.9 percent if it does. If the true value is anywhere close to these figures, it would clearly be a major mistake to assume that the government can spend a dollar at a cost to the public of only a dollar.

Two recent studies have used more elaborate methods to estimate the marginal welfare cost of taxation. Using a two-sector aggregate general equilibrium model, Charles Stuart estimated marginal welfare costs ranging from 7.2 percent to 133 percent. Using a multisector, dynamic computational general equilibrium model, Ballard, Shoven, and Whalley produced estimates ranging from 17 to 56 percent.[11] Although comparisons with the results of table 3–3 are difficult because a somewhat different range of assumptions was used in each case, these studies support the general conclusion that marginal welfare cost is probably substantial.

It should also be repeated that the approach used to develop the estimates in table 3–3 evaluates only the labor supply effect of higher tax rates. Since higher tax rates distort other economic decisions as well as labor supply, the estimates reported here probably understate the marginal welfare cost to some unknown degree.

## TABLE 3–3
### MARGINAL WELFARE COST PER DOLLAR OF REVENUE
(percent)

| | dt | m = 0.38 | | | m = 0.43 | | | m = 0.48 | | |
| --- | --- | --- | --- | --- | --- | --- | --- | --- | --- | --- |
| | | η = 0.2 | 0.3 | 0.4 | 0.2 | 0.3 | 0.4 | 0.2 | 0.3 | 0.4 |
| Earnings constant | 1.25dm | 9.9 | 14.9 | 19.9 | 12.2 | 18.3 | 24.4 | 14.9 | 22.4 | 29.8 |
| | 0.72dm | 17.3 | 25.9 | 34.5 | 21.2 | 31.8 | 42.4 | 25.9 | 38.9 | 51.8 |
| | 0.50dm | 24.8 | 37.3 | 49.6 | 30.5 | 45.8 | 61.1 | 37.3 | 56.0 | 74.6 |
| Earnings decline | 1.25dm | 11.0 | 17.6 | 24.9 | 13.9 | 22.5 | 32.4 | 17.6 | 28.9 | 42.7 |
| | 0.72dm | 20.9 | 35.1 | 53.1 | 27.0 | 46.9 | 74.3 | 35.1 | 64.1 | 108.9 |
| | 0.50dm | 33.2 | 59.8 | 100.0 | 44.1 | 85.2 | 159.7 | 59.9 | 128.7 | 303.4 |
| Average welfare cost | | 7.5 | 11.2 | 15.0 | 10.5 | 15.7 | 20.9 | 14.3 | 21.4 | 28.5 |

NOTE: $m$ = marginal welfare cost; $\eta$ = labor supply elasticity; $dt$ = change in average tax rate; $dm$ = change in marginal tax rate.

SOURCE: Browning, "On the Marginal Welfare Cost of Taxation," table 2.

## The Marginal Welfare Cost of Redistribution

Government expenditure policies, in combination with the taxes that finance them, are often intended to redistribute income from one group to another. For expenditure policies of this sort, the marginal welfare cost of raising revenue does not tell us how costly it is to transfer income from one group to another and therefore cannot be used directly in evaluating the redistributive aspects of expenditure policies. It is still important, however, to evaluate the marginal distorting effects associated with redistributive policies, and this section briefly discusses some of the issues involved.

Suppose a policy transfers $1 from person A to person B; how should the distortions produced by the redistribution enter into an evaluation of this policy? Assume that raising the dollar in taxes from A has a marginal welfare cost of 50 percent, so that the cost to A of providing the funds to be redistributed is $1.50. At the same time, the policy used to transfer the dollar to B is likely to distort his economic decisions in some way and therefore make the value of the subsidy to him less than one dollar; suppose the $1 transferred to B is worth only $0.75. Thus it costs A $1.50 to provide a benefit of $0.75 to B. We could describe this as a marginal cost of $2 to A per dollar of benefit to B or, equivalently, as a marginal welfare cost of redistributing income to B of 100 percent (it costs A 100 percent more than the benefit to B).

This way of conceptualizing the cost of redistributive policy is attractive since it emphasizes that redistribution is not a zero-sum game: to provide benefits to one person or group imposes larger costs on others.[12] We are then led to consider the relevant question: Is it desirable to expand or contract the amounts being redistributed when at the margin each dollar of benefit to B costs A two dollars? Note that recognizing the existence of a marginal welfare cost associated with redistribution does not prejudge the answer to this question. There is nothing logically inconsistent with recognizing that it costs A more than a dollar to provide a dollar in benefits to B and still concluding that the redistribution is worthwhile. In making such decisions, however, most people recognize the actual costs and benefits to the groups involved as relevant considerations, and that information is provided by the marginal welfare cost of redistribution.

Although the marginal welfare cost of raising tax revenue does not typically equal the marginal welfare cost of redistributing income, the two concepts are related. As the example above suggests, the marginal welfare cost of raising taxes is part of the overall story. In

FIGURE 3–2
## MARGINAL WELFARE COST OF REDISTRIBUTION

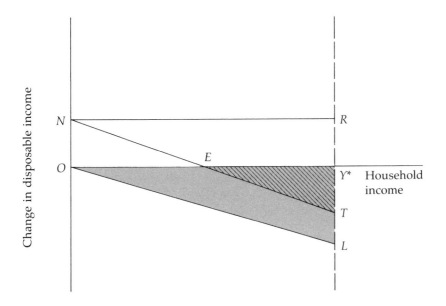

some cases, however, the connection is not quite so clear, as the following example will show.

Starting with the existing system of taxes and transfers, suppose that we evaluate a small increase in the amount of income redistributed in the following way: a flat 1 percent tax rate on labor income is added to the tax system, and the proceeds are spent by providing equal per household cash transfers. This tax-transfer program differs from the example above in that all households pay taxes and receive benefits. Nonetheless, this policy would effect a substantial redistribution of income since low-income households would pay less in taxes than they would receive in benefits, while the reverse would be true for high-income households. What we want to determine is the marginal welfare cost of redistributing income through this policy.

Figure 3–2 illustrates this tax-transfer operation, but with the magnitudes exaggerated for clarity. The tax is shown by *OL*, the vertical difference between *OL* and the horizontal axis measuring the additional tax liability at each level of income. The transfer is shown by *NR*, which is drawn parallel to the horizontal axis since the transfer acts to raise everyone's disposable income by the same amount, *ON*. What is important here, however, is the combined effect of the two policies, which is shown by *NET*. *NET* indicates that households with incomes below *OE* receive transfers greater than the additional tax they pay, while the opposite is true for those with higher incomes. In short, the policies redistribute income from upper-income households to lower-income households.

For this kind of policy the marginal welfare cost of redistributing income will be much larger than the marginal welfare cost of raising tax revenue considered alone. To see why, assume for simplicity that households are uniformly distributed between *O* and *Y\** in the figure. Then we can interpret areas as proportionate to the amounts of tax revenue and net gains and losses. For example, the gross tax revenue is proportional to the area *OY\*L*, while the amount actually redistributed is proportional to the area *EY\*T*. The amount actually redistributed is therefore a small fraction of the additional taxes raised. Whatever the additional welfare cost of raising this tax revenue is, its magnitude will bulk much larger in comparison to the amount redistributed than in comparison to the gross revenue raised.

To illustrate roughly the quantitative importance of this point, let us assume that the marginal welfare cost of raising revenue with this kind of tax change is 25 percent. (That would be the approximate value for $\eta = 0.3$ and $m = 43$ percent, since in this case the marginal tax rate and average tax rate both rise by the same proportion: see table 3–3.) In other words, the additional welfare cost is 25 percent of area *OY\*L* in figure 3–2. On the basis of the actual distribution of incomes in the United States, however, the area *EY\*T* is estimated to be only 22 percent as large as area *OY\*L*; that is, of the additional gross tax revenue only 22 percent is redistributed from upper- to lower-income households. Thus the additional welfare cost when expressed as a percentage of the amount redistributed will be 114 percent (0.25/0.22).

The 114 percent figure does not tell us the marginal welfare cost of redistribution as previously defined since that will depend on the division of the additional welfare cost between upper- and lower-income households. Suppose it is divided equally, so that the additional welfare cost per dollar of net tax to upper-income households is fifty-seven cents, while lower-income households also bear an additional welfare cost of fifty-seven cents per dollar of net transfer they receive. Then each dollar redistributed imposes a cost of $1.57 on upper-income households and results in a real benefit of $0.43 ($1.00 – $0.57) to lower-income households. The marginal welfare cost per dollar of benefit to lower-income households is 265 percent. Put differently, it costs upper-income households $3.65 to provide a transfer worth $1.00 to lower-income households.

Although this example is intended only to illustrate why the marginal welfare cost of redistribution is likely to be larger than the marginal welfare cost of raising tax revenue, the numbers used do not misrepresent the actual relationships very much. In a recent study William R. Johnson and I used a sample of about 50,000 households and a computer simulation to estimate the marginal welfare cost of redistribution carried out with policies like those discussed here.[13] Table 3–4 shows some of the results, expressed as the change in average real income (incorporating the additional welfare costs) per household for each quintile of households. Just as we saw earlier, the magnitudes depend on compensated labor supply elasticities and other factors (all cases shown in the table used marginal tax rates that averaged 43 percent). With the intermediate elasticity of 0.31, for example, households in the lowest quintile (ranked by household income) gained an average of $47.30, and changes for the other quintiles were $32.60, −$11.49, −$71.59, and −$196.21. Translated into the marginal welfare cost of redistributing income to the lowest two quintiles, this implies that the cost to the upper three quintiles of households is 249 percent greater than the benefit to the lowest two. Moreover, this outcome results from assumptions implying that the marginal welfare cost of raising tax revenue is only about 25 percent.

A change in the volume of income redistribution could be accomplished in many ways, and the marginal welfare cost is likely to depend on the kind of policies used, being in some cases higher and in other cases lower than for the policies examined here. The general point that would, I believe, remain true is that the marginal welfare cost of redistribution would be several times greater than the marginal welfare cost of raising tax revenue considered alone.

TABLE 3–4
CHANGE IN REAL INCOME PER HOUSEHOLD

| | | Quintile | | | | | Marginal Welfare Cost (%) |
|---|---|---|---|---|---|---|---|
| | Elasticity | 1 | 2 | 3 | 4 | 5 | |
| Benchmark | 0.31 | 47.30 | 32.60 | −11.49 | −71.59 | −196.21 | 249 |
| High elasticity | 0.47 | 38.55 | 18.07 | −30.32 | −93.45 | −222.00 | 511 |
| Low elasticity | 0.21 | 56.12 | 45.85 | 3.46 | −56.80 | −185.07 | 129 |

SOURCE: Edgar K. Browning and William R. Johnson, "The Trade-off between Equality and Efficiency," *Journal of Political Economy*, Vol. 92 (April 1984), tables 6, 8.

It is sometimes objected that the policies considered above are biased toward finding a high marginal welfare cost because the transfers are made not only to low-income households but to all other households as well. The assumption that everyone pays taxes and also receives transfers is used, however, to clarify the relationship between the marginal welfare cost of redistributing income and the marginal welfare cost of raising taxes; the policy need not operate in exactly this way. Note in figure 3–2 that identical results would be produced if the government levied taxes only on those earning above *OE*, as shown by *ET*, and used the proceeds to dispense transfers to low-income households, as shown by *NE*. This tax-transfer program is analogous to using the federal income tax (which exempts low-income households from payment of taxes) to raise revenue and then making transfers to low-income households through a negative income tax. The real economic effects, including the marginal welfare cost of the redistribution, would be the same as in the example. Thus policies that avoid making transfers to some or all of those who provide the tax revenues do not necessarily reduce the welfare costs involved.

Relatively little research has been done on the marginal welfare cost of redistribution, and the estimates given here should be considered merely suggestive. The major point to emphasize is that the marginal welfare cost of raising tax revenue is not directly relevant to the evaluation of redistributive policies. Instead, a related measure, the marginal welfare cost of redistribution, is needed, and it will usually be substantially larger.

## Conclusion

Economists often emphasize that it is essential to apply a marginalist approach to the study of economic problems. In most cases our concern is not with all-or-nothing alternatives but with the consequences of a little more or a little less. For example, we seldom consider eliminating educational subsidies or social security entirely. Instead, most policy questions center on whether a little less spending on education or a little more spending on social security is desirable. In this context, it is the marginal effects, the consequences of a small change from the current level, that are relevant. Moreover, marginal effects are often of quite different magnitude from the average effect. For instance, the average benefit (measured in some way) of higher education may be substantial, but a small expansion in resources devoted to higher education will almost certainly produce additional gains—marginal benefits—that are much lower.

This chapter applies this approach to certain questions concerning government taxation and expenditure policies. Surprisingly, only recently have economists systematically begun to study the marginal welfare costs associated with varying the levels of government policies. A major result of this work is the finding that the marginal welfare costs are quite substantial, both absolutely and in relation to the average effects of the policies being studied. Although the marginal welfare cost of raising tax revenue can be estimated only with a significant margin for error, values in the range of 30 to 40 percent are apparently not likely to overstate its size.

The body of research discussed here has important implications for at least two issues of current interest. First, it is relevant to evaluation of proposals to reform the tax system. The estimates reported here are based on the tax system as it is currently structured, and a reform of the system could affect the magnitude of the marginal welfare cost. For example, if the federal income tax were changed to a true flat rate tax (a single rate on a broad measure of income), the marginal welfare cost would be substantially reduced. This would not only reduce the effective marginal tax rate by perhaps eight to ten percentage points but would also mean that additional tax revenue would be raised with a nonprogressive increase in rates; these two factors together could reduce the marginal welfare cost by more than half. It is important to recognize, however, that most current reform proposals, such as the administration and Bradley-Gephardt proposals, are not true flat rate taxes. They approximately maintain the progressivity of the income tax and do not significantly reduce effective marginal tax rates. Therefore, they would not have much effect on the magnitude of the marginal welfare cost.

Second, recognition of the high cost of raising tax revenue is relevant for deciding whether to close the deficit by reducing expenditures or by raising taxes. Expenditures should be reduced unless their benefits exceed their budgetary cost by an amount at least as large as the relevant marginal welfare cost. Although this chapter does not attempt to estimate the benefits of any expenditure policies, it is clear that government spending policies must pass a stiffer test than normally thought for it to be preferable to raise taxes rather than cut expenditures to reduce the deficit.

## Appendix

To explain why equation 1 in the text measures the total welfare cost of a tax on labor earnings, consider figure 3–3. The worker's market wage rate (before tax) is assumed constant at $w$, and his compensated labor supply curve is shown as $S$. The compensated supply curve

## FIGURE 3–3
### Total Welfare Cost of Tax on Labor Earnings

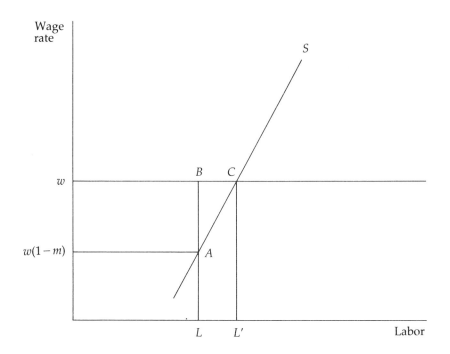

shows only the substitution effect of a tax-induced change in the net wage rate. With a marginal tax rate of $m$ on labor earnings, the net wage rate is $w(1-m)$, and the worker's equilibrium will be at point $A$ on the supply curve, supplying $L$ units of labor. If the marginal tax rate were reduced to zero (while continuing to collect the same tax revenue), the worker's net wage rate would rise to $w$, and he would choose point $C$ on his supply curve, supplying $L'$ units of labor. Thus his labor earnings would rise by $BCL'L$, but this would not be a net gain since $ACL'L$ would be necessary to compensate him for working the longer hours. His net gain from reducing the marginal tax rate to zero would therefore be area $ABC$; put the other way around, this is the net loss, or welfare cost, due to the tax which leaves the worker at point $A$ rather than at point $C$.

The formula used to calculate the total welfare cost, area $ABC$, is easily derived. Since $ABC$ is a triangle (assuming $S$ can be approximated as a straight line), its area equals one-half $BC \times AB$; $BC$ equals the change in the quantity of labor due to the tax, $\Delta L$, and $AB$ equals

100

the reduction in the worker's wage rate due to the tax, $wm$. Thus the welfare cost can be expressed as

$$W = \tfrac{1}{2}(\Delta L)wm \qquad\qquad (A-1)$$

Since the change in the quantity of labor supplied, $\Delta L$, can be expressed as the inverse of the slope of the supply curve, $\Delta L/\Delta w$, times the change in the wage rate, $wm$, (A–1) can be rewritten as

$$W = \tfrac{1}{2}\left[(\Delta L/\Delta w)\ wm\right]wm$$

Multiplying by $L(1-m)/L(1-m)$ and rearranging yields

$$W = \tfrac{1}{2}\left[\frac{\Delta L}{\Delta W}\frac{W(1-m)}{L}\right]\frac{m^2}{1-m}wL \qquad\qquad (A-2)$$

Note that the term in brackets is the percentage change in labor supply divided by the percentage change in the wage rate produced by the marginal tax rate; that is, it is the elasticity of the supply curve at point $A$ in the figure. Thus, using the symbol $\eta$ for the compensated labor supply elasticity, equation A–2 can be written as

$$W = \tfrac{1}{2}\,\eta\,\frac{m^2}{1-m}wL \qquad\qquad (A-3)$$

Equation A–3, the expression I set out to derive, can be used to estimate the total welfare cost of a tax on labor savings. A more complicated expression is required to estimate the marginal welfare cost of a tax.[14]

# Notes

1. Congressional Budget Office, *Revising the Individual Income Tax*, July 1983, p. 11.

2. Economic Report of the President (Washington, D.C., 1985), p. 72.

3. This analysis is based on the assumption that workers can adjust their hours of work to the level they desire given their net-of-tax wage rates. Even though individual workers seldom have such flexibility, this assumption is still appropriate in the present context because if taxes affect desired hours of work on average, employers have an incentive to cater to this change in conditions. Thus, even though the workweek may be fixed from the point of view of each individual worker, the level at which it is fixed is likely to reflect the preferences of workers on average.

4. The elasticities used here are what economists refer to as "compensated" elasticities. Roughly speaking, that means they refer to the change in labor supply produced when changes in marginal tax rates produce changes in net wage rates but do not change the amount of taxes actually paid. Thus they differ from elasticities that measure the effect of a change in market wage

rates. A higher market wage rate, for example, may not lead to an increase in the quantity of labor supplied because it has two opposing effects on labor supply. Workers do not need to work as hard because any given effort produces a higher income; this is the income effect, and it acts to reduce work effort. The higher wage rate also increases the pay for more work and encourages greater effort on this count; this is the substitution effect. It is the substitution effect that produces welfare costs, and that is what is measured by the compensated elasticity.

5. See Edgar K. Browning and William R. Johnson, "The Trade-off between Equality and Efficiency," *Journal of Political Economy*, vol. 92 (April 1984), table.

6. See the discussion in ibid.; Charles Stuart, "Welfare Costs per Dollar of Additional Tax Revenue in the United States," *American Economic Review*, vol. 74 (June 1984); and Charles L. Ballard, John B. Shoven, and John Whalley, "General Equilibrium Computations of the Marginal Welfare Costs of Taxes in the United States," *American Economic Review*, vol. 75 (March 1985), for references to the literature.

7. Joel Slemrod and Nikki Sorum, "The Compliance Cost of the U.S. Individual Income Tax System," *National Tax Journal*, vol. 37 (December 1984), pp. 461–74.

8. Suppose there is a one-hour reduction in labor supply when the marginal tax rate rises from 10 to 11 percent and also when the marginal tax rate rises from 40 to 41 percent. If the market wage rate is $10, the time gained would be worth $8.95 (89.5 percent of the $10 reduction in earnings) in the first case since it would be valued at the net-of-tax wage rate, and the additional welfare cost would be $1.05, the $10 loss in earnings less the value of the time gained. In the second case, the value of the additional hour would be $5.95, and the additional welfare cost would be $4.05.

9. Martin Feldstein, "Debt and Taxes in the Theory of Public Finance," National Bureau of Economic Research, Working Paper no. 1433, August 1984.

10. Marginal welfare cost can be evaluated for either a small increase or a small decrease in tax rates. For small changes in rates, the value will be approximately the same.

11. Both Stuart ("Welfare Costs") and Ballard et al. ("General Equilibrium Computations") use upper-bound estimates of compensated labor supply elasticities that are larger than those used here.

12. Most economists who have considered this matter have concluded that this is the proper way to pose the issue. For example, Arthur Okun suggests looking at redistribution as transferring income in a "leaky bucket," with part of the income taken from the taxpayer leaking out before the bucket reaches the recipient. He asks that we consider how large the leakage must be before we consider that the transfer is not worthwhile. A leakage of 50 percent (a $1 burden on the taxpayer yielding a $0.50 benefit to the recipient) is equivalent to a marginal welfare cost of 100 percent in the formulation suggested here. See Arthur M. Okun, *Equality and Efficiency: The Big Tradeoff* (Washington, D.C.: Brookings Institution, 1975).

13. See Browning and Johnson, "The Trade-off."

14. A more thorough discussion of the technical issues involved in estimating marginal welfare costs can be found in my paper "On the Marginal Welfare Cost of Taxation," Working Paper, Texas A&M University, 1985.

# 4

# The Evolution of
# Regulatory Activities in the
# 1970s and 1980s

*Bruce Yandle*

## Summary

*Presidents Ford, Carter, and Reagan have led major efforts to reform federal regulation, and each administration has made a significant imprint on the institutions that regulate major sectors and industries in the American economy. But even now, after ten years of reform activity, there is evidence that yet another wave of regulation may be forming.*

*Historians generally identify three major waves of federal regulation. Starting with the Progressive movement in the late 1800s when the Interstate Commerce Commission was established and the Sherman Antitrust Act was passed, the first wave brought the first full dose of federal regulation to the American economy.*

*The second wave broke surface during the New Deal period when a multitude of "alphabet" agencies were created. And the third wave, which by almost any measure surpassed the other two, came in the late 1960s and early 1970s. It was the third wave's burgeoning production of rules and regulations for practically every aspect of economic life that caused people far and wide to question the role of government and the extent to which intervention should reach into the economy.*

*If there is to be a fourth wave, evidence suggests it will be associated with regulation of the financial sector and international competition. Those two main features will be accompanied by renewed growth in environmental regulation. These predictions are based on analysis of relative employment growth in more than fifty federal regulatory agencies for the years 1975 through planned budgets for 1986. There is an obvious and systematic linkage between the employment of labor and the ability to produce and enforce rules. In fact, researchers have shown that the nation's overall productivity growth was adversely affected by employment growth in regulatory agencies and by the number of laws passed and enforced in that period. Although there are benefits associated with rules and regulations, they are often more speculative than the costs they incur. It remains to be seen if new learning about regulation and the increased use of such things as benefit-cost analysis in the preparation of rules will improve the outcomes.*

*Why is growth in regulation so hard to tame? In the language of economists, there is demand for regulation, which is to say regulation provides an interesting array of benefits valued by firms, by institutions, and by individuals. Since there is demand for the various rules produced by government, people are understandably willing to spend resources to obtain those rules. In fact, competition among regulation seekers for governmental favors can be a problem itself. Specialized resources that otherwise might be employed producing goods and services are used to seek government regulation, which in some cases adds another element of social cost to the economy.*

*A sizable amount of research completed over the past fifteen years indicates that some rules that appear to be the most burdensome to business, such as certain Environmental Protection Agency (EPA) and Occupational Safety and Health Administration (OSHA) regulations, often increase the value of some affected firms. In some cases, for example, the rules increase competitors' costs, making it easier for the benefited firms to earn higher profits.*

*Other rules that simply restrict entry into geographic markets or restrict domestic entry of lower-cost foreign goods are clearly valuable to regulated industries, and they logically seek those rules.*

*Even antitrust laws can be used beneficially by competitors. Suits may be brought against a firm that cuts price in another firm's market. Such actions chill competition while benefiting the firm that wishes to be insulated from its competitors.*

*It is little wonder that deregulators encounter difficulty when they seek to remove rules that are profit makers for the affected firms. And more often than not, a good public interest story accompanies all federal regulation.*

*An examination of the efforts by the Ford, Carter, and Reagan administrations to bring about regulatory reform provides encouragement for those who support the application of economic logic to government decision making. Each successive administration has brought innovative changes to management of the regulatory process, in some cases making significant changes in the incentives faced by regulators to induce cost-effective behavior. In other cases, outright deregulation of major industry sectors has occurred, as in trucking, rail and air transportation, and financial institution reform.*

*The culmination of the institutional reforms is seen in the Reagan administration's call for a review by the Office of Management and Budget (OMB) of proposed regulations coupled with the review of regulations already on the books. Going further, the Reagan administration now requires regulatory agencies to provide documentation and explanations of planned regulatory efforts as an integral part of the budget process. For the first time, the regulatory process is a part of the overall management process.*

*Recent reforms of regulation and the application of new learning to the enforcement of antitrust laws in some ways mirror changes brought about by technological change and international competition. These forces also affect the demand for regulation. Indeed, the rise and decline of some regulatory agencies seems to be explained partly by the economic fortunes of major economic sectors during the same period.*

*What about the apparent wave of regulation that appears to be forming? Will it rise to the level of the 1960s and 1970s? World competition is an important element in determining the answer to those questions. Competitive economies have little room for inefficient institutions, whether in the private or in the public sector. A protected economy will predictably have more regulation and less incentive to deal with related productivity problems in the short run. The adjustments now under way in the larger economy will largely determine the type and amount of future regulation.*

## Introduction

Economic historians and students of regulation frequently identify three distinct waves of federal regulation. The first wave is associated with the Progressive movement at the turn of the century. This was the period when the Interstate Commerce Commission (1887) was established, the Sherman Act (1890) was passed, and the Federal Trade Commission (1914) was formed. These first-wave agencies represent the three commonly identified categories of regulation: economic, social, and antitrust.

A second surge of regulation occurred during the New Deal and the 1930s. Generally explained as being a part of the medicine developed for treating the ills of the Great Depression, the second wave saw a large increase in economic regulation with the formation of such agencies as the Securities and Exchange Commission (SEC), the Federal Deposit Insurance Corporation (FDIC), and the Federal Power Commission (FPC) and a host of legislative actions designed to affect market prices, incomes, and income security.

The regulatory cauldron was relatively quiet through the 1940s and 1950s, when the nation was involved in two wars. The third wave of regulation broke surface in the 1960s and continued into the early 1980s.

The complex origins of the third wave had to do with strong perceptions that many ills of modern America could be redressed if only the right rules were written and enforced by government. Time and again, public leaders pointed to America's accomplishments in space and technology and asked why problems of pollution, poverty, worker safety and health, nutrition, and fairness in the marketplace

107

were not being addressed with the same commitment of resources and intelligence and sense of purpose.

Following the regulatory boom of the early 1970s when federal regulation expanded to include every industry and affected almost all economic decisions, the pendulum began to swing the other way. Government took actions to reduce the burden of regulation and to introduce competitive forces into longstanding regulated industries. Although the efforts of three administrations have resulted in the deregulation of major industries and the invention and installation of systems for managing the regulatory process, the impulse to regulate has not been eliminated. Nor will it be. There is demand for regulation, and it will likely be supplied.

This chapter first examines the surge of regulation that occurred in the late 1960s and 1970s and discusses the responses to that phenomenal period in regulatory history. A chief result of the reactions is the significant body of new learning that became embodied in reform initiatives developed by successive administrations.

This chapter also examines the evolution of reform institutions that emerged in the Ford, Carter, and Reagan administrations and identifies major features of those institutions and some of the resulting actions. It further focuses on the reform of antitrust law enforcement. The discussion and the analysis in the fourth section of the chapter identify elements of a fourth wave of regulation by analyzing the collection of federal regulatory agencies as an industry. Evidence on the relative growth of various agencies reveals empirically which sectors of the economy may have been deregulated and which are becoming more highly regulated. The last section summarizes the major points and issues discussed in the chapter.

### The Escalation of Regulation in the 1970s

A movement toward more regulation picked up steam as the nation entered the 1970s. New regulatory agencies were formed and old ones expanded. The expectations for social benefits loomed large, while the unknown social costs were placed in the category of being justified, no matter what the cost might be. With the passage of time, the real costs of regulation began to be registered in rising prices, plant closings, and new complexities in entering and doing business. By the mid-1970s, the purpose and usefulness of regulation were being seriously questioned. Even the more committed social regulators wondered how the regulatory process might be tamed and its attendant costs reduced. By 1978 *Time* magazine was writing about rising regulation and its risks.[1]

Still, while some viewed the new regulation of the 1970s as though it were crabgrass that somehow had taken root and was spreading in the lawn of the nation's economy, others saw regulation as the lawn and the unregulated transactions in the society as the crabgrass. The notion that effective government intervention could best resolve market-determined inequities and inefficiency and deal with problems such as worker safety and pollution competed politically with the theory that unfettered markets are more efficient than government in dealing with the same problems.

It was the third wave of regulation in the 1970s, perhaps more than the earlier ones, that established a veritable industry of regulatory analysts, scholars, reformers, and writers who began to examine intensely the nature, causes, and effects of federal regulation.

**The Nature and Magnitude of the New Regulation.** Because it was controversial and costly, regulation and what to do with it and about it took its place with inflation, unemployment, poverty, and national defense as major planks in presidential platforms. Attempts to reform and revise regulation became major efforts during the administrations of Presidents Ford, Carter, and Reagan.

The composition and kinds of rules promulgated in the late 1960s and since were markedly different from most of those announced in previous periods. Dominated by social regulation that addressed such things as safety, health, and the environment (as distinguished from economic regulation that set prices and controlled competitive entry into certain industries), the new regulation addressed functional activities across diverse firms and industries.[2] Since the newer regulatory agencies did not specialize in single industries, there was consequently no score card maintained on the total costs and number of rules imposed on major economic sectors by all regulators taken together. When buffeted simultaneously by major rules promulgated by agencies like the Environmental Protection Agency (EPA) and the Occupational Safety and Health Administration (OSHA), industries and sectors frequently carried their appeals to the president and Congress, while attempting to tell the world about their perceived problems. EPA, OSHA, NHTSA (National Highway Transportation Safety Administration), and CPSC (Consumer Product Safety Commission) became chief focal points of debate and analysis as the agencies and their output of social regulation expanded.

While this new third wave of social regulation tended to cut across industries, antitrust investigations during the third wave tended to be industry specific, as compared with the case-by-case approach taken earlier. The auto, steel, petroleum, and cereal industries became targets of mammoth investigations. And the Federal Trade Commission (FTC), armed with expanded procedural tools, proposed more than a dozen major sets of rules directed toward such nationwide groups as funeral homes, health spas, vocational schools, used-car dealerships, and antacid drug producers.[3] The massive nature of these undertakings caused progress to be measured over years.[4]

The selection of large industry-wide antitrust actions reflected a philosophical and theoretical position that identified bigness as badness. The focus was on concentration and size of the firm and revealed an underlying animus toward large business.

Major reforms of antitrust law enforcement were proposed that directly addressed concentrated industries. A 1968 task force on antitrust policy recommended that antitrust authorities be enabled to use divestiture orders for the purpose of reducing industry concentration.[5] The task force recommended levels of firm and industry concentration that would define certain oligopolies as automatic targets for antitrust actions. Some of the recommendations of the task force were incorporated into the proposed 1973 Industrial Reorganization Act that, among other things, placed a burden of defense against breakup on firms that earned more than 15 percent annually on net worth over a five-year period, or for industries in which the four-firm concentration ratio was greater than 50 percent.[6] Although that proposal was not passed into law, some of its underlying concepts were embodied in legislation. The 1976 Hart-Scott-Rodino Antitrust Improvements Act increased the investigatory powers of the antitrust enforcement agencies, set elaborate prenotification requirements for significant mergers, and gave state attorneys general the power to file treble damages suits on behalf of injured consumers.

The notion of no-fault monopoly, that firms could be found guilty of antitrust violations even in the absence of a finding of collusion or restrictive practices, emerged in the Carter administration, which appointed a national commission to review antitrust laws and procedures.[7]

The commission recommended amending the Sherman Act by strengthening antitrust statutes to deal with structural problems in the economy. Size itself was on the way to becoming a potential violation of federal law. The commission's report failed to bring about statutory changes but still reflected the attitude and approaches taken by the FTC in its industry-wide investigations and the Antitrust Division's new theory of shared monopoly. At the time, Joe Sims commented:

The report is yet another step in the transition of antitrust

## FIGURE 4–1
### A Decade-By-Decade Comparison of
### Major Regulatory Legislation, Pre-1900–1979

Major regulatory statutes

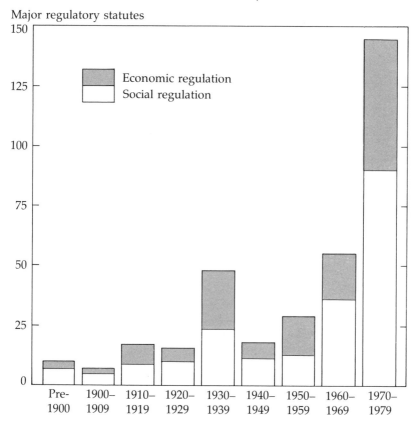

SOURCE: Center for the Study of American Business.

from negative second-guessing and post facto punishment
. . . to affirmative regulatory intervention.[8]

One measure of the relative magnitude of this third wave of regulation is seen in figure 4–1, which charts legislation that spawned social and economic regulation. From the chart it is obvious that the third wave strongly overshadows the previous two periods of surging activity. Although discussion of growth waves has generally not included antitrust actions, a similar pattern of activity is reflected in figure 4–2, which charts case activity at the Antitrust Division of the Department of Justice. There are striking similarities and an obvious

111

## FIGURE 4–2
### ANTITRUST ACTIONS, PRE-1900–1983

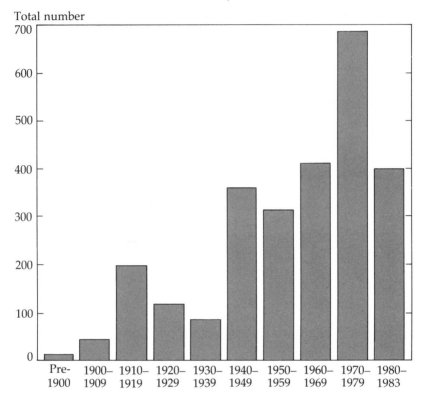

SOURCE: Data taken from Richard A. Posner, "A Statistical Study of Antitrust Enforcement," *Journal of Law and Economics,* vol. 13, no. 2 (October 1970), pp. 365-419, and from annual reports of the Antitrust Division of the U.S. Department of Justice.

difference observed when comparing the two figures. While the New Deal period was bringing a surge of economic regulation, antitrust enforcement was temporarily dormant. The National Industrial Recovery Act, the antithesis of antitrust, encouraged cartelization and price fixing.

Figure 4–2 shows Department of Justice actions increasing in the period 1910–1919 and again in the 1960s and 1970s. The data suggest that actions taken in the 1940s somehow compensated for the reduced antitrust activity in the previous periods.

**Reactions: New Theories and Learning.** Strong reactions are expected when a social system produces sharp and dramatic changes in the evolutionary path previously followed. The regulatory activity of the 1960s and 1970s set in motion several such reactions. Among these were political forces that called for a reexamination of government's role in the private sector and for modifications in how regulations were developed and implemented as well as in what was to be the domain of federal regulation. Important social phenomena also attract the attention of members of the academic community. In the case of third-wave regulation, those phenomena beckoned researchers in all disciplines, particularly economists. The resulting theoretical and applied research created an intellectual foundation for reform efforts later institutionalized by successive administrations.

The analysis of cost effectiveness of particular regulations and regulatory agencies, drawing heavily on the concepts of benefit-cost analysis and traditional economic models of efficiency, forms an important element in the first category of scholarly work. Not necessarily questioning the political-economic forces that gave rise to the growth of third-wave regulation, this body of work eventually fed into and then out of government agencies that emerged in the Ford, Carter, and Reagan administrations.

While benefit-cost analysis and project evaluation were becoming controversial methods of regulatory analysis in the federal government, advances were taking place in academic research that penetrated beyond the effects of regulation to focus on the behavior of regulators and government. Explanations of regulation prior to the early 1970s had relied primarily on public interest arguments, suggesting that government officials would not be severely affected by special interest demands, and that firms, industries, and regions of the country would not obtain regulation in pursuit of private interests. Drawing on theories of political economy reaching back to J. B. Say in the 1800s, the new empirical research provided explanations of regulatory behavior that could not be explained by the public interest theory.[9] A growing body of literature emerged that applied the basic concepts of supply and demand and the theory of firms and markets to regulatory phenomena.

Robust theories of public choice shed light on the incentives of regulators and legislators to expand bureaucracies and to regulate in specified ways.[10] New theories of regulation focused on the demand for regulatory-derived benefits and identified powerful forces that explained why regulation, while controversial and costly, could also be strongly supported by particular firms, industries, and sectors of the economy.[11] Gregg A. Jarrell, for example, found evidence that the early electrical utility industries sought and gained from regulation.[12] Looking back at a much earlier period in history, Howard P. Marvel found evidence that supported the theory that owners of capital-intensive English factories actively supported and gained financially when the factory acts were passed limiting the use of child labor.[13] And after examining safety and environmental regulation in the 1970s, Robert McCormick and M. T. Maloney found evidence that the stock values of particular firms in the copper and textile industries increased when tighter air pollution and safety standards were imposed.[14]

From the 1970s on, a wave of literature emerged that sought to explain, and in some cases to affect, the surging supply of regulations. But mounting empirical evidence made it clear that regulatory reform was no simple matter. For every regulation of importance there would likely be important groups supporting it, groups other than the expected public interest organizations.

A similar intellectual base formed in the area of antitrust. Scholars in law and economics developed new theories of antitrust that raised fundamental questions about the relevance and usefulness of the standard antitrust emphasis on size of firm, market concentration, and the anticompetitive effects of vertical mergers, resale price maintenance, and price discrimination.[15]

In 1970 Yale Brozen presented evidence on concentration and profits that showed a positive relationship when observed over a short period but that became less related through time. Even highly concentrated industries were characterized by competitive entry.[16] Breakup by antitrust authorities for the sole purpose of reducing concentration was therefore not necessarily a desirable policy.

A 1973 analysis by Harold Demsetz set the stage for further investigation. He provided evidence that showed size of firm to be highly correlated with efficiency of operation, which naturally led to higher concentration in an industry.[17] Demsetz argued that market concentration could no longer be said to lead automatically to collusive behavior and higher prices, a conclusion that formed the basis of a popular antitrust doctrine at the time. Indeed, he argued that breakup of highly concentrated industries would likely have negative economic effects. Prices would rise and profits fall. The focus on domestic over international markets was seriously questioned, and the findings of a large body of empirical work cast serious doubt on the usefulness of past efforts to limit the mergers of firms and attack internally driven expansions of markets.[18] Out of the burgeoning research on antitrust came a body of literature aptly titled "the new learning." This body of thought and related efforts to publicize and popularize the new findings were partly a reaction to the active antitrust efforts of regulators in the 1960s and 1970s. A new foundation for building public policy emerged as the third wave was reaching its peak.

Scholarly work applying models of political economy to antitrust developed more slowly than for other forms of regulation. To some extent, the Sherman Act has been, and most often is still, viewed as the sacred cow of regulation. How antitrust might be used to serve special interests presented a theoretical challenge. Work by Long, Schramm, and Tollison, as well as by John Siegfried, indicated a lack of empirical evidence supporting the notion that antitrust actions were actually targeted on firms having monopoly power.[19] William Baxter, later to be named assistant attorney general in the Reagan administration, offered suggestions as to how special interests might explain the variation in antitrust enforcement.[20] And Faith, Leavens, and Tollison found that FTC enforcement of antitrust actions was less likely to occur against firms headquartered in the regions of members of important congressional oversight committees than against firms in other areas.[21]

**The Focus on Costs.** Along with the development of theories and new learning about regulation and antitrust came studies designed to assess some of the costs imposed by the rush of regulation that had characterized the 1970s. Of course, it is only after several years' experience with regulations in place that the cost of living with them can be estimated. At the outset, however, regulatory analysts made estimates of the expected costs.

Even the very best estimates of regulatory costs often confused transfers of expenditures between consumers and producers with costs imposed on the overall economy. A part of all compliance and administrative costs raises prices to consumers, which transfers income from consumers to producers just as increased wages would do. But higher prices induced by regulation reduce the quantity of goods demanded, and that reduces output. Where regulation is not cost effective or where the benefits of regulation are less than the costs of inputs used to meet it, undue costs are imposed on the economy. To consider intelligently the question of social costs and benefits, it is useful to have estimates of costs in any way those estimates can be obtained. But caution must be applied in reaching overall conclusions about the effects of regulation on the economy.

Litan and Nordhaus surveyed several studies and assembled evidence on both prospective and experienced costs and provided a partial estimate of the cost of third-wave regulation.[22] Their analysis dealt with (1) the cost of administering agencies, (2) the cost incurred when firms and organizations comply with regulations, and (3) the costs imposed on the overall economy when regulations are in place.

Each of the cost categories is increasingly difficult to analyze.

Commenting on the first category, Litan and Nordhaus state:

The administrative costs are the best measured component. While these costs are only a small fraction of the total, their growth over the past decade is indicative of the increase in federal regulation. In fiscal year 1969, for example, major regulatory programs cost slightly less than $600 million to administer. By 1979, the sum had grown to just over $3 billion. Corrected for inflation, the growth of these expenditures is striking: going from $670 million in 1969 to $2 billion in 1981 (in 1972 dollars).[23]

Going on to survey prospective estimates of compliance costs made by various government agencies, the two authors found that from 1975 to 1980 major regulations—those requiring an estimated expenditure of $100 million or more annually—had a cumulative cost that ranged from $33.6 billion to $77.9 billion annually, which is from 2.2 to 5.5 percent of 1981 gross national product.

Estimation of the cost of compliance with regulations became something of a cottage industry in the late 1970s, as industries, universities, hospitals, municipalities, and other organizations attempted to communicate their concern to political decision makers. Of the various studies, one completed by Arthur Andersen for the Business Roundtable passed many tests for credibility and the use of appropriate methodology.[24] The Andersen study focused on incremental regulatory costs—those things regulation required that would not have been done in the same way or at all—for six regulatory areas: energy, environment, safety and health, trade, equal employment opportunity, and employment retirement security. The firm estimated 1977 operating and capital costs to be $2.6 billion for forty-eight of the 192 Business Roundtable members. Again, these were largely costs passed on to consumers in the form of higher prices. The costs of distortions imposed on the total economy were not estimated.

Murray L. Weidenbaum was the first to tackle the problem of estimating the combined administrative and compliance costs of government regulation.[25] His estimate included regulatory costs borne by both taxpayers and consumers. In 1978, after examining the relationship between the costs of complying with major regulations and the budgets of the federal agencies involved, he and Robert DeFina found a multiplier of 20. Using that multiplier on 1976 data, they reported compliance costs alone for all regulations to be $63 billion, or 3.6 percent of GNP.[26] On the basis of that relationship, they estimated administrative and compliance costs combined for all federal regulation to be $66 billion, or 3.8 percent of GNP.

Applying the multiplier in later work, Weidenbaum found the

1979 combined cost to be $102.7 billion, 4.2 percent of GNP.[27] Using his multiplier on 1980 costs he found the total of administrative and compliance costs to be $120 billion, or 4.5 percent of GNP.[28] Weidenbaum's analysis and the use of the multiplier drew considerable criticism, but they nonetheless provided a basis for further discussions and analyses.

Edward Denison led the way in performing a systematic analysis to estimate the overall effects of major regulations on the performance of the national economy. He examined growth in productivity from 1948 to 1973 and found that environmental and safety and health regulation constituted more than 10 percent of the two-percentage-point decline that occurred across the period. In a more recent study, Gregory B. Christensen and Robert H. Haveman examined productivity growth between 1947 and 1982 using three measures of regulatory intensity: (1) the cumulative number of major pieces of regulatory legislation in effect; (2) the volume of real expenditures by regulatory agencies; and (3) the total number employed in the regulatory agencies.[29] They found little effect of regulation on productivity until the mid-1960s, the time that is generally used to mark the beginning of the third wave of regulation. As growth in productivity diminished, the effects of expenditures by regulatory agencies began to lead the other two measures of regulatory effects in explaining productivity losses. Christensen and Haveman note:

> Setting each index equal to 100 in 1947, R1 (legislation) attained a level of 288.1 for the economy as a whole in 1980, while R2 (expenditures) and R3 (employment) reached 898.6 and 710.6, respectively, in the same year.[30]

In terms of effect on productivity growth, the two authors found regulation had practically zero effect from 1958 to 1965, a negative effect on productivity gains of from .1 to .3 percentage points from 1965 to 1973, and a negative effect of .2 to .3 percentage points from 1973 to 1977. The losses in productivity identified by the two authors account for 12 to 21 percent of the slowdown in labor productivity in the 1973–1977 period, relative to 1958–1965.[31]

Of course, the estimates of declines in productivity do not necessarily mean that regulation imposed net losses on the economy. As mentioned earlier, a benefit side to the ledger has to be considered, and unfortunately many of the presumed benefits from regulation are not measured in aggregate economic data. EPA emission regulations, for example, may independently reduce the levels of nitrogen oxides and the occurrence of harmful smog, which in turn may increase average life expectancies and the value of urban land. But these effects are not easily measured across the economy. Various studies of individual regulatory programs raise doubts about their overall effectiveness, but it is clear that each regulation has strong support from groups that provide public interest arguments. It was still the cost side of the equation that raised concerns about how to achieve the various regulatory goals and whether or not the benefits were really worth it.

Even with all the analyses performed, another form of regulatory-induced cost was overlooked. No estimate has been made of the private-sector costs incurred in the process of securing, resisting, and managing the regulatory process. In 1967 Gordon Tullock noted insightfully that economic agents could theoretically exhaust all possible gains from regulation in the process of seeking and obtaining it.[32] By the same token, those having secured profitable benefits from regulation would spend the value of those benefits fighting to maintain their favored positions. In other words, this is another element of cost that must be added to those that were estimated, and its magnitude is unknown.

The new theories and learning and the accumulated evidence on the higher-than-expected costs of regulation assembled in the 1970s became important arguments for regulatory reform. The plans and programs of successive administrations drew on the growing stock of knowledge, and in some cases called scholars into government service, as regulatory reform became institutionalized.

## The Beginning of Regulatory Reform

**The Ford Administration.** Regulatory reform began in earnest during the early days of the Ford administration. Its origins are traced to a series of inflation summit conferences held in the fall of 1974, which were attended by a cross section of the public, including economists and representatives of state and local governments.[33] At the time, President Ford's Whip Inflation Now program was in its formative stages. But burdensome and costly regulation was a chief concern identified by conference participants, who had been invited to bring ideas for solving the nation's economic problems. One petition calling for elimination of numerous regulations was signed by twenty-one of twenty-three economists attending a session. What was a macroeconomic problem—inflation—led to a microeconomic solution—deregulation.[34]

In November 1974, President Ford announced his Inflation Impact Statement program (later to be named Economic Impact Statement program) that would require executive branch agencies to assess the economic effects of newly proposed rules. Ford's Executive Order 11821 requiring the evaluation of major regulations became a model for two subsequent administrations.

The Council on Wage and Price Stability (CWPS), created by legislation in 1974 for the purpose of monitoring wages and prices, in 1975 was given responsibility for reviewing and commenting on proposed regulations whose economic effects triggered certain price and cost increases. Government agencies determined when the criteria were triggered and later certified their completion of the impact statement process when publishing final rules. Economists and lawyers at CWPS reviewed the impact statements, commented on proposed agency rules in official regulatory proceedings, and advocated the use of benefit-cost analysis in all government agencies.[35]

In all, some fifty-four impact statements were completed by federal agencies and reviewed by CWPS during the Ford years. CWPS also publicized any proposed regulation it found to be troublesome, whether it was major or not. Review by OMB of regulatory legislation was another piece of administrative machinery devised to establish a regulatory review process. Benefit-cost analysis, cost effectiveness, and consideration of alternative modes of regulations were on their way to becoming a permanent part of government's review of regulation.

The Domestic Council Review Group on Regulatory Reform was a final component of President Ford's reform mechanism. Composed of representatives from executive regulatory agencies, the Council of Economic Advisers, OMB, and the White House, the group identified regulations to be reviewed and coordinated the development of legislative packages aimed at deregulating particular industries.

The Ford administration counts several reform successes to its credit. It gained passage of legislation deregulating the brokerage industry, saw passage of the Railroad Revitalization and Regulatory Reform Act, gained repeal of federal fair trade laws, initiated legislation for reforming financial institutions, saw the beginning of hearings on deregulating the airlines, initiated the Motor Carrier Reform Act of 1975, and established the Commission on Federal Paperwork.[36]

**Regulatory Reform in the Carter Years.** The Carter administration added to the previous administration's regulatory reform efforts. In addition to expanding CWPS and issuing Executive Order 12044 containing a broader requirement for economic impact analysis of major rules, President Carter established the Regulatory Analysis Review Group composed of Cabinet and EPA representatives, chaired by the Council of Economic Advisers and administered by CWPS.[37] The Reg-

ulatory Analysis Review Group examined, commented on, and resolved differences concerning major rules; where problems were un-
resolved it called upon CWPS to prepare formal analyses to be placed
in the public record for comment. Finally, if issues were still unsettled,
the chairman of the Council of Economic Advisers entered the fray.
This approach to the review of regulation further institutionalized the
use of benefit-cost analysis.

In its intention to give OMB power to delay regulations that failed
to pass muster when reviewed for cost effectiveness, the Carter administration received considerable internal criticism. It therefore established a regulatory council, composed of heads of all executive
branch agencies and some independent agencies, which dealt internally with regulatory problems and overlapping rules. The council
also developed and provided a regulatory calendar, which gave a
more complete and consistent picture of future regulatory developments.

Picking up on some of the reform momentum of the Ford administration, adding new layers to the administrative machinery, and
setting new priorities for both expanding and contracting regulation,
the Carter administration saw the successful passage of major legislation deregulating trucking, railroads, and the airlines, gained revision of natural gas legislation that set specific dates for decontrol of
prices, obtained financial institution reform legislation, and pushed
the use of economic incentives in the application of environmental
regulation. Although major strides were made toward revising and
reforming economic regulation, social regulation expanded.[38]

While these changes were occurring on the traditional regulatory
front, the Carter administration focused its antitrust machinery on
large firms and major industries; it demonstrated concern about concentration as a measure of monopoly behavior by pushing the notion
of "shared monopoly" in the enforcement of antitrust statutes.

**Reagan Regulatory Reform.** Having established regulatory reform as
a major plank in its bid for office, the Reagan administration initiated
its most visible thrust in regulatory reform immediately upon taking
office.[39] On January 22, 1981, the new president appointed a cabinet-
level task force on regulatory relief led by Vice President George Bush.
Seven days later, the president issued a freeze on many of the regulations that had been pushed through during the last days of the
Carter administration. CWPS, which had expanded greatly in the
Carter years following its involvement with the management of voluntary wage-price guidelines, was eliminated. With it went the legal
authority of the White House to participate as a party in rulemaking

proceedings before various agencies. The CWPS regulatory analysis group, however, was moved to OMB to be a part of the new Office of Information and Regulatory Affairs and was given significantly expanded responsibilities for reviewing and approving agency rules.[40]

Consistent with the Ford and Carter administration approaches, President Reagan issued his Executive Order 12291, which was more stringent in its requirements for the use of benefit-cost analysis, cost effectiveness, and consideration of alternative approaches in the formulation of new rules than those in the previous administrations. With the issuance of the Reagan executive order, the reform vocabulary acquired one more name for the documentation of benefit-cost analysis by agency personnel. First had been the Ford administration's Inflation Impact Statement and Economic Impact Statement, then the Carter administration's Economic Impact Analysis, and now the Reagan Regulatory Impact Analysis.

Commenting on the Reagan executive order, George Eads, a member of President Carter's Council of Economic Advisers and chairman of the Regulatory Analysis Review Group, had this to say:

> Executive Order 12291 provides all the tools needed to accomplish [the] tasks. The order certainly is impressive both in its scope and in the extent to which it rearranges the power relationships that prevailed under previous administrations.[41]

President Reagan discontinued the Carter-organized Regulatory Analysis Review Group and Regulatory Council, making the structure of his reform apparatus thin. OMB, given authority to monitor all federal agencies in the normal course of managing budgets and approving programs, was the gatekeeper for regulation. Precise guidelines for the review of regulations were developed, and these were applied by OMB staff, under the direction of an assistant director of OMB, who was also named executive director of the Regulatory Relief Task Force. Importantly, the reviews of proposed regulations were to be done prior to their being announced publicly and again when being released.

Among other things, the guidelines took a dim view of all economic regulation. Attempts to control entry and price were clearly in disfavor. The guidelines called for flexible, cost-effective performance standards instead of the technology-based standards that had dominated third-wave regulation in the development of rules for safety, health, and environmental problems.

Picking up on an idea from the Carter administration, the deregulators developed a consolidated regulatory agenda, which twice annually gave a summary and schedule of planned regulatory actions for forty-four federal agencies. For the first time, a score card could be used managerially to determine the full range of regulations that might affect particular industries and sectors. Indeed, Reagan's executive order required agencies to take into account all proposed regulations that might affect a particular industry.

While working at the margin of newly proposed rules, the Reagan administration introduced another innovation: it authorized OMB to call for reviews of existing rules, which might mean the agency involved would have to work the rule through the new OMB requirements. Calling upon private sector organizations to communicate concerns about specific regulations, the task force identified 119 existing regulations for retrospective analysis.

The Reagan administration's last move to bring institutional changes to the regulatory apparatus set in motion an effort to gain regulatory reform legislation that would require independent as well as executive-branch agencies to review and justify all regulations. This effort was completely frustrated in the legislative process, however.

The Carter administration had achieved major deregulation in surface and air transportation, and financial institution reform was also progressing. At the time the Reagan administration took office, the Civil Aeronautics Board was already scheduled to go out of business in early 1985. Trucking and rail transportation had been pushed toward competitive rate making. Entry into and exit from those industries occurred practically on a carte blanche basis. To these reforms, the Reagan administration added deregulation of interstate bus lines and went on to gain passage of the Garn–St. Germain legislation, which accelerated the previous deregulation of financial institutions and eliminated controls on interest rates paid to savers and checking account customers. During the first month in office, the administration eliminated all remaining price controls on crude oil and petroleum products, an action that was highly controversial at the time but which proved to be one of the most positive actions taken by the deregulators.

By late 1983, OMB had completed its review of 76 of the 116 existing regulations targeted by the task force, gaining revisions of some and the elimination of others. Calling its mission complete, the task force disbanded, leaving the OMB regulatory review group on its own.

In its completion report, the task force indicated that some $14 billion annually in unnecessary regulatory costs had been eliminated along with an equal amount of one-time capital costs.[42] However, almost half of the one-time capital cost savings and one-third of the annual cost savings were associated with the deregulation of financial institutions, which some critics felt was the result more of efforts by earlier administrations than of the task force.[43]

The Reagan regulatory review program was buttressed in January 1985 by Executive Order 12498, which established a clear-cut planning process. Understandably controversial, the order requires executive-branch agencies to submit to the director of OMB an annual statement of policies and plans for the coming year along with a summary of regulations in process.[44] The director of OMB is authorized to return rules to agencies that do not satisfy the review process.

The first compilation of agency plans (616 pages) was submitted to Congress in August 1985 as a companion piece to agency budget requests. For the first time, Congress and all interested parties have available a coherent description of regulatory programs that can be compared directly to agency operating budgets.

**The Evolving Administrative Structure.** An interesting pattern of institutional development can be observed in the evolution of regulatory reform that took place in the third wave. The Ford administration's actions were at first largely reactionary, responding primarily to concerns about inflation. The Ford administration then turned to the development of institutions to review new regulations, promoted the concept of benefit-cost analysis, and openly battled regulatory agencies when seeking to bring change. It initiated and completed several major legislative reforms. Looking back, one can credit the Ford administration with setting in place the foundation for the managerial reforms that followed. At first, however, the use of regulation as a major device for solving all manner of problems was still widely supported and deeply ingrained across the economy and in government.

With the election of President Carter, institutions for regulatory reform became highly elaborate. Instead of doing battle publicly, CWPS, CEA, and OMB were used to bring about internal reform. The Regulatory Council provided a cushion for reform efforts, which probably blunted the effectiveness of some. Economic regulation became the focus of attention, as efforts to reform social regulation, a major thrust of the Ford initiatives, were relaxed. Social regulation expanded. Highly significant legislative gains were obtained during the Carter years in revising older economic regulations. The continued promotion of economic analysis of regulation during those years, particularly by the Council of Economic Advisers, brought increasing acceptance of the use of economic incentives in regulation and of the usefulness of benefit-cost analysis itself.

President Reagan made deregulation a major part of his campaign platform. As was pointed out earlier, the costs of regulation had become widely recognized. The surge of regulation of the third wave had been assessed and in many cases found wanting. High expectations for change caused the Reagan deregulators to reach back to the Ford period for reactionary approaches to reform and revision. They also picked up some of the elements of the Carter administration's managerial approach and discarded others. The Carter administration had focused successfully on the reform of economic regulation and moved much more gingerly on social regulation; the Reagan administration, however, first focused on social regulation and attempted to maintain the reforms in place at the economic regulatory agencies.

Plans for regulation are currently a routine part of the budget review and planning process. Policy makers now confront the full thrust of the hundreds of individual regulatory actions that previously fell randomly on the economy. Further, the executive branch can assess overall effects and be asked to answer for the overall effects rather than just for the effects of individual major regulations.[45]

Mancur Olson has made an important point about the implications of the kind of institutional change that has occurred in the regulatory process.[46] Understandably and quite logically, smaller interest groups seize upon regulation as a means for securing benefits that are important to them. Elected representatives in Congress predictably favor the interests they represent and have less incentive to gain and use information on the total effect of all regulation. The committee system used to manage regulatory agencies reflects this incentive structure and reinforces what some call a myopic view of the problem.

As Olson points out, once special interest effects become widespread and all encompassing, that is, when information on the effects is widespread, societies respond to the incentive to behave differently and to oppose the collection of individual special interests. When achieved, reform can bring reductions in costs all around, while special interest groups lose some of the gains they may have garnered at the expense of the larger society.

### The Status of Antitrust

The reform of economic and social regulation occurred at both the agency and central authority levels; however, reform of antitrust law enforcement during the past few decades has involved almost exclusively revisions in rules and case selection practices within the Antitrust Division of the Department of Justice and the Federal Trade

Commission. As much as anything, antitrust enforcement involves the application of agency discretion regarding firms, industries, and industry practices that will become the subjects of close scrutiny.

Because of the apparent flexibility available to agency heads in guiding the identification of priorities and the selection of cases, it might be expected that greater change could occur in the antitrust area than in an agency that is more tightly bound by precise statutory language. That conclusion, however, overlooks the intense interest and oversight influence exerted by Congress in its review of antitrust activities. And although the basic antitrust statutes have not been amended in decades, Congress has not been reluctant to proscribe the activities of the antitrust authorities through the use of the language of appropriations.

In any case, the magnitude of reform of antitrust law enforcement during the Reagan administration in some ways is more impressive than that in other regulatory areas. Because of the nature of the agencies, the record of change primarily reflects the direction given by Assistant Attorney General William F. Baxter and FTC Chairman James C. Miller III, both of whom established records as regulatory scholars and favored significant reform prior to their appointments to office.

During the Reagan years, the Department of Justice moved sharply away from the tendency to prosecute primarily on the basis of size of firm, as in the case of mergers, or on levels of concentration, where an industry might be dominated by a few domestic producers. Indeed, the department made headlines by closing down the thirteen-year-old IBM case, which had employed some 300 lawyers and generated 66 million pages of record.[47] The abandonment of that case, which reflected the emergence of new meaningful competition across IBM's major product lines, was accompanied almost simultaneously by the breakup of AT&T, the largest of all antitrust settlements in history.[48] Although at first the two events may seem to reflect virtual and total inconsistency in law enforcement, a deeper examination reveals the AT&T settlement was as much the deregulation of an industry that no longer fit the regulatory straitjacket in which it operated as it was an antitrust action. Nonetheless, the most powerful antitrust tool that can be applied—divestiture—was used forcefully in the case. Part of the AT&T issue related to separating firms that are regulated, such as local telephone companies, from those that had not been, such as AT&T's Western Electric Division. Another separation issue was associated with the AT&T longlines division, which had been bound partly to outmoded communications technology by regulatory decisions.

The simultaneous announcements of the AT&T and IBM decisions served notice that major competition would be emerging in the computer and communications industry. AT&T, which had previously been barred from operating in the computer industry, was released to draw on its Bell Laboratories expertise in squaring off against IBM, which was no longer under the antitrust shadow.

The Department of Justice emphasized strict enforcement of Sherman Act collusion cases, particularly against scores of firms charged with rigging highway construction bids. Along other lines, the department revised its 1968 merger guidelines, which set trigger points for investigating mergers. The new guidelines, revised again after Attorney General Baxter returned to university teaching in 1984, raised significantly the levels of concentration that would be accepted without investigation of a merger. New and rich consideration was given to the disciplining effects of potential competition when reviewing merger proposals.[49]

Along with the sharp change in direction taken in opening new cases at the Department of Justice, the agency undertook a review of hundreds of existing consent agreements that had been negotiated over the years when settling antitrust cases. In some instances, consent agreements had long outlived any meaning at all. A 1919 injunction against Armour, for example, limited its ability to compete in the changed market of the 1980s. The agency also took a strong stand opposing the per se enforcement of antitrust laws limiting the use of agreements between manufacturers and their retailers. On a separate front, the agency added flexibility for firms in the same industry to enjoy economies of scale in research by taking a more relaxed view of joint ventures organized exclusively for research and development purposes.

Of course, each of these actions was controversial and received scholarly and other criticism. The heightened enforcement of Sherman Act cases against bid rigging by construction firms, which could lead to the exclusion of firms from future state business, was criticized for eliminating future competition, thereby giving competitors an incentive to behave strategically in bringing action against other firms. Those fearing the threat of efficiency that accompanies competition among large firms in some cases objected to the new merger guidelines, and a host of critics, the most notable being congressional oversight committees, expressed concern about the introduction of a rule of reason in the review of vertical arrangements between producers and sellers.[50] Nonetheless, viewed in terms of change, it cannot be denied that reform came to antitrust law enforcement at the Department of Justice. And when considered in the light of the restructuring taking place in the U.S. economy, partly in response to new and intense international competition, a strong case can be made for the revisions undertaken.

The reform of antitrust law enforcement at the FTC during the Reagan administration to some extent parallels the experience recounted for the Department of Justice. The new learning in antitrust law and economics was reflected directly and immediately in two ways at the FTC. First, the commission voted to close its large investigations of the cereals and the petroleum industries. The notion of shared monopoly used to justify the cereals case could not be justified empirically or theoretically. And world competition in the petroleum industry, coupled with deregulation of petroleum pricing, eliminated the logic of the action. The second application of the new learning in antitrust was observed when the FTC published its statement on horizontal mergers, the counterpart to Justice's merger guidelines. Where Justice emphasized measures of concentration by using them, even at a reduced level, the FTC chose not to address such measures at all. Instead, the FTC focused on post-merger market conditions and the likelihood that collusion might occur or that artificial barriers to entry might limit future competition. These considerations were made in the light of potential consumer benefits that could accrue from reduced costs and prices that stem from efficiency-enhancing mergers.

The FTC had much to overcome when taking new directions in antitrust law enforcement. Between 1977 and 1983, the commission had lost twenty-two of thirty-five antitrust cases appealed to federal courts. The record, which included twenty-two merger cases, demonstrated partly the extent to which the thinking of appellate courts no longer matched the logic used by the FTC in bringing actions. In addition to the unimpressive record on past antitrust actions, the FTC was under the gun of Congress for having overreached in applying its rule-making authority in the discharge of its consumer protection mission. Indeed, the excesses and mismanagement of the agency in the late 1970s raised such a public uproar that in 1980 Congress ceased funding the agency and then put the agency on an extremely short leash in an attempt to control its activities.[51]

Both the antitrust and consumer protection missions at the FTC became subject to the application of strong economic logic when cases were being considered. The agency's approach to these missions was articulated in an October 1984 report on its actions, which stated: "The FTC cannot supplant the marketplace, nor should it attempt to do so. The economy is too complex, and the abilities of government regulators too limited, for such a task."[52] Put differently, benefit-cost analysis was applied regularly and systematically.

Because of its assignment under the antitrust liaison agreement with the Department of Justice, since 1981 the FTC has reviewed and acted upon some of the largest mergers in the nation's history—those involving the petroleum industry. In the process, the agency challenged and affected changes in the mergers of Mobil and Marathon, Gulf and City Services, Texaco and Getty, and Standard of California and Gulf. Like the Justice Department, the FTC undertook reviews of old antitrust orders and since 1981 has modified thirty-seven of them.

While modernizing the approach to antitrust law enforcement, the commission focused attention on services, the high-growth sector of the economy. Its most controversial actions in that endeavor involved the learned professions. Raising the wrath of Congress, the FTC brought complaints against medical societies that conspired to set fees and organize boycotts against health providers that refused to recognize fee structures. It challenged positions taken by professional associations to restrict the dissemination of truthful information and closely monitored market practices surrounding the emergence of newer, competitive health providers such as midwives who sought to practice in hospitals.

Pushing on into new territory, the FTC began investigations of trade associations and brought complaints when those organizations acted to restrain trade. Finally, the agency established procedures for examining the behavior of local governments in the granting of exclusive franchises to firms. The agency sued two cities for unduly restricting entry into the taxi cab business.

The FTC also expanded its program of intervening in the proceedings of other regulatory agencies. The agency reviewed newly proposed regulations of such agencies as the FCC (Federal Communications Commission), ICC (Interstate Commerce Commission), ITC (International Trade Commission), and OSHA and submitted formal comments to them. In a way, the FTC intervention program filled the vacuum left when the Council on Wage and Price Stability was eliminated in the first month of the Reagan administration. To illustrate the level of FTC intervention activity, more than sixty comments to other agencies were prepared by the FTC in fiscal 1984.

When viewed historically, the shifts taken by the FTC and the Department of Justice in antitrust law enforcement are dramatic and have prevailed long enough to have an effect on the competitive structure of the economy. By its very nature, antitrust law enforcement is slow and ponderous. A two-term presidency seems almost necessary to bring about new approaches. Yet, while changes have occurred, the direction of change can be altered quickly when new

administrations and appointees take charge of law enforcement programs. In the case of the Reagan administration's efforts, however,
it seems safe to say that the overwhelming logic of the new learning
in law and economics will prevail, no matter what the political leanings
of an incumbent administration. Antitrust reform was a phenomenon
whose time had come.

## The Fourth Wave of Regulation

The three previous waves of regulation had a beginning and an end,
at least in terms of the visible institutions that accompanied them.
Yet, cross currents were present during each one that finally broke
through to form the next wave of regulation. The genesis of these
currents was the distinctive feature of each. In simple terms, the first
wave set the beginning of federal regulation of all forms; the second
focused primarily on economic regulation; and the third saw the development of social regulation.

There is clearly a substantial fourth wave of regulatory activity
in today's economy. But this fourth wave has more to do with reforming the regulatory apparatus and eliminating obsolete regulatory
strictures than with adding new rules to the stock of regulation. Still,
there is new regulation. In some cases, there is a desire to return to
the more comfortable regulatory habits of the past, especially after
first experiencing the chaos that comes with fresh deregulation. In
other cases, there are newly developed special interest groups who
see opportunities to use regulation to redistribute income or to guard
their economic positions.

The task of discovering the elements of the fourth wave, while
assessing the effects of recent reform efforts, can be accomplished
partly by analyzing the regulatory sector as though it were an industry
operating under a single management. Employment and employment
growth in regulatory agencies provide direct indications of priorities
assigned to various sectors of the economy when the political mechanism responds to demand for regulation. There is also a direct link
between growth in regulation and growth in agency employment.

Just as additional staff can invent new rules and impose burdensome regulation on the economy, however, additional employees can
also bring cost-effective revisions to existing rules and deliver cost-
beneficial public services. In other words, employment data and page
counts of the *Federal Register* cannot be taken as the final word on
assessing regulatory reform. Still, it must be recalled that Christensen
and Haveman have shown that a systematic relationship exists between regulatory agency employment, pages of laws, and economic

performance as measured by productivity.[53] In any case, the relative rise and decline of the various agencies gives a direct reading of the results of political behavior, as opposed to rhetoric about reform intentions.

**Analysis of Regulation as an Industry.** The first evidence of the source of fourth-wave forces should be revealed by those agencies that held their ground during the years when the Reagan budget cuts were made. These are the agencies that presumably enjoyed the greatest demand for their services. To give background to the Reagan period, a first view of the regulatory industry seen in table 4–1 shows employment growth rates and rankings for forty-seven agencies for the period 1975–1980.[54] Average employment growth for all agencies during the period was 10.1 percent. Among the faster growing agencies are the social regulatory agencies, Nuclear Regulatory Commission (NRC), Equal Employment Opportunity Commission (EEOC), the Mine Safety and Health Administration, OSHA, Environmental Protection Agency (EPA), and Food and Drug Administration (FDA). The Antitrust Division is also in the top half of the table along with several economic and financial regulators such as the International Trade Administration (ITA), the International Trade Commission (ITC), the Comptroller of Currency, the National Credit Union Administration, the Federal Maritime Commission, and the Commodity Futures Trading Commission.

There is also diversity among the agencies that show relative losses during the period. The ICC, SEC, CPSC, and NHTSA, for example, all lost employees. If any conclusion can be drawn from the data, it is that the older economic regulators were on the decline. Social regulation was generally on the rise.

Table 4–1 also shows employment growth data for the 1980–1984 period. Here we see the imprint of Reagan regulatory reform: total employment in the regulatory industry fell 13.7 percent.

Looking at the top twenty agencies in the industry, we see *seven* financial market regulators, three economic regulators (FCC, the Federal Energy Regulatory Commission (FERC), and SEC), and three social regulators (FDA, EPA, and NRC). In the previous period, there were six social regulators in the top twenty. An examination of the rankings for the two periods shows considerable shuffling of position during which the FTC, FMC (Federal Maritime Commission), CPSC (Consumer Product Safety Commission), ICC, and CAB (Civil Aeronautics Board) were pushed to the bottom of the industry. Economic regulation is clearly declining. Financial market and international trade regulation is growing, however. Among the agencies sustaining heavier reductions in personnel in the period were OSHA, NTSA, FTC, FMC, CPSC, ICC, CAB, CEQ (Council on Environmental Quality) and the Antitrust Division.

Evidence of regulatory reform as revealed in the deployment of federal employees during this first Reagan period suggests three conclusions. First, financial market regulation is alive and well, as are environmental, nuclear, and international trade regulation. Second, deregulation of the older regulated industries, such as surface, water, and air transportation and some forms of energy, continues at a quickened pace. Third, regulation of product markets by the FTC and the CPSC is declining.

**A Further Identification of the Fourth Wave.** An examination of the rankings for proposed employment growth for the years 1984–1986 in table 4–1 further identifies the fourth-wave forces. Once again social regulation is in the top tier. EPA ranks third; NHTSA is eighth. Those two agencies join a nest of international trade and financial market regulators in the top twenty. Of agencies in the top ten for 1980–1984, only the two international trade agencies maintained their top-tier position. Ten of the top twenty agencies in 1980–1984 held their top-twenty position in the 1984–1986 rankings (the Federal Highway Administration, ITA, ITC, the Copyright Office, the Federal Energy Regulatory Commission, the Farm Credit Administration, CFTC, SEC, the Patent and Trademark Office, and EPA).

We can gain a final perspective on what has happened by placing all agencies into functional categories and considering growth in agency employment between 1970 and 1986.[55] The calculations show those agencies that fall into the consumer safety and health category were top gainers with employment growth of 384 percent. Environment- and energy-related agencies experienced 254 percent growth. Those agencies involved in job safety and working conditions grew 219 percent, while the finance-and banking-related agencies added 42 percent more staff. Those in the general business category grew just 23 percent, and the older industry-specific regulatory agencies lost 12 percent of their staff. The sixteen-year perspective masks the fact that agencies within these groupings were rising, declining, and again rising as old- and new-wave regulation interacted.

**Stability: A Reflection of Political and Economic Strength.** In some cases, as the new learning in law and economics suggests, the process of regulatory reform involves tough encounters with strongly entrenched interest groups who have fought hard political battles to bring about the formation of agencies to their liking. In other cases,

## TABLE 4-1
### GROWTH IN EMPLOYMENT IN REGULATORY AGENCIES, 1975–1986

| Agency | Rank 1975–1980 | Change (percent) | Rank 1980–1984 | Change (percent) | Rank 1984–1986 | Change (percent) |
|---|---|---|---|---|---|---|
| Federal Election Commission | 1 | 304.0 | 25 | -10.3 | 12 | 2.2 |
| Employment Standards Administration | 2 | 69.9 | 35 | -23.2 | 47 | -9.1 |
| Fish and Wildlife Service | 3 | 64.6 | 31 | -20.6 | 7 | 10.1 |
| Copyright Office | 4 | 54.0 | 16 | -5.3 | 19 | 0.9 |
| Nuclear Regulatory Commission | 5 | 51.1 | 6 | 9.5 | 21 | 0.5 |
| Equal Employment Opportunity Commission | 6 | 49.2 | 26 | -12.1 | 26 | 0 |
| Federal Railroad Administration | 7 | 34.5 | 42 | -30.9 | 20 | 0.8 |
| International Trade Administration | 8 | 32.9 | 3 | 14.0 | 2 | 78.2 |
| Antitrust Division | 9 | 31.3 | 38 | -25.0 | 44 | -7.8 |
| Mine Safety and Health Administration | 10 | 31.1 | 27 | -15.1 | 46 | -8.9 |
| Comptroller of Currency | 11 | 30.8 | 11 | -2.4 | 24 | 0 |
| Army Corps of Engineers | 12 | 30.5 | 23 | -9.3 | 25 | 0 |
| National Transportation Safety Board | 13 | 25.1 | 21 | -8.5 | 31 | -1.4 |
| Occupational Safety and Health Administration | 14 | 23.8 | 38 | -21.8 | 34 | -3.1 |
| National Labor Relations Board | 15 | 22.6 | 7 | 1.7 | 40 | -6.6 |
| Federal Energy Regulatory Commission | 16 | 21.3 | 12 | -2.5 | 17 | 1.4 |
| Environmental Protection Agency | 17 | 20.3 | 19 | -7.8 | 3 | 18.7 |
| National Credit Union Administration | 18 | 19.0 | 32 | -21.3 | 13 | 2.0 |
| Food and Drug Administration | 19 | 15.1 | 13 | -3.3 | 36 | -3.8 |
| Federal Maritime Commission | 20 | 13.1 | 43 | -35.7 | 42 | -7.3 |
| Commodity Futures Trading Commission | 21 | 10.6 | 8 | 1.2 | 15 | 1.7 |
| Farm Credit Administration | 22 | 9.5 | 5 | 13.8 | 16 | 1.7 |
| International Trade Commission | 23 | 7.3 | 10 | 0 | 6 | 10.5 |

| | | | | | |
|---|---|---|---|---|---|
| 24 | Federal Communications Commission | 6.6 | 20 | -8.3 | 39 | -6.4 |
| 25 | Federal Trade Commission | 6.1 | 41 | -30.3 | 37 | -5.0 |
| 26 | Federal Home Loan Bank Board | 6.3 | 18 | -7.7 | 23 | 0.2 |
| 27 | Federal Reserve Board | 5.3 | 4 | 13.0 | 28 | -0.2 |
| 28 | Federal Highway Administration | 5.0 | 17 | -7.1 | 10 | 4.4 |
| 29 | Civil Aeronautics Board | 4.8 | 47 | -51.7 | 50 | Sunset |
| 30 | Federal Deposit Insurance Corporation | 2.1 | 15 | -3.7 | 27 | 0 |
| 31 | Packers and Stockyards Administration | 0.9 | 22 | -8.6 | 43 | -7.5 |
| 32 | Animal Plant Health Inspection Service | -0.6 | 9 | .1 | 30 | -1.2 |
| 33 | National Highway Traffic Safety Administration | -0.7 | 40 | -26.7 | 8 | 10.1 |
| 34 | Consumer Product Safety Commission | -1.4 | 44 | -35.9 | 32 | -1.6 |
| 35 | Labor Management Services Administration | -1.7 | 29 | -15.9 | 41 | -6.8 |
| 36 | Securities and Exchange Commission | -2.3 | 14 | -3.7 | 14 | 1.9 |
| 37 | Occupational Safety and Health Review Commission | -4.0 | 45 | -41.8 | 38 | -6.2 |
| 38 | Federal Aviation Administration | -4.9 | 37 | -24.8 | 33 | -2.4 |
| 39 | Bureau of Alcohol, Tobacco and Firearms | -5.4 | 34 | -22.4 | 29 | -0.7 |
| 40 | Coast Guard | -6.5 | 28 | -15.7 | 45 | -8.0 |
| 41 | Patent and Trademark Office | -9.2 | 2 | 20.1 | 11 | 3.7 |
| 42 | Interstate Commerce Commission | -9.4 | 46 | -47.2 | 49 | -12.6 |
| 43 | Customs Service | -18.3 | 24 | -10.2 | 48 | -10.5 |
| 44 | Economic Regulatory Administration | -27.4 | 50 | -76.6 | 5 | 17.7 |
| 45 | Drug Enforcement Administration | -35.4 | 30 | -16.3 | 1 | 78.9 |
| 46 | Council on Environmental Quality | -36.0 | 49 | -65.6 | 4 | 18.1 |
| 47 | Agricultural Marketing Service | -54.7 | 1 | 49.6 | 22 | 0.5 |
| | Office of Surface Mining Reclamation | | 36 | -24.1 | 9 | 5.7 |
| | Food Safety and Quality Service | | 39 | -26.5 | 18 | 1.3 |
| | Federal Grain Inspection Service | | 48 | -61.3 | 35 | -3.2 |

SOURCE: Data on regulatory agency budgets and employment used throughout this section are those developed by the Center for Study of American Business, Washington University, St. Louis, Mo.

133

reform may come easier. That is, interest group support that at one time rallied around a particular agency or regulatory goal may have either withered away or simply been transferred to other more important political objectives. Accepting the notion that smaller variations in the growth of employment budgets reflect the relative strength and stability of interest group support, we can examine the relative stability of agencies between 1970 and 1986.

A simple measure of employment stability for each agency was obtained by calculating coefficients of variation for fifty-six agencies. This is the standard deviation of employment for the series of years divided by the mean level of employment for the full time period.

The results of the calculations are shown in table 4–2. The agencies having a smaller coefficient of variation have the most stable employment paths. In the top two tiers of the table are some financial sector agencies along with the food safety–related agencies and the FMC and the FCC. A wide-ranging mix of agencies is found at the bottom of the table, with no particular pattern revealed.

TABLE 4–2

COEFFICIENTS OF VARIATION FOR EMPLOYMENT IN
REGULATORY AGENCIES 1970–1986

(percent)

| Rank | Agency | Coefficient of Variation |
|------|--------|--------------------------|
| 1 | Safety and Quality Service | 3.08 |
| 2 | Commodity Futures Trading Commission | 5.83 |
| 3 | Packers and Stockyards Administration | 6.07 |
| 4 | Federal Reserve Banking System | 6.69 |
| 5 | Patent and Trademark Office | 7.30 |
| 6 | Renegotiation Board | 8.14 |
| 7 | Federal Communications Commission | 8.90 |
| 8 | Farm Credit Administration | 10.62 |
| 9 | Federal Highway Administration | 10.72 |
| 10 | National Labor Relations Board | 11.28 |
| 11 | National Transportation Safety Board | 11.69 |
| 12 | Securities and Exchange Commission | 12.03 |
| 13 | Federal Energy Regulatory Commission | 12.37 |
| 14 | Customs Service | 12.72 |
| 15 | Mine Safety and Health Administration | 12.95 |
| 16 | Federal Deposit Insurance Corporation | 13.13 |
| 17 | Federal Maritime Commission | 13.22 |
| 18 | Food Safety and Inspection Service | 13.46 |
| 19 | Bureau of Alcohol, Tobacco and Firearms | 14.16 |

## TABLE 4–2
### (Continued)

| Rank | Agency | Coefficient of Variation |
|---|---|---|
| 20 | Federal Trade Commission | 14.50 |
| 21 | Cost Accounting Standards Board | 15.49 |
| 22 | Coast Guard | 15.58 |
| 23 | Occupational Safety and Health Administration | 15.70 |
| 24 | Labor Management Services Administration | 15.77 |
| 25 | National Highway Traffic Safety Administration | 15.89 |
| 26 | Comptroller of the Currency | 15.99 |
| 27 | Federal Aviation Administration | 16.25 |
| 28 | Food and Drug Administration | 16.38 |
| 29 | Federal Reserve System Board of Governors | 17.15 |
| 30 | International Trade Commission | 17.22 |
| 31 | Employment Standards Administration | 17.40 |
| 32 | National Credit Union Administration | 18.07 |
| 33 | Antitrust Division | 18.13 |
| 34 | Copyright Office | 18.18 |
| 35 | Office of Surface Mining Reclamation and Enforcement | 18.83 |
| 36 | Environmental Protection Agency | 19.09 |
| 37 | Civil Aeronautics Board | 19.84 |
| 38 | Consumer Product Safety Commission | 20.61 |
| 39 | Federal Home Loan Bank Board | 24.21 |
| 40 | Federal Election Commission | 24.83 |
| 41 | Federal Railroad Administration | 25.58 |
| 42 | Interstate Commerce Commission | 26.34 |
| 43 | Nuclear Regulatory Commission | 30.18 |
| 44 | Drug Enforcement Administration | 30.39 |
| 45 | Fish and Wildlife Service | 31.24 |
| 46 | Equal Employment Opportunity Commission | 33.95 |
| 47 | Occupational Safety and Health Review Commission | 35.39 |
| 48 | International Trade Administration | 36.42 |
| 49 | Army Corps of Engineers | 36.49 |
| 50 | Federal Grain Inspection Service | 44.82 |
| 51 | Council on Environmental Quality | 53.72 |
| 52 | Animal and Plant Health Inspection Service | 63.40 |
| 53 | Agricultural Marketing Service | 83.67 |
| 54 | Council on Wage and Price Stability | 84.00 |
| 55 | Economic Regulatory Administration | 85.30 |
| 56 | Office of the Federal Inspector for the Alaska Natural Gas Transportation System | 106.01 |

SOURCE: Calculated from data provided by the Center for the Study of American Business, Washington University, St. Louis, Mo.

The relative employment stability of the various agencies can be explained by looking at economic growth: the composition of the regulatory industry in some sense mirrors the industrial makeup of the country. When major sectors are expanding in the economy, we would predict that the regulatory counterparts would either be expanding in an absolute sense or at least resisting wide swings in their levels of employment. In other words, the demand for regulation is affected by growth in economic activity. The explanation is consistent with theories of regulation that relate to the protection of private interests as well as with the public interest theory that suggests government responds to problems associated with private sector activities.

Table 4–3 shows growth in share of GNP for eleven major sectors of the economy from 1965 to 1982. As indicated, communications was the fastest growing sector in the economy, with services, finance, and wholesale trade following in that order. Construction ranked last in growth, with mining and manufacturing ranking just above it.

Looking back at table 4–2 and the rankings of stability, it can be seen that the FCC, the communications sector's regulatory agency, was very stable during 1970–1986. Six financial sector regulators are in the top half of the chart, corresponding to the economy's third fastest growing sector. EPA and CPSC were very unstable agencies during 1970–1986. Their instability relates directly to manufacturing,

TABLE 4–3
GROWTH IN REAL GNP CONTRIBUTED BY
MAJOR ECONOMIC SECTORS, 1965–1982
(percent)

| Sector | Growth | Rank |
|---|---|---|
| Communications | 415 | 1 |
| Services | 280 | 2 |
| Finance, insurance, and real estate | 261 | 3 |
| Wholesale trade | 220 | 4 |
| Utilities | 184 | 5 |
| Retail trade | 182 | 6 |
| Transportation | 167 | 7 |
| Agriculture | 134 | 8 |
| Manufacturing | 128 | 9 |
| Mining | 116 | 10 |
| Constuction | 103 | 11 |

SOURCE: Calculated from data from various issues of *Survey of Current Business* and *Census of Manufacturers*.

which ranked ninth in growth, and to mining, which ranked tenth.

Transportation was another slow-growth sector in the economy. Its regulatory agencies—CAB, ICC, the Federal Railroad Administration, and the Federal Aviation Administration—were subject to employment shocks in 1975–1986, with the CAB, ICC, and the Federal Railroad Administration exhibiting the greatest instability.

It is difficult to identify the regulatory counterparts for wholesale and retail trade and services, the second-, fourth-, and sixth-ranking growth sectors. But utilities, the fifth most rapidly growing economic sector, matches with the Federal Energy Regulatory Commission, which was relatively stable. Of course, one should also note the high instability of the Nuclear Regulatory Commission and the fall of nuclear power generation in the United States.

Although the data used for this comparison are highly aggregated and therefore crude, there is a strong indication that macro forces in the economy affect the growth and stability of employment in regulatory agencies. The analysis suggests that economic forces may be more important than ideology when one seeks to understand regulatory reform. This is not to say that strong-willed deregulators and political leaders who favor markets over government agencies for allocating resources do not matter. Quite to the contrary, the analysis suggests that the social system is a *system* that includes a political economy and all agents—political and otherwise—who work in it. In other words, the presence of deregulators at a time when the economy is restructuring because of international and domestic change is not merely a coincidence.

**Final Thoughts**

Since 1981 the American economy has sustained a major recession and experienced a strong recovery while also experiencing the effects of an accelerated restructuring of major sectors, industries, and firms. Much the same can be said of the nation's regulatory apparatus. The regulatory process is an integral part of the economic engine.

But regulatory activity can be countercyclical.[56] Rules can be devised to protect industries, firms, and organizations from the raw forces of economic change, and the rate at which existing rules are exercised can be increased. The regulatory process can preserve the wealth of special interests while postponing efficiency gains that might accrue to the larger community. In this situation, regulatory reform is an opening of windows and doors that allows the delayed ordeal of change to occur, some would say in a more timely manner.

Still there is more to the process of regulation, its management, and reform than a reflection of dominant economic forces in the economy. Regulation can be a substitute for market solutions to newly recognized, but not well-understood, risks. Ideally, simple rules can be constructed and enforced so that private markets can continue to function in the presence of fissionable materials, toxic chemicals, and highly complex technologies. When risks are better understood, the former crude and stringent rules can be relaxed somewhat. More flexible legal structures and recognizably cost-effective solutions can be adopted for managing risks. This process too gives the appearance of regulatory growth followed by regulatory reform. It suggests that the passage from ignorance to understanding coincides with regulatory reform.

Regulation is also a part of an evolving system of property rights. In the past two decades, for example, we have observed the slow development of the use of environmental resources as the right to use the environment has evolved and found its way into the market process. When environmental regulators finally allow individuals to exchange pollution rights and so to minimize their costs when controlling emissions, we also label those steps regulatory reform.

We would expect to observe a continuous waxing and waning of demand for regulation in an economy as dynamic and diverse as America's. Rapid technological change, often based on the use of hazardous materials, increases demand, as does a quickened pace of economic change driven by changing relative prices. When these cycles are in phase, we observe waves of regulation and regulatory reform.

This rather sanguine view of a process that eventually conforms to competitive forces may be a satisfactory description of long-run tendencies. But that is doubtful. It seems to suggest that we should not fret and worry about apparently wasteful regulation, that somehow OSHA, EPA, FTC, and all the rest are simply part of a natural system that ultimately maximizes the well-being of the human community. The view also suggests that institutional design does not matter a great deal.

But results over the long term are what is important about coordinated reform and management efforts. The agents that drive the regulation and regulatory reform process necessarily respond to incentives. Institutional change more often than not means that those incentives are changed.

Regulators understandably have no systematic incentive to minimize the social costs of their actions. Like all people, regulators minimize *their* costs. They receive no invoices for the resources employed by the regulated, and they are not driven out of business when their regulations fail to perform at lowest cost. In fact, regulators may be rewarded when their rules are most costly, since cost imparts the perception that much is being done, and higher cost standards are more effective barriers for protecting existing firms and industries from new competition.

The hard political struggles that ensue with any reform effort testify to the economic value of regulation. Once regulatory structures are in place it is costly to change them, even when they have become obsolete. The resistance to the move to review all regulation attests to the cost of the standard imposed by OMB relative to that used by the agencies themselves.

If the newly developed centralized review of regulation is beneficial, it will be because the review serves as a proxy for market forces that might be encountered if regulators were truly a part of a competitive industry. The risk of the review process is the possibility that zealous regulators, insensitive to the full implications of their actions, will use the review process strategically to guard themselves against the ordeal of change, just as other special interest groups sometimes use their regulators.

The fourth wave of regulatory activity in the United States finds the regulation industry in good health and apparently growing. As in all industries, growth is not uniformly distributed. Some sectors are expanding; others are declining. The relative fortunes of the various agencies reflect at least two components of demand. First, the external demand for particular regulations, as balanced politically, has either withered, flourished, or remained steady. Second, and holding the first constant, reforms have had varying degrees of success in introducing the logic of the market to the production of regulation. In some cases, reforms may have reached the limits of the laws enforced by certain regulators. It will take major legislative reform of air and water pollution control legislation, for example, to bring additional cost effectiveness to that regulation.

This chapter has focused on modern regulatory institutions, how they were formed and operated, and what they have accomplished. The story recounted here has emphasized elements of a process that led finally to the integration of regulation into the management of federal agency activities.

So what is the future of the fourth wave? As with the economy itself, the future of this regulatory wave will likely be determined by the extent to which competitive forces are allowed to guide future growth. World competition allows little room for obsolete structures and inefficient government processes. Protectionism and monopoly allow for much and keep reformers fighting an uphill battle.

# Notes

1. See, "Rage over Rising Regulation,"*Time*, January 2, 1978, pp. 48–50; and "The Rising Risk of Regulation," *Time*, November 27, 1978, pp. 85–87.

2. For discussion of this point, see Murray L. Weidenbaum, *Business, Government and the Public*, 2nd ed. (Englewood Cliffs, N.J.: Prentice-Hall, Inc., 1981), pp. 18–32. See also Bruce Yandle and Elizabeth Young, "Regulating the Function, Not the Industry," *Public Choice*, forthcoming.

3. For discussion of these and other rules, see Timothy J. Muris, "Rules without Reason—The Case for the FTC," *Regulation*, September/October 1982, pp. 20–26.

4. Documentation of the cost and record associated with one major FTC rulemaking is provided in Bruce Yandle, "The Cost of Getting Nowhere at the FTC," *Regulation*, July/August 1981, pp. 43–47.

5. Yale Brozen, "The Antitrust Task Force Deconcentration Recommendation," *Journal of Law and Economics*, vol. 12, no. 2 (October 1970), pp. 279–92.

6. For a more complete summary see, Peter Asch and Rosalind Seneca, *Government and the Marketplace* (Chicago: The Dryden Press, 1985), pp. 244-47. See also Joe Sims, "Report of the President's Commission on Antitrust," *Regulation*, March/April 1979, pp. 25-32.

7. See Joe Sims, ibid., p. 26.

8. Joe Sims, ibid., p. 32. John H. Shenefield, President Carter's head of the Antitrust Division of the Department of Justice, also commented on the shared monopoly and "big case" approach: "We cannot shrug our governmental shoulders and say that some cases are too big to touch. The Antitrust Division is ready and eager to try big cases." "Cracking the Whip at the Justice Department," *Business Week*, September 19, 1977, p. 44.

9. In discussing regulation, Say states: "Those engaged in the particular branch of trade are anxious to have themselves made the subject of such regulation; and the public authorities are very ready to indulge them in what offers so fair an opportunity of raising a revenue." See J. B. Say, *A Treatise on Political Economy*, translated from the 4th ed. by C. R. Prinsep (Philadelphia: Claxton, Remsen and Heffelfinger, 1880). Reprinted ed. (New York: Augustus M. Kelley, Bookseller, 1964), p. 176.

10. See, for example, William A. Niskanen, Jr., *Bureaucracy and Representative Government* (Chicago: Aldine-Atherton, 1971); James M. Buchanan, Robert D. Tollison, and Gordon Tullock, eds., *Toward a Theory of the Rent Seeking Society* (College Station: Texas A&M Press, 1980); for a more recent application of these theories, see Roger G. Noll and Bruce M. Owen, *The Political Economy of Deregulation* (Washington, D.C.: American Enterprise Institute, 1983).

11. Principal literature in the area includes: George J. Stigler, "The Theory of Economic Regulation," *Bell Journal of Economics and Management Science*, vol. 2, no. 1 (Spring 1971), pp. 3–21; Sam Peltzman, "Toward a More General Theory of Regulation," *Journal of Law and Economics*, vol. 19, no. 2 (August 1976), pp. 211–40; and Richard S. Posner, "Taxation by Regulation," *Bell Journal of Economics and Management Science*, vol. 2 (Spring 1976), pp. 21–50.

12. See Gregg A. Jarrell, "The Demand for State Regulation of the Public Utility Industry," *Journal of Law and Economics*, vol. 21 (October 1978), pp. 269-95.

13. Howard P. Marvel, "Factory Regulation: A Reinterpretation of Early English Experience," *Journal of Law and Economics*, vol. 25 (April 1982), pp. 99–121. Discussion of other early examples of regulation that strongly suggest the influence of special interests is found in Bruce Yandle, "Intertwined Interests, Rent Seeking, and Regulation," *Social Science Quarterly*, vol. 65, no. 4 (December 1984), pp. 1002–12. See also Bruce Yandle, "Bootleggers and Baptists—The Education of a Regulatory Economist," *Regulation*, May/June 1983, pp. 12–16.

14. See Robert E. McCormick and M. T. Maloney, "A Positive Theory of Environmental Quality Regulation," *Journal of Law and Economics*, vol. 25, no. 1 (April 1981), pp. 99–123.

15. Seminal work in this area includes: Robert H. Bork, *The Antitrust Paradox* (New York: Basic Books, Inc., 1978); Richard A. Posner, *Economic Analysis of the Law* (Boston: Little, Brown and Company, 1972); collected articles in Yale Brozen, *The Competitive Economy* (Morristown, N.J.: General Learning Press, 1975); and Harvey J. Goldschmid, H. Michael Mann, and J. Fred Weston, *Industrial Concentration: The New Learning* (Boston: Little, Brown and Company, 1974).

16. See Yale Brozen, "The Antitrust Task Force Deconcentration Recommendation," in *The Competitive Economy*.

17. Harold Demsetz, *The Market Concentration Doctrine* (Washington, D.C.: American Enterprise Institute, 1973).

18. For a recent discussion and analysis of this point, see B. Espen Eckbo and Peggy Weir, "Antimerger Policy under the Hart-Scott-Rodino Act: A Reexamination of the Market Power Hypothesis," *Journal of Law and Economics*, vol. 28, no. 1 (April 1985), pp. 119–41.

19. See, William F. Long, Richard Schramm, and Robert D. Tollison, "The Determinants of Antitrust Activity," *Journal of Law and Economics*, vol. 16 (October 1973), pp. 351–64, and John J. Siegfried, "The Determinants of Antitrust Activity," *Journal of Law and Economics*, vol. 17, no. 2 (October 1975), pp. 559–73.

20. William Baxter, "The Political Economy of Antitrust," in Robert D. Tollison, *The Political Economy of Antitrust: Principal Paper by William Baxter* (Lexington, Mass.: D.C. Heath & Co., 1980), pp. 3–49. For a summary of research along these lines, see William F. Shughart II and Robert D. Tollison, "The Positive Economics of Antitrust Policy: A Review Article," *International Journal of Law and Economics*, forthcoming.

21. See Roger Faith, Donald Leavens, and Robert D. Tollison, "Antitrust Pork Barrel," *Journal of Law and Economics*, vol. 25, no. 2 (October 1982), pp. 329–42. William Comanor, director of the FTC's Bureau of Economics during the Carter administration, provides interesting insight into the political forces that affect the antitrust environments; see William S. Comanor, "Antitrust in a Political Environment," *The Antitrust Bulletin*, vol. 27, no. 4 (Winter 1982), pp. 733–52).

22. Robert E. Litan and William D. Nordhaus, *Reforming Federal Regulation* (New Haven: Yale University Press), 1983.

23. Ibid., p. 19.

24. See Michael E. Simon, "What We Did," *Regulation*, July/August 1979, pp. 20–21, which describes the methodology and findings. See also Marvin H. Kosters, "Counting the Costs," *Regulation*, July/August 1979, pp. 17–19, 22–25 for a discussion of some of the problems associated with estimating regulatory-induced costs.

25. For an interesting discussion of the Weidenbaum estimates, see George C. Eads and Michael Fix, *Relief or Reform?* (Washington, D.C.: The Urban Institute Press, 1984), pp. 28–34.

26. Murray L. Weidenbaum and Robert DeFina, *The Cost of Federal Government Regulation of Economic Activity* (Washington, D.C.: American Enterprise Institute, 1978).

27. See Murray L. Weidenbaum, "The Costs of Government Regulation of Business," Joint Economic Committee, 95th Congress, 2d session, 1978.

28. See Murray L. Weidenbaum, *Business, Government, and the Public*, 2nd ed. (New York: Prentice-Hall Inc., 1981), p. 344.

29. See Gregory B. Christensen and Robert H. Haveman, "The Reagan Administration's Regulatory Relief: A Mid-Term Assessment," in George C. Eads and Michael Fix, eds., *The Reagan Regulatory Strategy: An Assessment* (Washington, D.C.: Urban Institute Press, 1984), pp. 49–80. The work by Denison is found in Edward F. Denison, "Explanations of Declining Productivity Growth," *Survey of Current Business* (August 1979), pp. 1–24.

30. Ibid., p. 59.

31. Ibid., p. 77. The two authors report similar findings when using a different method of analysis and also examine 1981–1982 data, which showed a small increase in the rate of growth in productivity.

32. See Gordon Tullock, "The Welfare Costs of Tariffs, Monopolies, and Theft," *Western Economic Journal*, vol. 5 (June 1967), pp. 224–32.

33. See James C. Miller III, "Lessons of the Economic Impact Statement Program," *Regulation*, July/August 1977, pp. 14–21, and *The Challenge of Regulatory Reform*, A Report to the President from the Domestic Council Review Group on Regulatory Reform, Washington, D.C., January 1977.

34. See Gottfried Haberler, *The Problem of Stagflation*, Washington, D.C.: American Enterprise Institute, 1985. Haberler discusses "supply-oriented" policies, as distinguished from a supply-side economics, in the context of macroeconomic performance. He includes regulatory reform as one policy that adds valuable flexibility to an economy.

35. A collection of CWPS comments was subsequently edited and published. See James C. Miller III and Bruce Yandle, eds., *Benefit-Cost Analysis of Social Regulation* (Washington, D.C.: American Enterprise Institute, 1979).

36. For a summary of these actions, see *The Challenge of Regulatory Reform*.

37. For discussion of these actions as well as an excellent review of regulatory reform during the Carter administration, see Larry J. White, *Reforming Regulation* (Englewood Cliffs, N.J.: Prentice-Hall, Inc., 1981). See also, "After

Economic Impact Statements—What?" *Regulation,* January/February 1978, pp. 12–13.

38. It has been argued that President Carter appointed dedicated deregulators to head the older economic regulatory agencies and advocates of regulation to lead the social regulatory agencies. The same source indicates the Reagan administration did just the reverse. See Martha Derthick and Paul J. Quirk, *The Politics of Deregulation* (Washington, D.C.: The Brookings Institution, 1985), pp. 33–34.

39. The discussion here is drawn from Presidential Task Force on Regulatory Relief, "Reagan Administration Regulatory Achievements," August 11, 1983. Other historical details are taken from George C. Eads and Michael Fix, eds. *The Reagan Regulatory Strategy* (Washington, D.C.: Urban Institute Press, 1984), especially chap. 1. See also W. Kip Viscusi, "Presidential Oversight: Controlling the Regulators," *Journal of Policy Analysis and Management,* vol. 2, no. 2 (1983), pp. 157–73.

40. The role played by OMB was comparable to its role in determining agency budgets. For the first time, OMB had authority to return rules in their formative stages and to require revision before the rules were approved and released. For discussion, see George Eads, "Harnessing Regulation," *Regulation,* May/June 1981, pp. 19–26.

41. Ibid., pp. 19–20.

42. See, Presidential Task Force on Regulatory Relief, "Reagan Administration Regulatory Achievements."

43. There is also a problem with counting increased payments of interest to consumers as a savings. For discussion of this point, see George C. Eads and Michael Fix, *Relief or Reform?* p. 241.

44. The executive order and its product drew fire from congressional oversight committees and consumer advocacy groups. The additional element of executive branch control implied by the order disturbs previously arranged structures for influencing and controlling regulatory programs by interest groups. See David Burnam, "Reagan Specifies What Regulations Will Be Issued in the Year," *The New York Times,* August 9, 1985, p. A-10; and Henry Boyd Hall, "Who's Going to Regulate the Government's Regulators?" *The Washington Post National Weekly,* August 26, 1985, p. 32.

45. On June 23, 1983, in the *Chadha* decision, the Supreme Court struck down the legislative veto, which had been a major congressional tool for managing regulatory processes. The action by the Court effectively shifted power from the legislative to the executive branch of government, adding further accountability for and control of regulation by the president and his appointees. The legislative veto had been included in various legislative actions over the course of six decades and gave Congress an opportunity to stop action when agencies undertook to implement laws assigned to them. For example, the FTC was required to submit to Congress rules approved by the commission, at which time action by both houses could override the commission. The invention of the legislative veto was applauded by many during the regulatory excesses of the 1970s, but it raised serious questions

about the separation of powers. The constitutional question was settled by the Court, and Congress was sent back to the legislative drawing boards to develop alternative devices for controlling regulatory agency actions as well as the activities of other departments. See Theodore B. Olson, "Restoring the Separation of Powers," *Regulation*, July/August 1983, pp. 19–22, 27–30.

46. See Mancur Olson, *The Rise and Decline of Nations* (New Haven: Yale University Press), 1983.

47. See "Rewriting Antitrust Rules," *Business Week*, August 29, 1983, pp. 50–52. In describing the IBM episode, Schnitzer points out that the Department of Justice concluded that the previous accusation that IBM had gained market position through illegal means was without merit. The firm's 1960s 75-percent share of market had fallen to 68 percent in 1980. Nine new computer firms entered the industry while the case was being litigated. See Martin Schnitzer, *Contemporary Government and Business Relations* (Boston: Houghton Mifflin Company, 1983), pp. 168–71.

48. The AT&T decision obviously was long in arriving. Technological change was driving the firm to seek revisions in regulation in the early 1970s, and a series of FCC decisions predestined the antitrust outcome. See Derthick and Quirk, *The Politics of Deregulation*, pp. 174–202.

49. For discussion of the Department of Justice guidelines, see Eleanor M. Fox, "The New Merger Guidelines—A Blueprint for Microeconomic Analysis," *The Antitrust Bulletin*, vol. 27, no. 3 (Fall 1982), pp. 519–91. The author reviews Supreme Court case law under section 7 of the Clayton Act as amended by the Celler-Kefauver Amendment in the light of the 1982 merger guidelines and identifies those cases that likely would not have been brought. Of twenty cases assessed, she determined the government would not have sued either initially or upon remand in fourteen.

50. Both the Department of Justice and the Federal Trade Commission received language in their 1984 appropriations bill barring the use of any funds for the purpose of overturning or altering per se interpretation of antitrust law barring agreements between producers and sellers that establish retail prices.

51. Discussion of episodes leading up to the congressional action is found in Ernest Gellhorn, "The Wages of Zealotry: The FTC Under Siege," *Regulation*, January/February 1980, pp. 33–40. See also, Bruce Yandle, "Regulatory Reform at the FTC," *Business*, July-August-September 1984, pp. 53–57.

52. "Federal Trade Commission Law Enforcement in the 1980s," Federal Trade Commission, Washington, D.C., October 1984, p. 1.

53. The link between employment and the production of regulation is fairly straightforward when examined in terms of pages printed in the *Federal Register*. When the log of total pages by year is regressed on the log of employment in all regulatory agencies for the years 1970 through 1985, with data for 1985 estimated by doubling that of the first six months, the $R^2$ is .52, and the coefficient on employment is significant at the 5 percent level. The estimate indicates there is a .7 percent increase in pages published for a 1 percent increase in employment. It should be recalled that Christensen and Haveman use employment in regulatory agencies as one measure of regulatory intensity

in their study of regulation's effect on productivity and found a highly significant relationship. See Christensen and Haveman, "The Reagan Regulatory Relief," pp. 49–80.

54. Data on regulatory agency budgets and employment used throughout this section are those developed by The Center for Study of American Business, Washington University, St. Louis, Mo.

55. The growth agencies of both the third and fourth waves have a common characteristic: the focus is on functions within firms such as credit, personnel, manufacturing, and marketing, rather than on regulating entire industries. This relationship was observed when growth in employment for six categories of regulatory agencies including some fifty individual agencies was examined statistically across the years 1970–1986. The categories of regulatory agencies were: (1) consumer and safety; (2) job safety; (3) environment and energy; (4) finance and banking; (5) industry specific; and (6) general business. The statistical tests sought to determine which categories grew faster, using general business as the benchmark, and if the mean rate of growth was alternatively higher or lower during the Carter and then during the Reagan years. The regression results indicate that consumer and safety, job safety, and environment and energy grew significantly faster and in that order over the 16-year period. Growth was found to be no higher or lower than average during the Carter years and lower during the Reagan years. Larger agencies were also found to grow more slowly than smaller ones, as one might have expected. See Bruce Yandle and Elizabeth Young, "Regulating the Function, Not the Industry," *Public Choice*, forthcoming.

56. On this point, see W.F. Shugart II and R.D. Tollison, "The Cyclical Charactor of Regulatory Activity," *Public Choice*, vol. 45, no. 3 (1985), pp. 303–11, and Anthony Brown, "The Regulatory Policy Cycle and the Airline Deregulation Movement," *Social Science Quarterly*, vol. 66, no. 3 (September 1985), pp. 552–63.

# 5

# Financial Deregulation

## David H. Pyle

### Summary

*The Reagan administration came into office with a philosophical commitment
to less regulation and more competition in financial markets. Despite this
commitment, there is little to point to in the way of concrete accomplishments.*

*The major explicit change in financial regulation, deregulation of deposit
interest rates, was under way when President Reagan entered office. The root
cause of the decision to remove interest rate ceilings was their growing ineffectiveness in achieving deposit and earnings stability at thrifts. The growth
of money market mutual funds from insignificance in 1978 to a $240 billion
financial intermediary in 1982 precipitated the almost complete elimination
of ceilings on deposit interest rates by 1983. An effect of this deregulation
has been an increase in interest expense per $1 of assets at depository insti-
tutions by about 300 basis points and an increase in the correlation between
deposit interest expense and short-term market rates of return. During the
period of ceilings on deposit interest rates, banks and thrifts experienced
increases in noninterest expenses as they substituted nonprice for price competition. With the sharp increase in interest expenses, these institutions are
faced with the problem of reducing those noninterest expenses or increasing
service charges. Both processes are going on, but neither has proceeded very
far to date. Between 1966 and 1981, total bank and thrift offices increased
from 3.3 to 4.9 per 10,000 adult population. At year end 1984, this figure
for per capita deposit offices was 4.7. Bank employment has been essentially
stable since 1981, but employment at savings and loan associations has continued to rise at approximately the rate experienced during the period of ceilings
on deposit interest rates. The disparate behavior of savings and loans with
respect to employment undoubtedly resulted from their response to new asset
and liability opportunities granted as part of the deregulation package.*

*A comparison of price deregulation in the securities industry with de-
regulation of deposit interest rates may be useful. The dismantling of fixed
brokerage commissions began in 1968 and full deregulation was completed in
May 1975. Between 1968 and 1978, per capita branch offices of securities
brokers and dealers decreased by 40 percent and employment in the industry*

*decreased by over 60 percent. Although recovery in employment by securities brokers and dealers began in 1978, it remains almost 40 percent below the levels reached before price deregulation. These data suggest that the process of adjustment to deregulation of deposit interest rates at banks and thrifts may have some way to go before it is finished.*

*The adjustment problems facing banks and thrifts have raised questions about the advisability of removing ceilings on deposit interest rates. The fact that the solvency problem of thrifts was not solved by those ceilings, and was perhaps exacerbated by them, makes a strong case against reregulation.*

*The new asset powers at thrifts combined with their ability to increase their deposit base rapidly by offering competitive interest rates have serious implications for the deposit insurance system. Deregulation of thrift assets was intended to increase their earnings capacity and to reduce the mismatch of their asset-liability maturity. Between the end of 1980 and the first quarter of 1985, savings and loan associations acquired almost $440 billion in new assets. Only 29 percent were residential mortgages, and almost 60 percent were newly permitted assets such as direct investment in real estate, investment in corporate securities, and investment in service corporations engaged in a variety of nontraditional activities. An increasing fraction of the failures and potential failures of savings and loans is attributable to bad loans and investments rather than to interest rate spread problems. This change in investment policies of the thrift industry is supported by deposit insurance guarantees. Although commercial banks were not given significant new asset powers in federal legislation, they too have been permitted to adopt investment strategies that depend in great part on federal guarantees of their deposits. These explicit and ad hoc forms of asset deregulation are a mistake without concomitant changes in the deposit insurance system.*

*Neither geographic expansion nor the intermingling of commercial and investment banking has been addressed in financial deregulation legislation. Nonetheless, the interstate activities of depository institutions have increased substantially over the past two decades as has the competition between commercial banks and securities firms. The case can be made that this ad hoc deregulation is frequently inefficient and that it leads to differential regulation of functionally similar institutions. The Reagan administration expressed strong interest in addressing Glass-Steagall reform issues and put forward the Financial Institutions Deregulation Act as a basis for this reform. This proposal has not resulted in legislation, and there is some doubt that the administration is prepared to continue to press for this reform. The idea of an explicit move to full interstate banking seems to have been stifled by the Supreme Court ruling that regional reciprocal banking laws (interstate banking is allowed on a regional basis while excluding entry by banks from outside that region) are legal.*

*The most pressing need for financial reform is a reformation of the federal deposit insurance system. The situation at the Federal Savings and Loan Insurance Corporation (FSLIC) has become especially critical. At year end 1984, the ratio of FSLIC reserves to insured deposits was just under 0.8 percent compared with a peak ratio of 2.14 percent in 1969. Congress has held hearings on deposit insurance reform. A number of reform schemes have been discussed, including recapitalization or merger of the insurance funds; various forms of risk-sharing involving uninsured depositors, subordinated debt holders, and private insurers; and risk-related deposit insurance. It is argued here that without a change in the way in which insolvent institutions are closed, from a rule based on book value to a rule based on market value, none of these approaches will prove to be an adequate solution to the deposit insurance problem.*

*The Bush Task Group on Regulation of Financial Services was intended as a major step in the simplification of financial regulation. The Reagan administration hoped to use the task group to put together a proposal that would substantially consolidate the financial regulatory agencies and address Glass-Steagall issues. A clear goal was to relate federal financial regulation by a given agency to the functions of the firms it regulates. The report produced by the task group bears little resemblance to these reform suggestions, and, although over a year has passed since the report was signed, there is no sign of legislation based on it.*

## Introduction

This review of recent financial deregulation in the United States emphasizes the deregulation of depository institutions. Deregulation in some industries, for example in the airline and trucking industries, appears to have been an attempt to improve economic efficiency through increased competition. Has financial deregulation been a program to reduce government intervention and permit more competition in financial markets? The conclusion reached here is that this is not a good explanation of the financial deregulation that has taken place. Two other considerations are more important reasons. One is the attempt to support the thrift industry through a stressful period; the second is the case-by-case response to innovation in the financial services industry. The failure to find a consensus for a general reformation of U.S. financial regulation has resulted in explicit deregulation that is limited in scope and to some extent dysfunctional. Meanwhile, market innovators continue to find ways around existing restraints, creating an increasingly uneven application of financial regulation across functionally similar institutions.

The second section of this chapter covers deregulation of deposit interest rates resulting from the bank acts of 1980 and 1982 and the actions of the Depository Institutions Deregulation Committee in 1982 and 1983.

Product and geographical deregulation are then discussed in the third section. The new asset powers for thrifts in the 1980 and 1982 acts were intended to improve thrift diversification and earnings. They also provided new opportunities for risk taking. In addition to this explicit deregulation, changes in technology and in business practices have led to a substantial amount of ad hoc deregulation of depository institutions. This ad hoc deregulation has undermined two of the major pillars of regulation of U.S. depository institutions, the McFadden Act and Douglas Amendment and the Glass-Steagall Act.

The Bush Task Group on the Regulation of Financial Services was to have been the basis of a major financial policy initiative by the Reagan administration. The Bush report is largely a discussion of how regulatory responsibilities should be redistributed among the various federal and state financial regulatory agencies. There is also a brief discussion of deposit insurance reform in the report. These two topics are addressed in the fourth section.

Some conclusions are drawn in the last section.

### Deregulation of Deposit Interest Rates

The elimination of ceilings on deposit interest rates is the centerpiece of recent financial deregulation. This deregulation began in earnest during the Carter administration. Neither of the two bills that authorized it were Reagan administration bills. Deregulation of deposit interest rates was a reaction to thrift industry problems rather than a decision to promote competition and economic efficiency.

The secular increase in interest rates that began in the early 1960s decreased spreads between interest rates on fixed-rate mortgages in thrift portfolios and current deposit interest rates. Congress reacted to this threat to the solvency and vitality of the major home mortgage suppliers by passing the Interest Rate Adjustment Act of 1966. The provisions of this act put ceilings on deposit rates at all federally insured depository institutions.[1]

Paul Cootner made a prescient comment on the potential for this legislation to achieve its goal:

> Whatever merits one may find in rate regulation, it cannot be accomplished by one sector of a highly competitive market. It is true that when the regulation was first attempted, neither the commercial bank sector nor the debt securities markets were as competitive as they gradually became, and so the prospects for success were more sanguine at the outset

than they were in retrospect—but that is an outstanding characteristic of partial price regulation. . . . There is some serious question about the merits of attempting to control soundness . . . by rate controls because of its tremendous impact on liquidity problems.[2]

The attempt to maintain thrift profitability through ceilings on deposit rates might have worked had the need to do this been short-lived. As it turned out, the interest rate levels of the 1960s were mild compared with those that followed, and the interest cost control strategy unraveled. Market interest rates in excess of ceiling rates led to two competitive responses, the substitution of unregulated securities for regulated deposits and nonrate competition among depository institutions.

**Disintermediation and Deregulation of Deposit Interest Rates.** As shown in table 5–1, interest expenses per $1 of assets at commercial banks and savings and loan associations grew slowly from 1965 through the mid-1970s despite substantial, cyclical increases in market interest rates, as shown by the certificate of deposit (CD) rate. Increases in short-term money market rates above deposit rate ceilings in 1968–1970, however, led to disintermediation at banks and thrifts. Depositors substituted unregulated money market securities for rate-controlled deposits. Innovative banks created unregulated substitutes, such as offshore deposits and commercial paper, which the regulators then tried, with limited success, to bring under the rate ceilings. By 1969, there were serious liquidity problems at many depository institutions due to deposit losses. Large banks were especially hard hit as corporate depositors found it easy to substitute Treasury Bills and commercial paper for negotiable certificates of deposit. The resulting liquidity problems led to the first step in dismantling ceilings on deposit rates, the 1970 removal of ceilings on interest rates of large ($100,000 + ) CDs.

Throughout the 1970s, deposit growth fluctuated with changes in market interest rates. There were substantial savings inflows at savings and loan associations in 1971–1972 and again in 1975–1978 when short-term market rates were close to the ceilings on deposit rates (see figure 5–1). The resulting growth in assets occurred mainly during periods of relatively lower interest rates, an outcome inconsistent with the desire to maintain thrift solvency. There were attempts to stabilize deposit flows at thrifts during the late 1970s by introducing new types of deposits, notably the aborted "wild-card" experiment in 1973, the six-month money market certificate (MMC) in 1978, and the small saver certificates (SSC) in 1979. Minimum size restrictions

151

for the MMCs and minimum maturity restrictions for the SSCs were set to prevent these new deposit types from "cannibalizing" existing lower-rate accounts. Between 1978 and 1981 interest expense per $1 of assets increased by over 60 percent at savings and loan associations and more than doubled at commercial banks. Despite the higher rates, the restrictions on the new accounts reduced their effectiveness in combating unregulated substitutes. Money market mutual funds, which were insignificant competitors in 1978, grew rapidly from approximately $50 billion total assets in 1980 to $240 billion by 1982.

Congress and the administration were faced with the growing ineffectiveness of ceilings on deposit interest rates. These ceilings were

TABLE 5–1

INTEREST EXPENSE PER DOLLAR OF ASSETS (IE/A) FOR

COMMERCIAL BANKS (CB) AND

SAVINGS AND LOAN ASSOCIATIONS (SL), 1965–1984

| | IE/A (%) | | | | $\Delta IE/\Delta CD$ | |
| | CB | SL | CB (col. 1) to SL (col. 2) | 3 mo. CD Rate | CB | SL |
| | (1) | (2) | (3) | (4) | (5) | (6) |
|------|------|------|------|-------|-------|-------|
| 1965 | 1.56 | 3.46 | 0.45 | 4.35 | — | — |
| 1966 | 1.68 | 3.73 | 0.45 | 5.47 | 0.11 | 0.24 |
| 1967 | 1.92 | 3.87 | 0.50 | 5.02 | −0.53 | −0.31 |
| 1968 | 1.95 | 3.91 | 0.50 | 5.86 | 0.04 | 0.05 |
| 1969 | 2.33 | 3.96 | 0.59 | 7.77 | 0.20 | 0.03 |
| 1970 | 2.42 | 4.04 | 0.60 | 7.57 | −0.45 | −0.40 |
| 1971 | 2.39 | 4.14 | 0.58 | 4.99 | 0.01 | −0.04 |
| 1972 | 2.44 | 4.22 | 0.58 | 4.67 | −0.16 | −0.25 |
| 1973 | 3.51 | 4.42 | 0.79 | 8.41 | 0.02 | 0.05 |
| 1974 | 4.44 | 4.75 | 0.94 | 10.24 | 0.51 | 0.18 |
| 1975 | 3.83 | 4.87 | 0.79 | 6.44 | 0.16 | −0.03 |
| 1976 | 3.98 | 5.00 | 0.80 | 5.27 | −0.13 | −0.11 |
| 1977 | 3.98 | 5.03 | 0.79 | 5.64 | 0.00 | 0.08 |
| 1978 | 4.49 | 5.10 | 0.88 | 8.22 | 0.20 | 0.03 |
| 1979 | 5.79 | 5.67 | 1.02 | 11.22 | 0.43 | 0.19 |
| 1980 | 7.10 | 6.77 | 1.05 | 13.07 | 0.71 | 0.60 |
| 1981 | 9.06 | 8.31 | 1.09 | 15.91 | 0.69 | 0.54 |
| 1982 | 8.47 | 8.23 | 1.03 | 12.27 | 0.16 | 0.02 |
| 1983 | 6.84 | 7.15 | 0.96 | 9.07 | 0.51 | 0.34 |
| 1984 | 7.28 | 7.34 | 0.99 | 10.37 | 0.34 | 0.15 |

SOURCES: FDIC Annual Report, various issues and Combined Financial Statements: FSLIC Insured Institutions, FHLBB, various issues.

FIGURE 5–1
NET SAVINGS FLOWS AT
SAVINGS AND LOAN ASSOCIATIONS, 1960–1983

Dollars per year (billions)

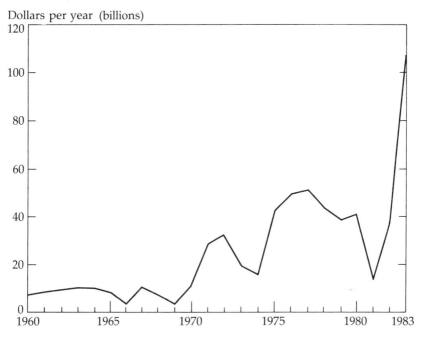

not protecting thrift solvency, nor were they stabilizing mortgage flows. Some depository institutions wanted an account that would compete with money market mutual funds. The first deregulatory response was the Depository Institutions Deregulation Act of 1980. This act called for the elimination of all ceilings within six years under the supervison of the Depository Institutions Deregulation Committee (DIDC).[3] In early 1981, the Reagan administration took charge of this deregulation process by transferring the chairmanship of the DIDC from the Federal Reserve System chairman to the secretary of the Treasury. The administration, through Secretary Regan, expressed a strong commitment to proceed with the deregulation of deposit interest rates as rapidly as possible. The continuing growth of the money market funds increased the pressure for this price deregulation and led the DIDC to introduce a series of small-denomination, market-rate time deposit accounts in 1982. Two additional accounts, money market deposit accounts (MMDAs) and super-NOW accounts, were authorized by the Garn–St Germain Act of 1982 and introduced near the end of 1982. There are no interest rate ceilings on these accounts

153

as long as the specified minimum balances (initially $2,500, subsequently $1,000) are maintained. Transactions, including check writing, are permitted. By early 1983, depository institutions were providing a package of return and liquidity on these accounts that was competitive with money market mutual funds.

The introduction of the MMDA in December 1982 was the most important event in this series of price deregulations. Within three months over $300 billion was deposited in MMDAs. Total MMDA balances are currently in excess of $450 billion, and super-NOW deposits total almost $60 billion. Only part of this deposit growth came from money market mutual funds, as described below.

In 1983, the DIDC removed interest ceilings on all time deposits with original maturities more than thirty-two days and on time deposits with original maturities from seven to thirty-one days with minimum balances of $2,500. The final step in the deregulation of time and savings deposit interest rates, the elimination of rate ceilings on savings deposits, is scheduled for 1986.

The move to almost complete deregulation of deposit interest rates by 1983 went faster than was expected by many observers in 1980. The sharp increase in short-term interest rates in 1981 and the resulting pressure on deposit accounts from unregulated substitutes played the major role in hastening this deregulation. The Reagan administration's commitment to restore unregulated price competition on deposit accounts deserves some credit for the outcome. A recent "supervisory bulletin" sent out by the Federal Home Loan Banks, however, suggests this commitment may be weakening, at least at that agency. Thrift directors were ordered to review their firm's interest rates and how they are set and to compare their rates with those of other institutions. The management of the Federal Home Loan Bank system does not seem convinced that all savings and loan associations can be trusted to set deposit rates without supervisory oversight.

**The Effects of Deregulation of Deposit Interest Rates.** Price deregulation has increased the market rate sensitivity of interest expenses at banks and thrifts. Changes in interest expense began to have a consistently positive relation to changes in short-term market rates in 1979 (see columns 6 and 7 of table 5–1). Even before the introduction of MMDAs in late 1982, interest expense per $1 of assets at savings and loans had increased by over 300 basis points from 1978 levels and by almost 400 basis points at banks. The decrease in market rates in 1983 and their increase again in 1984 were mirrored by similar changes in bank and thrift deposit interest rates. Interest expenses per $1 of

154

assets remained at levels approximately 300 basis points higher than those before deregulation.

Michael Keeley and Gary Zimmerman have analyzed the effects of introducing MMDAs at commercial banks.[4] Banks attracted a significant amount of deposits from money market mutual funds in the period immediately following the introduction of MMDAs; the Keeley and Zimmerman estimate is $90 billion. There was only a modest increase in total bank deposits, however.[5] The increase due to MMDAs was largely offset by decreases in small-denomination time deposits and in wholesale CDs. Neither savings deposits nor transaction accounts showed statistically significant changes as funding sources.[6]

Keeley and Zimmerman argue that aggressive bank promotion of MMDAs implies that "banks faced substantial costs in their non-price competition for retail accounts and in the substitution of whole-sale for retail accounts" and conclude that the substitution "of retail for wholesale deposits and price competition for non-price competition . . . secur[ed] . . . a more stable and lower cost source of deposits."

These two cost reductions do not have equal effects on a given institution, nor are their effects uniform across depository institutions. Once past the initial period of high MMDA rates, the substitution of price-deregulated retail deposits for wholesale deposits produces an immediate reduction in interest expense, probably without a significant increase in operating expense. On the other hand, banks and thrifts that substituted price-deregulated retail deposits for price-regulated retail deposits must reduce their noninterest costs (or charge more for services) to benefit from the deregulation. These adjustments to price deregulation are proving painful for many retail-oriented depository institutions, and it appears that more cost adjustments in banks and thrifts will be needed before a new equilibrium is established.

One dimension of this adjustment problem can be illustrated by looking at data on noninterest expenses. Figure 5–2 shows noninterest operating costs per $1 of assets for commercial banks and for savings and loan associations. Between 1965 and 1984, noninterest expense per $1 of assets increased by fifty-one basis points at savings and loan associations and ninety-four basis points at commercial banks.[7] These increases in per unit operating costs went against the trend in data processing and communication costs. The increase in costs for commercial banks is particularly notable. Commercial bank per unit noninterest expenses were about twice those at thrifts when price ceilings were introduced. To a large extent, this difference reflected the more labor-intensive nature of commercial bank services, especially demand

## FIGURE 5-2
### PER UNIT OPERATING COSTS, 1960-1984

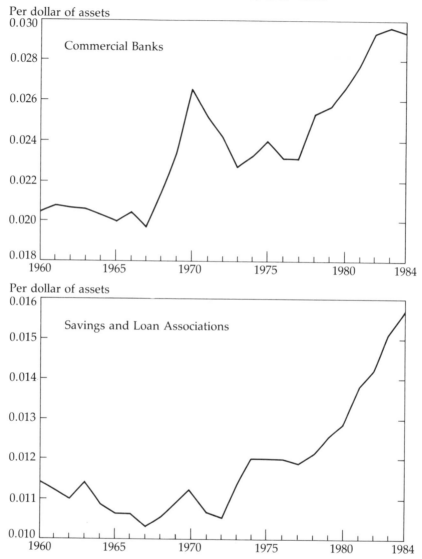

Per dollar of assets

Commercial Banks

Per dollar of assets

Savings and Loan Associations

deposit services. The ninety-four-basis-point increase in per unit non-interest expenses at banks occurred despite a large reduction in the fraction of bank liabilities held as demand deposits from just under 50 percent in 1965 to less than 17 percent in 1983. Furthermore, as shown in column 4 of table 5-1, interest expense per $1 of assets

156

increased more rapidly for banks than for thrifts. Instead of a substantial interest expense advantage for banks (approximately 50 percent lower), as was the case in 1965, bank and thrift interest expense per $1 of assets were at parity in 1984.

The increases in per unit noninterest costs reflect increases in deposit offices and employees. Between 1965 and 1981, total commercial bank and savings and loan association offices doubled and total employees more than doubled (see figures 5–3 through 5–6). The average annual growth rate over this period was 4.4 percent for total deposit offices (figures 5–3 and 5–5) and 4.9 percent for total employees of banks and S&Ls (figures 5–4 and 5–6) while the growth in adult population (twenty years and older) averaged only 1.8 percent per year. The physical capital and labor services available to depositors (that is, deposit offices and depository institutions' employees per capita) thus increased substantially over the period.

Price deregulation should change this, and there is evidence that the adjustment process has begun. The number of bank offices fell in 1982 for the first time in the postwar period. Bank offices per capita, which peaked at 3.5 offices per 10,000 adult population in 1981, had fallen to 3.4 offices per 10,000 by year end 1984. Savings and loan association offices continued to increase in 1982, but then fell in 1983

FIGURE 5–3

OFFICES AT COMMERCIAL BANKS, 1960–1984

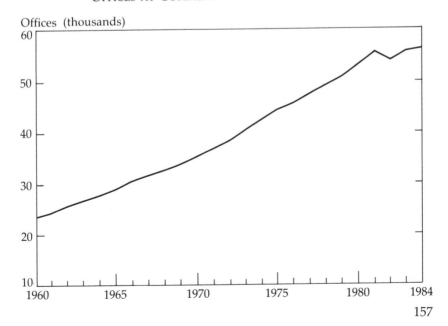

Offices (thousands)

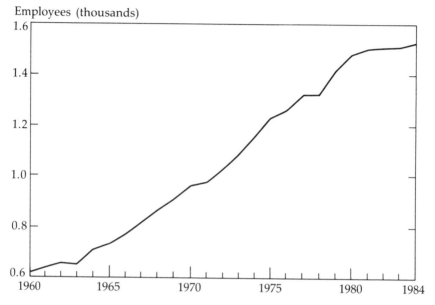

FIGURE 5–4

EMPLOYEES AT COMMERCIAL BANKS, 1960–1984

Employees (thousands)

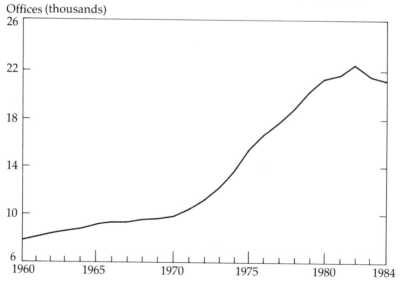

FIGURE 5–5

OFFICES AT SAVINGS AND LOAN ASSOCIATIONS, 1960–1984

Offices (thousands)

FIGURE 5–6

EMPLOYEES AT SAVINGS AND LOAN ASSOCIATIONS, 1960–1984

Employees (thousands)

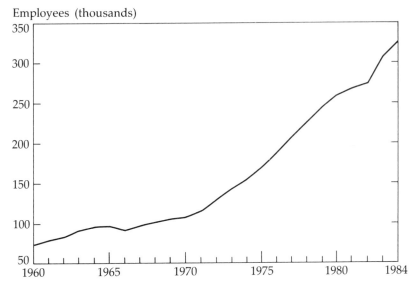

and 1984 to the level reached in 1980. In per capita terms, savings and loan offices went from 1.4 per 10,000 adult population in 1982 to 1.3 at year end 1984. Both of these responses to price deregulation are particularly striking when we observe that total bank and thrift offices per capita increased every year between 1966 and 1981 from 3.3 per 10,000 adult population in 1966 to 4.9 in 1981.

Total bank employment has been essentially stable since 1981. In contrast, employment at savings and loan associations has continued to grow. Between 1981 and 1984, savings and loan association employment grew at an average annual rate of 6.3 percent, almost exactly the average rate of growth for the 1965–1981 period. This difference in adjustment to interest rate deregulation by banks and thrifts is reflected in differences in their per unit noninterest expenses. Since 1982, noninterest expense per $1 of assets has stabilized at commercial banks but increased by fourteen basis points at savings and loan associations.[8]

Overall, the impression given by these data is that banks and thrifts responded to price regulation by providing depositors with more service. Although there are indications that these institutions are now responding to price deregulation by cutting back on nonprice competition, there has not been a dramatic reduction in noninterest costs. It is important to remember that this adjustment process, when

159

## FIGURE 5-7
### PER UNIT SERVICE CHARGES AT COMMERCIAL BANKS, 1960–1984

Per dollar of deposits (basis points)

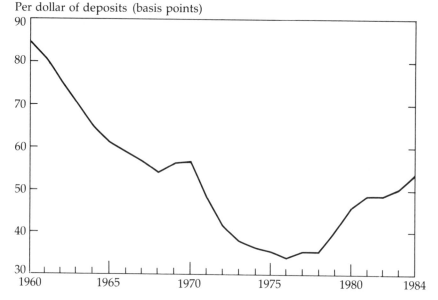

it comes, will fall more heavily on those institutions that were forced to rely on nonprice competition to avoid disintermediation (typically retail-oriented firms) than it will on those that substituted wholesale CDs for retail deposits in the 1970s.

Service charge increases are an alternative response to price deregulation. Figure 5–7 shows service charges per $1 of deposits for commercial banks from 1960 through 1984. As noted earlier, demand deposits were a decreasing fraction of bank deposits over this period; thus it is not surprising that per unit service charges fell until 1979. The beginning of significant price deregulation in 1978–1979 is marked by the start of a trend toward higher per unit service charges. So far the adjustment, an increase of approximately nineteen basis points per dollar of deposits, seems modest.

Attempts to adjust to price-deregulated retail deposits are meeting with consumer and legislative resistance. The attempt to increase the price of services and to weed out less profitable accounts has led to demands for "lifeline" banking services (that is, low- or zero-cost demand deposit accounts for individuals of modest means). Legislation requiring banks to provide lifeline services has passed the Massachusetts and New York legislatures and is under consideration in other states. The Massachusetts statute prohibiting fees on the accounts of persons over sixty-five or under eighteen years of age is striking in its simplicity:

> Paragraph 1 of section 2 of chapter 167D of the General Laws, as appearing in section 2 of chapter 590 of the acts of 1983, is hereby amended by inserting after the word "bank," in line 5, the words: provided, however, that no bank shall impose any fee, charge or other assessment against the savings account or checking account of any persons sixty-five years of age or older or eighteen years or younger. . . .

Regulators and legislators are also concerned about deposit office closures. In February 1985, the Office of the Comptroller of the Currency issued a circular instructing banks considering branch closure to have objective policies in place that take into account the effects of the closure on the community and its residents. An amendment to an interstate banking bill (H.R. 2707) passed by the House Banking Committee on June 12, 1985, gives federal banking authorities the right to deny interstate mergers and acquisitions if the applicant has a record of closing deposit facilities in a manner that disadvantages low- or moderate-income neighborhoods.[9]

These concerns about service fees and branch closures are certain to complicate the process of adjusting to price deregulation. On one hand, banks and thrifts will find it difficult to shift the costs of responding to these concerns to other depositors, since those depositors still have the opportunity to move to unregulated alternatives such as money market mutual funds. On the other, nonbank firms seem willing to provide lifeline services if the existing depository institutions will not. Sears, for example, has suggested the authorization of "consumer banks" that would make only consumer, small business, and family farm loans, that would be required to lend in the community, and that would provide basic checking services with no fees and no minimum balances.[10]

The pending price deregulation of savings accounts in 1986 will further complicate this adjustment process. Keeley and Zimmerman argue that the remaining savings depositors are those who prefer implicit interest in the form of nontaxable service rather than taxable interest and that this explains the lack of a significant shift from savings accounts to MMDAs. It is not certain, however, that the competitive solution for price-deregulated savings will result in the same relation of interest rate to service yield that prevails under price regulation. Past changes in ceilings on savings deposit interest rates led to increases in the rates offered by banks and thrifts. If interest expenses on savings deposits at banks and thrifts increase when interest rate ceilings on savings deposits are removed, additional reductions in service or increases in service charges will be necessary, and an additional group of disaffected consumers (who would like to have their interest and service, too) will be heard from.

**Price Deregulation in the Securities Industry.** The effects of price deregulation in the securities industry may provide clues on the pace and scope of the adjustment facing depository institutions. Before 1968, in fact for over 150 years, securities brokers carrying out trades on national exchanges were paid according to commission schedules set by the exchange. This led to the provision of a variety of non-transaction services as "soft-dollar" offsets to the fixed commissions and to price cutting through such devices as commission give-ups and the uncompensated sale of client products (for example, mutual funds). It also led to the growth of "third market" firms specializing in arranging trades off the organized exchanges. In other words, the governmentally sanctioned price cartel in the securities industry produced nonprice competition among regulated firms and competition from unregulated firms just as the governmentally imposed price cartel did in the market for deposit services.

Deregulation of fixed brokerage commissions began in 1968. Pressure from the Securities and Exchange Commission (SEC) and from institutional brokers led to the introduction of volume discounts (for orders over 1,000 shares) in that year. In 1972, a new commission schedule that lowered rates on all multiple round lot orders was adopted, and negotiated commissions for transactions in excess of $300,000 were authorized. On May 1, 1975, ("Mayday"), SEC rule 19b-3 became effective, and the exchanges were prohibited from setting commissions. Thus, price deregulation for securities brokerage began more than sixteen years ago, so that a decade has passed since full price deregulation became effective.[11]

The securities industry experienced sharp decreases in the number of broker-dealer branch offices and in total employment until 1979 (see table 5–2). Between 1969 and 1978, branch offices decreased by over 30 percent. Total employment by broker-dealers peaked in 1972 and by 1978 had fallen to 41 percent of that peak level. These reductions in service inputs occurred while share volume was increasing, for example, by a factor of 2.5 on the New York Stock Exchange. Since 1978, there has been a steady increase in both the number of branch offices and total broker-dealer employment. To put this adjustment process into perspective, we must consider its effect on broker-dealer per capita inputs. The decrease in offices per capita between 1969 and 1978 was fully restored by 1983, but employees per capita remain almost 40 percent below pre-deregulation levels.

TABLE 5–2
SECURITIES BROKER-DEALERS: BRANCH OFFICES AND EMPLOYEES
PER 10,000 ADULT POPULATION

|  | 1969 | 1978 | 1983 |
|---|---|---|---|
| Branch offices | 6.7 | 4.0 | 7.0 |
| Employees | 29.1 | 10.8 | 18.1 |

SOURCE: SEC Annual Report, various years.

This evidence suggests that adjustment to deregulated prices in the securities industry took about ten years to work itself out. It is useful to note that the stock market was strong in the years immediately following "Mayday." The resulting strength in brokerage income probably sheltered the securities industry from the immediate effects of full price deregulation. If we take 1980 as the beginning of retail price deregulation for depository institutions, the securities industry experience suggests that it may be some time before we see the end of the depository institutions' adjustment process. Again, as in the experience of the securities industry, the recent strength of the U.S. economy may be slowing the rate at which that adjustment is taking place.

Important changes in the structure of the brokerage industry have also taken place as a result of deregulation. One such change is the growth of retail discount brokers. Having entered the industry without the capital and labor encumbrances that full-line brokers built up during the fixed-commission period, these discount brokers have been quite successful in obtaining a significant market share. The Securities Industry Association estimated that the discounters' share of retail brokerage commissions was 8.4 percent in 1982. Since discount commission rates are less than half those at full-line brokers, the discounters' share of retail transactions was on the order of 20 percent in 1982 and has undoubtedly increased since then. Institutional investors also have a choice between minimum-cost brokers and those who continue to provide other services along with the transactions services. Institutional brokers specializing in research (the so-called research boutiques) have become an endangered species, however. The disappearance of a number of major broker-dealers as independent entities in recent years suggests that the market has become less tolerant of management mistakes by securities firms than it was when the price cartel cushioned them against the resulting losses. The change in the pattern of employment at broker-dealers is also instructive. Almost 75 percent of the reduction in broker-dealer employment between 1972 and 1978 was a reduction in the number of registered representatives.

These structural changes in the deregulated securities industry have implications for depository institutions. Where entry into the provision of deposit services is easy, including entry by unregulated firms, low-cost competitors will force the pace of cost reduction by existing firms. Pressure from these competitors and the absence of the cushion afforded by ceilings on deposit interest rates have made banks and thrifts more susceptible to the effects of their management mistakes, as high failure rates of banks and thrifts show.

Employment changes in the securities industry emphasized reductions in higher-cost personnel, research workers, and sales representatives. Post-deregulation employment changes in depository institutions are unlikely to be as effective in producing cost reductions. The limited information that is available seems to bear this out. Real wages per employee increased from 1981 to 1984 by about 10 percent at commercial banks and by almost 17 percent at savings and loan associations.

**Deregulation of Deposit Interest Rates and Financial Policy.** Critics argue that removal of ceilings on deposit interest rates endangers bank and thrift soundness through its adverse effect on costs and by promoting undue risk taking.

Industrywide ceilings on deposit interest rates were introduced to alleviate solvency problems at thrifts. The secular rise in market interest rates led to nonprice competition and competition from unregulated securities. This caused the strategy to fail. The thrift solvency situation is worse today than it was when price regulation began. Edward Kane estimates aggregate thrift net worth after deducting unrealized mortgage losses at − $16 billion in 1971 and − $86 billion in 1983.[12] This is not a phenomenon concentrated in a small number of institutions. Using a year end 1980 sample of 1,919 insured savings and loan associations, Fred Balderston found that 1,902 had negative net worth after deducting unrealized portfolio losses.[13] Aggregate net worth of thrifts in market value terms has undoubtedly improved since 1980, especially with the recent fall in mortgage rates, but not enough to pull many thrifts back to positive economic net worth. Furthermore, there is no assurance that mortgage interest rates will stay at current levels (or lower) indefinitely. Even if they do, the solvency problems of thrifts may not improve dramatically. The disinflation instrumental in the fall of interest rates has a depressing effect on the inflation premium in housing values and tends to make fixed-debt payments more burdensome. This has already led to mortgage default rates in excess of those experienced in recent decades (S&L losses and provisions for losses on real estate loans tripled between 1982 and 1984) and to the refinancing of high fixed-rate mortgages. Both of these outcomes offset some of the net worth gains to be realized from lower mortgage rates.

The solvency of thrifts remains a critical and largely unsolved financial policy issue, and serious solvency problems at commercial banks have been added to it.[14] Although the adjustment to deregulated prices is contributing to the distress of depository institutions, it is not the fundamental source of the insolvency problem, and reregulation of deposit interest rates is not a realistic solution. As Cootner suggested in 1969 and subsequent events confirmed, partial price regulation is not effective in a competitive market. It leads to the substitution of a liquidity problem for the solvency problem and to inefficient nonprice competition.

Has price deregulation promoted risk taking? The usual argument is that depository institutions lend at higher rates to try to offset increased interest costs. To get higher returns, the depository institution is forced to invest in higher-risk assets. This is not a sound strategy in an efficient capital market. Liability costs, including the required return on equity, would rise with the increase in risk offsetting the improvement in nominal interest margins. Of course, banks and thrifts might be following suboptimal strategies, such as maximizing short-run earnings, in which increased risk taking would follow the deregulation of the deposit interest rates.

A more important reason for a link between price deregulation and risk taking is the market imperfection introduced by the deposit insurance system.

Deposit insurance premiums that are not risk related create an incentive for insured institutions to increase risk.[15] Part of any increase in asset risk is borne by the federal government through the deposit insurance agencies. This federal subsidy to risk taking increases expected equity return more than enough to compensate the equity holders in an insured institution for the increased risk they bear. Insured banks and thrifts will take on as much risk as they are permitted in this situation, with or without ceilings on deposit interest rates.

To argue that risk taking results from price deregulation, one must presume that depository institutions earned economic rents (or quasi-rents) under price regulation. The reliance on nonprice competition with its emphasis on locational advantage and the presence of entry barriers in some banking markets make the existence of such rents likely. Since a knowledgeable manager would stop short of full exploitation of the deposit insurance subsidy in order to protect future rents that would be lost in a failure, removal of the source of the rents via deregulation of deposit interest rates would induce a move toward riskier assets. The extent to which this is occurring would not be easy to determine, since other factors such as product deregulation are also involved. In any case, the main culprit is surely not price deregulation but a deposit insurance system with perverse risk incentives.[16]

## Deregulation of Financial Products and Markets

The markets for financial services have changed significantly over the past two decades. New products and services have been introduced. The extent of competition among depository institutions and between depository institutions and other financial firms has increased. Geographic barriers to entry have been eroded. Most of these changes result from innovation and unregulated entry rather than from explicit financial deregulation. In some cases innovators found an opportunity not covered in the existing law, for example the invention of "nonbank banks."[17] In others, for example the underwriting of Eurobonds by U.S. bank subsidiaries, the regulatory authorities permitted new products and services to develop under existing laws. These and other forms of ad hoc deregulation have had a more profound effect on the market for financial services and on the problems facing financial regulators and policy makers than the limited amount of explicit product and market deregulation that has taken place. The discussion that follows concentrates on the explicit and ad hoc deregulation of asset powers at banks and thrifts to illustrate this point. The section concludes with a brief discussion of the deregulation of transaction accounts and of geographic deregulation.

**The Deregulation of Asset Powers.** New asset powers for thrifts were first introduced during the Carter administration in the Depository Institutions Deregulation and Monetary Control Act of 1980 (DIDMCA). The Treasury under Secretary Regan supported the additional thrift powers in the Garn–St Germain Act of 1982 (Garn–St Germain), but had little role in setting this policy. A Reagan appointee, Comptroller of the Currency Conover, did play an active role in the ad hoc deregulation of commercial banking especially, in the chartering of nonbank banks. The Reagan administration, however, has been ineffective in articulating and finding support for a deregulation plan that addresses the major reform issues including Glass-Steagall reform. Their major financial deregulation initiative was the Financial Institutions Deregulation Act, a bill introduced but not enacted in the ninety-eighth Congress. As noted below, the Treasury under Secretary Baker appears to be backing away from some of the key elements of that proposal.

*Thrift asset powers.* Title IV of DIDMCA included provisions liberalizing regulations governing thrift assets, and this asset deregulation for federally chartered thrifts was extended in the Garn–St Germain Act. State authorities gave similar privileges to state-chartered institutions and in some important cases carried the asset deregulation process further.

Table 5–3 lists the major new asset powers granted federally chartered thrifts in the Federal Home Loan Bank Board (FHLBB) implementation of the 1980 and 1982 acts. A California law (Assembly Bill AB3469) passed in fall 1982 is illustrative of the more extreme asset deregulation undertaken by some states. AB3469 permits California-chartered savings and loan associations to hold up to 15 percent of their assets as commercial loans (rising to 20 percent in 1985) and 25 percent in consumer loans. More important, all other percent-of-assets limitations were eliminated including those on direct investment in real estate, commercial real estate lending, and investments in service corporations. State-chartered savings and loans were permitted to invest in corporate debt securities without percent-of-assets restrictions. Under Garn–St Germain federally chartered thrifts are also allowed unlimited investment in corporate debt, but there is an important difference. No limitations on quality were set for institutions chartered by California while bond-rating restrictions similar to those applicable to national banks were imposed on federally chartered thrifts. State-chartered thrifts in other states, notably Arizona, Florida, New York, Ohio, and Texas, were also given asset powers that go

TABLE 5–3
MAJOR NEW ASSET POWERS FOR FEDERALLY CHARTERED THRIFTS
AS OF JANUARY 1, 1984

| New Asset Type | Maximum Percentage of Assets Allowed |
|---|---|
| Consumer loans | 30 |
| Commercial loans | |
| Real estate | 40 |
| Other | 10 |
| Corporate securities | 100 |

SOURCE: "FHLBB Final Rules on New S&L Powers," *Washington Financial Reports*, vol. 40, no. 22, p. 1160–1206.

significantly beyond those granted federally chartered institutions. Savings and loan investment was predominantly in fixed-rate residential mortgages before the passage of DIDMCA. The resulting portfolios were sensitive to interest rate risk, and thrift investment opportunities were tied to housing market fluctuations. The deregulation of thrift assets cannot be seen as an attempt to increase competition in the markets that were opened to thrifts. No investigation of the need for such competition was made. Rather, it was a response to the thrift earnings crisis resulting from the high and variable interest rates of the 1970s. The new assets were intended to redress the lack of diversification in thrift portfolios and to provide thrifts with high return opportunities outside housing.[18]

The effect of asset deregulation on the acquisition of savings and loan assets is shown in table 5–4. The comparison between 1975–1979 and 1983–first quarter 1985 is probably the most relevant one to make.[19] Recent investments by savings and loans in residential mortgages occurred at about half the pre-deregulation rate. Investment in traditional assets of savings and loans has been replaced by investment in consumer loans, in commercial mortgages, and especially in other assets. Other assets include most of the investments permitted under more liberal state regulations, namely direct investment in real estate, investment in corporate securities, and investment in service corporations.

The new asset powers produced significant changes in thrift investment strategies. As thrifts became less dependent on residential mortgages as their investment vehicle, they shortened investment maturities. The problems created by the deregulation of thrift assets

TABLE 5–4

NET ACQUISITION OF FINANCIAL ASSETS BY
SAVINGS AND LOAN ASSOCIATIONS, 1975–1985

| Period | Total Assets Acquired (billions) | Total | Distribution (percent) | | | |
|--------|--------|-------|-------------|------------|----------|--------|
| | | | Residential mortgages | Commercial mortgages | Consumer credit | Other assets |
| 1975–1979 | $277.2 | 100 | 72.4 | 6.9 | 2.7 | 17.9 |
| 1980–1985ᵃ | 438.9 | 100 | 28.8 | 6.5 | 6.4 | 58.3 |
| 1983–1985ᵃ | 293.6 | 100 | 33.5 | 11.6 | 7.0 | 48.0 |
| 1984ᵇ–1985ᵃ | 137.8 | 100 | 39.7 | 12.3 | 8.8 | 39.2 |

a. First Quarter 1985.

b. Second Quarter 1984.

SOURCE: Flow of Funds Accounts, First Quarter 1985, Board of Governors of the Federal Reserve System.

have also become apparent. Increasingly, failures and potential failures of savings and loans are attributable to bad loans and risky investments rather than to interest rate spreads. On July 25, 1985, FHLBB Chairman Gray predicted that 117 insured savings and loans would need FSLIC aid over the twelve months from June 1985 to June 1986 and indicated that 74 percent of these cases involved asset problems. All seventeen FSLIC-insured thrift failures between January and June 1985 were "directly attributed to asset quality, with no significant spread problems noted."[20] Most of the current problems with thrift assets are associated with real estate investments, but the potential for major losses on nontraditional investments—for example on low-grade corporate debt securities—is there.[21]

Nontraditional asset growth at thrifts was supported by federal deposit guarantees. The guarantee was crucial. Let us suppose a large number of thinly capitalized, nondepository institutions were able to raise debt funds at relatively low interest cost to finance large (fivefold, for example) increases in assets in less than five years using investment vehicles and strategies that were new to them. Without a federal guarantee of their liabilities, it is doubtful that any of them could pull this off; with FSLIC deposit insurance over a hundred thrift institutions, and probably many more than that, have done so.[22]

Deregulation of thrift assets without reform of deposit insurance was a mistake. The FHLBB recognizes this and has been trying hard to reregulate. The somewhat narrow emphasis of this attempt is to force state-chartered thrifts to conform to the less liberal federal regulation of assets. On June 12, 1985, the House Banking Committee approved a bill (H.R. 20) that would allow the FHLBB to determine permissible activities for state-chartered, federally insured savings and loans. A FHLBB proposal to restrict investments in low-grade corporate securities was put out for comment on July 10. These reregulation proposals are strongly opposed, and their enactment is far from certain. Even if the FHLBB gets these regulatory powers over state-chartered firms, the reregulation will only constrain the more obvious exploitation of deposit insurance guarantees. Any significant freedom-of-asset choice for insured institutions, including that granted to federally insured thrifts under the 1980 and 1982 acts, is incompatible with the existing deposit insurance system.

It is not just the explicit deregulation of thrift assets that is at issue. The investment strategies followed by insured commercial banks— for example, the commitment of large fractions of a bank's capital to developing-country lending or the extensive sale of standby letters of credit—have produced problems with asset quality (and therefore problems with deposit insurance) without any significant changes in the explicit powers of bank assets.[23] It did not require deregulation for the Financial Corporation of America to "bet the bank" on an interest rate decline or for Continental Illinois to overextend in energy lending. The fundamental flaw is mispriced deposit insurance and not asset deregulation. Deposit insurance reform is a necessary condition for asset deregulation without concommitant economic inefficiency and problems of insurance fund solvency. This point is taken up again later.

*Securities activities of commercial banks.* The Banking Act of 1933 (Glass-Steagall Act) was intended to separate commercial and investment banking.[24] Commercial banks were stripped of many, but not all, of their securities activities. They continued to underwrite, distribute, and trade in U.S. government and municipal general obligation securities and to participate in the private placement of other securities and in corporate financial advising (for example, merger and acquisition services). Trust departments continued to manage investment accounts. Beginning in the 1970s, commercial banks became more aggressive in finding new securities activities that avoided the Glass-Steagall restrictions. As table 5–5 indicates, they convinced federal regulators and federal courts to permit a number of these new activities. These activities reflect only some of the inroads of the commercial banks into investment banking markets. Large banks have increased their participation in the private placement of corporate securities and in the provision of corporate financial advisory services.[25] They are active in the market for interest rate and currency swaps in which they act as agents for agreements between firms to exchange fixed for variable interest payments or payments in one currency for payments in another. The agent bank is often the residual guarantor of the swap. Most important, U.S. commercial bank affiliates are major participants in underwriting and distributing U.S. corporate securities in the Euromarket. A regulatory system that permits the underwriting of U.S. corporate debt in the Eurobond market by a U.S. bank subsidiary and denies the bank the same subsidiary activity in U.S. capital markets is strikingly ad hoc.

Affiliations between investment firms and savings and loan associations were approved by the FHLBB on the basis that the Glass-Steagall Act does not apply to savings and loans. Given the new asset and liability powers granted to savings and loan associations under the 1980 and 1982 banking acts, this is a legal but not a functional distinction. Affiliations such as that between Allstate Savings and Dean Witter Reynolds are difficult to distinguish from the commercial bank and investment firm affiliations that Glass-Steagall supposedly

TABLE 5–5
COMMERCIAL BANK SECURITIES ACTIVITIES
APPROVED SINCE THE PASSAGE OF GLASS-STEAGALL

| Activity | Year Approved |
|---|---|
| Underwriting, distributing, and trading municipal housing revenue bonds | 1968 |
| Sponsoring closed-end funds | 1974 |
| Financial advising for mutual funds | 1974 |
| Automatic investment services | 1974 |
| Dealing in commercial paper | 1978 |
| Investment management of IRA comingled accounts | 1982 |
| General retail brokerage | 1982 |
| Trading financial and precious metals futures | 1983 |

SOURCE: Adapted from George Kaufman, "The Securities Activities of Commercial Banks," in Richard Aspinwall and Robert Eisenbeis, eds., *The Banking Handbook*, New York: John Wiley & Sons, Inc., 1984.

prohibits. A proposal by the FDIC to exempt state-chartered insured banks from Glass-Steagall restrictions would further compromise the original intent of that act.

Erosion of the line between commercial and investment banking has not come solely from the commercial banking side. Provisions of the Glass-Steagall Act and of the Bank Holding Company Act of 1970 appear to prohibit affiliations between all types of investment companies and commercial banks. Some investment companies have taken advantage of the technical definition of a commercial bank to obtain permission to acquire a commercial bank and qualify it for nonbank bank status by selling off the commercial loan portfolio.[26] Another ruling by the comptroller of the currency allowed mutual funds to affiliate with nonbank banks, thereby gaining access to federally insured deposits, the national payments clearing system, and wider trust powers while regular commercial banks remain prohibited by Glass-Steagall from affiliating with investment firms, including mutual funds. The comptroller of the currency's chartering of nonbank banks is the major item of financial deregulation directly attributable to the Reagan administration.

Investment banks are moving in on commercial loan markets in a number of other ways. The development of mortgage-backed securities and consumer receivable-related securities and the growth of commercial paper as a substitute for bank loans provide good examples.

The arguments for and against commercial bank and investment bank affiliation are well known.[27] They involve questions of economic efficiency, commercial bank stability, and conflicts of interest. The gradual erosion of the line separating commercial banking and investment firms has little to do with a considered attempt to deregulate financial markets in response to the arguments and counterarguments about the usefulness of Glass-Steagall in today's financial environment. It has much more to do with legal contrivance and regulatory acquiescence to market innovations. The affiliations of investment firms with nonbank banks and with savings and loan associations are clear cases in which a legal or regulatory loophole has been used to avoid Glass-Steagall restrictions. A few additional examples from the commercial banking side will support this point more generally.

Attempts by commercial banks to gain a foothold in heretofore prohibited types of security underwriting provide another example. Bankers Trust (New York) began to deal in third-party commercial paper in 1978. The nonbank securities industry challenged this as a violation of Glass-Steagall, but the activity was ultimately approved by the Federal Reserve Board. The issue was taken to the federal courts. A final decision on the legality of Bankers Trust's current commercial paper activities has not been given. Meanwhile, the bank continues to deal in (its opponents say "underwrite") commercial paper. The issue in the pending case depends to some extent on the fact that Bankers Trust has been dealing in commercial paper through a bank subsidiary. While awaiting the final decision in this case, Bankers Trust and J. P. Morgan have applied for permission to carry out this activity through nonbank subsidiaries.[28] If the Federal Reserve Board grants this permission, Bankers Trust should have a few more years to deal in commercial paper even if the Court of Appeals does not rule in its favor on the current case.

In another effort to bypass Glass-Steagall, Citicorp applied for permission to underwrite commercial paper and other nonpermissible securities in a nonbank subsidiary, Citicorp Securities, Inc. By limiting the proposed activities to 20 percent of the subsidiary firm's total activity (which was to include a large volume of permissible activities such as underwriting and dealing in U.S. government securities), it was claimed that Citicorp Securities would escape Glass-Steagall restrictions by not being "principally engaged" in prohibited underwriting activities. The original proposal was withdrawn when a Federal Reserve preliminary analysis proved unfavorable.[29] The latest episode in this effort is an application for Citicorp Securities, Inc., that drops commercial paper and corporate debt from the underwriting proposal but retains a request to underwrite and deal in municipal revenue bonds, mortgage-related securities, and consumer-receivable-related securities. The Federal Reserve decision on this is still pending, but approval is thought likely by some legal experts.[30]

The acquisition of retail brokerage firms by commercial banks follows a similar pattern of an aggressive move to circumvent Glass-Steagall by a regulated firm that is later ratified by the regulators and the courts.

The ad hoc nature of these changes in commercial bank securities activities and in investment firm affiliations with banklike financial firms has produced an uneven application of financial regulation across functionally similar institutions and has led to proposals to repeal or reform the Glass-Steagall Act. The Financial Institutions Deregulation Act is the Reagan administration's policy response on this reform issue and, as of fall 1985, its only legislative proposal for financial deregulation. In the act, the administration proposed a significant overhaul of the restrictions on commercial bank activities involving securities, insurance, and real estate. Bank and thrift holding companies would have been permitted to

- underwrite and deal in municipal revenue bonds
- underwrite and advise mutual funds
- engage in insurance underwriting and brokerage
- engage in real estate investment, development, and brokerage
- engage in activities that the Federal Reserve Board determines are "of a financial nature"

The legislation would also have allowed for bank holding companies to own thrifts and for thrift holding companies to own banks. It would have brought insured nonbank banks and state-chartered banks under bank holding company law (but curiously would not have brought a nonbank firm that acquired a thrift under that law). The legislation did not directly address the question of commercial bank and investment bank competition for corporate debt obligations, although it seemed to have left an opening for these activities in the activities "of a financial nature" clause.[31]

Secretary of the Treasury Baker recently endorsed broader banking powers in Senate Banking Committee testimony but backed away from endorsing some of the powers advocated in the 1983 Treasury bill. It is not clear from Secretary Baker's statement to the committee that the administration is prepared to push for serious Glass-Steagall reform at this time.[32]

A failure to enact explicit changes in Glass-Steagall will not stop erosion of the separation between commercial banking and investment banking. As George Kaufman aptly put it, "Aggressive commercial banks and aggressive investment banks [can] offer almost as many 'prohibited' activities as they wish as long as they are willing to incur the potentially large legal expenses involved."[33] This is an expensive and economically dangerous way to deregulate.

**The Deregulation of Transaction Accounts.** The pattern of regulatory ratification of market innovations traced in the review of asset deregulation holds for the deregulation of transaction accounts. A provision of the Banking Act of 1980 permitted all banks and thrifts to issue Negotiable Orders of Withdrawal (NOW accounts), an interest-bearing account on which the depositor can write drafts that are functionally equivalent to checks. This established nationally the 1972 innovation of NOW accounts by mutual savings banks in Massachusetts and New Hampshire. These transaction accounts have not been completely deregulated since they still carry an interest rate ceiling. An account offering a limited number of transactions with no ceiling (the super-NOW account) became available to banks and thrifts through the 1982 act, and thrifts were also granted a noninterest-bearing demand deposit account.

The availability of transaction accounts at thrifts has further blurred the distinction between banks and thrifts and buttressed the case for depository institution regulation along functional lines.[34] As discussed below, this issue was addressed by the Bush Task Group on Regulatory Reform, but the proposed rearrangement of regulatory authority along functional lines did not survive in the final report.

The invention of overnight repurchase agreements (zero balance accounts) for corporate transaction balances was a second important innovation to avoid the prohibition of interest on demand deposits. Under these cash management schemes, corporate treasurers who will have positive demand deposit balances (in excess of agreed-upon minimums) at the close of business can have those balances automatically transferred to an interest-bearing repurchase agreement. With overnight repurchase agreements, these balances become available to meet cash outflows the next day if needed.

These and other transaction account innovations have led to concern about their effect on the conduct of monetary policy. An extensive discussion of this issue is beyond the scope of this essay. There is, however, considerable empirical evidence supporting the conclusion that these changes in financial markets have altered the relation between money stock measures and the level of economic activity.[35] As one might expect, this evidence has not convinced everyone.[36] Even among those economists and policy makers who accept the conclusion that unusual variations in monetary velocity are caused by explicit and ad hoc transaction account deregulation, there is debate on whether this instability is transitional or permanent.[37]

Regardless of one's conclusion regarding their effects on monetary policy, improvements in payments systems technology and the development of interest-bearing substitutes for demand deposits have made the prohibition of demand deposit interest increasingly dysfunctional. Sophisticated depositors earn an explicit return on transaction balances, but at the unnecessary cost of setting up and maintaining elaborate cash management systems. The effects of this outmoded regulation also show up in banks' exposure to costs and risks. In 1973 the turnover rate on demand deposits was about 100 times per year at all insured banks and 250 times per year at major New York City banks; in 1984 these rates were approximately 450 and 1,900 respectively.[38] This turnover rate is contributing to the banks' exposure to risks from interbank overdrafts that occur during a business day and to bank operating costs. Recently, Congress has shown interest in considering more fundamental deregulation of transaction accounts: the authorization of interest rates on demand deposits.

**Geographic Deregulation.** The McFadden Act and Douglas Amendment restrictions on interstate banking are in almost complete disarray. Geographical expansion was accomplished without any significant changes in the federal laws governing interstate banking activities. It is true that the Garn–St Germain Act authorized interstate acquisitions of failed and failing banks and thrifts, but even this was a confirmation of an extraordinary acquisition procedure already in use. Notable examples include the 1981 acquisition of thrifts in New Jersey and Florida by the California-based Citizens Savings (since metamorphosed into First Nationwide Savings) and the Citicorp acquisition of Fidelity Savings and Loan of San Francisco immediately before the Garn–St Germain Act passed.

Donald Whitehead has provided a thorough summary of the interstate activities of banks and bank holding companies.[39] Using data from a Federal Reserve Bank of Atlanta survey, he identified almost 7,600 interstate offices of U.S. banks (as of 1983). Every state had at least one of these interstate offices. Approximately 5,500 of these offices are subsidiaries of bank holding companies engaging in activities the Federal Reserve Board has determined to be "a proper incident" to banking. This includes out-of-state ownership of mortgage banking firms, finance companies, industrial banks, credit card operations, and a host of other consumer finance services as well as some commercial financial services such as factoring. Loan production

175

offices (202 in thirty-four states) and Edge Act offices (143) add to the interstate presence of banks engaged in commercial lending. When the interstate activities of nonbank banks and thrift affiliations with national retailers (such as Sears and K-Mart) and with the credit subsidiaries of durable goods manufacturers (such as the acquisition of First Nationwide Savings by Ford Motor Company) are added to the list, it is clear that most consumer and commercial lending can be done by firms operating interstate.

Some of these developments, especially the activities of nonbank banks, have also contributed to the capacity for interstate deposit gathering. Furthermore, money center banks and large regional banks have tapped a national market for corporate and institutional time deposits since the mid-1960s using negotiable certificates of deposit. Since 1982, smaller banks and thrifts have escaped branching restrictions on their ability to raise out-of-state time deposit funds by using deposit brokers and 800 phone numbers.

McFadden Act and Douglas Amendment restrictions on bona fide interstate bank deposit offices without explicit approval by the state involved remain in effect. It is sometimes suggested that these branching restrictions are now only a minor annoyance to banks. There is a measure of truth in this, but the continued, costly efforts by some money center banks to extend their explicit interstate powers suggest that the annoyance may still be more than minor. Until very recently, these efforts and the economic pressures on state authorities seemed to portend a complete breakdown of interstate banking restrictions. Bank and thrift insolvencies in their states and ad hoc entry by out-of-state banks and nonbanks induced nineteen states to pass new laws between 1982 and 1984 permitting additional out-of-state entry, bringing the total number of states allowing some form of explicit interstate banking to twenty-two.[40] Reciprocal laws that allow interstate banking on a regional level while excluding money center banks have been passed by more than ten states. More are expected following the June 10, 1985, Supreme Court ruling that such pacts are legal.[41] It was widely thought that these regional pacts might not be approved, and Congress appeared poised to consider federal legislation to introduce nationwide interstate banking. The momentum for a nationwide interstate banking trigger has been blunted by the Supreme Court decision.

**Regulatory Reform**

Financial deregulation and changes in the financial services industry are forcing the administration and Congress to consider deposit insurance reform and the restructuring of the federal regulatory system. The deposit insurance system has been put under considerable stress by the systematic depletion of the insurance funds. The resulting changes in the deposit insurance system have been limited to date, but substantive deposit insurance reform is on the administrative and legislative agenda. The ability of the federal regulatory system to cope with its responsibilities in the current financial environment and its efficiency in doing so were the subjects of a Reagan administration initiative, the Task Group on Regulation of Financial Services. The initiative has not produced any completed or even any pending legislation to date.

**Deposit Insurance Reform.** The federal deposit insurance system has served this country well for over fifty years. The weak condition of that system today is making it difficult to continue financial deregulation and is providing critics of deregulation with the strongest case for reregulation. As noted throughout this review, changes in the financial services industry and in the economic and regulatory environment in which it operates have strained the resources of the deposit insurance system. The adequacy of the insurance funds to meet potential claims and the ability of regulators to monitor and control risk have been called into question. The 1984 year end ratio of book value reserves to insured deposits at the Federal Savings and Loan Deposit Insurance Corporation was just under 0.8 percent (compared with a peak ratio of 2.14 percent in 1969). This ratio has decreased steadily since 1969 except for modest increases in 1979 and 1980. The comparable ratio for the Federal Deposit Insurance Corporation was about 1.2, up from a low of 1.16 percent at year end 1980.[42] These ratios understate the weakness of the insurance funds. They are measured in terms of explicitly insured deposits. Deposit guarantees in practice have often been extended to uninsured liabilities. The denominator of the ratio should be larger to reflect this. Furthermore, reserve book values overstate market values, so the numerator should be smaller. Even if we corrected the ratio of insurance reserves to insured liabilities for these effects, the weakness of the insurance funds would still be understated, since we would be counting only realized losses. There are major unrealized insurance fund losses because some insured banks and thrifts continue to operate with negative market net worth.

The Ninety-seventh Congress responded to this situation in March 1982 by passing a joint resolution (H.R. 290) placing the "full faith and credit" of the U.S. government behind the deposit insurance agencies' guarantees.[43] The continuing depletion of the insurance funds since 1982 has made deposit insurance reform an important financial policy issue. Congressional hearings on this subject began in the summer of 1985. An administration task force has been at work on a deposit insurance reform for over a year but has yet to put forward a legislative proposal.

It has long been recognized that the federal deposit insurance system is flawed by having deposit insurance premiums that are not risk related.[44] This flaw leads to perverse incentives for insured firms to take risk and to economic inefficiency as the subsidy to risk taking is passed on to borrowers. The importance of this problem has increased with increases in the risk-taking potential of insured institutions, with increases in their leverage, with decreases in the dependence of institutions on core deposits, and with increases in the competitiveness of financial markets. Critics of the existing system suggest that the failure to keep portfolio risk and leverage commensurate with the statutory premium has contributed to the current situation in which the unrealized liabilities of the insurance funds outstrip the assets in those funds.[45] The systematic failure to close or reorganize insured institutions before the market value of their assets falls significantly below the value of covered liability claims, however, is a more important and fundamental cause of the perilous condition of the insurance funds.[46]

The reform proposals discussed in the 1985 congressional hearings fall into four categories: insurance fund proposals, risk-sharing proposals, risk-related deposit insurance, and market value accounting.

*Insurance fund proposals.* Fund recapitalization and fund merger have been proposed as ways to improve the deposit insurance system. There is a sense in which either of these steps would be cosmetic. They will not change the reality of depositors' claims on the deposit insurance system and ultimately on the U.S. taxpayer. Nevertheless, there are questions about the current status of the 1982 "full faith and credit" resolution and concerns over its ambiguity, so there may be merit in any step that will reinforce small depositors' confidence in this guarantee.

More important, as an insurance fund gets smaller, decisions on how to deal with weak and failed institutions are increasingly directed toward preserving the fund in the short run rather than at minimizing the ultimate cost to the government. Fund recapitalization and, to a lesser extent, fund merger may have a role to play here. An alternative view is that the potential for an insurance fund to run out of reserves is a strong political incentive for Congress to enact substantive legislation reforming deposit insurance and that fund merger or recap-italization before the reform is undertaken would blunt that incen-tive.[47]

*Risk-sharing proposals.* The current risk-sharing proposals include the modified payoff plan, reduction in deposit insurance coverage from its current level of $100,000 per account, increased use of sub-ordinated debt capital, and various private deposit insurance schemes. The idea behind each of these risk-sharing proposals is to get agents other than the federal government to share in the risk of depository institution failure and to assist in the monitoring of insured institu-tions.

A modified payoff plan has been put out for public comment by the FDIC.[48] Under this plan, the FDIC would pay uninsured depositors and general creditors of a failed bank a percentage of their claims immediately, rather than after transferring deposits to some other bank or paying them off after asset liquidation has taken place. In large bank crises, this procedure would be substituted for the usual practice of having all deposits, insured or not, assumed by a successor institution.

Most critics of the existing system would agree that the situation in which uninsured depositors do not fully price the risk of failure is undesirable. Any scheme that depends critically on putting uninsured depositors at risk, however, will work only if the regulators and mem-bers of Congress are willing to tolerate bank runs. Deposit runs have been rare at federally insured institutions because almost all depositors have been fully insured, either explicitly or implicitly. Once they conclude they are not fully protected from loss, uninsured depositors will try to remove their funds from institutions that they perceive to be in trouble. These runs are not likely to be as rapid or dramatic as the recent thrift runs in Maryland and Ohio, but we have seen in the case of the Continental Illinois Bank that a so-called silent run can precipitate a liquidity crisis. Of course, this could be just what the financial doctor ordered. The regulators' attention is drawn to a serious solvency problem by alert private sector depositors, and the chartering agency moves rapidly to close or recapitalize the institution while there are enough uninsured deposits still around to absorb a signif-icant fraction of any loss. It did not work that way at Continental Illinois, however, so there have to be doubts whether regulators and legislators will accept bank runs, silent or noisy, no matter how ca-thartic they might be.[49]

It is not clear that reducing the deposit insurance coverage per account would do much to increase market discipline. There is a cost to maintaining more than one account to stay fully insured, but not a cost that would induce currently insured depositors to accept a share of the risk of failure. A limit on the deposit insurance coverage per individual would be more effective in reducing system exposure if a workable method of controlling individual coverage could be devised. It is not clear what that maximum coverage should be, however. It cannot depend only on the effect on institutional risk taking. The optimal amount of deposit insurance per individual must also depend on total monitoring costs. More uninsured depositors would mean more total monitoring costs.

One of the clearest congressional concerns is the use of brokered deposits by insured institutions. A deposit broker obtains funds from investors throughout the country and channels them to client depository institutions, assigning title for the deposits in separate units, up to the $100,000 insurance limit, to a number of different investors. Banks and thrifts can offer higher yields on these brokered deposits as an enticement. Those institutions that want to engage in increased risk taking need not wait for local deposit growth to provide the funding, nor do they have to consider depositor concerns about the riskiness of their portfolio. Financial regulators and members of Congress are legitimately concerned over the insured risk taking that results from deposit brokerage.

Reducing the maximum coverage per account would constrain and perhaps eliminate the brokerage of insured deposits by making reallocations of a large investment into fully insured accounts more costly. Eliminating insurance coverage on brokered funds would be an even stronger step to stop this source of insured risk taking. Whether it is desirable to eliminate deposit brokerage by these methods or any other is another question. Insured deposit brokerage gives smaller institutions access to national markets in much the same way that direct sale and brokerage of negotiable CDs have given larger institutions national access to corporate, institutional, and individual savings. Both markets work because depositors have little concern about losses due to bank and thrift failure. In this sense, the implicit guarantee of the liabilities of large institutions is functionally equivalent to the explicit insurance of the deposits of smaller institutions at an account size that permits brokerage to take place. Moreover, there is an alternative solution to the brokered deposit problem. An actuarially sound system of deposit insurance would solve it without interfering with the access to national deposit markets.

Subordinated debt has distinct advantages over uninsured deposits as a method of risk sharing. Until the maturity of subordinated debt gets short, the regulator has time to discover a troubled bank or thrift before the debt holder can slip away. Subordinated debt holders have good reason to monitor the bank or thrift whose debt they hold, and the effect of that monitoring on the price of the debt is a useful signal for the institution's regulator. Furthermore, truly subordinated debt can be forced to absorb losses up to the amount of that debt rather than to share those losses *pari passu* with the federal insurer, as is the case for uninsured depositors and other general creditors. Of course, subordinated debt will not be of much help to an insurance fund if the debt holders get bailed out along with the depositors as they were in the Continental Illinois failure.

Private deposit insurance is a fourth approach to risk sharing.[50] Proponents of this approach argue that private insurance would necessarily be actuarially sound and that monitoring by private insurers would reduce and perhaps eliminate the need for bank regulation. Critics have expressed doubts that private insurance can succeed except perhaps as a supplement to federal guarantees. Viewed as a supplement to federal deposit insurance, private insurance provides added depositor protection similar to that provided by subordinated debt capital, except that insurance company reserves rather than the value of a subordinated debt claim are providing the backup. Whatever the merits of a well-conceived private deposit insurance plan, the recent failures of private plans in Maryland and Ohio have created an adverse political environment for this approach to risk sharing.

Risk sharing alone will not solve the risk incentive problem. Although an effective risk-sharing scheme imposes costs on riskier institutions that would probably reduce their propensity to take risks, an incentive to take risks remains unless deposit insurance premiums and the risk of insured losses are appropriately related.

*Risk-related deposit insurance.* The risk incentive in flat rate deposit insurance can be eliminated either by making the risk to the insurance fund commensurate with the statutory premium or by charging variable premiums that are commensurate with the risk imposed on the fund. Since the risk is made up of two components, portfolio risk and leverage, the regulator has both of these tools as well as the size of the insurance premium to work with. The major reform proposals for improving the link between risk and insurance premiums are risk-related premiums, risk-related capital requirements, and intensified supervision. Risk-related premiums use the insurance premium as the control variable, and risk-related capital uses leverage while intensified supervision focuses on bringing portfolio risk in line with the statutory premium.

In principle, the deposit insurance premium can be brought into line with the deposit insurer's liability from a given institution by using these controls in different combinations or by the use of any one alone. The decision on which to use should be based on the costs of implementing the policy, and it is not obvious which method or combination of methods would be least costly. There is an extensive literature on the pricing of deposit insurance.[51] These models are useful in demonstrating the critical control variables in a risk-related deposit insurance system and for making estimates of the adequacy of the existing premium or of proposed risk-related premiums. They have not been used to address the important question of the overall cost to society of a given set of controls.

The enthusiasm of the financial regulators for risk-related premiums is restrained. The Federal Home Loan Bank Board was the only agency that gave a strong endorsement to this approach in the reports to Congress on deposit insurance reform.[52] The leadership of that agency has since changed, and the FHLBB has backed away from that endorsement. More recently, the FDIC proposed a limited form of risk-related premiums in which banks in the three poorest risk classifications would not receive rebates from the statutory premium. If adopted, this would result in a maximum insurance premium difference of five basis points between the less risky (categories one and two) and more risky (categories three, four, and five) banks. A comparison of this risk differential with estimates of the actuarial insurance premium suggests that an added five basis points will not remove much of the risk incentive in the deposit insurance system.[53] Industry critics of risk-related premiums recognize the power to discriminate among competing institutions that this approach would give the regulators and are concerned that this discrimination might not always be on the basis of true risk differences.

Capital regulation has natural advantages as a control variable, at least at institutions with publicly traded debt and equity. The argument for this centers on the cost of capital regulation for the insured institution and on monitoring costs.

A case can be made that capital, especially subordinated debt capital, is not costly compared with properly priced deposits.[54] This view is often countered by appeals to the reluctance of management to add capital. Using standard capital structure arguments, institutional reluctance to add debt capital is seen largely as a response to the risk subsidy the current deposit insurance system provides on implicitly insured negotiable CDs and other money market liabilities. Since that subsidy is what we are trying to eliminate, the claim that debt capital is costly compared with deposits is not a valid argument against this approach. Within reasonable limits, the addition of subordinated debt will improve the quality of uninsured deposits, so that increased capital need not be costly to the institution. The higher debt cost is offset by a lower cost on uninsured deposits. In contrast, a risk-related insurance premium in excess of the proper risk-adjusted premium is a cost without an offset.

A second advantage of capital regulation in the case of publicly traded firms is that the market value of that capital and its price volatility provide a low-cost monitoring device. In contrast, greatly intensified supervision in the form of onsite examinations would significantly increase the cost of managing the deposit insurance system. With a low-cost monitoring device, it is economical to use monitoring frequency as a risk-related control. Institutions that are perceived to be taking greater portfolio risk based on the price volatility of their traded capital would be required to meet a capital test more frequently.

Discussions of alternative systems for reducing the risk incentive in the deposit insurance system are frequently marred by arguments that portfolio risk and the market value of capital are too difficult or too costly to measure. It is important to recognize that any control system that removes the risk incentive, including the improved supervisory risk control that would be needed to make the current system work, requires someone to make reliable estimates of portfolio risk and of the market value of assets of insured institutions. The alternative is to leave the system with an inefficient risk incentive that will continue to threaten the solvency of the insurance funds.

*Market value accounting.* Whatever set of controls is used to remove the risk subsidy, it is also essential to adopt a market value rule for the closure decision.[55] Paul Horvitz made a thoughtful case against risk-related premiums in which he said, "The key point . . . is that if insured institutions are operating with positive net worth, and the insurance agency is able to monitor their condition, then risk of loss to the agency is low, *regardless of the riskiness of individual institutions."*[56] The idea that the regulators will not allow institutions with negative market net worth to continue to operate is implicit in Horvitz's remark. The experience has been quite different; closure has consistently been delayed until market net worth was significantly negative.

A closure policy that systematically results in asset realizations that are less than covered deposit claims greatly increases the deposit insurance subsidy. This effect is substantially more important than excessive portfolio risk in increasing the federal deposit insurance liability.[57] The use of book value standards of net worth virtually ensures that the market net worth of insured institutions that are closed will be systematically and significantly negative. The policy proposals in this area are usually stated in terms of market value accounting. Market value accounting may be useful in conditioning institutional behavior and in providing better information to depositors. It is not really the basic issue. An appropriate closure policy need not involve market value accounting on the part of the institutions; it only requires the regulators to monitor capital on the basis of their best estimates of the market value of that capital with the clear legal authority to demand recapitalization or, failing that, closure on the basis of those estimates.

*Current initiatives in deposit insurance reform.* The major administrative response to the federal deposit insurance crisis has been the establishment by the FDIC of a 6 percent minimum capital requirement for insured institutions. This is a positive step to the extent that it has resulted in actual increases in the difference between the market value of an institution's assets and the covered deposit claims on that institution. As long as the capital rule is based on book values, however, these increases in capital will often prove illusory. For example, two responses to the new capital requirements have been the sale of bank buildings and increases in accounting reserves against loan losses. The sale of bank real estate on the books at depreciated historical cost results in an increase in measured capital but not in a commensurate increase in the market value of the bank's assets. Similarly , an increase in reserves against loan losses increases regulatory capital (because regulatory capital is defined to include reserves against loan losses) without changing the ratio of bank assets (at market value) to the face value of depositor claims. Even where the increase in capital requirements actually resulted in an increase in the ratio of asset market value to insured claims, the increases will prove illusory in the long run for institutions that experience future declines in the market value of assets, unless those losses are promptly recognized and the institution is required to recapitalize.

The report of the Bush Task Group on Regulation of Financial Services, *Blueprint for Reform*, includes a section on reform of the deposit insurance system.[58] This short section of the report stands as the public statement of the Reagan administration's policies on this critical topic, although as noted earlier specific legislative proposals have been anticipated for over a year. The Bush task group recommendations may give us a clue to those legislative proposals. They are:

• no insurance fund merger at this time
• risk sharing via modified payout on uninsured deposits
• authorization of, but not a requirement for, risk-related premiums

- common minimum capital standards and common accounting rules for FDIC- and FHLBB-insured institutions

Assuming that this does represent the framework around which the administration's deposit insurance reform proposals are being written, the most important omission is the absence of any reference to market value accounting or, more important, to market value closure rules.

**Regulatory Reform.** On December 10, 1982, the Reagan administration announced the formation of the Task Group on Regulation of Financial Services to be chaired by Vice President Bush with Secretary of Treasury Donald Regan as vice chairman. Secretary Regan's October 20 memorandum calling for establishment of such a task force and subsequent statements from the vice president's office and from the task force staff make it clear that the administration hoped to consolidate substantially the bank and thrift regulatory agencies and to address issues associated with the banking and securities industry interface.[59] In August 1983, it was reported that the regulatory consolidation option favored by the staff (headed by the deputy counsel to Vice President Bush) was to centralize banking regulation in a new banking commission while expanding the powers of the Federal Home Loan Bank Board to include small community banks and all thrifts. This was intended to be consistent with the reform principle of splitting regulatory responsibility along functional lines. The regulatory responsibilities of the Federal Reserve System were to be eliminated.[60] The elimination of Federal Reserve System responsibility for regulation and supervision to allow it to concentrate on its responsibilities for monetary policy has long been advocated by some monetary economists. The Federal Reserve, on the other hand, has consistently argued that regulatory and supervisory authority are essential adjuncts to its responsibility for economic stabilization.

The final recommendations of the task group in *Blueprint for Reform* bear only a slight resemblance to these sweeping reform suggestions. The only federal agency slated to lose regulatory and supervisory authority was the FDIC. Division of regulation across functional lines was more a symbolic than a real outcome of the task group's work. The Federal Reserve retained major regulatory and supervisory responsibilities, along with its role in monetary policy. There is an even more striking indicator of the failure of the Bush report to affect financial regulatory reform. Over a year has passed since the report was signed, and no legislation based on it has been introduced in Congress.

## Conclusion

The case is made in this essay that market innovation and the thrift crisis have forced the pace of financial deregulation. Virtually all the deregulation of depository institutions has been ad hoc and not a considered attempt at financial reform. Despite a philosophical commitment to fewer regulations and more competition in financial services, the Reagan administration has little to show in the way of concrete financial deregulation.

The elimination of ceilings on deposit interest rates is the major achievement in the deregulation of depository institutions. Despite the adjustment problems created by this deregulation, it should prove to be a permanent change for the better by removing an inefficient and largely ineffective regulation. With the price deregulation of the securities industry as a guide, it may take another five to seven years to realize the full effects of the deregulation of deposit interest rates on the structure of the financial services industry. The failures and consolidations that result may constrain the pace of explicit deregulation, but not the ad hoc deregulation of financial products and markets. It will take leadership in financial deregulation to put forward a general plan of deregulation, or we will continue to experience the inefficient, uneven, and potentially dangerous process of piecemeal deregulation through regulatory forbearance and legal contrivance. The source of that leadership is not evident today.

The most pressing problem facing the makers of federal financial policy is the growing insolvency of the deposit insurance funds. It is becoming increasingly clear that product deregulation at thrifts is contributing to the deposit insurance crisis. Here again it is tempting to reregulate. Some reregulation, especially with respect to the more liberal state regulations on permissible assets, may be necessary. A more general attempt at asset reregulation would not be likely to succeed in the long run, because the problem lies in a deposit insurance scheme with perverse risk incentives and not in the specific means by which that risk incentive is exploited. Deposit insurance reform should be the first order of business. The conclusion reached here is that adoption of market value closure rules is a necessary first step in that reform.

# Notes

1. Regulation Q deposit interest rate ceilings for member banks existed before 1966 but did not apply to all insured depository institutions. The 1966 act established the first industrywide deposit rate ceilings.

2. Paul Cootner, "The Liquidity of the Savings and Loan Industry," *Study of the Savings and Loan Industry* (Washington, D.C.: Federal Home Loan Bank Board, 1969), p. 289.

3. At the time, critics of interest rate ceilings noted that this undertaking was not a particularly encouraging sign of the will to get rid of these ceilings, because it could be interpreted as the longest renewal of the authority for ceilings since their "temporary" establishment in 1966.

4. Michael Keeley and Gary Zimmerman, "Competition for Money Market Deposit Accounts," *Economic Review* (Federal Reserve Bank of San Francisco), no. 2 (1985), pp. 5–25.

5. Money market mutual fund managers responded to the challenge presented by MMDAs at banks and thrifts by taking various steps to improve their product. As a result, their loss of funds to MMDAs was a one-time shift, and MMMF assets have recovered to their pre-MMDA levels.

6. Savings and transaction balances appeared to decrease slightly, but not significantly, following the introduction of MMDAs. Keeley and Zimmerman suggest the decline in these accounts was actually a runoff of balances from maturing time deposits and securities held temporarily in liquid form to await the availability of MMDAs.

7. It is not clear that these accounting cost figures fully reflect true economic operating costs, especially capital costs such as the cost of bank and thrift offices.

8. The increases in employment at savings and loan associations may reflect changes in their asset and liability composition, a point we will return to in the next section.

9. Bureau of National Affairs, Inc., *Washington Financial Reports*, hereafter *WFR*, vol. 44, no. 9, p. 368, and no. 24, p. 1025.

10. "Financial Services: Guidelines for a New Regulatory Framework," Sears, Roebuck & Co., undated.

11. See Arie Melnik and Aron Ofer, "Price Deregulation in the Brokerage Industry: An Empirical Analysis," *The Bell Journal of Economics*, vol. 5; (1978), pp. 633–41, for an empirical analysis of the effects of negotiated commissions on commission rates. Their results show "that price competition has led to lower prices and to a rate structure that reflects the costs of executing different types of transactions."

12. See tables 4.5 and 4.6, pp. 101–102, in Edward Kane, *The Gathering Crisis in Federal Deposit Insurance* (Cambridge, Mass.: MIT Press, 1985), hereafter Kane. I used the maximum of Kane's two savings and loan net worth estimates in forming the 1983 estimate of aggregate thrift net worth. The 1971 vs. 1983 comparison was necessary because Kane's savings and loan association net worth estimates do not begin until 1971. His estimate of mutual savings bank net worth (after mortgage losses) is − $1.8 billion for 1966 compared with − $4.8 billion for 1971. Extrapolating from the mutual savings bank data gives a 1966 savings and loan association net worth estimate of − $4.2 billion or an aggregate thrift net worth of − $6.0 billion for that year.

13. See Figure 3B-1, p. 47, in Fredrick Balderston, *Thrifts in Crisis: Structural Transformation of the Savings and Loan Industry* (Cambridge, Mass.: Ballinger Publishing Co., 1985).

14. The FDIC problem bank list had 251 banks on it in 1971. At year end 1984, it had 847. See table 3.1, p. 61, of Kane.

15. See Thomas Mayer, "A Graduated Deposit Insurance Plan," *Review of Economics and Statistics*, vol. 47 (1965), pp. 114–16.

16. The need for deposit insurance reform is discussed below.

17. The legal definition of a commercial bank under the Bank Holding Company Act is a bank that accepts deposits that a depositor can withdraw on demand and engages in the business of making commercial loans. By acquiring an insured commercial bank and stripping off one of these two functions, a firm can have an insured institution and not run afoul of bank holding company and other federal banking laws.

18. Ironically, by the time the asset deregulation legislation was passed, the need for risk diversification in interest rates in thrift assets had been reduced by extensive use of adjustable rate mortgages and interest rate hedging strategies.

19. The asset acquisition data for 1980–1982 reflect the special effects of the strong deposit disintermediation at thrifts during that period. Furthermore, the new asset powers were not fully available until 1983.

20. *WFR*, vol. 45, no. 9, p. 302.

21. The FHLBB believes that "junk bond" holdings by FSLIC-insured thrifts were about $5 billion in June 1985 with about half of that total concentrated in a small number of institutions. *WFR*, vol. 45, no. 9, p. 303.

22. Using Gray's estimate, approximately eighty-six FSLIC-insured institutions are in trouble due to poor asset quality and another seventeen failed for this reason. This undoubtedly underestimates the number of institutions that aggressively exploited their new asset powers on the basis of federal deposit guarantees.

23. See A. James Meigs, "Regulatory Aspects of the World Debt Problem," *Cato Journal*, vol. 4 (1984), pp. 105–24; and Michael Goldberg and Peter Lloyd-Davies, "Standby Letters of Credit: Are Banks Overextending Themselves?" unpublished manuscript, Board of Governors of the Federal Reserve, September 1983.

24. This section draws heavily on an excellent review of commercial bank securities activities by George Kaufman, "The Securities Activities of Commercial Banks," in Richard Aspinwall and Robert Eisenbeis, eds., *The Banking Handbook* (New York: John Wiley & Sons, Inc., 1984).

25. A 1977 survey by the Federal Reserve System found that commercial bank private placements were less than 10 percent of total private placements. It seems likely that this activity has grown since that time.

26. Comptroller of the Currency, "Decision of the Comptroller of the Currency on the Application to Charter J & W Seligman Trust Company N.A.," February 1, 1983, and "Decision of the Comptroller of the Currency to Charter Dreyfus National Bank and Trust Company," February 4, 1983.

27. See, for example, pp. 42–51 of Kaufman.

28. *WFR*, vol. 45, no. 1, p. 7.

29. *WFR*, vol. 44, no. 9, pp. 373–74.

30. *WFR*, vol. 44, no. 14, pp. 604–605 and no. 16, p. 675.

31. *WFR*, vol. 41, no. 3, pp. 53–55.

32. *WFR*, vol. 44, no. 24, pp. 1023–24.

33. See p. 61 of Kaufman.

34. Transaction accounts at S&Ls increased sharply after 1980, reaching a total of $23.4 billion or 3 percent of total liabilities at FSLIC-insured institutions by the end of 1983. Their growth, however, appears to have slowed, and the S&L share of the transaction account market is less than 6 percent. At year end 1984, total transaction accounts at S&Ls were $28.9 billion or 3.1 percent of total liabilities as compared with $491.1 billion or 21.7 percent at commercial banks. *Federal Reserve Bulletin*, vol. 71, no. 7, table 1.25, p. A18, and *Combined Financial Statements: FSLIC-Insured Institutions*, FHLBB, 1984, table vi, p. ix.

35. See John Judd and John Scadding, "The Search for a Stable Money Demand Function: A Survey of the Post-1973 Literature," *Journal of Economic Literature*, vol. 20 (1982), pp. 993–1023, and Thomas Simpson, "Changes in the Financial System: Implications for Monetary Policy," *Brookings Papers on Economic Activity*, vol. 1 (1984), pp. 249–72.

36. See Milton Friedman, "Why a Surge in Inflation Is Likely Next Year," *Wall Street Journal*, September 1, 1983, and J. Tatom, "Was the 1982 Velocity Decline Unusual?" *Review of the St. Louis Federal Reserve Bank*, vol. 65 (1983), pp. 5–15.

37. John Karaken, in "Bank Regulation and the Effectiveness of Open Market Operations," *Brookings Papers on Economic Activity*, vol. 2 (1984), pp. 405–55, raises the interesting point that bank deregulation more generally conceived may significantly affect the Federal Reserve's resolve to control inflation if it faces the board with the Hobson's choice of a liquidity crisis brought on by bank failures. See also James Tobin's discussion of this point in the same volume.

38. See Almarin Phillips and Donald Jacobs, "Reflections on the Hunt Commission," in G. Benston, ed., *Financial Services: The Changing Institutions and Government Policy* (Englewood Cliffs, N.J.: Prentice-Hall, Inc., 1983), pp. 235–65. Data for 1984 are from *Federal Reserve Bulletin*, vol. 71, no. 7, table 1.22, p. A15.

39. Donald Whitehead, "Interstate Banking: Probability or Reality?" *Economic Review*, Federal Reserve Bank of Atlanta, May 1985, pp. 6–17.

40. See p. 9 of the reference in footnote 39.

41. *WFR*, vol. 44, no. 24, p. 1050.

42. *WFR*, vol. 44, no. 9, p. 364.

43. The legal status of this resolution is not clear. There appear to be differing opinions on whether a resolution passed by one Congress is binding on later Congresses. Few, if any, informed observers doubt that Congress would honor insured depositors if an insurance fund was unable to. As Kane (see p. 4 of Kane) points out, however, the resolution does not state how the government's obligation would be discharged, leaving some uncertainty at least about the timeliness of the payoff.

44. Guy Emerson, "Guaranty of Deposits under the Banking Act of 1933," *Quarterly Journal of Economics*, vol. 48 (1934), pp. 229–44.

45. See Kane, for example.

46. By covered liability claims, I mean claims that are legally insured plus uninsured liabilities that have been guaranteed in fact.

47. I am grateful to Robert Cooter for this point.

48. "FDIC Request for Comments on Market Discipline," Federal Deposit Insurance Corporation, May 1985. The full text is in *WFR*, vol. 44, no. 18, pp. 807–809.

49. The FDIC was conducting an experiment with modified payoffs before the beginning of the uninsured deposit runoff at Continental Illinois. After that runoff was under way, the FDIC announced that "all depositors and other general creditors of the bank will be fully protected," thus undermining the modified payoff scheme.

50. See Catherine England and John Palffy, "Replacing the FDIC: Private Insurance for Bank Deposits," *Heritage Foundation Backgrounder*, December 2, 1982, p. 229.

51. See Kane, chapter 4, for an extensive review of these models.

52. The three reports are "Deposit Insurance in a Changing Environment," (Washington, D.C.: FDIC); "Agenda for Reform," (Washington, D.C.: FHLBB, 1983); and "Credit Union Share Insurance: A Report to Congress," (Washington, D.C.: NCUA), all published in 1983.

53. See Robert Merton, "An Analytical Derivation of the Cost of Deposit Insurance and Loan Guarantees," *Journal of Banking and Finance*, vol. 1 (1977), pp. 3–11; and David Pyle, "Pricing Deposit Insurance: The Effects of Mismeasurement," Federal Reserve Bank of San Francisco working paper, October 1983.

54. Black et al. make this case in Fischer Black, Merton Miller, and Richard Posner, "An Approach to the Regulation of Bank Holding Companies," *Journal of Business*, vol. 51 (1978), pp. 379–412.

55. The term "closure decision" in this context does not necessarily mean a decision to shut down the institution in question. Rather, in most cases, it would be a decision to force recapitalization through a capital infusion by existing owners or through acquisition by new owners or by some other means.

56. See Paul Horvitz, "The Case against Risk-Related Deposit Insurance Premiums," *Housing Finance Review*, vol. 2, pp. 253–63, p. 257 (his emphasis).

57. David Pyle, in "Capital Regulation and Deposit Insurance," *Journal of Banking and Finance* (forthcoming), has made estimates of the effect of closure rules that are not based on economic insolvency assuming a constant asset risk. In fact, the tendency of the management of insured institutions that are in financial difficulty to "bet the bank" to try to escape that difficulty makes the cost of these closure rules even greater than those estimates.

58. "Blue Print for Reform: The Report of the Task Group on Regulation of Financial Services," July 2, 1984.

59. *WFR*, vol. 39, no. 22, p. 997; and vol. 39, no. 24, p. 1122.

60. *WFR*, vol. 41, no. 8, p. 261.

# 6

# The Changing Structure of the Health Care System

*Jack A. Meyer and Rosemary Gibson Kern*

## Summary

*After many years of sharp cost escalation, health care spending increases decelerated in 1984. The moderation reflects the slowdown in general inflation, significant public policy changes, altered payment practices in the private sector, and the growing supply of physicians.*

*While the health care sector is experiencing a shake out and a period of restructuring, longer-term forces are developing that portend a rising price tag for health care in years to come. The aging of our population, breakthroughs in medical research and technology, and the desire to provide access to care for as many people as possible will drive up spending in the future.*

*Government policy toward health care is undergoing a major change in the 1980s. The government is concentrating more on getting its own house in order—with major new policy thrusts in Medicare and Medicaid—and less on regulating private sector activities. The rate and entry controls of the 1970s are giving way to incentive-based reforms. These reforms have marketlike features but also incorporate quasi-regulatory aspects.*

*Instead of offering 1970s-style national blueprints purporting simultaneously to solve the problems of high cost and access to care for the medically indigent, the government is now overhauling the way Medicare pays hospitals, limiting physician reimbursement under public programs, and opening up Medicaid to local experimentation with a variety of payment mechanisms. Prospective payment, deregulation, and decentralization are the building blocks of a streamlined, but limited public policy. The government now believes that the private sector can redesign employee group health insurance on its own to achieve cost discipline that proved so elusive to federal control in the past. The private sector employers—the major purchasers of care—are encouraging the appropriate use of the health care system and the substitution of outpatient for institutional care. They are also obtaining better information on variations in provider practice patterns and charges and are steering workers toward cost-effective health plans.*

*These trends are eliminating some of the waste and inefficiency from the health care system. But they do not address the nagging problems of how to subsidize those whose low income or high-risk health status makes it difficult to obtain private insurance, but whose family or work status arbitrarily excludes them from coverage under the public safety net.*

*Thus, a more competitive marketplace is shaving costs, offering consumers more choices while undermining the dominance of service providers and eroding the cross-subsidies through which indigent care and medical education were financed in the past. What is needed now is a system of direct subsidies for the worthy social objectives that would be underfunded in a more competitive market. Such subsidies would complement the incentive-based reforms that offer a promising alternative to the controls of the past that concealed the defects in the health care finance system.*

*Information is a key ingredient in making these reforms work, and information on both the cost of care and the quality and outcomes associated with health care is increasingly sought by both public and private sector bill payers. Recent regulatory changes strengthening requirements that institutional providers disclose information such as mortality rates for selected procedures will give patients the tools to make more informed choices about the care they receive.*

*The reforms in public and private sector payment systems are also causing providers to reevaluate the way in which the provision of health care is organized. The financing and delivery of health care are increasingly being integrated. Hospitals are marketing the services offered by their physicians, and insurers and employers are also interacting in new ways with the provider community. Institutional providers themselves are selling insurance packages, including health maintenance organizations (HMOs) and preferred provider organizations (PPOs) in addition to traditional insurance arrangements. In this way, providers are assured of patients and revenues. Physicians are reconfiguring themselves, as well. Solo practice is giving way to PPOs and other organized delivery system models. The result is systems of integrated care replacing a string of unrelated components.*

## Introduction

The health care system is undergoing rapid changes. For two decades increases in health care outlays outpaced the growth of GNP, and health care expenditures rose from 6.1 percent of GNP in 1965 to 10.8 percent in 1983. In 1984, however, health care expenditures as a percentage of the GNP dropped for the first time, to 10.6 percent. They grew 9.1 percent, the lowest rate in twenty years. This trend reflects the slowdown in general inflation. It also reflects changes in the methods, introduced by both the government and the private sector, of paying doctors, hospitals, and other providers of health services.

Although it could be the beginning of a more lasting slowdown in the rate of growth of health care expenditures as a percentage of GNP, it is likely that the recent trend constitutes a one-time shake out of the industry. In this chapter, we analyze the forces that have contributed to recent expenditure patterns, tracing both the new pressures applied by purchasers of health services and the responses of physicians, hospitals, and other providers of health services to these mounting pressures.

The state of flux in the health care sector of the economy reflects a virtual revolution in the way government and the nation's employers—the major purchasers of care—pay those who provide the care. Traditional payment systems that rubber-stamped and passed through costs that providers incurred are inexorably yielding to more incentive-based payment systems with prospective payments to providers. This chapter outlines and explains the basic elements of this wholesale change.

The health care industry is reconfiguring itself to meet the challenges imposed by more aggressive purchasers. Physicians who provide cost-conscious services are joining forces to bargain with the bill payers; hospitals are trimming their staffs, advertising services, requiring their medical staffs to limit unnecessary use of health care services, and engaging in new ventures. Employers are obtaining data that they never examined before on prices and provider practice patterns in their communities. These and other trends are discussed here.

In recent years, the federal government has stimulated this new climate by changing policy in several important ways. First, Medicare, a $67 billion program financing health care expenditures of the elderly, has converted from an open-ended, cost-based hospital payment system to a prospective payment system with strict limits. Second, the government has abandoned, for the present, past efforts to enact a national health plan that would combine coverage for uninsured citizens with a nationwide regulatory system for establishing allowable fees and charges throughout the health care industry. Third, the government has begun to decentralize authority under the Medicaid program, a joint federal-state effort to help low-income persons meet health care expenses. Fourth, the applicability of antitrust law to health care delivery and other professions has challenged and sent into retreat prior practices that tended to insulate the dominant mode of health care practice and financing from competitive challenges.

The Reagan administration has led the way on some of these changes, and the Congress has been an active participant in creating the new landscape. The administration has changed the focus of national health policy, so that instead of devising "solutions" for the whole industry, it helps implement cost controls in federal programs, allowing the private sector and, to a certain extent, the states to develop their own cost-control mechanisms. The dimensions of the federal deficit make a reexamination of the basic rules of the game under Medicare and Medicaid imperative. The private sector has also been making corresponding changes that are substantially altering employees' access to health care services and their use of them.

Congress has balked at some of the administration's cost-control initiatives but has rarely retreated to the status quo or to a defense of the orthodox payment system. For example, disputes between the administration and Congress have generally involved congressional preferences for cost controls that bear down primarily on providers. Congress has shielded Medicaid recipients from some of the blows of the budget axe. It moved rapidly to install prospective payment for hospitals under Medicare in 1983 and is now considering important changes limiting physician reimbursement under that program. Recent changes in Medicare, however, have increased the out-of-pocket costs for Medicare beneficiaries.

The shake out under way in the health care industry is the result of the interaction between these new developments in government policy and employer behavior, on the one hand, and an "overbuilt" industry, on the other. The ratio of physicians to the population has been rising steadily and is projected to continue to climb. Hospitals are typically only about two-thirds occupied. These trends on the supply side of the market make the sellers of health services more receptive to buyer pressure.

While we have clearly achieved a slowing in the explosion of health care costs that characterized the past two decades, some long-term trends now under way portend future health care spending increases in the future. The most important trends are the aging of the U.S. population and the rapid development of new technology. Unless the gains from an improved payment system—significant as they are—exceed our expectations, these long-term forces will continue to pose difficult choices for the United States, as we are forced to choose between increasing the resources devoted to health care and limiting access to care and quality of care.

The proportion of our population sixty-five years of age and over is projected to rise from 11.3 percent in 1980 to an estimated 19.5 percent in the year 2025. Moreover, the population eighty-five years old and over (sometimes referred to as the "old-old") is projected to increase from about 2½ million people today, or about 1 percent of the population, to about 16 million people or 5 percent of the population in the year 2050 (See table 6-1). People in this age bracket

TABLE 6–1
GROWTH OF THE POPULATION AGED 65 AND OVER
IN RELATION TO TOTAL POPULATION, 1950–2050
(percent)

| Year | 65 and older | 65–74 years | 75–84 years | 85 years and over |
|------|------|------|------|------|
| 1950 | 8.1 | 5.6 | 2.2 | 0.4 |
| 1960 | 9.2 | 6.1 | 2.6 | 0.5 |
| 1970 | 9.8 | 6.1 | 3.0 | 0.7 |
| 1980 | 11.3 | 6.9 | 3.4 | 1.0 |
| 1990 | 12.7 | 7.2 | 4.1 | 1.4 |
| 2000 | 13.1 | 6.6 | 4.6 | 1.9 |
| 2010 | 13.9 | 7.2 | 4.3 | 2.4 |
| 2020 | 17.3 | 10.0 | 4.8 | 2.5 |
| 2030 | 21.1 | 11.3 | 6.9 | 2.9 |
| 2040 | 21.6 | 9.5 | 8.0 | 4.2 |
| 2050 | 21.7 | 9.7 | 6.8 | 5.2 |

SOURCES: U.S. Bureau of the Census, Decennial Censuses of Population 1900–1980 and Projections of the Populations of the United States: 1982–2050 (Advance Report); Current Population Reports, Series P-25, No. 922, October 1982.

require more health and social services than younger people. While there will also be more younger people in absolute terms, the ratio of older citizens to working-age citizens will rise beginning in the early part of the next century. For example, in 1900, there were about seven elderly persons for every hundred aged eighteen to sixty-four years. By 1982, there were nineteen elderly people per hundred working-age persons. By the year 2000, the ratio is projected to increase to twenty-one per hundred and, in 2050, will grow to thirty-eight per hundred.[1]

## The Health Sector of the Economy:
## Background and Recent Trends

Between 1964 and 1983, the average annual increase in total national health expenditures was 12.5 percent, as compared to an average annual increase in nominal GNP of 9.0 percent. Per capita spending for health care in constant dollars has increased about two and a half times since 1965, rising from $599 in 1965 to $1,580 in 1984.[2]

In 1965 health care was a $42 billion industry, and the government—federal, state, and local—financed 26.2 percent of this total. By 1984 the industry had grown to $387 billion, and the total government spending had risen to $160 billion. In 1980, total government spending as a percentage of national health expenditures reached a high point of 42.7 percent. Since then, government expenditures as a percentage of total national expenditures have been decreasing (see table 6-2).

The largest portion of health expenditures, 41 percent, is for hospital care. There are approximately 5,800 nonfederal, short-term general hospitals in the United States. Of these, 3,300 are nongovernmental not-for-profit, 760 are investor owned, and 1,700 are state and local government hospitals.

The second largest item of health care expenditures is for physician services, which account for another 19 percent of national health expenditures. There are now about half a million doctors in the United States. The supply of physicians is expected to grow 27 percent between 1981 and 1990 and 51 percent between 1981 and 2000.

These long-term trends in expenditures for health services, however, mask some recent developments that presage a significant deceleration in the rate of growth in health care spending. In 1984, for example, health care outlays grew by only 9.1 percent, the lowest rate of increase in many years. Similarly, outlays for Medicare and Medicaid, the government's programs for assisting the elderly and low-

TABLE 6–2
SELECTED MEASURES OF NATIONAL
HEALTH CARE EXPENDITURES, 1929–1984
(percent)

| Year | Total National Health Expenditures/ GNP | Public Expenditures/ Total Health Expenditures | Private Expenditures/ Total Health Expenditures |
|------|------|------|------|
| 1929 | 3.5 | 13.9 | 88.9 |
| 1950 | 4.4 | 26.8 | 72.4 |
| 1960 | 5.3 | 24.5 | 75.5 |
| 1965 | 6.1 | 26.2 | 73.8 |
| 1970 | 7.6 | 37.0 | 63.0 |
| 1975 | 8.6 | 42.5 | 57.5 |
| 1980 | 9.4 | 42.7 | 57.3 |
| 1981 | 9.7 | 42.6 | 57.5 |
| 1982 | 10.5 | 42.1 | 57.9 |
| 1983 | 10.7 | 41.7 | 58.1 |
| 1984 | 10.6 | 41.4 | 58.6 |

SOURCES: National Health Expenditures, *Health Care Financing Review* (Fall 1985), and "National Health Expenditures," *Health Care Financing Review* (Winter 1984).

income households, have begun to rise at a more manageable pace in recent years. For example, Medicare outlays rose fivefold between 1970 and 1980, from $7.5 billion to $36.8 billion. But, from 1982 to 1986, outlays rose by about 3 percent, from $52.4 billion to an estimated $68.6 billion (see table 6–3). Medicaid outlay increases also decelerated considerably in the mid-1980s from the pace of increase in the prior decade. This is not to argue that health care spending increases no longer constitute a problem, but rather that the magnitude of this problem has recently begun to diminish.

It is likely that the moderation in public spending for health care under the Medicare and Medicaid programs will continue in the near future, as more cost discipline is introduced into the programs and inflation remains at lower levels than rates that prevailed in the 1970s. In the longer term, however, other forces are likely to continue to drive up spending under Medicare and Medicaid, particularly the demographic trends and technological developments noted earlier. The aging of our population will affect both programs, as Medicare will be serving the acute medical care needs of a higher proportion of our population (if the eligibility age remains constant), and the growing Medicaid spending will rise with the growing demand for long-term care. Medicaid is the principal vehicle for government support of nursing home care.

The slowdown in health spending increases reflects not only the deceleration of inflation noted earlier, but also the decrease in the volume of hospital services provided. Hospital admissions fell by 1.5 million between 1983 and 1984, and the average length of stay edged downward from 7.0 days in 1983 to 6.6 days in 1984. In addition, the number of hospital employees has dropped. From 1960 to 1982, the number of full-time equivalent hospital personnel per 100 patients more than tripled, from 114 to 376. For the first time, in 1984, the

TABLE 6–3
GROWTH IN FEDERAL OUTLAYS FOR MEDICARE
AND MEDICAID, 1970–1987
(billions of dollars)

|          | 1970 | 1975 | 1980 | 1981 | 1982 | 1983 | 1984 | 1986ᵃ | 1987ᵃ |
|----------|------|------|------|------|------|------|------|-------|-------|
| Medicare | 7.5  | 16.3 | 36.8 | 44.7 | 52.4 | 58.8 | 64.6 | 68.6  | 70.2  |
| Medicaid | 3.0  | 7.9  | 14.5 | 17.3 | 18.0 | 19.3 | 20.9 | 24.6  | 24.7  |

a. Fiscal years, estimated.

SOURCES: Health Care Financing Administration and Office of Management and Budget, budget for fiscal year 1987.

number of full-time equivalent employees dropped 2.3 percent after rising 1.4 percent in 1983.[3]

Looking only at hospital use, however, can be misleading, as the decline in hospital use may be partially offset by a greater use of alternatives to hospital care such as nursing homes, doctors' office visits, hospices, and home health care. Nevertheless, the aggregate figures on health spending are decelerating, suggesting that the extra spending outside of hospitals does not fully offset the decline in inpatient hospital care spending.

The nation's physicians have also begun to feel the pinch. Increases in doctors' incomes have tapered off, at least in terms of available measures, which may not fully reflect earnings from nonpractice sources. Indeed, physician incomes actually fell slightly in real terms during the 1970s. Average real net income of physicians (in 1970 dollars) was $39,400 in 1981, or 4 percent *below* the level in 1971 ($43,400). In 1983 the current dollar average income of physicians was $106,000.[4] In part, the leveling of doctors' incomes in real terms reflects both the new cost-control measures introduced in the public and private sectors and the rising number of doctors relative to the population. In the year 2000, there are expected to be 260 doctors per 100,000 people, compared with 199 in 1981.[5] Some areas of the country are already experiencing a "doctor glut," with a ratio of physicians per 100,000 as high as 600.

It is important to note the probable relationship between trends in physician incomes and the tightening rein on the industry held in the hands of government officials and private sector decision makers. It used to be said of the health care industry that doctors controlled the health care market, not patients, and that they simply ordered tests, visits, and prescriptions to reach a target income. While debatable, it is doubtful that the system ever worked in just this fashion. Yet, it is true that with inherently cost-generating payment systems that rewarded more spending with more reimbursement, doctors could, to a large extent, call the tune.

Today's climate is different. Not only are there more doctors competing for a given number of patients, but also passive buyers have turned into tough bargainers. The market power of doctors has diminished and is being met with the strong market power of health care purchasers. Government, as payer of two-fifths of health care expenditures, is acting in ways that limit doctors' ability to generate income as they see fit, and employers are banding together in coalitions that enhance their ability to confront organized medicine effectively. At the same time, consumers are being required to seek "second opinions" and are becoming better educated about the dangers of overusing the health care system. Thus, trends in supply and demand are likely to continue eroding physician real incomes, or at least check any substantial increases in the foreseeable future.

## Basic Problems in Our Health Care System

Inefficiency Resulting from Faulty Reimbursement Systems and Regulation. In this section we focus on some of the basic problems with the way we have financed and subsidized health care in the United States. Subsequent sections examine the recent responses of the major actors in the system to these problems.

Many health care analysts have attributed the rapid growth of health care costs simply to the *growth* of health insurance. It is also a reflection, in part, of the *nature* of health insurance. It is not just insurance, per se, but the special relationship between the service providers—in this case, doctors, hospitals, and other health professionals—and the insurers who pay their claims that makes the difference.

The hallmark of traditional systems for paying doctors and hospitals has been a failure by the bill payers to distinguish adequately between cost-conscious and profligate providers of care. Long before the days of Medicare and Medicaid, Blue Cross, Blue Shield, and commercial health insurers were reimbursing health care providers on a cost-plus basis, a system that rewarded and underwrote the higher-cost providers and constituted a handicap for the innovative, cost-reducing provider. As long as the doctor who charged twice as much as his colleagues could pass his charges through, without question, to a third-party payer, the basic ingredient of cost discipline—and of a real market—was missing.

Medicare and Medicaid copied the payment systems developed in the private sector, ratifying and shoring up the prevailing fees in a community and offering no advantages to newly developing delivery systems with the potential to undercut the dominant cost structure. Until recently, both government programs and private insurance failed to install incentives for the cost-conscious use of health services. Government left intact the faulty payment system just described, which inflated the demand for health services at the same time it attempted to mask this flaw through regulatory controls on doctors, hospitals, and other providers of health care. The government fed these health care costs and utilization increases through an open-ended reimbursement system under Medicare and Medicaid and the open-ended, preferential tax treatment of employer contributions to private health insurance premiums.

In an effort to contain the excesses of its own policies, the federal government created an elaborate regulatory apparatus built along the lines of a public utility model of rate and entry controls. The rate controls consisted of various restrictions on allowable hospital revenue increases ranging from the formal wage-price controls of the early 1970s through the revenue caps called for under the 1982 Tax Equity and Fiscal Responsibility Act (TEFRA) legislation. The entry controls consisted of measures such as state certificate-of-need programs mandated by federal law, restrictive occupational licensure laws, and scope-of-practice limitations at the state level.

Three distressing features resulted from this paradox of both pumping up and capping the health care system. First, doctors, hospitals, and other health care providers were caught in a schizophrenic squeeze. Through the use of price controls, revenue caps, fixed budgets, and capital expansion controls, the government attempted to make the providers of care do *less* for patients while at the same time, through forces operating on the demand side, the government encouraged patients to get *more* things done in the medical system.

Second, patients were not discouraged from seeking unnecessary care and were not rewarded for seeking less expensive care. As a result, providers had no incentives to be efficient or to develop innovative, cost-effective patterns of care.

Third, the "control the providers" strategy made doctors and hospitals into scapegoats for the government's own inflationary policies. The "villain" mentality led policy makers to attack symptoms rather than causes.

The evidence suggests that the controls used in health care in the 1970s had little effect on spending. If the effects had been greater, of course, they would have been accompanied by undesirable side effects. Other studies have shown that the certificate-of-need regulation has had little or no effect on hospital capital expansion, while utilization review and rate regulation have had a positive, but rather limited impact in some regions and no discernible effect in other areas.[6]

The deceptive nature of regulation is that, even as the evidence mounts that it is not working, it may appear to be working as costs are temporarily buried or shifted among groups. For example, some states employ certain rigid limits on what they pay hospitals under Medicaid that saves the government some money. Hospitals, in turn, offset this shortfall through higher charges to private patients. Private health insurance premiums rise as that portion of care not reimbursed by Medicaid is charged to privately insured persons. Also, Medicaid discourages physicians from participating by limiting how much it pays physicians. Medicaid beneficiaries sometimes, then, receive nonemergency care in the emergency room at several times the cost of receiving care in a physician's office because relatively few physicians are willing to render care to those eligible for Medicaid. The same reaction could occur among physicians regarding Medicare eligibles, if Medicare continues to squeeze physician fees.

**Imbalance in Coverage.** In addition to the basic flaws in the way we have paid for health care, there is also an imbalance in the pattern of coverage across various types of health services and an inequity in the distribution of government subsidies. Our health care system covers some services very generously at the same time as other services are covered in a skimpy fashion or excluded altogether. And, too often the services that are poorly covered are either the ones performed in a lower-cost setting or the ones that are vital to good health and really a bargain from the viewpoint of cost-effectiveness.

Both government programs and many private insurance policies have underemphasized the prevention of disease by not providing sufficient benefits for screening and diagnostic services. While billions are spent for curing the disease after it occurs, the nation's bill payers have often scoffed at laying out small fractions of these amounts for prevention. Even though all preventive measures are not cost effective, smoking cessation, screening for cardiovascular disease, and treatment for hypertension can have a sizable return in terms of good health and lower expenditures.

There is also a bias in the system against financing care for long-term or chronic illnesses vis-à-vis acute or short-term care. Reimbursement stipulations tend to be overly generous in financing acute care but fall short in financing long-term care. To be eligible for any public assistance for institutional long-term care, a person has to become pauperized and, in some cases, endure the indignity of a waiting list. Elderly persons may even be charged large advance payments by long-term care institutions, since government payment rates are substantially below the market rates.

Moreover, nonmedical, custodial care, which may enable a person to remain at home rather than be cared for in a nursing home, is typically not covered by public programs. At the same time, as they deny coverage for home care or routine therapy for a seriously disabled patient, public programs are reimbursing up to 80 percent of a routine visit to the doctor and paying almost all the hospital bill.

**Inequitable Distribution of Public Subsidies.** In addition to the imbalanced nature of coverage under public and private health insurance programs, inequities also exist in public expenditures for health care.

201

Some people with no particular financial need, such as middle- and upper-income taxpayers, receive large subsidies through the exclusion from income tax of employer-paid health insurance while persons with inadequate resources are completely excluded from government programs.

The inequity in public spending for health care reflects fundamental inequities in the welfare and tax systems. The welfare system arbitrarily limits coverage to people who are categorically eligible on the basis of family and work status. For example, low-income households with two parents present, one of whom is working, are generally screened out of the Aid to Families with Dependent Children (AFDC) program and, hence, Medicaid. Even single-parent families headed by an adult who is working usually lose AFDC coverage after four months of work, as a result of changes introduced by Congress in 1981. These changes substantially tightened allowable deductions related to work expenses and limited the exclusion of one-third of earnings from "countable" income to four months. As a result of these changes, most low-wage workers have countable income that exceeds the thresholds established by states for the receipt of AFDC benefits. Moreover, the loss of AFDC coverage for low-wage workers often makes them ineligible for Medicaid, and many jobs of this type do not provide employee health benefits. Thus, these workers often lack health care coverage of any kind.

In fact, an estimated half of those who are uninsured at some point during the year (about 12 to 17 million people) are employed, but do not receive health benefits.[7] Many of these people would have difficulty affording a health insurance policy at nongroup rates.

In some states, lower-income people who are categorically eligible for AFDC and Medicaid but whose incomes are above the threshold for eligibility can be eligible for Medicaid after they "spend down" to the poverty threshold by incurring large health care expenses. Also, some states provide optional Medicaid coverage to people who have incomes low enough to qualify for public assistance, but who are excluded from regular coverage because of their work status or family configuration. But many states do not offer either of these extra provisions. As a result, there are sharp geographic inequities involved in public assistance for health care.

Subsidies to middle- and lower-income people remain intact even as eligibility has been restricted under the Medicaid program. Given the progressive nature of the income tax system, the subsidy associated with the full employee tax exclusion of the employer contribution to health insurance is worth more to workers with higher earnings.

## New Developments in the Finance System

Until this point we have been describing the health care finance system as it existed throughout most of the postwar period. In recent years, however, the system of paying for health care has been changing significantly, and in the mid-1980s the pace of change has accelerated dramatically. In the following sections we briefly describe the most important changes that are occurring and suggest ways in which recent innovations could be extended to achieve further improvements in the fairness and efficiency of our health care system.

**Medicare.** One of the most important changes in recent years is Medicare's new way of paying hospitals. The 1983 social security amendments directed the U.S. Department of Health and Human Services (HHS) to establish a prospective payment system for Medicare reimbursement of hospitals. In September 1983 the department began to implement a system of fixed, prospectively determined rates based on diagnostic-related groups, or DRGs. The new system establishes a separate rate of payment for each of 467 diagnoses, based on communitywide averages. Hospitals that hold down costs below these rates may retain the difference while hospitals whose costs exceed these rates must absorb the difference.

It is important to understand that this approach, whatever its drawbacks, is a dramatic departure from the old allowable cost payment system that was built on the existing cost base of every hospital, no matter how efficiently or inefficiently the hospitals used their resources. It was a giant step away from a public utility type of rate review process that determined if costs were really incurred and which of the costs fit within the "allowable base" and then paid those costs in full. Under the new system, hospitals that are high-cost relative to a community norm are squeezed, while those that beat that norm are rewarded.

Various adjustments are made to the communitywide average to allow for the special circumstances of various types of hospitals. Hospitals in a rural rather than an urban area receive adjustments, and teaching hospitals receive an extra payment to compensate them for some of the extra costs of training doctors. In addition, proposals are now under consideration to make further adjustments in the DRG payment rates to account for the differential burden of uncompensated care that hospitals in a given area bear.

In theory, these adjustments are designed to ensure that hospitals will be reimbursed for conditions "beyond their control," while at the same time holding them accountable for costs that are out of line for controllable reasons. In other words, a hospital that treats a more seriously ill mix of patients should not be compensated at the same rate as one that sees less severely ill patients.

The DRG system is to be updated annually for inflation and for technological change. Although there are methodologies available to perform these calculations, they are also subject to fiscal and political pressures. The temptation to make upward adjustments smaller than those called for by the statistical measurements in order to hold down federal spending will be strong. This has already occurred, as the DRG rates initially implemented were lowered in September 1984 and increased by only 1 percent a year later. The effect of the Gramm-Rudman-Hollings legislation will most likely result in a further racheting down of rates for the foreseeable future.

Thus, there are a number of problems with the new approach despite its obvious superiority over the old system. The system will work only if the adjustments described above prove to be a reasonably accurate proxy for a market price and if the rates are adjusted fairly over time to reflect the cost of providing a given service. Furthermore, as complex as the new system is, it is still incomplete as a cost-control measure because it sets prospectively determined rates once a patient is in a hospital but does not give physicians an incentive to be cautious about admitting patients to the hospital.

One criticism of DRGs is that they are just another form of government rate controls. While there is some truth to this assertion, it is an overstatement. DRGs do have the defects of any system based on average-cost pricing, and the federal determination of the payment levels is subject to a complicated, bureaucratic process. The new system, however, is less a price-control system than some previous proposals by virtue of allowing private payers to establish their own rates of payment without any government guidelines. Mandatory all-payer rate-setting mechanisms employed in some states do not have this virtue. Also, by establishing payment norms for each illness, however crudely, the new system does reward cost reductions and penalize excessive costs, which cannot be said of the old "allowable cost" system.

Another step toward an improved payment system under Medicare involves the prospective payment of competitive medical plans such as health maintenance organizations (HMOs). Beginning in January 1985 the federal government began paying competitive medical plans 95 percent of the average cost in an area of serving Medicare patients. After calculating an average cost adjusted for various factors, Medicare pays, in advance, the amount to qualifying plans.

Under this new arrangement, Medicare shares the savings associated with lower costs of these alternative health plans with Medicare enrollees. The government enjoys the 5-percentage-point savings realized by paying only 95 percent of the areawide "norm." Beneficiaries receive extra benefits from the HMOs, which must offer such added coverage in an amount equal to the extent to which their costs are lower than 95 percent of the overall average. It would be preferable to allow HMOs the flexibility either to add such extra benefits as eyeglasses or dental care (not covered by Medicare) or to reinvest some of the cost savings by modernizing facilities, hiring more specialized or highly trained physicians, or providing beneficiaries with cash rebates.

One way to move beyond these two policy changes toward a more fully competitive Medicare payment system is a voucher plan. The new approach to paying HMOs just described is a step in this direction, but a voucher approach would not limit consumer choice to plans like HMOs. Other health plans that combine the features of HMOs and fee-for-service could also join the competition.

Under the voucher approach, Medicare would make a fixed payment on behalf of each beneficiary to the health plan that the beneficiary selects from a pool of qualifying plans. The government could screen these plans to ensure that they compete mainly on price, and not by offering unduly skimpy coverage. Beneficiaries selecting a plan with a premium above the government payment, which might be set in line with the cost of a cost-effective plan in the area, would have to add the difference. Similarly, those choosing a plan with a premium below the voucher amount would receive a rebate. The voucher payment would be adjusted for age (65–69, 70–74, etc.), sex, and region and would be updated annually for inflation.

Critics of this approach have contended that it would reward the healthier elderly and penalize those with higher expected health outlays. It is feared that the healthier elderly will select HMOs or other alternative health plans while the "poor risks" join the more traditional plans. Critics also fear that the voucher amount would not be set or updated in a fair way, but would be used to ratchet down Medicare spending. The Medicare beneficiary would be more directly burdened by fiscal pressure, whereas when payments are made to providers the fiscal pressure is more directly borne by them. Moreover, trying to set the level of a voucher to reflect the variations in expected health care outlays among the elderly would be difficult.

Advocates of the voucher claim that such problems as adverse selection could be limited by a minimum benefit requirement, open enrollment, and the careful screening of plans. They also argue that by allowing Medicare beneficiaries to select among a variety of alternatives, a voucher would permit them to choose plans that have some of the cost-control features of HMOs, but still retain aspects of fee-for-service models that some patients prefer. Medicare could reap the savings over time from the more wide-open competition among health plans for enrollees. The competition would force plans with open-ended utilization of the health care system to install a better system for monitoring claims and preauthorizing the use of high-cost services.

**Medicaid.** Medicaid expenditures have been the fastest-growing item in many states' budgets. States have responded, as the federal government has done with Medicare, by holding down payments to hospitals and physicians, imposing restrictions on benefits, tightening eligibility criteria, and setting limits on rates.

These measures, however, do not address some of the underlying forces that drive the growth in expenditures. Instead, as benefits and eligibility are restricted, costs are shifted onto patients who forgo or delay receiving care. Other costs are shifted onto those providers who render care not covered by Medicaid. Counties, which in many states are the providers of last resort, also bear some burden as states limit the scope of their programs. Furthermore, as states limit fees paid to physicians, they deter providers from caring for Medicaid beneficiaries. Decreasing physician participation requires patients to seek alternative and more expensive care in hospital outpatient departments and emergency rooms. Hence, short-term measures to stave off budget crises limit Medicaid beneficiaries' access to providers and lead to higher expenditures in the long run.

Some states have recognized the need to redress the Medicaid incentive structure, which leads to overspending, and to encourage providers and patients to use health care resources more cost effectively. Several states and counties have changed the way they organize the delivery and financing of health care for at least a portion of their Medicaid beneficiaries. Some have contracted with HMOs to render care to beneficiaries. But in areas where there are no HMOs or where HMOs do not want to participate in Medicaid, states and counties are setting up programs that incorporate some of the features of HMOs.

For example, in Santa Barbara County, California, and in Missouri, Medicaid beneficiaries may choose a solo practice physician or a physician in a community health clinic to serve as primary provider. The physician oversees all the care the beneficiary requires, either providing the care directly or referring the patient to the appropriate physician. The most important feature of these programs is the ability of the physician to "manage" a patient's care. At a minimum, this approach discourages patients from physician shopping and self-referral.

By controlling unnecessary use of health care services, resources are freed up and can be used to offer physicians an extra financial benefit. In some programs, physicians may also be at some minimal financial risk as a means to encourage them to provide cost-effective care. Medicaid eligibles benefit since they have a regular point of access to the health care system, a feature that some do not have because of the low physician participation rate in many communities.

Other states have recognized the need to redress the gaps in coverage in the Medicaid program. Currently only about half of those persons with incomes below the federal government's poverty threshold are eligible for Medicaid. In Tennessee, for example, a four-person family can qualify for Medicaid only if its income is less than 35 percent of the federal poverty level.

Several states are trying to ease Medicaid eligibility requirements and expand benefits to fill in some of the gaps in coverage. They have begun to realize that the lack of coverage may actually increase costs for state- and county-funded programs. Hence, some states are considering discrete, limited additions to Medicaid, which are partially funded by the federal match.

Florida, for example, has recently expanded its Medicaid program to include more persons whose incomes are less than the poverty level. Some states are targeting extensions of their programs to children and pregnant women. On the federal level, the 1984 Deficit Reduction Act extended Medicaid coverage to first-time pregnant women and to children up to age five. These trends are promising; yet as health care providers become increasingly competitive and as payers no longer subsidize care rendered to the poor, many gaps in coverage among those with below-poverty incomes remain.

Changing the finance and delivery arrangements to control expenditures for acute care is, however, only part of the states' battle with growing Medicaid expenditures. Medicaid payments for long-term care, as a portion of total Medicaid expenditures, rose from 34.9 percent in 1973 to 42.5 percent in 1980. In 1984 about 50 percent of Medicaid expenditures were allocated for long-term care. Meanwhile, the portion of total Medicaid payments for inpatient hospital services decreased from 30.8 percent to 26.9 percent during the same period. Also, physician payments decreased as a portion of total expenditures from 10.7 percent to 8 percent.[8] Hence, states' efforts to control hospital and physician expenditures are addressing a decreasing portion of total Medicaid spending.

States have adopted a variety of approaches for controlling their expenditures for long-term care for the elderly. Both price and supply constraints have been used. First, some states have placed controls on Medicaid's nursing home reimbursement rates. This pressure has discouraged nursing homes from admitting Medicaid patients, when they can otherwise have private paying patients at a higher reimbursement rate. Since most nursing homes are proprietary, the low reimbursement rates also discourage investors from investing in nursing homes. In this way, states constrain the supply of nursing home beds for which they would have to pay.

Second, some states like Wisconsin, which have a large older population, have imposed moratoriums on nursing home construction. Even if reimbursement rates were sufficient to attract capital, entry controls would preclude investment in nursing homes. These constraints account for the average nationwide occupancy rate of nursing homes of 91 percent.

States also have had the incentive to keep Medicaid patients who are eligible for Medicare as well in hospitals rather than in nursing homes, because under Medicare the federal government assumes a larger portion of a patient's hospital expenditures. Otherwise, if the patient were in a nursing home, the state would have to pay anywhere from 22 to 50 percent of the cost, depending on the federal-state matching rate. These incentives account for the large number of days that some patients spend in the hospital unnecessarily. Hence, states' entry controls help maintain a bottleneck at the end of a patient's hospital stay. They also preclude patients from being cared for in nursing homes where payment rates are much lower than hospital rates.

Some states have taken steps in the Medicaid program to encourage alternatives to hospital and nursing home care for elderly persons. Oregon, for example, is "channeling" long-term care patients to the most appropriate and cost-effective setting. Mathematica Policy Research is conducting a multiyear longitudinal study of the effectiveness of this channeling approach. States are also attempting to transfer seriously disabled children from institutional settings to their homes, which often requires a waiver from the federal government to permit Medicaid reimbursement of home care. Similarly, Medicare is now paying for hospice care as an alternative to institutional care. Together, these measures begin to address the institutional bias in reimbursement policies.

The fastest-growing part of Medicaid expenditures, however, is for long-term care for the mentally retarded. The reason for this growth is that states have gradually deinstitutionalized the mentally retarded from their own facilities, for which they pay 100 percent of the cost. Many of these patients are now in nonstate facilities where the federal government pays a portion of the expenditures under the Medicaid matching formula. States have therefore tried to control their expenditures for the mentally retarded, but in doing so have shifted a portion of their costs onto the Medicaid program and the federal government.

**Private Sector Reforms.** The public sector is not the only arena in which the delivery and financing of care are undergoing change. Changes are being made in the private sector, driven by employers' concern with the rising cost of health care coverage.[9] Employers are offering more choices of health plans to employees and steering them toward the more cost-effective plans; they are redesigning benefits within health plans to encourage the delivery of care to their workers in the lowest-cost safe setting; some are paying more attention to worker safety, health promotion, and disease prevention, in addition to encouraging rehabilitation and return to work by those with extended health-related absences; they are introducing more employee cost sharing and taking a second look at promises made to their retirees who remain in the company health plan; and they are compiling data on the charges and practice patterns of providers to guide their employees toward the most cost-conscious doctors and hospitals in the community.

A number of the largest companies are self-insuring for at least a major portion of their employees' health expenses. By self-insuring, employers avoid state regulations that mandate benefits in insurance packages and premium taxes imposed on commercial insurers. The Employee Retirement and Income Security Act (ERISA) preempts states from extending fiduciary and other requirements imposed on third-party payers to self-insured employers managing health and welfare funds.

Unions are also more active now in efforts to contain health care costs. These activities include a growing interest in mandatory second opinion programs for surgery, negotiation of doctors' charges that appear to be out of line, bulk purchasing of pharmaceuticals, and programs that allow workers to share in the savings when they discover overcharges on their medical bills.

Employers and unions are also redesigning benefits to encourage cost-effective care. Employers are increasingly reimbursing outpatient care more generously and, at the same time, introducing various checks on the use of the relatively more expensive inpatient care. A recent survey of employers conducted by Louis Harris & Associates for the Equitable Life Assurance Society found that 70 percent of employers report changing their health care plans in the past three years. The most frequent change was the introduction of second opinion programs.[10]

Some employers are mandating the use of second opinions before nonemergency surgery can be performed and reimbursed under the employer's health benefit plan. Other employers allow employees to decide whether they wish to obtain a second opinion, but they set the reimbursement rules in favor of using this option. For example, a company plan might pay 100 percent of an elective surgical procedure if a second opinion is sought and it confirms the initial recommendation for surgery, but only 80 percent or less of the bill if the employee chooses not to obtain the second opinion.

Similar incentives are being adopted regarding the setting in which care is delivered. Traditionally, health plans would pay 100 percent of the bill for surgery performed in a hospital and less than full amounts for the same procedure in a less expensive outpatient setting. This encouraged the patient to use the high-cost alternative because it was that choice that cost him nothing. Currently, a number of health plans are reversing these incentives and are paying a higher proportion of the tab for surgical procedures performed in a free-standing "surgicenter" or a doctor's office. Of course, these incentives are only appropriate for surgical procedures that can be safely done in either a hospital or an outpatient setting.

Some employers are also introducing wellness programs and disease prevention programs for their employees. They are taking a greater interest in the rehabilitation of disabled or injured workers. In short, the business community is beginning to view health care cost management as more than effective claims monitoring. They are taking a more comprehensive view of health, one that includes prevention as well as cure, disabled as well as healthy workers, and retirees as well as active workers.

### The Effect of Changing Public and Private Sector Purchasing Policies on the Structure of the Health Care Sector

The previous section described the rapidly changing purchasing patterns of both federal and state governments and the nation's employer community. We have traced the beginnings of what appears to be a steady movement away from the old "blank check" methods of paying doctors and hospitals toward payment systems that set fixed budgets and gear reimbursement to the charges and practice patterns of the more cost-conscious providers of health care in the community.

In this section we analyze the changes in the systems of delivering health care that are accompanying, and in many cases responding to, the new payment systems. How are the nature and structure of the health care market changing as the bill payers take a tougher line on the costs that they will reimburse?

Health care markets, like other markets, can work properly only if some of the basic ingredients of competition are included in the recipe. Perhaps the most crucial ingredient is reliable information in a usable form, and the following section will discuss efforts under way to make such information available.

**Information.** Traditional payment systems in health care have required very little information about provider charges for the same service, variations across a community in hospital admission rates, or length of stay for the same illness. These comparisons, in one sense, simply did not matter, as most payers were reimbursing some stipulated percentage of costs, ex post, and that percentage was the same for all providers. Thus, after a determination of what cost items were to be included in the allowable cost base, providers had only to submit and document their allowable costs to be paid. Simply stated, comparisons did not matter in this environment. The goal of the game for providers was to get as many items of cost (including common costs or overhead) into the allowable cost base, while the objective of the bill payers was to exclude such items as research and development, bad debts, or the lawn and maintenance budget from the cost base. Then, in the fashion of public utility regulation, allowable costs were filed and reimbursed. This habit, along with entry controls that blocked out innovative providers, wove a protective cocoon around traditional providers.

As the goals of the game are changing, so are the information requirements. As Medicare, Medicaid, and employers shift from the allowable cost game to prospective budgeting and establish "allowable" costs on the basis of the most cost-effective providers in the community, there is a corresponding need for information systems that permit and facilitate cross-provider comparisons of the price and quantity of health care services.

Until recently the major payers of health care costs—federal and state governments and employers—paid little attention to the fact that the cost for a given day in the hospital can vary by hundreds of dollars. For example, the cost of a semiprivate hospital room and board in suburban Washington, D.C., can range from $176 to $452, depending on whether the hospital is a teaching hospital that tends to render care to patients with complicated illnesses or a hospital that handles more routine cases.[11] Yet, now that payers have a vested interest in

211

controlling health expenditures, they are paying for information that will help them determine the lower-cost providers of care.

The actions of a group of employers in Iowa exemplify the trend toward development of new data bases. Interested in acquiring information on the cost of care in their state, they encouraged the governor to establish an organization for collection and analysis of information on hospitals and physicians. Information on hospitals' charges, the number of admissions for different diagnoses, and the length of a patient's stay is collected. With this information, employers are better equipped to bring pressure on providers to render cost-effective care.[12]

Until recently, purchasers paid little attention not only to variations in the cost of services, but also to variations in the kinds of services rendered to treat a given diagnosis. Health researchers have documented some of the variations in the way different physicians treat patients with a certain illness. For example, a comparison of two communities in Maine showed that hysterectomies were performed in one community at a rate such that 70 percent of the women would have had one by the time they reached age seventy. In a neighboring community, 25 percent of the women would have had a hysterectomy by the time they reached age seventy. The study concluded that no medical reasons explain the difference in the rates of surgery. Rather, they show that physicians' responses to a given diagnosis vary tremendously, based on community standards and the way physicians are trained. The extra cost associated with the higher rate of hysterectomies in the first community exceeded $2 million in one year.[13]

Payers are also interested in the quality of care rendered by providers. Although the quality of patient care is difficult to define, employers, states, and Medicare administrators are interested in having some indicators of quality of care. For example, payers have recognized that those hospitals in which a certain procedure is performed more frequently have lower mortality rates. Hence, payers are interested in determining the number of procedures performed in a given year at different hospitals.

The Department of Health and Human Services has recently issued new regulations that give the public access to statistics that offer some indication of the quality of patient care in hospitals.[14] For example, prospective patients and payers can have access to information on mortality rates for certain procedures, the frequency with which a given procedure is performed, the average length of stay, infection rates, and the cost of different procedures. Some concern does exist that the information could be distorted by simplistic analysis. For example, some hospitals may have higher mortality rates because they treat sicker patients, not because their health professionals are less skilled.

The disclosure of information on the health care market will have a tremendous impact on hospitals. Those hospitals that perform certain procedures infrequently may discontinue those procedures and specialize in others. This specialization may lead to greater regionalization of some health services, like trauma centers, burn units, and open-heart surgery centers.

While there is a trend toward specialization in hospital care, there are limits to the extent of specialization and regionalization desirable. If efficiency measures are taken to an extreme, some areas may be without some services. Hence, there may be a trade-off between efficiency considerations and access to certain services.

**Marketing and Advertising.** Until recently, hospitals did very little marketing and advertising. One reason is that physicians, rather than patients, chose the hospital where care would be provided. Yet, as consumers have become more health and cost conscious, they are participating more in the selection of the hospital. Hence, hospitals have to attract prospective patients as well as their physicians. To do this, some hospitals have established "guest relations" programs. A favorable antitrust climate has permitted advertising outreach programs that may have been proscribed in years past.

Other marketing strategies aimed at prospective patients include targeting specific population groups. Urban hospitals, for example, may try to attract suburban residents who are likely to be privately insured. These patients offer some financial stability to a hospital that may serve a large number of patients who do not have the means to pay for their care.

Already, some hospitals are contracting with organizations that market their physicians with admitting privileges. "Dial-a-Doc" services offer prospective patients information on the physicians' training, specialty, office hours, and fees. In this way, hospitals increase the number of patients their physicians can admit and, therefore, their occupancy rates.

Some hospital systems are developing campus-like facilities that feature an entire continuum of care for the elderly who may be less able to travel distances to receive care. Some may waive Medicare cost-sharing requirements. Other hospitals offer medical credit cards, extended hours, and house calls, which may appeal to families with two working parents.

Few hospitals advertise the price of their services. The few surveys performed on patients' choice of hospitals indicate that cost is not an

213

important factor. This is not surprising since many patients have third-party insurance to cover the cost of hospital care. Hence, there is little need for the patient to comparison shop for hospital care on the basis of price. Moreover, patients have little information on prices to do comparison shopping. The disclosure requirements imposed by DHHS should make more cost data available.

**Reorganization of Delivery and Financing.** The pressure from the public and private sectors to control expenditures and disclose information on cost and quality requires providers to rethink the manner in which they organize the provision of care. It also changes the way patients use the health care system. Providers are responding to these pressures by integrating the delivery and financing of health care services. The major components in the health care system include hospitals and other health facilities, insurers, and physicians and alternative delivery systems. Some of these components have joined in varying contractual arrangements to form an integrated health care system.

*Hospitals.* The nation's hospitals are undergoing tremendous reorganization. Approximately one-third of the hospitals have formed multihospital systems to take advantage of bulk purchasing of supplies and insurance. Motivating the horizontal integration and the development of multihospital systems is the access to capital such arrangements can bring to capital-poor hospitals, and access to patients and revenues. In contrast to the 1940s and 1950s when hospitals could receive federal funding under the Hill-Burton program, they must now seek capital for renovation and construction from private sources. In the case of proprietary hospitals, their access to private capital markets has given them powerful clout.

Moreover, hospitals are vertically integrating as they develop a range of prehospital and posthospital services, including ambulatory care and diagnostic services, which serve as a source of patients and revenues for in-hospital care. For posthospital care, hospitals are establishing or linking up with existing nursing homes, home health facilities, rehabilitation centers, and hospices. Eventually, hospitals will become places of care only for acutely ill patients. With vertical integration, the hospital can separate health care services to avoid having to add expensive inpatient hospital overhead costs onto outpatient care. Primary care can be provided, for example, at rates competitive with primary care providers in the community who do not bear a portion of hospital overhead in their charges to patients.

Hospitals are exploring other possibilities for vertical integration. The foiled attempt by Hospital Corporation of America (HCA), a large for-profit hospital chain, to acquire American Hospital Supply, one of the largest distributors of hospital equipment, is an example of possible combinations in the health sector. As such mergers occur, some clear guidance on antitrust should permit combinations that do not hinder competition while discouraging combinations that thwart competition.

*Insurers.* A second component of the health care system, the commercial insurers and Blue Cross and Blue Shield, are now performing more entrepreneurial rather than simply administrative functions. Traditionally, health insurers have distributed risk over beneficiaries and served as intermediaries between the patient and provider. They did little to mitigate the problem of "moral hazard" whereby patients use more medical services than they would use if they were paying for care out of pocket.

Insurers now are being pressured by employers and other payers to become more aggressive actors. Some are offering health insurance packages that incorporate measures to control unnecessary use of health care services, such as requiring that certain procedures be performed on an outpatient basis if the patient's health would not be adversely affected. Other insurers are negotiating discount rates with hospitals and physicians in return for giving those providers a guaranteed volume of potential patients. The insurers can then offer employers a reduced premium on the condition that employees use the providers selected by the insurer.

Hospital systems, whose objective is to ensure a flow of patients for their facilities, are also entering the business of insurance. By offering insurance packages to employers at rates below those offered by other insurers, the hospitals can increase their patient volume. Moreover, revenue from insurance premiums guarantees a substantial cash flow. For example, HCA, with more than 63,000 beds in the United States and abroad, is beginning to market a variety of insurance arrangements. These include an HMO, a traditional health insurance plan, a self-funded plan for employers with adequate cash flow, and a preferred provider organization. They will be offered to employees in the sixteen major markets where HCA has most of its facilities.

*Physicians.* Physicians are responding to these pressures, as well as competition from their growing numbers, by organizing themselves in a variety of configurations. Increasingly, physicians are moving away from the solo practice provider model to the organized delivery system model. Some physicians are forming groups of "preferred providers" and marketing themselves at cut rates to insurers or, in some cases, directly to employers or unions.

Hospitals are increasingly relying on physicians to attract patients and, hence, increase revenues. The move toward hospitals' building office space for physicians as part of their "campus" facilities reflects hospitals' efforts to cultivate relationships with physicians.

*Alternative Delivery Systems.* Alternative delivery systems include a variety of models, such as HMOs, primary care networks, and preferred provider organizations. Each of these models has some features in common. First, they receive premiums in return for providing or arranging for all patients' services. The systems operate within a fixed budget, and providers have incentive to use resources judiciously. They can exercise management control over both quality and cost. Second, patients enrolled in alternative delivery systems accept a limited choice of doctors in return for comprehensive services at no or minimal out-of-pocket costs. Third, physicians may be salaried or may receive a per capita payment plus a portion of the program's net income.

HMOs, as one model of an alternative delivery system, were given impetus in 1973 with the federal HMO act that offered funds for HMO market surveys and development. The act also mandated certain requirements, including risk reserves, and required employers with more than twenty-five employees to offer an HMO option to their workers if the community had any HMOs. Yet now that HMOs have gained a stable foothold in health care delivery, Congress may repeal the act.

In 1973, thirty-three HMOs served 3 million enrollees. In 1984, 306 HMOs served 15 million people, about 7 percent of the total insured population (see table 6–4). From December 1983 to December 1984, HMOs experienced record-breaking growth. The number of HMOs increased 16.2 percent and the number of enrollees increased 22.4 percent. All states but seven have at least one HMO, although

TABLE 6–4
SUMMARY OF HMO GROWTH, 1981–1984

|  | June 1981 | June 1982 | June 1983 | June 1984 |
|---|---|---|---|---|
| Total number of HMOs | 243 | 265 | 280 | 306 |
| Number of new HMOs | 20 | 38 | 24 | 40 |
| Total enrollment (in millions) | 10.2 | 10.8 | 12.4 | 15.1 |

SOURCE: 1984 National HMO Census, Interstudy.

a few states account for a substantial portion of HMO enrollees. California, Wisconsin, Florida, and Massachusetts have more than a quarter of all HMOs.[15] This rate of growth may decelerate as some employees perceive that HMOs may not ease employee health benefit expenditures as traditional health insurance plans become more price competitive.

The increase in the enrollment is accounted for by Medicare and Medicaid and by private payers wanting to stabilize health expenditures. In 1984, Medicare beneficiaries accounted for 4.4 percent of all HMO enrollees. This figure will increase since the new HMO payment plan under Medicare, described earlier, encourages HMOs to enroll Medicare beneficiaries. Only about 2 percent of HMO enrollment consists of Medicaid beneficiaries, although this figure represents a 35 percent increase from 1983 to 1984.

Two evident trends in the HMO market mirror trends in the overall health sector. As HMOs have grown larger and the level of capital investment in HMOs has increased, multistate HMO firms have been developed. Multistate firms are characterized by networks of HMOs often affiliated by owernship or management. Currently, there are fourteen major chains in the United States representing for-profit and not-for-profit HMOs. The second trend in HMOs is not-for-profit HMOs converting to for-profit status. While for-profit HMOs were rare in the mid-1970s, almost sixty HMOs—about one-fifth of the total—currently operate on a for-profit basis.

HMOs are not the only model of alternative delivery systems. A primary care network (PCN) is another model that has been widely used in the Medicaid program and in the private sector as an alternative to HMOs. PCNs have several common characteristics. Primary care, solo practice physicians serve as "managers" and agree to provide all services and arrange referrals. This is in contrast to some HMOs, which hire their own physicians. In the PCN model, physicians continue to practice in a private office. Second, beneficiaries choose a physician in the network and must pay for any care they receive outside the network. Third, a management organization oversees the working of the PCN by reviewing providers' use of services for cost effectiveness and monitors the quality of patient care. Whereas in an HMO model these functions would be performed by the internal management, in PCNs the managing entity may be the state or a county-designated local authority. Fourth, an account is set up for each participating physician with a fixed payment made for each enrolled patient. Bills for all referral services are debited to the account, and physicians share any surplus or deficit with the entity managing the PCN.

The growth of PCNs has been rapid in recent years. Between 1981 and 1984, eighteen state Medicaid programs initiated PCNs with more than 350,000 enrollees. In addition, thirteen different projects designed to develop PCNs have been sponsored by the Robert Wood Johnson Foundation. PCNs are an attractive model since, unlike HMOs, they can be started with a minimum of investment and disruption of established practice patterns. They can also be tied to existing group insurance arrangements.

*Substitution Effects.* HMOs, PCNs, and other alternative delivery systems embrace the efficiencies of substituting care rendered in lower-cost settings for care in higher-cost settings. Medicare, which now reimburses for home health care visits without a prior hospital stay, recognizes the efficiencies of lower-cost settings. Alternatively, Medicare would be paying for more expensive care in hospitals or nursing homes for a rapidly growing elderly population when patients could be otherwise treated at home.

The recent surge in proprietary and not-for-profit home health care agencies is, in part, a consequence of Medicare's DRG payments, which encourage substitution of home care for hospital care. In 1983, Medicare expenditures for home health services grew 30 percent over 1982. Where the substitution of home care for hospital care can be desirable for health and financial reasons, there is concern that home care services will become an added benefit rather than a substitute for more expensive care.

Also, home care services are more readily available as technology is adapted to the home environment. For example, specially made beds for patients with tecubitus, or skin breakdowns, are available for patients who are then able to remain at home rather than in a hospital or skilled nursing facility. The technology for renal dialysis at home is also available as a substitute for hospital-based dialysis.

A key to encouraging providers to use cost-effective technology in home settings, however, is whether payers offer incentives to providers to use cost-effective technology. Reimbursement policy under Medicare, which pays for services to all renal dialysis patients on a fee-for-service basis, has for many years offered little incentive for providers and patients to use available technology in the home.

In addition to home care, outpatient care can serve as a cost-effective substitute for inpatient care. Between 1979 and 1983, the volume of outpatient surgery procedures rose 77 percent. Currently, there are 249 free-standing surgical centers in the United States, twice the number in 1980. Some observers project that this number will increase to 600 in 1988.[16]

The major attraction of outpatient centers is that their charges average less than 55 percent of hospital rates. Generally, they have a faster admitting process and conduct fewer lab tests. The cost saving associated with outpatient care partially accounts for the 7.4 percent decrease in hospital admissions and the 22 percent drop in the average number of inpatient days for federal workers in the Blue Cross-Blue Shield plan.

Other insurers are responding to the pressure from their paying customers by encouraging their subscribers to use outpatient services. Some plans cover 80 percent of inpatient care and 100 percent of outpatient services in cases where the procedure can be safely performed on an outpatient basis. While these settings offer lower-cost services, free-standing surgical centers do not have overhead associated with emergency or other services that patients may need during or after outpatient care.

## Ongoing Reform

The "bottom line" mentality increasingly adopted by employers and government agencies in paying for health care is shaking up the market in a number of favorable ways. It is important to observe, however, that these events also produce some casualties. While the traditional systems shielded certain inefficient medical practices, it also shielded certain "services" that were buried in the cost base. For example, the costs of training doctors at teaching hospitals and the costs of providing indigent care for the poor who are ineligible for Medicaid were typically imbedded in the bills paid by Blue Cross and commercial insurance carriers. Medicare, and to some extent Blue Cross, would use their market power to exclude some of these overhead items from their cost base. In general, however, while costs were shifted around among payers based on relative market power, cross-subsidies enabled the cost of training physicians and providing health care services to the uninsured poor to be reimbursed.

In the new environment, the desire of bill payers, including self-insured employers, to escape these "extra" charges has been heightened. As those bearing the cross-subsidies recoil at the competitive disadvantage they create, there is a tendency for some of these common costs to go unreimbursed. As this occurs, the capacity of a hospital to continue to provide care to the uninsured poor or to offer what amounts to equally uncompensated training costs is eroded. Hospitals accepting nonpaying patients are handicapped in competing with those who do not, and thus the objective is to shun such patients or steer them to others. Thus, as Professor Uwe Reinhardt has observed, we are now beginning to shift patients instead of costs.

From 1980 to 1982, a small number of hospitals were accepting a disproportionately large share of patients who were uninsured and denied care elsewhere. Public hospitals increased their volume of free care 5.6 percent while a few private urban hospitals increased their volume of free care 6.7 percent.[17] This increase in volume could be attributed, in part, to persons losing health insurance during the period of high unemployment in the early 1980s, rather than to a competitive marketplace. More recently, however, anecdotal evidence indicates that hospitals, under pressure from the marketplace, are increasingly "dumping" uninsured patients onto public hospitals and certain private hospitals committed to serving the uninsured.

The challenge facing the health care industry today is to devise new, more efficient ways of subsidizing the training of doctors and care for the poor. It is tempting but foolhardy to return to the old, inefficient ways of paying for care even though they brought with them the side benefit of covering the cost of care rendered to the uninsured. But to ignore the dislocations and hardship (as well as the undervaluing of the future that accompanies a reduction in research or training) involved with a more sensible payment strategy is also unfair and imprudent. An adequate safety net to assume access for those who cannot afford basic health care services is a necessary complement to a movement toward a more efficient health care system.

So that these direct subsidies for indigent care can be financed, health care benefits provided by government could be targeted more directly to those in need. At the same time that a large segment of the poor are without any health care coverage, many Americans with substantial means receive large government subsidies through tax preferences and direct government expenditure programs. Capping these subsidies or varying the contributions that recipients of government-provided insurance make given their financial resources can help to redistribute a given amount of public health care dollars fairly.

It would also be sensible to make government assistance more neutral regarding the type of health services covered. In practice, this means to redesign public benefits in a way that provides protection against any type of catastrophic illness expense—regardless of whether it is for heroic surgical measures provided in a hospital or chronic illness and custodial outlays associated with long-term care. The additional coverage for long-term care would be financed for the most part by greater "front-end" contributions by patients, scaled to their ability to pay. In other words, the combined Medicare and Medicaid programs would be based on the standard principles of risk and insurance more than they are at present; people would pay a portion of routine expenses out-of-pocket according to their income but would be fully protected from unforeseen and unusual outlays for medical care.

The public sector safety net should also be supplemented more than it is currently with a combination of private saving and private insurance. A variety of private financing mechanisms—including insurance for long-term care, reverse annuity mortgages, IRA accounts and the like, and employer-provided pensions—can play some role in helping to meet the medical bills of the elderly.

In the future, health care expenditures will continue to grow as a percentage of GNP, accelerated by the aging of the population. These trends could be ameliorated somewhat by continued pressure on the part of private and public sector payers. It will also be contingent upon the degree to which existing gaps in the safety net are filled.

# Notes

1. *Aging America: Trends and Projections*, U.S. Senate Special Committee on Aging in conjunction with the American Association of Retired Persons, 1984, p. 18.

2. *Economic Report of the President, 1985*, p. 133.

3. *Statistical Abstracts of the United States, 1984*, U.S. Department of Commerce, Bureau of the Census, p. 106.

4. American Medical Association, *Profile of Medical Practice 1981*, Chicago, 1982; American Medical Association, *Journal of American Medical Association*, vol. 244; No. 22 (December 5, 1980); American Medical Association, *SMS Report*, vol. 1, no. 5 (June 1982).

5. *Projections of Physician Supply in the U.S.*, U.S. Department of Health and Human Services, Public Health Service, March 1985, p. 18.

6. Frank Sloan, "Rate Regulation as a Strategy for Hospital Cost Control: Evidence from the Last Decade," *Milbank Memorial Fund Quarterly, Health and Society*, vol. 61 (Spring 1983), pp. 195–217.

7. Gail Wilensky, "Uncompensated Hospital Care: Targeting Providers or Individuals," adapted from a paper presented at a symposium entitled, "Uncompensated Hospital Care: Defining Rights and Assigning Responsibilities," Vanderbilt University, April 6–7, 1984, p. 4.

8. Darwin Sawyer, Martin Ruther, Aileen Pagan-Berlucci, and Donald Muse, *The Medicare and Medicaid Data Book*, 1983, U.S. Department of Health and Human Services, p. 26.

9. See Sean Sullivan, *Managing Health Care Costs* (Washington, D.C.: American Enterprise Institute, 1984).

10. "Options for Controlling Costs," Louis Harris and Associates, for the Equitable Life Assurance Society, August 1983.

11. *News*, Blue Cross & Blue Shield of the National Capital Area, 3rd Quarter 1985, p. 2. Note that the variation is also due to hospital accounting practices.

12. Nancy S. Bagby and Sean Sullivan, *Employer Strategies for Managing Health Care Costs* (Washington, D.C.: American Enterprise Institute, forthcoming).

13. J. Wennberg and A. Gittlesohn, "Variations in Medical Care among Small Areas," *Scientific American*, vol. 246 (1982), pp. 120–34; J. Wennberg, K. McPherson, and P. Caper, "Will Payment Based on Diagnosis-Related Groups Control Hospital Costs?" *New England Journal of Medicine*, vol. 311 (August 2, 1984), pp. 295–99.

14. *The Federal Register*, April 17, 1985.

15. *National HMO Census, 1984*, Interstudy, Excelsior, Minnesota, 1985, pp. 2–5.

16. "Outpatient Surgery Rises as Firms Push to Reduce Health Care Costs," *The Wall Street Journal*, February 20, 1985, p. 35.

17. Judith Feder, Jack Hadley, and Ross Mullner, "Falling Through the Cracks: Poverty, Insurance Coverage, and Hospitals Care for the Poor, 1980 and 1982," *Milbank Memorial Fund Quarterly*, vol. 62 (Fall 1984), pp. 544–66.

# 7

# Farm Policy and the Farm Problem

*Bruce L. Gardner*

## Summary

*Federal budgetary expenditures on farm price support programs are estimated at $18 billion in 1985; and indirect support for sugar, tobacco, and peanuts adds another $4–5 billion to consumers' costs. These figures together amount to about $10,000 per U.S. farm. Current intervention in farm commodity markets is as massive as it has been since farm programs were introduced in the 1930s.*

*At the same time, a substantial number of farms—perhaps 100,000 to 150,000, although estimates are imprecise—are in a precarious financial situation. Farmers are producing far more than can be sold at the support prices for grains, cotton, and milk. The U.S. export market has shrunk because of increased production abroad and the high value of the dollar in terms of foreign currencies. And most important for the financially pressed farmers who are heavily indebted, land values have fallen about 30 percent on average since their 1981 peaks.*

*Farm programs have provided a palliative for U.S. agriculture, but their costs to consumers and taxpayers are far more than the corresponding benefits to farmers. Moreover, most of the benefits—about three-fourths according to estimates of the U.S. Department of Agriculture (USDA) for 1984—go to farmers who are not in financial trouble. And the programs have done nothing to resolve the underlying problem of overproduction. That problem can be resolved by improving farm export markets or by adjusting U.S. production. Farm programs are unhelpful in dealing with the macroeconomic and international factors that have caused the weak export market and reduced land values, and they are counterproductive in that they encourage farmers to keep up their production capacity to qualify for deficiency payments and other program benefits.*

*The main commodity programs expired in 1985, and Congress had the opportunity to replace them with legislation that would be more pertinent to the current situation. In the farm bill debate a wide-ranging consensus of congressional and USDA staff experts, academic economists, agribusiness* *interests, and many farm groups, particularly those representing livestock producers but also some crop-growing interests, appeared to exist for a reduction in intervention. The principal recommended features were phased cuts in Commodity Credit Corporation (CCC) loan prices, target prices guaranteed by deficiency payments, and movement away from acreage controls. The Reagan administration supported such reforms and, indeed, recommended faster cuts in support (target and loan) prices than a consensus perhaps would have favored. In the end, the fears of producers of supported commodities about economic losses under even modest cuts in income protection prevailed politically. The new farm bill will freeze the target prices and hence the incentives to overproduce. We can expect farm programs to cost taxpayers and consumers $15 billion to $20 billion again in 1986. The reductions in loan prices, however, begin to address the underlying economic problems of agriculture.*

*The consensus remains that further policy reforms in the direction of market orientation are wise and indeed appear inevitable in the longer run. Events of 1985, however, give us no reason for confidence that when now-distant decision points arrive in 1986, 1987, or 1988 the policy outcome will be different from that in 1985.*

## Introduction

The Reagan administration's initial views on agriculture were that governmental intervention in that sector, as elsewhere in the economy, should be reduced. Yet, it refrained from pressing Congress, in the 1981 farm bill debate, for agricultural reforms that it favored, particularly for peanut and sugar programs, in return for congressional help on the general tax and spending proposals that were thought to be more important. The administration acquiesced in signing the Agricultural and Food Act of 1981, which ended up costing about $12 billion annually in direct budget costs, with additional billions of indirect costs to consumers of sugar products, peanuts, and tobacco. Yet, upon the expiration of the 1981 act in 1985, the U.S. farm sector was in perhaps its worst financial shape in the post–World War II period. These events can best be understood in the context of a "farm problem" in which needed adjustments in product and factor markets were coupled with farm policies that over the years hindered rather than promoted adjustment.

Agriculture, as is typical of U.S. industries, has undergone continual adjustment throughout history. Since it is costly, adjustment creates problems; but it also creates opportunities. Although over the long term agriculture has been a viable competitive industry with a high rate of technical progress, adjustment in U.S. agriculture is viewed in the policy arena more as a problem than as an opportunity. Probably this perception results because public officials do not hear from farmers who do well under changing circumstances but instead from those for whom the costs of adjustment exceed the returns.

This paper reviews the recent economic history of adjustment in agriculture and the political responses to it, attempts a critique of the resulting policies, and discusses policy options for farm legislation today in light of this background.

## A Brief History of Adjustment in U.S. Agriculture

Some farm spokesmen would deny that the farm problem is an adjustment problem. A popular view among farmers, and therefore among politicians, is that the problem is low prices for farm commodities. What is meant is that net returns to producers of commodities are low because, however low a price may be, it does not cause problems for producers if costs are lower. Moreover, returns must be low in relation to some alternative or opportunity return for resources used in agriculture. How can we tell if returns are low in this sense? We would observe resources moving from agriculture to other employment. That is, we would observe adjustment in factor markets. Resource adjustment is a necessary condition to show that a meaningful farm problem exists. It is not, however, a sufficient condition because resource adjustment is not only a symptom of low returns, it is also a solution to the problem of low returns. Moreover, resources might leave agriculture when nonagricultural opportunities improve, as when farmland is sold at a high price for development in an expanding suburban area. Here adjustment indicates not a problem but a new opportunity. This ambiguity about the relation between resource adjustment and low returns is important to keep in mind in interpreting the history of resource adjustment in U.S agriculture.

A key statistic in many discussions of the farm problem is the number of farmers, the decline in which is taken to reflect the farm problem (figure 7–1). What this statistic really shows, however, is the decline of labor relative to capital in farming and the increasing size of farm operations. While labor in agriculture is declining, purchased inputs, especially those associated with technical progress in agricultural production, are increasing rapidly (table 7–1). The overall picture of U.S. agriculture as a sector is best shown by the aggregate indexes of farm inputs and outputs (figure 7–2). U.S. agricultural output has risen about 2.2 times since 1940 while aggregate input has remained about constant. The implied rate of sustained productivity growth since 1940 is impressive. The annual rate of growth in total

FIGURE 7-1
U.S. FARM POPULATION AND FARM LABOR, 1929-1984

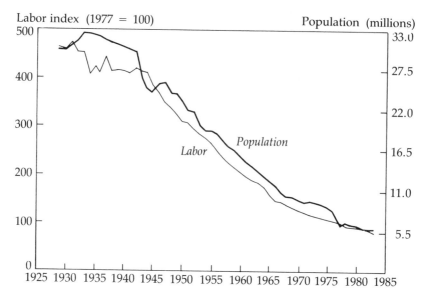

NOTE: Farm population refers to all people who live on farms, according to the U.S. Census definition. Farm labor refers to USDA's index of hours worked on farms to produce agricultural products.

SOURCE: U.S. Department of Commerce, Bureau of the Census, and U.S. Department of Agriculture.

factor productivity (aggregate output index divided by aggregate input index) is 1.8 percent. The labor productivity index more commonly calculated for manufacturing industries (aggregate output index divided by the labor input index) has since 1947 grown 5½ percent annually in agriculture compared with a 2 percent rate in nonfarm business.

The short-term variations in these trends indicate the ability of U.S. agriculture to adjust to improved opportunities. Farm inputs, especially investment in machinery and equipment, increased during the 1970s when commodity markets were booming. In the 1973–1975 crop years, U.S. grain acreage was 12 percent higher than in the three years prior to the grain price shock triggered by the Soviet purchases of July 1972 (while at the same time worldwide grain acreage increased only 4 percent). The decade with the largest decline in farm labor and number of farms was the 1940s, while the movement off farms in the 1930s was the slowest of any decade in the century. Indeed, despite the dustbowl picture painted in *The Grapes of Wrath* and the like, the number of farms increased overall in the early 1930s. The data suggest that opportunities elsewhere, more than economic distress on farms, direct the ebb and flow of labor out of agriculture.[1]

## The Role of Policy in Agricultural Adjustment

U.S. agricultural policy has not always focused on price supports. In the establishment of the Department of Agriculture, the land grant universities, the Homestead Act, and the Federal Extension Service, all in the last half of the nineteenth century, policy followed up on Jeffersonian ideas of encouraging technical progress, new farming enterprises, and agricultural expansion. Federal policy had an agenda that would be pleasing to modern advocates of "industrial policy." At the same time, especially after 1870, farmers experiencing commodity price declines generated a rising clamor for governmental intervention to improve matters. This discontent focused not on regulating the commodity markets but on breaking the monopoly power of railroads and "Eastern" capital generally and made its greatest mark in the movement for easy money against the gold standard.[2] Still, this perceptual change of government's role from one of greasing the skids of agriculture to one of harrying the enemies of agriculture provided a political setting in which the twentieth-century commodity programs were a natural step to take. Moreover, the advocacy of protective tariffs arose as soon as efficient competitors and cheaper

TABLE 7–1

U.S. FARM INPUT USE, 1910–1980

(Index 1910 = 100)

| Year | Labor | Real Estate | Mechanical Power and Machinery | Agricultural Chemicals | Feed and Seed |
|------|-------|-------------|-------------------------------|------------------------|---------------|
| 1910 | 100 | 100 | 100 | 100 | 100 |
| 1920 | 106 | 105 | 159 | 167 | 135 |
| 1930 | 102 | 104 | 200 | 200 | 159 |
| 1940 | 91 | 106 | 212 | 300 | 229 |
| 1950 | 68 | 108 | 424 | 633 | 341 |
| 1960 | 45 | 102 | 488 | 1067 | 453 |
| 1970 | 28 | 104 | 506 | 2500 | 565 |
| 1980 | 20 | 101 | 618 | 4000 | 635 |

SOURCE: U.S. Department of Agriculture.

FIGURE 7–2

FARM PRODUCTIVITY, OUTPUT, AND INPUT, 1929–1984

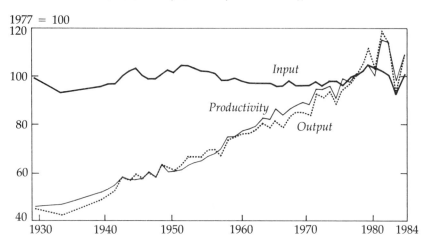

SOURCE: *Economic Report of the President, 1985*, pp. 339, 340.

transportation became a real threat to U.S. agricultural producers.[3]

The promotion of agricultural production through research, education, and information has continued to the present. Indeed, the surge in productivity that began in the late 1930s has been attributed to the government-funded research program of the preceding two decades.[4] In addition, policy has worked to promote agriculture since the New Deal era by largely exempting farmers from Fair Labor Standards legislation and by permitting farmers special dispensations to import guest workers when tight immigration restrictions were binding in other industries.

Nonetheless, the main thrust of agricultural policy since the 1930s has been to regulate commodity markets in an attempt to place a floor under farmers' receipts. This approach, from the beginning of the New Deal programs in 1933, took forms that unfortunately hindered the adjustments that would have to be made to provide a long-term remedy to the farm problem. Instead of providing aid to farmers and farm workers who were leaving agriculture, we tried to keep them in farming. Instead of encouraging production in new areas and expansion of smaller farms, we tried to keep as many as possible in business at a smaller scale and keep farming in the traditional areas.

When the wheat growers rejected mandatory production controls in 1963 and rice and cotton allotment systems were being phased out by 1975, the anti-adjustment wave in farm policy seemed to be over.

The Food and Agriculture Act of 1977 provided an opportunity to consolidate these policy reforms in a market-oriented program, consistent across commodities, that could finally put the New Deal supply management approach behind us.[5] It did not happen. An unfortunate precedent had been set during the Ford administration, which—in response to a felt economic emergency during the 1976 campaign—gave the wheat loan rate its largest one-time increase ever. The Carter administration in 1977 and 1978 acquiesced in substantial further rises in both target prices and loan rates. Even more significant than the 1977 act was the Emergency Agricultural Act of 1978, passed just six months later. The 1978 act was the federal government's payoff to the demonstrating farmers organized by the American Agriculture Movement during the winter and spring of 1978. In addition to allowing higher support prices, the 1978 act moved farm policy back into paid acreage diversion and created a new program of $6 billion in Economic Emergency loans at subsidized rates.

To grasp the economics of these programs, one must examine the programs in more detail. The policy decisions of 1976–1978 adjusted four important policy instruments—loan rates, target prices, acreage diversion, and subsidized credit—in ways that forestalled adjustment where it was needed, in the farm economy. I will consider these measures in turn.

**Loan rates.** The loan rate is not an interest charge but the payment per bushel that a farmer receives as a loan from the Commodity Credit Corporation (CCC). The grain that serves as security for the loan must be stored on the farm or in commercial storage. The farmer has the choice within nine months of the date at which the loan is taken out of redeeming the grain by repaying the loan—with interest at a rate based on the government's cost of borrowing—or of forfeiting the grain as full payment (including interest) of the CCC loan. The farmer benefits from forfeiting grain to the CCC whenever the market price obtainable is less than the loan rate plus interest. Consequently, one does not expect to observe market prices much below the loan rate. The government has in effect made an unlimited offer to buy grain at a minimum price equal to the loan rate. (This is what the CCC does directly for dairy products at the dairy support prices of butter, cheese, and powdered milk.)

Raising the loan rate raises the floor under the market price. Because no significant export taxes or restrictions exist, the loan rate also supports grain prices in world trade. Grain is diverted to CCC stocks until the world price rises to the loan rate (or U.S. exports go to zero). The problem this diversion has created since 1981 is that excess supply at the loan rate has been large enough to cause CCC accumulation beyond the levels at which any reasonable prospects for future commercial sales or even subsidized food aid exist. Moreover, because of the strong dollar, the U.S. loan rate in terms of the currencies of competing grain exporters is high enough to encourage continued output expansion abroad while the United States is looking for ways to cut production. Therefore, economists, commodity group spokesmen, and legislators widely agree that a way to cut loan rates should be found. Indeed, the 1985 farm legislation will cut the 1986 loan rates for the major commodities as much as 30 percent.

A related longer-term problem with the U.S. price support system was its effect on the U.S. position in General Agreement on Tariffs and Trade (GATT) negotiations in the 1940s and 1950s. At that time, as has continually been the case for dairy products, prices at support levels were high enough to attract imports. Consequently, the United States pressed for a waiver of GATT rules to permit restrictions of imports that section 22 of the Agricultural Adjustment Act of 1933 requires to prevent disruption of U.S. domestic farm programs. Since then, however, the European Community and Japan have become the primary restrictors of trade in farm commodities in which the United States has turned out to have a continuing comparative advantage. Now the United States would gain from liberalization of trade in agricultural commodities and would like to see agricultural products back on the table in GATT. Although this sketch is off the main subject, it is pertinent in illustrating how apparent policy imperatives can create long-term problems not visible at the time the policy decision is made.

**Target Prices.** These legislated prices provide price insurance to farmers by making payments to supplement their market receipts. The payment per bushel is the difference between the target price and the higher of the average price received by farmers or the CCC loan price. The payments are roughly sufficient to guarantee producers the target price—"roughly" because (1) the payments are made on a farmer's base acreage and base yield, not on actual current output; (2) the payments are based on U.S. average prices, not on each producer's actual price; and (3) farmers sometimes have to hold acreage idle to qualify for payments. When target prices were introduced in their present form, in the Agriculture and Consumer Protection Act of 1973, they were below market prices. The Rice Production Act of 1975 established a target price above the market price but, like the 1973 act, made payments only on long-established base acreage so that payments would not create a direct production incentive (no subsidy at the margin). The 1977 act made the fateful change of paying on a current-production basis and with a target price level already above the market price for wheat, grain sorghum, and barley. By 1982 target prices were above market prices for all the covered crops (see figure 7–3 for corn and wheat). The target price level consequently turned into a production incentive program, which further increased CCC stock buildup at the loan rates. At its original level in the 1977 act, the $3.00 wheat target price would probably not have created problems; but the boost to $3.40 in early 1978 sent the wrong message to producers.

**Acreage Controls.** Payments made to farmers for not growing crops were introduced in the first New Deal farm program (the Agricultural Adjustment Act of 1933), were a mainstay of programs in the 1950s (the Soil Bank), and evolved into the "set-aside" and voluntary (paid) diversion program of the 1960s; but they were phased out in the 1970s with Secretary of Agriculture Butz's injunction to plant fence row to fence row. Nonetheless, by 1977 we were back in the set-aside business for wheat, in response to accumulating CCC stocks. Set-asides require farmers to idle a fraction, typically 10 to 20 percent, of their acreage base for a crop to qualify for target prices and CCC loans. In the spring of 1978, the government reestablished paid diversion programs, which are essentially offers by the government to rent a farmer's land, which is then left idle. Farmers prefer this approach compared with set-asides. Because winter wheat had already been planted, the 1978 act included a unique haying and grazing plan that paid farmers to use their growing wheat crops for livestock forage or pasture rather than to harvest for grain. The average reductions actually induced, however, were quite small in both 1978 and 1979, and the production effects were not noticeable. Still, by 1978 the machinery was back in place for various acreage control measures.

**Subsidized Credit and Insurance.** In the mid-1970s, a new "disaster payment" program and an emergency loan program under the Farmers' Home Administration (FmHA) were established. By 1978 the disaster payment program was paying out about $500 million per year to compensate farmers for yield shortfalls due to conditions preventing a farmer from planting a field that would normally have been planted. For risky production areas in the Western Plains, these payments amounted to about 20 percent of the rental value of cropland and must have been a significant incentive to grow grains instead of leaving pasture for cattle or to take a chance on riskier but normally higher yielding crops (corn instead of sorghum). The emergency loans pro-

231

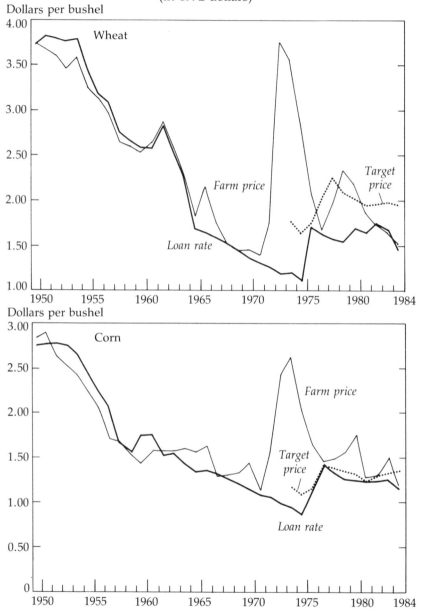

FIGURE 7–3
WHEAT AND CORN PRICE SUPPORTS, 1950–1984
(in 1972 dollars)

SOURCE: U.S. Department of Agriculture, Agricultural Stabilization and Conservation Service.

232

vided about $6 billion in subsidized credit by 1977 to farmers in counties declared disaster areas. In addition, the Emergency Act of 1978 established a new $6 billion program of economic emergency loans, basically to save overextended farmers from business failure. This set of credit and insurance programs permitted some marginal lands and farmers to remain in production through the weak prices of 1977–1979.

## Farm Policy and Adjustment in the 1980s

The preceding discussion indicates how U.S. agricultural policies enabled farmers by and large to ignore the market signals of the late 1970s, which should have caused a reversal of the output expansion of the mid-1970s. The need for such adjustment was temporarily obscured by the renewed large-scale entry of the Soviet Union into the grain markets and the substantial price increases that resulted for the crops of 1979 and 1980. These circumstances not only bailed out the farm sector from what was being called the worst agricultural recession since the 1930s but confirmed the scarcity syndrome that led experts to fear chronic food shortages and farmers to bid land prices to an all-time peak in 1981 (figure 7–4). Moreover, this environment permitted Congress to maintain target prices for wheat and rice and to increase them substantially for corn and cotton, without undue threat of high budgetary costs, in the Agriculture and Food Act of 1981. Budget projections for fiscal year 1982 were under $2 billion for all the USDA farm commodity programs.

In the event, the 1982 crops were large, export demand declined, commodity prices fell to the loan levels, CCC stocks bulged, and the budgetary costs soared to $18 billion. Some of the main commodity detail is shown in table 7–2. By late 1982, it was apparent that modest acreage controls implemented on 1982 crops and planned for 1983 were unlikely to prevent still larger and more costly surpluses in the 1983–1984 crop year. The escalation of target prices over the four-year period mandated in the 1981 act threatened to establish deficiency payments substantially above those shown in table 7–2 for 1982 crops. The $3.03 target price for corn in prospect for 1984, with the market price at a $2.55 loan rate, would generate $3.4 billion in payments on 7 billion bushels for this crop alone. This situation and outlook led to the Payment in Kind (PIK) program.

**The PIK Program.** PIK was the largest U.S. acreage control program ever, with 77 million acres enrolled. It gave producers the opportunity to add to acreage diverted under other provisions a further 10 to 30

FIGURE 7–4
AGRICULTURAL REAL ESTATE VALUE, 1950–1985

Index (1977 = 100)

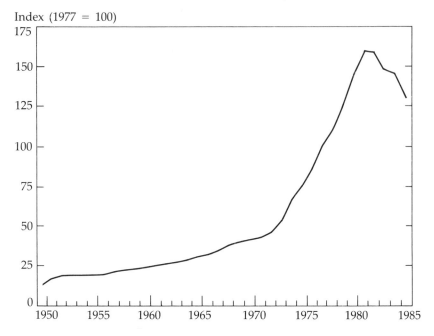

SOURCES: *Historical Statistics of the United States* and the *Economic Report of the President, 1985,* p. 341.

percent of their base acreage. The payment to farmers for this diversion consisted of commodities held by the CCC. The program differed slightly from commodity to commodity; its workings can be explained with reference to corn. The 1983 corn program had three acreage-control components. First, a 10 percent acreage reduction (from the producer's established prior-year base) was required for the producer to qualify for deficiency payments. Idling this acreage is costly to the farmers in that the rental value of the land is lost. Consider a farmer with a yield of 120 bushels per acre, whose annual returns to land are expected to be $80 per acre on 100 acres. By idling ten acres, the farmer becomes eligible for a deficiency payment the expected value of which is $0.21 per bushel (in 1983 the target price was $2.86 and the loan rate, $2.65 per bushel). On the ninety acres the payment amounts to $2,268. The rental value of the land is $800, so the farmer makes a $1,468 profit, or $0.136 per bushel produced. By idling a second 10 percent of base acreage, the farmer could earn $1.50 per bushel as a diversion payment for corn that the farmer would have

234

produced. In our example, this payment would be $1,800 for ten additional acres, again exceeding the $800 rental value of the land.

PIK acreage consists of another 10 to 30 percent, at the farmer's option. The government's payment on this acreage consisted of 80 percent of the corn that could have been grown. In our example, if the farmer idled an additional 30 percent, the payment would be 96 bushels per acre on thirty acres or 2,880 bushels which, at the loan rate of $2.65 per bushel, is worth $7,632. The rental value of the thirty acres is $2,400, so that the producer does well.

The PIK program consists of a package deal of acreage diversion as outlined. In the example, the producer idles 50 percent of acreage, at a cost to him of $4,000 in fixed resources that cannot be transferred to other uses. In return, the producer receives $7,632 in PIK corn, a $1,800 diversion payment, and $1,260 (0.21 × 50 × 120) in deficiency payments. Thus the farmer earns $6,692 or $0.56 per bushel more than by producing normal output and selling at the loan rate.

Alternatively, a farmer could offer to lease the government the whole farm at a PIK payment rate that the farmer chooses, not to exceed 80 percent. There is no guarantee, however, that such an offer would be accepted. The purposes are to give the USDA flexibility in choosing how much acreage to idle and to give farmers an incentive to bid less than 80 percent (to increase the odds of the offers being accepted).

As it turned out, 32 million acres of corn land were enrolled in

TABLE 7–2
DEFICIENCY PAYMENTS AND CCC OUTLAYS FROM
SELECTED U.S. CROPS, 1982

| Crop | Payments (millions of dollars) | Payments as Percentage of Market Value | Net CCC Outlays (millions of dollars) |
|---|---|---|---|
| Corn | 291 | 1.3 | 4,281 |
| Wheat | 414 | 4.2 | 1,595 |
| Cotton | 467 | 19.2 | 625 |
| Rice | 267 | 21.2 | 150 |
| Sorghum | 64 | 7.1 | 989 |
| Barley | 60 | 5.2 | 129 |
| Milk | NA | NA | 2,592 |
| Wool | 41 | 98.7 | NA |
| Total | 1,604 | | 10,361 |

NOTE: NA = not applicable.
SOURCE: U.S. Department of Agriculture.

235

the 1983 program, and 45 percent of 1982 corn acreage was harvested. This participation entitled producers to 2.1 billion bushels of CCC corn worth $5.6 billion at the loan rate. Since the CCC did not own this much corn, deals were struck with farmers along the following lines: A farmer who had one-half of his acreage in PIK was due 40 percent of his normal crop from CCC; but the CCC said, "We'll accept your growing crop in the loan program, pay you the loan rate on 40 percent of your normal crop, and then just give the growing crop back to you as your PIK payment." This action essentially cashed out the program.

In other instances, because PIK participants had the right to delivery of PIK grain at certain locations of their choice where the CCC did not necessarily have enough grain, the CCC had to buy grain from some farmers to deliver to others. There was some controversy over premiums the CCC paid to acquire such grain. Cashing out did not work here because some recipients, by insisting on delivery where they wanted grain, could receive transportation and storage services in addition to the grain itself.

As is typical with acreage control programs, there was "slippage" in PIK in the sense that some acreage was enrolled that would not, in fact, have produced the farmer's established program yield had it been planted. Program yield is the same for a whole farm; but most farmers have some land that is significantly less productive than their average land, which is naturally the land to enroll in PIK. In the Midwest, 1983 was a wet planting season, tempting farmers to enroll low-lying areas, including ponds. This strategy backfired, however, as a late-summer drought caused the sharpest corn yield decline since World War II. (Slippage should have increased measured yields.) In retrospect, the farmers should have planted low-lying areas and placed droughty hilltops in PIK.

In a more global retrospect, the poor weather made PIK unnecessary and, with PIK, meant larger effects than had been anticipated. The carryover of corn fell from a record high 3.1 billion bushels from the 1982 crop to 0.7 billion bushels from the 1983 crop. The average farm price rose from $2.68 to $3.25 per bushel. Consequently the real value of commodities paid to farmers was about 20 percent above the $9 billion budgetary cost assessed to PIK by valuing commodities at the loan rates. The shock to livestock producers buying feed was sufficient to bring them in force into the lobbying process for the 1985 farm bill.

How does PIK fit into the adjustment discussion? It might be viewed as a program to foster farmers' adjustment to a situation of oversupply, indeed perhaps a case of overadjustment. But in a more fundamental sense the program was a major obstacle to adjustment. It kept returns to producers high so that oversupply sent no market signals. The secretary of agriculture explained PIK as a one-time program to get U.S. agriculture back on track. Instead it was a signal to producers that the best strategy is to maintain a high acreage base because the government will take as strong steps as are necessary to prevent prices falling and the higher one's base, the greater the eligibility for diversion payments and other benefits. A slightly different picture emerges from consideration of policy for three other commodities in the 1980s: tobacco, milk, and sugar.

**Tobacco.** Another problem with PIK is that it raised world prices by means of U.S. production controls. Use of production controls places the United States in a position similar to that of Saudi Arabia in oil. Other countries can prosper under the price umbrella that the United States maintains. Tobacco is a commodity for which this problem has become chronic. The United States has had marketing controls on flue-cured tobacco for twenty years and on burley tobacco for fourteen years. These establish an output quota each year aimed at increasing the market price to the legislated support level. The market for sale and lease of these quotas indicates a wedge of 25 to 30 percent on average over this period between the supply price of tobacco and the market price. Yet maintenance of these rents necessitated a substantial scaling back of aggregate quotas as cigarette companies economized on tobacco and turned increasingly to imports, while the export market for U.S. tobacco shrank. Between 1960–1964 and 1982, the U.S. share of flue-cured exports fell from 52 to 25 percent and of burley from 57 to 25 percent.

The tobacco program is a no-adjustment program in maintaining quota ownership in small units reflecting the tobacco farming patterns of the 1950s or earlier. Transfers of quotas have permitted considerable consolidation of tobacco-farming enterprises, but they remain small on average by the standards of other commodities. The transfers via lease have created a political problem by placing ownership of the rent-generating program assets in the hands of nongrowers. By 1981 only 24 percent of flue-cured tobacco and 48 percent of burley was grown by a quota owner or an immediate relative.[6] This means that the majority of tobacco is grown by people for whom the tobacco program has become a source of costs, not benefits.

**Milk.** The market for dairy products has been heavily influenced by price support programs, especially since the mid-1960s. Milk producers have become more politically organized since that time, having formed one of the earlier large political action committees (PACs), with the dairy PAC still in the top ten in funding. Political action is probably the principal reason that the dairy support price has had the largest real increases of any major commodity in the past twenty years. Consequently, the dairy sector has not only failed to adjust to market conditions, in the past seven years especially it has also consciously attempted to move against market signals. International events and other random shocks are in part responsible for grain stock accumulation and policy problems, but in dairy the stocks and costs are essentially a direct creation of policy. Since 1979 returns to dairying rose as price supports were maintained and feed prices fell, inducing an expansion of U.S. milk production from 122 billion pounds annually to 139 billion, with essentially all the increase going into CCC stocks of butter, cheese, and milk powder (table 7–3).

Dairy policy also reveals the added costs of maintaining overpricing for too long. Now plants have been built in the Pacific region for processing milk just for purchase by the CCC. This excess capacity will make it doubly painful for policy adjustment to reduce the surpluses.

When in 1983 it became apparent that a $2–3 billion annual budgetary cost of dairy price supports had no prospects of decreasing and every prospect of increasing, Congress enacted the Dairy Production Equalization Act of 1983. Its essential feature was a payment to milk producers of $10 per hundredweight of milk that a farmer agreed not to produce from January 1984 through March 1985, between 5 and 30 percent below a 1982–1983 base. This program was of greatest interest to farmers who were producing less than 5 percent of their base period anyway, since they could receive payments for doing what they were already doing. The program seems to have reduced milk production in 1984 by about 2 percent. The payments were financed in large part by a $0.50 per hundredweight assessment on producers, which amounts to a reduction in the support price. Moreover, following the expiration of the program in April 1985, the support price has been cut to $11.60, compared with $13.10 in 1982–1983. So some real adjustments are beginning to be made in dairy policy.

**Sugar.** The policy picture for sugar is simpler but also shows firm resistance to market realities. Sugar policy in 1985 generated New York duty-paid prices of raw sugar of $0.18 to $0.22 per pound, while the offshore world price ranged from $0.025 to $0.065. This policy makes sugar by far our most protected agricultural commodity. Here, though, congressional urgency is lacking for policy reform because the roughly $3 billion cost of the program is borne directly by consumers in the form of higher prices for sweetener-containing products. This passing along the costs is possible because the United States imports a declining but still substantial fraction of its sugar.

In 1974 the Sugar Act expired, and it appeared that, along with the grains, sugar policy might move to a free-market basis. But as soon as sugar prices weakened, sugar programs returned. CCC loans and target prices with deficiency payments have been tried, but we have returned to primary reliance on import quotas, with the price level goal for quotas set by a legislated loan rate converted to a market support price (MSP) on a New York basis. In the 1980s, the sugar support level is the only important commodity price support to increase in real terms, rising from $0.15 in 1980 to $0.21 in 1985.

Problems of adjustment in sugar policy, as in dairy policy, are exacerbated by investment in processing facilities. This situation is especially important for some sugar beet–growing areas. Here farmers could readily switch to other crops—entry is free in sugar beet growing, and the rents are probably not large. But with the demise of beet growing, almost certain if sugar progams were abandoned, the processing plants would become essentially valueless.

A related problem is the creation, largely in response to high U.S. sugar prices, of an industry to produce high-fructose corn syrup (HFCS) as a substitute for sugar. HFCS accounts now for 25 percent of sweeteners, compared with 2 percent in 1973, and for some 250 million bushels or 5 percent of U.S. corn consumption. This industry would take substantial losses and perhaps die if the sugar program were ended.

In connection with sugar, I mention the honey program. This program had been moribund for twenty-five years, but amid the Reagan deregulatory revolution the honey market somehow was re-regulated. The support price rose from $0.44 per pound in 1979 to $0.66 per pound in 1984, and the CCC acquired one-half of U.S. honey output in the past two years. We can look for increasing amounts of honey in school lunch and food aid programs in the next few years.

### Policy Reforms for Fostering Adjustment

**The Mirage of Stabilization Policy.** Before discussing the prospects for changes in commodity programs that seem most promising, one view of adjustment in agriculture that is plausible but turns out to be unhelpful should be considered. This idea is to key farm policy to the stabilization of annual agricultural price fluctuations. This approach goes back to President Hoover's Federal Farm Board of 1929 and extends through the Carter administration's position that the Farmer-

## TABLE 7-3
## U.S. Dairy Program, 1972–1985

| | Support Price (dollars per cwt.) | Price Received by Farmers (dollars per cwt.) | Milk Production (billions of lbs.) | USDA Net Market Removals, Milk Equivalent (billions of lbs.) | Net Expenditures on Dairy Price Support (millions of dollars) |
|---|---|---|---|---|---|
| **1972–1973** | | | | | |
| April 1–March 14 | 4.93 | | | | |
| March 15–March 31 | 5.29 | 5.22 | 119.1 | 4.9 | 264.6 |
| **1973–1974** | | | | | |
| April 1–August 9 | 5.29 | | | | |
| August 10–March 31 | 5.61 | 6.95 | 114.9 | 0.7 | 77.0 |
| **1974–1975** | | | | | |
| April 1–January 4 | 6.57 | | | | |
| January 5–March 31 | 7.24 | 6.87 | 115.6 | 2.4 | 318.7 |
| **1975–1976** | | | | | |
| April 1–October 1 | 7.24 | | | | |
| October 2–March 31 | 7.71 | 8.12 | 116.4 | 0.9 | 256.9 |
| **1976–1977** | | | | | |
| April 1–September 30 | 8.13 | | | | |
| October 1–March 31 | 8.26 | 8.52 | 120.9 | 3.4 | 302.4 |

| | | | | | |
|---|---|---|---|---|---|
| 1976–1977[a] | | | | | |
| October 1–March 31 | 8.26 | | | | |
| April 1–September 30 | 9.00 | 8.65 | 122.2 | 6.9 | 714.3 |
| 1977–1978 | | | | | |
| October 1–March 31 | 9.00 | | | | |
| April 1–September 30 | 9.43 | 9.30 | 121.7 | 3.2 | 451.4 |
| 1978–1979 | | | | | |
| October 1–March 31 | 9.87 | | | | |
| April 1–September 30 | 10.76 | 10.86 | 122.5 | 1.1 | 250.6 |
| 1979–1980 | | | | | |
| October 1–March 31 | 11.49 | | | | |
| April 1–September 30 | 12.36 | 11.75 | 127.3 | 8.2 | 1,279.8 |
| 1980–1981 | 13.10 | 12.71 | 132.0 | 12.7 | 1,974.8 |
| 1981–1982 | | | | | |
| October 1–October 20 | 13.49 | | | | |
| October 21–September 30 | 13.10 | 12.68 | 135.0 | 13.8 | 2,239.2 |
| 1982–1983 | 13.10 | 12.66 | 139.0 | 16.6 | 2,600.4 |
| 1983–1984 | | | | | |
| October 1–November 30 | 13.10 | | | | |
| December 1–September 30 | 12.60 | 12.42 | 137.4 | 10.4 | 1,597.5 |
| 1984-1985 | 12.60 | | | | |

a. The designated marketing year for dairy products was changed from April-March to October-September at this time.

SOURCE: U.S. Department of Agriculture, Agricultural Stabilization and Conservation Service.

owned Reserve Program (FOR) was the "cornerstone" of its agricultural policy.[7]

These remedies derive from a diagnosis of the farm problem as one of annual or business-cycle-length fluctuations in commodity prices. The means of adjustment are a mechanism for smoothing out the peaks and valleys by buffer stocks of commodities. The FOR elaborated this idea. To encourage farmers to hold stocks, the federal government gives them storage subsidy payments. The government achieves control by setting a minimum price, based on the CCC loan rate, which the farmer receives as a loan for stored commodities. But here the loan is for three to five years, and the farmer has to agree not to redeem the grain until the market price reaches release levels that the government establishes (generally 140–160 percent of the loan rates). Two difficulties with this program, which has been operating from 1977 to the present under an evolving set of rules, are that it replaces unsubsidized storage by farmers and commercial interests and that establishing criteria for floor prices, release prices, call prices (at which the farmer not only may but *must* repay the loan), maximum size of the reserve, the size of the subsidies, is difficult. Two problems are more fundamental, however.

The first is that the establishment of floor prices became an adjunct to the income support function of farm programs. Stabilization, although invoked as a goal useful to both producers and consumers, is dominated politically by the desire to support farm income. Consequently the floor price in the FOR became a vehicle to offer farmers higher market prices than the loan rate guaranteed. By 1982 the price for wheat going into the FOR was $4.00 per bushel, while the regular CCC loan rate was $3.55. Although the Reagan administration has maintained the FOR, the initial enthusiasm for it has dissipated.

The second problem of the buffer stock approach is that the adjustment problem in agriculture is not a matter of annual or three- to four-year cycles. Instead we see a pattern of periodic sharp rises in commodity prices followed by long periods of lower prices. So far in the twentieth century, we have experienced three such commodity booms—World War I, World War II, and the mid-1970s (figure 7–5). The adjustment problems of agriculture involve coping with the years between the booms and with long-term trends and structural changes. Buffer stocks are quite useless for these purposes.

**Progress toward Reform in 1985 Legislation.** In the debate on the 1985 farm bill a remarkably wide consensus that substantial reforms were needed in farm programs existed. This consensus is evident in assessments by experts, testimonies by farm spokesmen, and state-

## FIGURE 7–5
## U.S. DEPARTMENT OF AGRICULTURE CROP PRICE INDEX, 1915–1984
(1967 = 100)

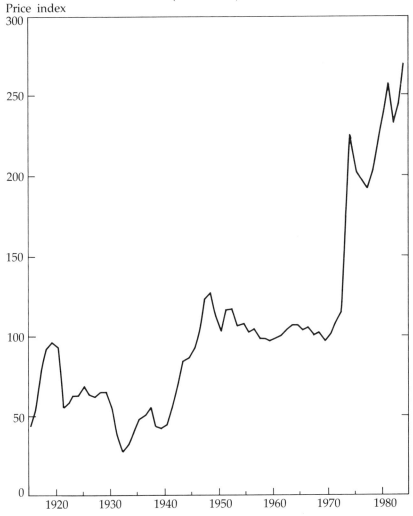

SOURCE: *Historical Statistics of the United States.*

ments by congressional and executive branch policy makers.[8] The dominant reason given for changes in farm programs was the need to make the United States more competitive in world commodity markets. An obvious hindrance to U.S. exports has been U.S. loan rates, as discussed earlier. It is difficult, however, to reduce loan rates

243

without changing other aspects of commodity programs, particularly the target prices. Maintaining target prices while loan rates are cut increases deficiency payments, which adds to the federal budget deficit that is already thought to be too large. As an example, the corn loan rate may have to be reduced to about $2.00 per bushel to clear the market without additions to CCC stocks under normal yield and demand.[9] If the target price is maintained at its current level of $3.03 per bushel, the potential budget exposure for deficiency payments is about $8 billion for this crop alone.

The Reagan administration's proposed legislation, as well as several other bills introduced in both houses of Congress early in 1985, reduced target prices along with loan rates. Not only does this reduce government outlays, it also reduces the incentive to produce that contributed to surpluses under the 1981 act. As the congressional debate wore on in mid-1985, cuts in target prices became increasingly problematic politically. The main reason was low farm income and particularly the financial plight of farmers with large debts and insufficient cash flow to cover debt service. The Department of Agriculture estimated that 93,000 or 14 percent of commercial farmers were under severe financial stress in early 1985, with perhaps another 50,000 having serious difficulties. Because of continuing land price declines as weak export demand extended expectations of low commodity prices, more farm businesses became regarded as bad credit risks and the Farm Credit Administration lending agencies experienced a worrisome deterioration in their balance sheets. About forty agricultural banks (those with more than 25 percent of their loan portfolios in farm loans) were liquidated in the first eight months of 1985. A cut in target prices would reduce the cash flow of farms in trouble and push more of them, and more of their lending institutions, over the brink.

The cold-blooded and, for the long run, economically sensible view for the farm sector as a whole would be to let the liquidations and failures occur, as normally happens with other small-business industries. Keeping failing farms in business is a matter of postponing the inevitable by and large. And keeping those farms in business by maintaining producer prices 20–30 percent above the prices at which quantities produced will clear the market only compounds overproduction problems. Moreover, in aggregate the farm sector is not in a crisis situation. Farm debts of $210 billion are still well below the $800 billion in farm assets. Most of the farms, producing most of the U.S. farm output, could survive and prosper without a new governmental bailout for agriculture. Nonetheless, the evident pain and hardship of the farmers who desperately need help is clearly the politically dominant force. This force doomed pro-adjustment reforms in the 1985 farm legislation. Both House and Senate have adamantly refused to cut target prices for 1986; and, despite initial opposition, the administration has accepted this freeze.

Because adjustment by means of cuts in target prices was ruled out politically, the feasible options for 1985 farm legislation consisted of close continuations of the 1981 act. But the budgetary exposure this continuation entailed gave renewed impetus to acreage control measures. The idea behind those measures is to cut supplies so that CCC stocks will not accumulate and to drive up market prices so that deficiency payments are diminished. This approach is the opposite of that which the four former secretaries of agriculture recommended. It is anti-adjustment in that it keeps intact the economic incentives to overproduce while suppressing output via acreage diversion. It hinders U.S. exports by providing a worldwide price umbrella under which other countries can expand production and European Community export subsidy costs are reduced. To counter these effects, new programs of export subsidies and subsidized export credit will be instituted (some have already been introduced).

In short, from the point of view of long-term efficiency of resource allocation within agriculture and between the farm and nonfarm sectors, the new legislation will rival the most costly of past farm programs. The reductions in low rates will permit adjustments in demand and a reduction of CCC stocks. But the target price freeze dominates the budget picture. Nonetheless, considerable sentiment remains in both Congress and the White House for cutting target prices in the future. But even if the legislation does contain future reductions in support levels, the legislation can readily be amended if the political situation in 1987 or 1988 demands. We need only recall the significant changes in the supposedly four-year 1977 act that took place in 1978. Given the lack of reform in the outcome of this year's debate, it is hard to see why future debates should have a different outcome. In any case, the surprising result is in: five years into the "Reagan Revolution," a juggernaut on so many domestic and foreign policy fronts, U.S. farm policy remains firmly in the New Deal mold.

# Notes

1. Further evidence on this point is developed in my "Farm Population Decline and the Income of Rural Families," *American Journal of Agricultural Economics* (August 1974), pp. 600–606.

2. Mary Elizabeth Lease's famous recommendation to raise less corn and more hell, the Populist party platform of 1982, and Bryan's campaign of 1896 were the political peaks of this thinking. Even with the modern-day farm protests of 1977, 1978, and 1979, however, the hell raising ended as the planting season arrived.

3. H. L. Mencken, on the Tariff Act of 1922: "It put a duty of 30 cents a bushel on wheat. . . . Danish butter was barred out by a duty of 8 cents a pound. . . . Potatoes carried a duty of 50 cents a hundredweight. . . . High duties were put, too, upon meats, upon cheese, upon wool—in brief, upon practically everything that the farmer produced. . . . One might almost argue that the chief, and perhaps even only aim of legislation in these States is to succor and secure the farmer." *Prejudices: A Selection* (New York: Vintage Books, 1958), pp. 160, 163.

4. For a review of evidence on this connection, see R. Evenson and Y. Kislev, *Agricultural Productivity and Research* (New Haven: Yale University Press, 1972).

5. See the discussion in Don Paarlberg, ed., *Food and Agricultural Policy* (Washington, D.C.: American Enterprise Institute, 1977).

6. For this and other aspects of tobacco, see Daniel A. Sumner and Julian M. Alston, "Effects of the Tobacco Program" (Occasional Paper, American Enterprise Institute, Washington, D.C., November 1984).

7. U.S. Senate, Committee on Agriculture, "Statement of Secretary of Agriculture Bob Bergland," January 24, 1979.

8. See, for example, "Joint Statement on Agricultural Policy by former Secretaries of Agriculture Freeman, Hardin, Butz, and Bergland," U.S. Department of Agriculture, July 1985. These men represented the Kennedy-Johnson, Nixon, Ford, and Carter administrations; and the extent of their agreement and willingness to publicize it is remarkable. For a summary of views of economists see K. Price, ed., *The Dilemmas of Choice* (Washington, D.C.: Resources for the Future, National Center for Food and Agricultural Policy, 1985).

9. See Bruce Gardner, "U.S. Agricultural Policies and World Commodity Prices" (World Bank, Washington, D.C., August 1985, Mimeographed).

# 8
# Containing Inflation
*Phillip Cagan*

## Summary

*As inflation escalated in the 1970s well into double-digit rates, it seemed out of control. Various studies concluded that subduing inflation would impose severe costs of unemployment, perhaps above the threshold of political acceptability, while an inability to control inflation implied ominous consequences for the future of the monetary system. Nevertheless, the inflation rate came down sharply from 1980 to 1983 and, in contrast to its past cyclical behavior, stayed down in the business expansion of 1984–1985. What explains the apparent change in the control of inflation?*

*Although the sharpness and the persistence of the disinflation were a surprise, a change in policy had indeed been indicated. The Federal Reserve had changed its operating procedure in October 1979 with the expressed purpose of gaining control over monetary growth, and both the Federal Reserve and the new Reagan administration seemed determined to subdue inflation. These policy changes raised the possibility of benefiting from credibility effects. An offshoot of the theory of rational expectations claims that the credibility to the public of an anti-inflationary policy affects the trade-off between inflation and output. Normally such a policy first contracts output, inasmuch as prices respond sluggishly to the reduction in aggregate demand. But if a restrictive policy were expected and believed to be permanent by the public, prices and wages could in this view respond very rapidly to achieve disinflation with little effect on output.*

*The disinflation of 1980–1985 offers an opportunity to evaluate the output costs of reducing inflation, the role of credibility, and the contribution of the concurrent large appreciation of the dollar.*

*The output costs of disinflation are measured by the sacrifice ratio, defined as the shortfall from a potential full-employment output divided by the concurrent reduction in the inflation rate. Based on estimates of the relation between inflation and employment since World War II, the sacrifice ratio by the 1970s appeared forbiddingly high. According to Arthur Okun's well-known estimate, the ratio was 10, which means that 10 percent of one year's*

My thanks to Maryam Homayouni and Kenneth Couch for research assistance.

*real gross national product would be given up for each one-percentage-point reduction in the annual inflation rate. At such a cost the pursuit of disinflation would be extremely painful and perhaps politically unattainable. Yet this prognosis turned out to be excessively pessimistic for the recent disinflation. The actual cost, despite the deep and prolonged recession of 1981–1982, came in at half of Okun's estimate when based on the same method of measurement. Earlier measurement of the inflation-employment relation did not describe the 1980s, mainly because the pre-1980 rising trend of inflation did not indicate revisions in the measurement needed to apply as well to a declining trend.*

*Even this revised estimate of the sacrifice ratio, moreover, could be viewed as too high. The full employment output on which it is based was unrealistically high compared with the reduced trend of output since the early 1970s, owing to lower productivity growth and capital formation. If the cost of the recent disinflation is measured by shortfalls from an actual growth trend of output that is adjusted only to remove cyclical fluctuations, the sacrifice ratio was less than 2, half as high as the low level of the revised estimate. Measured by the actual trend of output, the total six-percentage-point decline in the underlying inflation rate from 1980 to 1983 cost less than 12 percent of one year's output, far less than previous pessimistic estimates, which ranged from 24 to 60 percent. A good case can be made for this lower figure of the sacrifice ratio.*

*The lower estimate presented here also indicates that the cost of disinflation was somewhat lower in 1980–1983 than in 1973–1975. Whether the lower cost was the result of greater credibility is examined. The costs of the two disinflations can be compared by means of an updated Phillips curve. A standard version of this curve is presented, in which wage increases from 1953 to 1980 are regressed on a linear unemployment variable and adaptive expectations of inflation. Simulation of the regression equation for 1980–1985 tracks the decline in inflation very well. As unemployment fell in the cyclical recovery of 1983–1984, the reason that wage increases did not speed up is that expectations of inflation, based on the previous declines, continued to fall. Nevertheless, these simulations of the annual inflation in wages are too high in 1983–1985 by an average of over one percentage point. This discrepancy can be attributed to the effects of credibility and a strong dollar. It is possibly an overestimate of their effects, because some studies find little or no discrepancy in the equation in those years when it includes other demographic and economic variables. Whether these other variables belong in the equation and therefore properly account for the discrepancy remains an unsettled question. I remain skeptical that they do because they contribute little to the fit for the pre-1980 period.*

*On the presumption that the 1983–1985 discrepancy reflects a nonnegligible effect of credibility or dollar appreciation, the possible dollar effect was tested by examining comparative wage increases in industries most heavily involved in foreign trade. Forty-odd industries with the highest percentages of imports and exports to shipments (and with available data on selling prices and wages) showed considerably more than the economywide disinflation for prices but not for wages. This evidence suggests that foreign competition was and is squeezing profit margins in these industries as their wages remain in line with the total economy.*

*If the strong dollar did not add to wage disinflation, the 1983–1985 discrepancy from past behavior of the Phillips curve points to a credibility effect. The existence of such an effect, however, does not support the optimistic hopes that it appreciably reduces the costs of disinflationary policies. Its estimated contribution of one percentage point out of a six-percentage-point reduction in inflation from 1980 to 1983 came after a severe recession and three years of disinflation. Here credibility responded to the performance of policy and not to announced intentions, although it apparently helped sustain a reduced inflation rate after the disinflationary policy proved successful. Yet, although a credibility effect does not mitigate the cost of disinflation, the recent experience demonstrates that monetary policy can reduce inflation with far less cost than had earlier been predicted.*

*The question for 1986 is whether monetary policy will sustain or lose the reduction of inflation so far attained.*

## Introduction

The high inflation rates of 1979 and 1980 were cut in half in two years by the 1981–1982 business recession. In many previous recessions inflation was also cut in half, only to climb back to high rates in the subsequent business expansions. Yet, since the 1981–1982 recession, inflation has so far not escalated for three years (at the end of 1985). Compared with the string of failures since the mid-1960s to contain inflation, the recent reduction of inflation is a great success. But with the annual rate still about 4 percent in 1985, inflation remains a concern, and whether its reduction can be maintained and extended is in question.

The nation's ability and willingness to contain inflation depend on the perceived costs. The recent disinflation was accomplished with lower costs in lost output than had previously been thought possible. Had the costs been overpredicted, or were they reduced by the credibility of monetary policy or the strong dollar? This essay addresses these questions and their implications for the future containment of inflation.

The first section of the essay reviews similarities and differences between the recent decline of inflation and the temporary decline that occurred in the 1973–1975 recession. The cost of the recent disinflation in lost output is measured and compared with earlier estimates and previous experience. The second section updates the Phillips curve to test whether unemployment and expectations fully account for the decline in inflation. The third section investigates whether the strong dollar had differential effects on wages in industries heavily involved in foreign trade. The concluding section sums up the preceding evidence on the extent to which the credibility of monetary policy hastened the transition to lower inflation.

## Output Cost of the Disinflation

**Disinflation and Recessions.** The inflation that began in the mid-1960s has been interrupted four times by anti-inflationary efforts that contracted economic activity. Inflation subsided in the minirecession of 1967 and the full-fledged recessions of 1970 and 1973–1975, but each time only temporarily. The recent disinflation was the fourth interruption. Figure 8–1 shows cyclical fluctuations in the inflation rate since 1952 as represented by the deflator for GNP.[1] Business recessions are shaded to show their role in reducing inflation and its revival in each subsequent business expansion except for 1962–1964 and 1983–1985.

Inflation escalated sharply in two waves during the 1970s, both intensified by oil price increases, first in 1973 and again in 1979. The first wave, which subsided in the 1973–1975 recession, was followed by a sharp escalation of inflation in 1978, well before an additional surge from the second oil price increase. Although the Federal Reserve changed its operating procedures in October 1979 to gain tighter control over monetary growth, this change had no immediate effect in curbing inflation. As a result, expectations of runaway inflation spread. The prices of gold and silver on commodity exchanges soared in early 1980, and panic selling hit the bond and foreign exchange markets. In March 1980, to arrest a declining dollar and to calm financial markets, the administration implemented a package of measures, the most potent of which were controls limiting consumer installment credit. These remained in force until May, precipitating a sharp recession as retail sales collapsed. Business recovered quickly and completely from the recession in the second half of 1980. Although inflation escalated no further in 1980, neither did it really subside. The consumer price index (CPI) decelerated from high double-digit rates during 1980, but most of the decline reflected the diminishing push of energy costs as the 1979 oil price increase subsided and of housing costs as rising mortgage rates stabilized.[2] The broader inflation index for GNP shown in figure 8–1 did not start down until the first quarter of 1981. Only

# FIGURE 8-1
## INFLATION RATE, QUARTERLY, 1952–1985

Percent per year

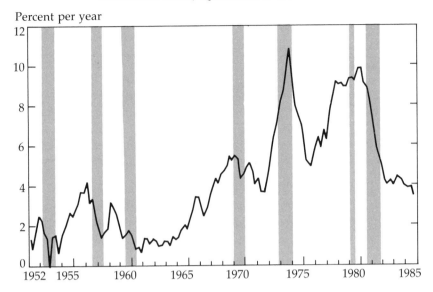

NOTE: Half-year rates of increase in GNP deflator, fixed-weight version since 1959, by Moore formula (see note 1). Shaded areas are business recessions.
SOURCE: Bureau of Economic Analysis.

an extended period of monetary restraint was able to subdue the inflation.

In measuring the reduction of inflation it is important to focus on the *underlying* rate. Transitory surges in oil and food prices and mortgage rates pushed the inflation in the CPI to double-digit peaks in 1974 and 1980, but these prices and interest rates soon stabilized to end their effects on the inflation rate. The underlying rate should be viewed as independent of temporary supply shocks whose effects die out within a year or so. It reflects the more persistent increases in input costs that are supported by the ongoing rise in aggregate demand. Its definition and measurement are somewhat arbitrary, to be sure, since what is persistent and what is temporary in the inflation rate are imprecise, but the concept is useful. Otto Eckstein constructed an underlying or "core" index of inflation based on costs of labor and capital.[3] Since labor costs are the major item, an underlying rate of inflation can be approximated by the increase in wages. Figure 8–2 shows the rate of increase of average hourly earnings of production workers and total labor compensation since 1953 and the employment cost survey since 1976. The last, though more reliable because it is

251

## FIGURE 8–2
## WAGE INFLATION, QUARTERLY, 1953–1985

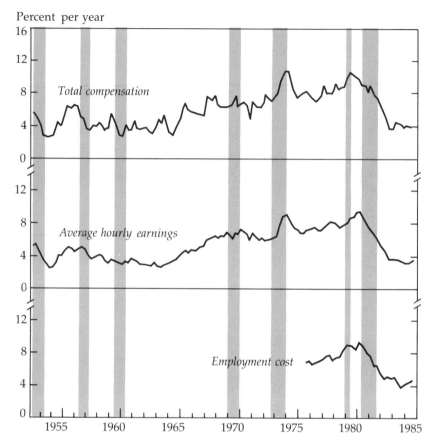

NOTE: Half-year rates of increase by the Moore formula (note 1). Total compensation per hour covers wage and salary income (including fringe benefits) of business nonfarm workers based on national income accounts. Average hourly earnings is an index of monthly wages of production workers in the private nonfarm sector adjusted for interindustry shifts and overtime in manufacturing (before 1964 an annual BLS series with quarterly interpolation based on Robert J. Gordon, "Inflation in Recession and Recovery," *Brookings Papers on Economic Activity*, no. 1 [1971], pp. 105–58, app. C). Employment cost is the BLS survey of private industry workers for wages and salaries only. Shaded areas are business recessions.
SOURCES: Bureau of Economic Analysis and Bureau of Labor Statistics.

unaffected by shifts among occupational groups, is not available for earlier years.

In the recent disinflation, wage increases peaked in early 1981 at a 10 percent annual rate and declined fairly steadily to between 3 and

## FIGURE 8-3
## MONETARY GROWTH (M1), QUARTERLY, 1972–1985
Percent per year

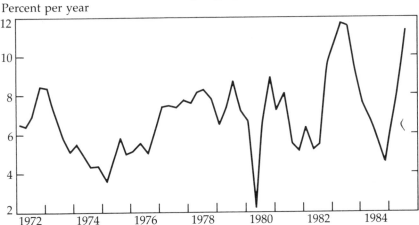

NOTE: Half-year rates of change by the Moore formula (note 1).
SOURCE: Federal Reserve Board.

4 percent by mid-1983. Although the disinflation began before the business recession of 1981–1982, it was steepest during the recession. The recession can be attributed to a failure of monetary growth to keep pace with the escalating inflation. Although annual monetary growth had fluctuated around a high 7¼ percent for four years to mid-1981 (figure 8–3), it did not rise to accommodate the escalating inflation rate, and real money balances available to the public steadily declined. When this restraint on aggregate demand finally turned business activity down after July 1981, monetary growth contracted sharply to deepen and prolong the recession. Although probably more severe than necessary to reduce inflation, the monetary contraction could be justified as a way to counter public skepticism that monetary policy would carry through with disinflation.

The 1973–1975 recession was started by a similar decline in real money balances. A decline in monetary growth began in 1973 only a few months before the recession and could not have precipitated it. The recession reflected instead an inflationary surge produced by the oil price increase and other supply-induced price pressures that outpaced monetary growth and restrained aggregate demand by reducing real money balances. Both the 1973–1975 and 1981–1982 recessions recorded roughly the same declines in the major indicators of economic activity and the same duration of sixteen months.[4] Both also cut the inflation rate in half. As already noted, however, the two

253

recessions differed in that inflation escalated sharply after the 1975 trough but has stayed down after the 1982 trough.

**Measuring the Output Gap.** The 1981–1982 recession, though not deeper, has nevertheless been called more severe than the 1973–1975 and other post-1930s recessions because of the greater and longer departure from a hypothetical full employment. In the 1981–1982 recession economic activity declined early and sharply, whereas in 1973–1975 activity remained on a plateau for eleven months before plunging. The implication was widely drawn that a greater loss of output in the recent recession was due to the accompanying disin-flationary policy, reflecting a trade-off in which the reduction of in-flation produces a period of depressed output.

Disinflation depresses output in relation to the potential output that economic resources are capable of producing when fully em-ployed at an unchanging rate of inflation. In each year that actual output falls below potential output, the difference can be expressed as a percentage shortfall or gap from potential. The once official meas-ure of potential output published by the Council of Economic Advisers (CEA) was based on an estimated growth trend of real GNP projected forward from 1955, a year viewed as having full employment.[5] Al-though the CEA has discontinued publishing this or any measure of potential GNP since 1980, others have used an extension of it to measure the cost of the recent disinflation. By one estimate for the six years 1979–1984, the cumulative output cost of the disinflation derived from the CEA measure, expressed as the sum of the annual gaps, totaled "40 percent of a year's potential aggregate supply," a quite high cost indeed.[6]

The CEA potential GNP is no longer viewed as indicative of the economy's capacity to produce. It has been consistently above actual GNP since 1973. The lower actual growth reflected a slowdown in productivity growth, and what the potential output could have been is unclear.

Two alternative measures of the GNP gap are presented in table 8–1, along with the old CEA measure, for the periods of disinflation in the mid-1970s and early 1980s. The first alternative assumes that the full-employment rate of unemployment increased after the 1950s to 6 percent in the 1970s, the consensus of numerous studies of the labor force. On the basis of this assumption and the relationship between unemployment and GNP, a GNP gap can be estimated.[7] Compared with the old CEA gap, the 6 percent full-employment gap is much lower, because it incorporates a lower full-employment level and the 1970s slowing of productivity growth.[8] The second alternative,

254

based on cycle averages of actual real GNP, is discussed below. The periods of disinflation covered in table 8–1 for the 1970s and 1980s begin with the first appearance of a positive gap according to the 6 percent full-employment assumption. These periods begin a few months earlier than the start of disinflation. Two endings of the periods are shown: one when the disinflation has largely ended, and the other when the gap first either turns negative or reaches its cyclical trough. The trough date is used to end the period when a cyclical expansion begins to reduce the gap and signals the end of disinflationary pressures.

To compare the costs of different disinflationary periods, Arthur Okun introduced the concept of the "sacrifice ratio," the cumulative gap in actual GNP from its potential that accompanies a per unit reduction in the inflation rate.[9] This ratio divides the cumulative percentage gap in annual GNP by the corresponding reduction in the

TABLE 8–1
ESTIMATES OF THE COST OF RECENT DISINFLATIONS, 1974:III–1984:II

|  | 1974:III–1976:III | 1974:III–1978:I | 1980:I–1983:II | 1980:I–1984:II |
|---|---|---|---|---|
| Cumulative GNP gap (percent) |  |  |  |  |
| Old CEA potential | 13.1 | 18.2 | 26.0 | 32.8 |
| 6 percent full employment | 8.8 | 10.8 | 19.0 | 25.0 |
| Midexpansion | 7.5 | 7.7 | 8.7 | 10.5 |
| Disinflation in GNP deflator[a] | −5.8 | −5.8 | −5.8 | −5.8 |
| Sacrifice ratio[b] |  |  |  |  |
| Old CEA potential | 2.3 | 3.1 | 4.5 | 5.7 |
| 6 percent full employment | 1.5 | 1.9 | 3.3 | 4.3 |
| Midexpansion | 1.3 | 1.3 | 1.5 | 1.8 |
| Disinflation in AHE[a] | −2.3 | −2.3 | −4.9 | −5.9 |
| Sacrifice ratio[b] |  |  |  |  |
| Old CEA potential | 5.7 | 7.9 | 5.3 | 5.6 |
| 6 percent full employment | 3.8 | 4.7 | 3.9 | 4.2 |
| Midexpansion | 3.3 | 3.3 | 1.8 | 1.8 |

NOTE: Periods begin with initial positive value of GNP gap according to 6 percent full-employment assumption and end, for the shorter period, with first reversal of decline in GNP deflator (figure 8–1) and, for the longer period, with either the final positive value of the gap or its cyclical trough, whichever came first.

a. Change from peak to minimum within the period in annual percentage rate. GNP deflator and average hourly earnings (AHE) are the series shown in figures 1 and 2 based on the Moore formula (note 1).

b. Percentage gap divided by decline in percentage inflation rate.

SOURCES: Council of Economic Advisers and Bureau of Economic Analysis (see note 8).

percentage annual rate of inflation. Writing in 1978, Okun estimated the U.S. sacrifice ratio to be 10, ranging from 6 to 18. That is, each one-percentage-point reduction in the annual inflation rate would require a depression of output equivalent to 10 percent of real GNP for one year. His estimate was based on prior studies of the relationship between inflation and unemployment. Some updated versions of this relationship—the Phillips curve—are presented in the next section.[10] A sacrifice ratio of 10 was a pessimistic and forbidding prognosis of efforts to combat inflation.

Okun's estimate of the cost of disinflation turned out to be far too high, however, even by the old CEA potential, which exaggerates the gap. Table 8–1 gives sacrifice ratios for the two disinflations of the 1970s and 1980s. Judged by the GNP deflator, the annual inflation rate had a maximum decline of 5.8 percentage points, by coincidence the same in both periods. The corresponding sacrifice ratios for different measures of the gap in table 8–1 are generally much lower than Okun's. Only the longer period for the 1980s based on the old CEA potential comes up to the lower range of Okun's estimate of the sacrifice ratio.

One reason for the difference is that the GNP deflator overstates the decline in the underlying inflation rate. After excluding transitory increases and decreases in the inflation rate, its decline appears somewhat less, particularly for the 1970s. Wages are a better representative of the underlying rate, and the disinflation based on average hourly earnings in table 8–1 gives larger sacrifice ratios except for the last period. But even then Okun's ratio appears too high, compared with ratios based on the 6 percent full-employment gap. One reason for the difference is that most of the earlier studies on which Okun's estimate was based related wage changes to the reciprocal of the unemployment rate. This convex relationship assumes that declines in wage inflation become smaller as the unemployment rate increases, which appears to understate the effect. For this and other possible reasons discussed further later, the earlier studies overstated the trade-off between unemployment and disinflation.

Although table 8–1 shows larger sacrifice ratios based on the GNP deflator for the later than for the earlier disinflationary period, there is little difference in the ratios based on wages. The GNP deflator overstates the 1970s disinflation in the underlying rate based on wages. The sacrifice ratio of about 4 to 4½ for wages based on the 6 percent full-employment gap is only slightly below later revisions of Okun's estimate.[11]

Hindsight casts doubt, however, on even the sacrifice ratios based on 6 percent full employment. At the beginning of 1985 this measure of the gap implied that the economy was 5 percent below potential. Yet after the 1981–1982 recession the economy recovered sharply during the first two years of expansion (despite a slowing at the end of 1984). Such a large gap for 1985 seems inconsistent with the strong cyclical recovery. One deficiency is that it does not allow for any change in the 6 percent assumption of full employment. Although this gap does make an adjustment for the productivity slowdown of the 1970s, it does not fully allow for effects of changes in capital and labor growth, productivity, and resource supplies. Furthermore, such measures of potential output assume that the economy could, if aggregate demand grew appropriately, expand along the potential path indefinitely.[12] This is most doubtful. The economy reaches the potential path only at the top of cyclical movements. The feverish activity of cyclical booms and even the late stages of ordinary business expansions are not sustainable, and the long-run additions to capital and technology that provide for growth would probably be about the same whether the rate of growth fluctuated or not. If so, potential output may be better approximated by the actual growth over the business cycle, abstracting from cyclical fluctuations.

Such a measure of cyclically adjusted output has recently been provided by the Bureau of Economic Analysis.[13] The measure is derived by taking the geometric average of output in the midexpansion stages of cycles and assuming constant growth between their midpoints. Midexpansion stages are found by dividing business cycles into four parts: contraction from peak to trough, recovery from the trough to the attainment of the previous peak level of output, midexpansion covering the subsequent twelve quarters, and late expansion thereafter to the next cyclical peak. If the midexpansion ends with another peak in less than twelve quarters, the period is truncated at the peak. Before the latest midexpansion stage ends, its midpoint level is partly based on forecasts. Subsequently, until the next cycle unfolds, the most recent years are estimated by projecting an assumed growth trend. Actual output in relation to the cyclically adjusted level becomes negative at times as well as positive as the economy fluctuates around the trend, and the cumulative gap over a full-cycle is approximately zero.

There are two reasons for focusing on this midexpansion measure of the gap. First, it clearly does not exaggerate the sustainable growth trend. To be sure, it also assumes that long-run economic growth could not have been greater than was actually achieved, and thus it is a lower bound of potential growth. Conceivably a felicitous monetary and fiscal policy could improve economic performance and produce a higher growth path than is usually achieved. But the degree of improvement is highly conjectural, and a lower bound is a solid estimate.

Second, the midexpansion gap is in theory the best estimate of average growth under a constant inflation rate. In economic theory escalating inflation raises output temporarily but not permanently and indeed is seen as detrimental to long-run growth. It is inconsistent with this theory to view the recent or any disinflation as reducing long-run average growth. The cost of disinflation measured by the sacrifice ratio is viewed instead as a delayed payment for the temporary increase in output from a prior escalation of inflation. This justifies a midexpansion measure of the gap, which averages zero over the long run.

The midexpansion gaps in table 8–1 are well below the other two measures. The sacrifice ratio for the midexpansion gap in the recent disinflation is below 2, which implies that the six-percentage-point reduction in the inflation rate cost less than 12 percent of a year's GNP. This is an optimistic view of disinflation compared with the other sacrifice ratios of 4 to 6 or Okun's 10, which imply that the disinflation cost 24 to 60 percent of a year's GNP. The GNP loss from disinflation, therefore, is very much a matter of the assumptions about the economy's potential. Although the midexpansion gap may be an underestimate, the others appear unrealistically high.

Because of the small difference in depth between the recessions of 1973–1975 and 1981–1982, the midexpansion gap assigns only a slightly larger cumulative gap to the latter, and the midexpansion sacrifice ratio based on wages (and all but one of the others) is actually smaller for the later disinflation. This raises the question whether anti-inflationary policies were more credible in the 1980s than they had previously been. Credibility can be relevant because it can influence the expected rate of inflation, which in turn influences the setting of wages and prices. If a credible policy leads to expectations of reduced inflation, wages and prices will reflect such expectations and adjust more quickly to disinflation with less disruption of output and employment. Thus a firm policy to reduce inflation, if widely believed, might be managed with a very low sacrifice ratio.[14] The anti-inflationary policies of the early 1980s indeed raised hopes of instilling high credibility. Both the Federal Reserve and the new administration taking office in 1981 expressed a strong determination to reduce inflation. The subsequent outcome provided a test of the effect of credibility.

Apart from the slightly lower sacrifice ratios based on wages in table 8–1, the recent disinflation is distinctive in that prices did not accelerate after business recovered from the recession. Besides greater credibility, a possible explanation for the absence of resurgence is the concurrent appreciation of the dollar, which reduces the underlying inflation rate by reducing input costs. The next two sections assess the roles of credibility and the strong dollar in the recent disinflation.

## The Phillips Curve in the Recent Disinflation

**Comparison of the 1980s with Previous Years.** The Phillips curve expresses a trade-off between inflation and the GNP gap or amount of unemployment. In the early versions it implied that unemployment could be made permanently lower by tolerating higher inflation. Such a permanent trade-off between unemployment and inflation is no longer viewed as possible. But in the short run the Phillips curve predicts the reduction in employment produced by disinflationary policies. Recent studies of expanded versions of the Phillips curve show that it tracks the data through the 1980s disinflation without major shifts.[15] An updated examination of this relationship shows whether it can track the recent disinflation and the absence of a resurgence of inflation without introducing a role for credibility or the dollar appreciation.

The original Phillips curve made wage increases solely dependent on unemployment, but a variable for expected inflation had to be added to explain developments during the 1970s, and recent versions include other variables as well. These other variables account for special influences on wages such as from social security contributions, minimum wages, and the wage controls of the early 1970s. None of these variables is particularly important for the 1980s disinflation, although collectively they can affect the results and are considered later. To avoid complicated and possibly spurious relationships, table 8–2 presents a simplified version of the Phillips curve to compare the recent and past periods. The table also gives the postsample errors in the regression forecasts for the subsequent period of reduced inflation after the business peak in the first quarter of 1980 and a later subperiod beginning in the second quarter of 1983, when the period of rapid disinflation ended. The regression fit therefore ends with the first quarter of 1980. It begins with the second quarter of 1953 and thus avoids the inflationary aftermath of the Korean War period. A graph of the actual and predicted values of one of the regressions for the period of fit and postsample forecasts is shown in figure 8–4.

The simplified relationship of table 8–2 involves wage increases, unemployment, and the expected rate of inflation. Wages are measured alternatively by average hourly earnings and total labor compensation (the same basic series as in figure 8–2). The unemployment

## TABLE 8–2
### Estimated Phillips Curves, 1953:II–1980:I, and Forecasts, 1980:II–1985:III

| Dependent Variable | Regression Coefficients (and t-statistic) | | | | $\overline{R}^2$ / DW | Average Forecast Error[a] | |
| --- | --- | --- | --- | --- | --- | --- | --- |
| | Constant | Unemployment | Expected inflation | Social security | | 1980:II–1982:IV | 1983:I–1985:III |
| Change in total compensation | 5.4 (10.0) | −0.71 (5.3) | 0.92 (13.3) | 1.13 (5.8) | .66 1.82 | +0.61 | +1.13 |
| Average hourly earnings | 5.1 (15.1) | −0.69 (7.9) | 0.85 (19.1) | — | .77 1.56 | +0.53 | +1.34 |

NOTE: Regression equation, fitted by ordinary least squares, is WAGE CHANGE = constant + $a_1U + a_2\,p^e + a_3\,SS$, where dependent variable is WAGE CHANGE at percentage annual rate (same series as cited in figure 8–2, quarterly rates of change *not* smoothed by the Moore formula), $U$ is unemployment percentage adjusted for composition of labor force (note 16), $p^e$ is expected rate of inflation equal to fifteen quarters' distributed lag (with linear declining weights) of personal consumption deflator (annual percentage rate), fixed-weight after 1958, and $SS$ is increase in employer contributions to social security relative to the trend in total compensation (note 17). $\overline{R}^2$ is squared correlation coefficient, and $DW$ is the Durbin-Watson statistic.

a. Forecast minus actual value, annual percentage rates. The ratios to the average forecast giving the average percentage forecast error are as follows: $0.61/8.88 = 6.9$ percent; $1.13/5.12 = 22.1$ percent; $0.53/8.13 = 6.5$ percent; $1.34/4.61 = 29.1$ percent.

FIGURE 8–4

ACTUAL AND PREDICTED AVERAGE HOURLY EARNINGS, 1953–1985

Percent per year

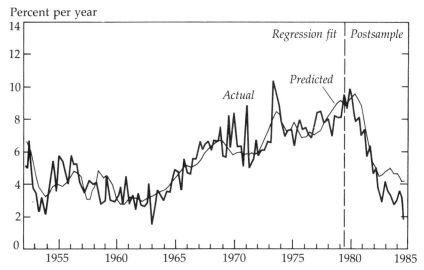

SOURCE: Regression equation of table 8–2.

series is adjusted for changes in the composition of the labor force, which have raised its level over time independently of market demand.[16] The expected inflation rate is a weighted average of actual past rates and is discussed in detail later. The only other variable included is increases in employers' social security contributions, which are part of the fringe benefits covered by total labor compensation.[17] When social security tax rates have increased, total compensation shows a sharp one-quarter increase, which is not offset by a corresponding decline in wage and salary payments. (This variable is therefore not needed to account for movements in average hourly earnings.)

Total compensation is more comprehensive than wage and salary earnings and hence is ordinarily a preferable measure of labor cost, except that its coverage of fringe benefits requires the use of less reliable data. Measurement error is suggested by its greater variability (figure 8–2) compared with the earnings series and by the lower correlation coefficient of its regression fit.[18] Despite the differences between these two series, they give comparable declines for the 1980s (table 8–2).

The regression forecasts (figure 8–4) demonstrate that the pre-1980 relationship accounts for the initial rapid deceleration of wages through early 1983 reasonably well, though with a lag at first. But the forecasts overstate the annual wage increases thereafter, by an average

261

of over one percentage point.[19] This overstatement could be due as noted to greater credibility or the strong dollar or both. Of the total actual wage deceleration of six percentage points, the five points forecast by the regression can be attributed to the Phillips curve trade-off. According to this trade-off, the rise in unemployment reduced wage increases, and by the time unemployment subsequently declined as business recovered, inflationary expectations subsided to hold the wage increases down and even reduce them further. (The wage change below 2 percent per year for 1985:III shown in figure 8–4 may be atypical. A preliminary figure for 1985:IV, not shown, is back up to 3¼ percent.)

There are two hard-to-verify features of the Phillips curve in table 8–2 that are critical for its forecast of most of the recent disinflation: the measurement of unemployment and the expected rate of inflation. These are discussed below.

*Unemployment.* This variable enters the regression here in linear form, despite the usual practice in earlier studies of an inverse relation. An inverse relation, which gives the trade-off between inflation and unemployment a convex shape, was appealing in theory but was never clearly shown to fit the data more closely than the linear form does.[20] The large rise in unemployment in 1981–1982 fits the rapid disinflation better with a linear than with a convex relationship. In the forecasts for 1983–1984 the linear form again appears to fit the data slightly better.

The technical choice between linearity and convexity bears on an important policy issue. "Gradualism," which became a tenet of macroeconomic policy in the 1960s, was based on convexity. A convex Phillips curve implied that higher unemployment rates would have diminishing effects in reducing inflation. To avoid inefficiently high costs of disinflation, therefore, it seemed to make sense to disinflate with moderate rates of unemployment maintained for a longer time— a policy of gradualism. If the trade-off relationship in fact is linear, gradualism is of no benefit, except to avoid the social disruption of extremely high unemployment. A given disinflation by high unemployment for a short period or by moderate unemployment for a longer period will cost the same in the cumulative total of unemployment months. A preference for gradualism would still be established if changes in expectations of inflation were less than proportional to the discrepancy between actual and expected rates of inflation, thus implying that speeding up the adjustment of expectations would involve disproportionate costs. But how expectations change is hard to pin down and too uncertain to base policy decisions on. Although the severity of the 1981–1982 recession exceeded what was generally thought desirable for a gradualist policy, it produced disinflation apparently in proportion to its severity to justify a nongradualist policy.

*The expected rate of inflation.* Earlier studies generally used changes in the consumer price index over the previous year or two to represent the expected rate, and its regression coefficient came out well below unity. Recent studies use the personal consumption deflator combined with a distributed lag of several years or more. The statistical significance of the latter variable in the regressions is about the same as the former, but its regression coefficient no longer differs significantly from unity.[21] Unity is consistent with the theory that expectations are not biased and no long-run trade-off exists between inflation and unemployment. Of course, this theory is supported but not proved by a regression coefficient close to unity, because these results can also be rationalized as statistical consequences of the long distributed lag and smaller volatility of the personal consumption deflator than of the CPI. The CPI is more volatile because of the larger weight it assigns to mortgage interest rates and some special components such as used cars. Given the relatively low variability of the wage series, the lower variability of the personal consumption deflator and of the long lag necessarily produces a larger regression coefficient for this variable than for the CPI. Despite the possible statistical basis for its better performance, the personal consumption deflator is used here to put the best possible light on the Phillips curve forecasts. Moreover, some of the greater volatility in the CPI was a misleading indicator of the underlying inflation rate and, even if accepted by the public as accurate, was probably still viewed as transitory and hence not incorporated into expectations of future inflation.

The calculation of the expected rate of inflation uses fifteen quarters of lagged inflation rates with linear weights declining into the past. The average length of the lag is two years. Such a distributed lag can be rationalized as the way expectations are probably formed. Moreover, the regression coefficient is near its theoretical value of unity, while coefficients of expected inflation with much shorter lags are significantly below unity.

The length of this lag has an important effect on the forecasts of disinflation. A shorter lag would bring the forecast values down faster in the disinflation and reduce the one-percentage-point average discrepancy shown in figure 8–4 for 1984–1985 (assuming the regression coefficient of the expected inflation variable is not smaller). Given the consistency of the fifteen-quarter lag with past experience,[22] the forecast errors suggest that in 1984–1985 expectations adjusted faster than

263

previously,[23] which could be attributed to an early perception of the continued success of the anti-inflationary policies (a delayed credibility effect) and perhaps also to the effects of the rising dollar.

**Comparison of the 1980s with Pre-1970 Years.** By fitting the regressions to an earlier segment, we can see whether forecasts based on the earlier period are different. Table 8–3 compares the results of fitting the regressions of table 8–2 for a shorter segment that ends with 1969 as well as for the full period up to 1980. The regressions for both periods of fit are used to predict wage changes for the 1980s. The predictions cover the same two periods for the 1980s disinflation as in table 8–1 except that, as indicated in the note to table 8–3, they give the total decline in the inflation rate from the beginning to the end of the periods and thus differ from the average of quarterly forecast errors in table 8–1. The first period of 1980–1983 covers the rapid part of the disinflation, when unemployment rose sharply. The second period extends the first to 1984 to cover the further moderate disinflation when unemployment recovered and the expected inflation variable continued to decline. The predicted changes show how far these developments are consistent with the experience of both the previous full sample period and its initial segment.

The predictions for both sets of regressions are consistent with the results for table 8–2 in failing to show as much decline as actually occurred for total compensation in the two postsample periods and for average hourly earnings in the extended period 1980–1984. In this respect the two periods of fit give the same results. The underprediction for the extended period 1980–1984 is greater for the regressions fitted to the initial segment, however, especially for total compensation and moderately for average hourly earnings.

The explanation of the greater understatement for the regressions fitted to the initial segment can be found in their coefficients, reported in the note to the table. Compared with the regressions for the full sample period reported in table 8–2, the shorter fits have much smaller regression coefficients for expected inflation and somewhat larger (negative) coefficients for unemployment. The smaller coefficients for expected inflation from the initial segment presumably reflect the smaller effect of that variable. It has a smaller effect in the initial segment perhaps because inflation was not yet perceived as a persistent phenomenon and expectations were less focused. In any event, for 1983–1984 the full period regressions assign a greater effect on wages to the continuing decline in expected inflation and less effect to the recovery of unemployment.

The regressions for average hourly earnings are of special interest because they have the same dependent variable as those that underlie Okun's estimate of the sacrifice ratio. Although neither of these regressions underpredicts the first part of the disinflation, both underpredict the full period of disinflation 1980–1984 by about one percentage point. This points, as noted, to an additional influence coming in at that time, such as greater credibility or a rising dollar. The similar forecasts of this dependent variable from the fits for the shorter and longer periods imply, however, that Okun's overestimate of the sacrifice ratio is primarily attributable not to the unavailability of later data but to the earlier pessimistic interpretations of the Phillips curve regressions.

Unlike the good fit for the rapid part of the disinflation in 1980–1983, therefore, the forecast errors for 1984–1985 imply a departure from past behavior. To be sure, these errors could reflect an omission of other variables in the regressions. It appears possible to eliminate much of these forecast errors in 1984–1985 by adding certain variables to the regressions, at least for total compensation.[24] Since variables can usually be found to improve any regression, however, the validity of such additions is difficult to determine. Confining the regression to the variables of the basic theory is a precaution against a spurious accuracy. Forecast errors are indeed evidence of other influences, but

TABLE 8–3
FORECASTS FROM PHILLIPS CURVES, 1980:I–1984:II

| Dependent Variable | Period of Fit | Predicted (and Actual) Change in Wage Inflation[a] | | | |
|---|---|---|---|---|---|
| | | 1980:I–1983:II | | 1980:I–1984:II | |
| Total Compensation | 1953:II–1969:IV | − 3.8 | ( − 5.0) | − 1.3 | ( − 5.4) |
| | 1953:II–1980:I | − 4.3 | | − 3.7 | |
| Average hourly earnings | 1953:II–1969:IV | − 3.9 | ( − 3.6) | − 3.6 | ( − 4.6) |
| | 1953:II–1980:I | − 3.8 | | − 3.8 | |

NOTE: Regression equations fitted to extended period are reported in table 8–2. For the initial segment they are as follows (variables described in note to table 8–2):

| Total compensation | = | 7.1 | − 0.84$U$ | + | 0.24$p^e$ | + | 1.09$SS$ | $\bar{R}^2$ = .36 |
|---|---|---|---|---|---|---|---|---|
| | | (7.9) | (4.9) | | (1.0) | | (3.5) | $DW$ = 1.84 |
| Average hourly earnings | = | 5.6 | − 0.75$U$ | + | 0.68$p^e$ | | | $\bar{R}^2$ = .59 |
| | | (11.1) | (7.7) | | (4.8) | | | $DW$ = 1.41 |

a. These are changes in annual percentage rates from beginning to end of the periods indicated by the Moore formula (note 1). Actual changes differ from those in table 8–1, which gives changes from the peak to minimum rates within the periods.

Predicted changes are based on changes in predicted values from regression equations. The changes were converted to levels needed to calculate the rates of change from the beginning to the end of the periods by the Moore formula.

## FIGURE 8–5
### Dollar Exchange Rate and Prices of
### Foreign-traded Goods, 1979–1985

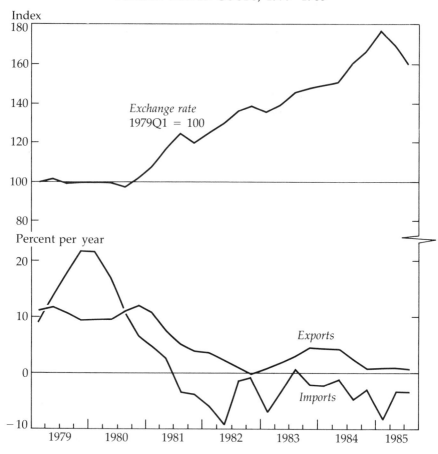

Source: Trade-weighted exchange rate, Federal Reserve Board. Half-year rates of change by Moore formula (note 1) of price deflators for imports and exports, National Income Accounts, Bureau of Economic Analysis.

these are not necessarily best identified by adding variables to the regression. This is especially true of unmeasurable influences such as credibility. It is important to examine other evidence. As a first step the next section examines evidence on the behavior of wages in industries especially subject to foreign competition for the effects of the strong dollar.

## Disinflation and the Appreciation of the Dollar

Figure 8–5 shows the extent to which the appreciation of the dollar since 1980 has disinflated import prices. They went from increases of over 20 percent per year in early 1980 to rates of *decline* over 5 percent per year two years later. Export prices have been less affected, decelerating more in line with the general price level in figure 8–1. The presumption here is that appreciation of the dollar developed from a foreign capital inflow owing to the federal budget deficit and therefore has largely contributed to rather than reflected the disinflation. The strong dollar put downward pressure on prices and wages in industries subject to import competition and to some extent in those that are heavy exporters. This kind of pressure may exceed what is predicted by the Phillips curve based on changes in unemployment or in the expected rate of inflation. The appreciation of the dollar may, therefore, help account for the positive forecast errors of the Phillips curve in 1983–1985 (figure 8–4). While some studies have added the foreign exchange rate as a separate variable to a Phillips curve wage equation,[25] time series regressions for prior periods give mixed results and may not be applicable to the 1980–1984 rise in the exchange rate, inasmuch as this rise far exceeds the comparable short-run changes of the post–World War II period.

Alternative evidence on the effect of the appreciation of the dollar on inflation is provided by examining industries subject to substantial foreign competition. These industries were selected according to their involvement in foreign trade. Data on the ratios of exports to total shipments and of imports to total domestic supply (shipments plus imports) were used to identify manufacturing industries (four-digit standard industrial classification) in which the sum of these ratios exceeded 25 percent in 1983 (the latest year available). There were 102 such industries, which account for 23 percent of the gross value of shipments in all manufacturing industries and compete against 35 percent of total merchandise imports. Figure 8–6 compares price and wage inflation in the general economy with forty of these industries for which individual price and wage series are available; these forty industries account for 59 percent of the shipments by the 102 industries.

In the top panel the comparison shows the additional disinflationary effects of foreign competition produced by the strong dollar. The forty industries on average disinflated more rapidly and further than the GNP deflator after 1980 as the dollar rose.[26] Their prices reinflated moderately during the business recovery of 1983 and early 1984 but remained below the 4 percent rate of the GNP deflator and

267

## FIGURE 8–6
### Comparative Price and Wage Inflation of
### Foreign-competing Industries, 1980–1985

Percent per year

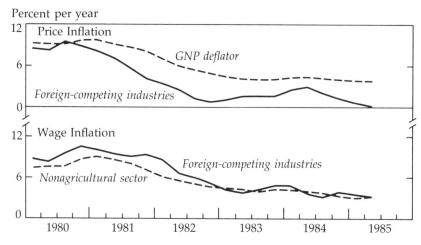

NOTE: Half-year rates of increase by Moore formula (note 1). The series for foreign-competing industries is an unweighted average of 40 industries with available data, selected from 102 (four-digit SIC) industries in which the sum of ratios of exports to shipments and of imports to domestic supply exceeded 25 percent in 1983. The GNP deflator is the same as figure 8–1, and nonagricultural sector wage inflation is based on the unadjusted version of average hourly earnings in figure 8–2.

SOURCES: Bureau of Economic Analysis and Bureau of Labor Statistics.

by mid-1985 had disinflated to almost a zero rate. Overall from the third quarter of 1980 to the second quarter of 1985 the prices for the forty industries rose on average only 12 percent, compared with 30 percent for the GNP deflator. They could have risen another 16 percent, therefore, to match the rise in the GNP deflator.

The bottom panel of figure 8–6 makes the same comparison for wages. It plots the inflation of average hourly earnings in the forty industries and in the entire nonagricultural sector. In contrast to prices, annual wage inflation disinflated only one additional percentage point in the forty industries from the first quarter of 1980 to the end of 1982 and none thereafter to mid-1985, even though some industries may show larger effects. This small effect of foreign competition on wages does not appear to reflect bias in the coverage of industries. A wage index available for most of the 102 industries exhibits the same pattern (not shown) and in particular rises within a band of 3 to 4½ percent per year from 1983 to mid-1985. This suggests that the forty are probably representative of the 102 industries in price behavior as well.

The substantial disinflation in prices and relatively little in wages for the forty industries implies a squeezing of their profit margins. The alternative explanation that there was a compensating increase in productivity is not plausible. Why wages have not disinflated more, even temporarily, where foreign competition has been strongest is not clear. Perhaps labor market adjustments have worked to prevent such wage differentials. Employment in the forty industries declined by more than in all manufacturing in the recession year 1982 but, surprisingly, has behaved the same since then. In any event, the profits squeeze suggests that these industries have been contracting now and that their prices will later reinflate whenever the dollar declines.

If the strong dollar is not responsible for reducing wage inflation in 1983–1985, some other special influence was at work to explain the positive forecast errors of the standard Phillips curve. This suggests a residual influence from enhanced credibility, but the influence was clearly less and came later than optimistic views of its potential effect had initially predicted.

**Conclusion: Disinflation and Monetary Policy**

Discussions of inflation in the 1950s and 1960s emphasized its trade-off with unemployment. The Phillips curve implied that the reduction of inflation required an increase in unemployment in the short run if not in the long run. After it became clear in the 1970s that expectations of inflation also affected the trade-off, the concept of the credibility of anti-inflation policy was introduced, raising the question whether a policy of disinflation would entail less unemployment if widely believed. The reasoning was that expectations of reduced inflation would influence the setting of prices and wages and speed their adjustment, thus avoiding much of the price stickiness that results in reduced output.

Two developments seemed to enhance the credibility of anti-inflationary policy at the start of the recent disinflation. First, in October 1979 the Federal Reserve adopted a new operating procedure designed to exert tighter control over monetary growth.[27] Second, the new administration taking office in early 1981 emphasized its commitment to containing inflation. These actions reflected an effort to enhance the credibility and thus the effectiveness of the planned anti-inflationary measures. It was not clear, however, how long it might take for the public to learn of the new measures and for credibility to affect price and wage behavior.

The cost of the ensuing disinflation, as measured by deviations of

269

actual from potential full employment output, was approximately the same in the early 1980s as in the 1970s. In both cases the cost per unit of disinflation—the sacrifice ratio—was actually only about half of a widely noted 1978 estimate based on existing studies of wage-price behavior. The measured cost was even lower and less forbidding when based on a more realistic measure of potential output. Moreover, the more realistic measure—the midexpansion gap—gives a sacrifice ratio that is lower for the 1980s than for the 1970s. This indication that greater credibility had reduced the cost for the 1980s disinflation is only partially confirmed by the behavior of wages, however.

Wages are a good indicator of the underlying rate of inflation, whereas price indexes are more subject to temporary disturbances. The Phillips curve was examined to provide evidence on the behavior of wages. A simple version of the Phillips wage equation fitted to past behavior and used to predict ahead accounts for all the decline in wage inflation from 1980 to the end of 1982. The equation also predicts the absence of rising inflation in the business expansion after 1982. Although the expansion reduced unemployment and worked to raise inflation, the expected rate of inflation in the equation continued to decline, predicting little net change in inflation. The equation overpredicted the annual wage increases in 1983–1985, however, by over one percentage point. This small but not inconsequential residual can be attributed to increased credibility and suggests that it had a belated effect in the reduction of inflation.

The main alternative for explaining the one-percentage-point discrepancy is foreign trade competition due to the strong dollar. But wages in industries most subject to foreign competition do not show the additional disinflation consistent with this explanation.[28] Foreign-competing industries did have more disinflation in prices but little more in wages and thus suffered a profits squeeze. How wages in these industries will behave in the future is unclear, but in the meantime the profits squeeze points to contraction and, should the dollar decline sufficiently, to a later reinflation of prices.

Taken all together, the evidence suggests that credibility had an effect, but only after the anti-inflationary policy had already demonstrated its persistence and effectiveness for almost three years. Credibility is apparently not easy to influence and depends on demonstrated performance rather than on announcements or intentions. Part of the difficulty in influencing expectations is that, apart from some dramatic step such as adoption of the gold standard, monetary policy cannot readily induce a skeptical public to take anti-inflationary intentions seriously. Furthermore, the actual initial decline of inflation raises the demand for money and requires a moderation of the contractionary monetary path that might otherwise strengthen the credibility of policy. The signals of monetary policy can be misleading. They have been particularly hard to interpret since 1979. Upon the adoption of the new operating procedure in 1979, the pattern of monetary growth became highly volatile and not well suited to inspire confidence in its future path. Although the disinflation of the early 1980s can be attributed to monetary tightening, policy did not follow a steady, predictable path. As shown in figure 8–3, monetary growth was highly expansionary from the mid-1970s through the first half of 1981 except for a brief contraction owing to the credit controls of early 1980. The recession beginning in July 1981 cannot be attributed to a prior contraction in monetary growth. It reflected instead a failure of monetary growth to match the escalation of inflation during 1980 from the second oil price increase, which reduced real money balances and thereby contracted aggregate demand. When business turned down in mid-1981, monetary growth contracted sharply for a year to deepen and prolong the recession. In late summer 1982 monetary growth expanded sharply to stimulate activity. When the economy responded to this stimulus in 1983, monetary policy tightened sharply to restrain the economic recovery, then just as sharply expanded again during 1985. The ups and downs of monetary growth have made it difficult to predict the future course of inflation. The expansion of monetary growth in 1985, undertaken to reduce interest rates and thus ease the plight of foreign-competing industries and debtor countries, added to concerns over the sustainability of the recent disinflation.

The reduction of inflation, though not initially helped by greater credibility, has gradually strengthened public confidence in the anti-inflationary policy. But the contribution of credibility to reducing output costs was belated and limited. Whether a steadier monetary policy would have produced more credibility is a debated issue. The steadiness of policy aside, recent experience suggests that reducing inflation requires an extended period of contractionary monetary pressure, and possible influences on expectations are not likely to reduce the associated costs by much. Once a reduction in the underlying inflation rate has been achieved, however, credibility can help to hold it down in the face of temporary upward pressures. Contrary to original hopes, credibility has developed too slowly to help reduce inflation, but in time it can help build protection against temporary new outbursts.

# Notes

1. The rates of change in this figure and others in this essary are calculated by a formula due to Geoffrey H. Moore to reduce short-run volatility with a minimum of smoothing. The formula is the difference in natural logarithms between the current quarter and an average of the preceding four quarters. The log difference has a span of two and one-half quarters and so is multiplied by 4/2.5 for conversion to an annual rate.

2. In the other direction, the used car component of the consumer price index has spuriously overstated inflation by more than usual since 1981 because of the increased importance of omitting a quality adjustment for used cars. The GNP and personal consumption deflators cited later give very little weight to used car prices. See Robert T. Mcgee, "Why Have Used Car Prices Risen So Fast?" *Quarterly Review* (Federal Reserve Bank of New York) (Autumn 1984), pp. 25–26.

3. Otto Eckstein, *Core Inflation* (Englewood Cliffs, N.J.: Prentice-Hall, 1981).

4. Actually, the recent recession was less severe in magnitude of decline. Between peaks and troughs of the two recessions, the unemployment rate rose 3.8 percentage points in the earlier and 3.5 percentage points in the later recession, industrial production fell 14.8 percent earlier and 11.3 percent later, and real GNP fell 4.9 percent earlier and 2.8 percent later. For the world economy, however, the later recession was more severe according to most indicators.

5. See *Annual Report of Council of Economic Advisers*, January 1981, p. 181.

6. Otto Eckstein, "Disinflation," in *Inflation: Prospects and Remedies* (Washington, D.C.: Center for National Policy, 1983), p. 20, based on CEA potential real GNP, projected after 1980 at 2.7 annual growth by Data Resources Inc. (Eckstein, *Core Inflation*, p. 45).

7. The relation between unemployment and GNP is based on "Okun's law" (see Arthur M. Okun, "Potential GNP: Its Measurement and Significance," *Proceedings of the American Statistical Association, Business and Economic Statistics Section, 1962*, pp. 98–104).

8. The 6 percent full-employment gap used below is from Thomas M. Holloway, "Cyclical Adjustment of the Federal Budget and Federal Debt: Detailed Methodology and Estimates," Bureau of Economic Analysis Staff Paper 40, June 1984 and update November 1984. (For the productivity adjustment see page 231 of the June 1984 publication.) See also Frank de Leeuw and Thomas M. Holloway, "Cyclical Adjustment of the Federal Budget and Federal Debt," *Survey of Current Business*, vol. 63 (December 1983), pp. 25–40.

9. Arthur M. Okun, "Efficient Disinflationary Policies," *American Economic Review*, vol. 68 (May 1978), pp. 348–52.

10. A sacrifice ratio is derived from the Phillips curve by calculating the additional unemployment it predicts from a given reduction in the inflation rate. The additional unemployment can be translated into an output loss, expressed as a percentage of potential real GNP. Dividing this percentage loss of real GNP by the reduction in the annual percentage inflation rate gives

the sacrifice ratio. Since the Phillips curve also contains the expected inflation rate, the effect of the reduction in inflation on expectations and the feedback of expectations on the inflation rate must be taken into account.

11. See Stanley Fischer, "Contracts, Credibility, and Disinflation," National Bureau of Economic Research Working Paper 1339, April 1984; Robert J. Gordon and Stephen R. King, "The Output Cost of Disinflation in Traditional Vector Autoregressive Models," *Brookings Papers on Economic Activity*, no. 1 (1982), pp. 205–42.

12. William Fellner objected to the concept of potential real GNP because it implied that the potential could be achieved by a proper management of aggregate demand only, without regard to other government policies. See "The High-Employment Budget and Potential Output: A Critique," *Survey of Current Business*, vol. 62 (November 1982), pp. 26–33.

13. See references in note 8.

14. This is a proposition implied by the theory of rational expectations. See, for example, Bennett McCallum, ed., *Rational Expectations*, a conference of the American Enterprise Institute, *Journal of Money, Credit, and Banking* (November 1980), pt. 2.

15. A. Steven Englander and Cornelis A. Los, "Recovery without Accelerating Inflation?" *Quarterly Review* (Federal Reserve Bank of New York), vol. 8 (Summer 1983), pp. 19–27, and "The Stability of the Phillips Curve and Its Implications for the 1980s," Federal Reserve Bank of New York Research Paper 8303 (February 1983); Steven Braun, "Productivity and the NIIRU (and Other Phillips Curve Issues)," Board of Governors of the Federal Reserve System Working Paper, Series 34 (February 1984); and Oliver J. Blanchard, "The Lucas Critique and the Volcker Deflation," *American Economic Review*, vol. 74 (May 1984), pp. 211–15.

For evidence that the Phillips curve predicts inflation better than other models, see David J. Stockton and James E. Glassman, "An Evaluation of the Forecast Performance of Alternative Models of Inflation," Board of Governors of the Federal Reserve System Working Paper, Series 53, July 1985.

16. The adjusted series of unemployment is from George L. Perry, "Changing Labor Markets and Inflation," *Brookings Papers on Economic Activity*, no. 3 (1970), p. 415; updated series kindly provided by him.

17. Increases in the contributions are expressed as a percentage of the trend growth in total compensation. This series, used by Braun ("Productivity and the NIIRU") and kindly provided by him, is from the Board of Governors of the Federal Reserve System's quarterly model.

18. Greater measurement error may explain why the total compensation regression does not exhibit significant serial correlation, a problem in the regression for average hourly earnings, as shown by the Durbin-Watson statistic.

19. A similar overprediction is produced by the Phillips curves estimated by Braun ("Productivity and the NIIRU") and Blanchard ("The Lucas Critique") and was tentatively noted by Phillip Cagan and William Fellner, "The Cost of Disinflation, Credibility, and the Deceleration of Wages 1982–1983,"

in Fellner, ed., *Essays in Contemporary Economic Problems: Disinflation* (Washington, D.C.: American Enterprise Institute, 1984), pp. 7–19.

20. Confirmation of linearity was recently reported by David T. Coe and Francesco Gagliardi, "Nominal Wage Determination in Ten OECD Economies," OECD, Economics and Statistics Department, Working Paper no. 19, March 1985.

21. Tests supporting a unity coefficient are reported by Braun ("Productivity and the NIIRU") and Englander and Los ("The Stability of the Phillips Curve").

22. The goodness of fit is not sensitive to moderate changes in the length of the lag. The fifteen-quarter lag was selected by Braun ("Productivity and the NIIRU") and Englander and Los ("The Stability of the Phillips Curve").

23. Inflationary expectations based on surveys record a sharp decline from 1980 to 1983, but whether this was unusually rapid is not clear.

24. No postsample overpredictions are reported for total compensation by Englander and Los ("The Stability of the Phillips Curve") or for prices by Robert J. Gordon, "Understanding Inflation in the 1980s," *Brookings Papers on Economic Activity*, no. 1 (1985), pp. 263–99.

25. See Rudiger Dornbusch and Stanley Fischer, "The Open Economy: Implications for Monetary and Fiscal Policy," National Bureau of Economic Research Working Paper 1422, August 1984; and Gordon, "Understanding Inflation," p. 274.

For a succinct survey of recent studies, see Charles Pigott and Vincent Reinhart, "The Strong Dollar and U.S. Inflation," *Quarterly Review* (Federal Reserve Bank of New York), vol. 10, no. 3 (Autumn 1985), pp. 23–29.

26. The average wage of the forty industries is unweighted, each industry wage being treated as an equally important observation, to avoid dominance by a few particularly large industries. Nevertheless, a weighted index gives similar results.

27. Interest rate responses to money supply announcements before and after October 1979 suggest that the Federal Reserve's new policy changed expectations in financial markets. See William T. Gavin and Nicholas V. Karamouzis, "Federal Reserve Credibility and the Markets' Response to the Weekly M1 Announcements," Federal Reserve Bank of Cleveland Working Paper 8502, July 1985; and Jan G. Loeys, "Changing Interest Rate Responses to Money Announcements: 1972–1983," *Journal of Monetary Economics*, vol. 15 (May 1985), pp. 323–32.

28. The unprecedented phenomenon in recent years of union concessions on wages as well as fringe benefits and work rules in many industries may perhaps have been influenced by foreign competition in the economy at large even when the competition was not directly important in most of the influenced industries.

# 9

# Job Changes and Displaced Workers: An Examination of Employment Adjustment Experience

### Marvin H. Kosters

## Summary

*Although employment increased rapidly enough to absorb most of the unusually large increase in the working-age population and the labor force during the past two decades, there were major differences among sectors of the economy. Most of the employment growth occurred in service-producing industries; there was little growth in goods-producing industries, especially in manufacturing. The manufacturing share of employment, for example, declined from 40 percent in the early 1970s to 30 percent in the mid-1980s.*

*These trends generated concerns about the health of basic industry, about implications for real wages, and about the effects on workers displaced from industries with declining employment. The employment adjustments involved were significant, but some of the concerns appear to have been exaggerated in view of the evidence on adjustment experience.*

*Although real earnings have increased less rapidly during the past decade then earlier in the postwar period, changes in real earnings trends cannot be traced to a declining share of manufacturing employment. A small but persistent component of overall real wage trends can be accounted for by shifts in employment shares away from relatively high-wage industries. Changes in real earnings trends, however, have been the result of other factors since shifting employment shares have been quite stable in relation to differences in wage levels among industries. Individual workers displaced from jobs have, of course, experienced unemployment and real wage changes as part of the adjustment process.*

*Estimates of numbers of workers displaced from jobs have often been misleading because insufficient attention has been given to the distinction between gross job changes and net changes in employment levels. Workers*

I am indebted to Murray N. Ross for assistance in analyzing the data discussed in this essay.

*who are permanently separated from their jobs account for only a small share of the employment adjustments going on in the economy. Although permanent job separation means that a worker cannot return to a particular job, it is the disappearance of the job that is permanent, not the opportunity of the worker to fill a new job. Experienced workers who are displaced from jobs could, nevertheless, face disproportionately serious problems, with their severity depending on their adjustment experience.*

*Careful examination of the characteristics and experience of displaced workers indicates some systematic differences from other workers in the economy who experience unemployment and job change. Most of these differences are not very pronounced, however. Major reductions in real earnings are not, in general, experienced by workers permanently displaced from jobs. Some unemployment for most of these workers, quite lengthy periods of unemployment for some, and withdrawal from the labor force for a small component were the main economic effects. Adjustment problems of displaced workers do not, however, appear to be sufficiently sharply distinguished from those of other workers making adjustments to merit consideration of special programs contingent on specific events, such as plant closure.*

## Introduction

Job creation in the U.S. economy in recent years has compared very favorably with earlier experience and with recent experience in other industrial countries. Despite unusually rapid growth in the working-age population and in the labor force, the fraction of the working-age population employed is at a record high level. Employment growth, although interrupted periodically by recessions, has been sufficient to absorb nearly all of the unusually large additions to the work force during the past twenty years (table 9–1).

Although overall employment growth has been quite strong, it has been uneven over time and among sectors of the economy. Cutbacks in employment by major firms and slow growth or even declining employment in some industries attracted so much media attention that the fact that such changes were much more than offset by additional new jobs in other sectors was often almost overlooked. The employment adjustments involved were so extensive, however, that it seemed possible that more, and more persistent, unemployment might be the result.

Industrial plant closings, for example, attracted a great deal of public attention during the recessionary period from 1980 through 1982. Layoffs and plant closings in the manufacturing industries were sufficiently widespread to generate discussion at the political level of the need for an "industrial policy" and of its potential merit. The need to foster "reindustrialization" was often emphasized to mitigate or reverse the "deindustrialization" that was perceived to be under way. Workers affected by sharp reductions in employment or plant closures—"dislocated" or "displaced" workers—also received increased attention.

During the general economic recovery after 1982 many new job opportunities became available, and in some instances workers were recalled who had earlier regarded their separation from a job as permanent. Nevertheless, severe competition from imports and weak demand for exports associated with the strong dollar and large balance of payments deficits kept employment from expanding or led to further job losses in certain industries, firms, and plant locations.

Adjustments in jobs and employment are, of course, the norm in a dynamic and changing economy. In general, the market system has proved to be quite effective as a mechanism for inducing resource reallocation in response to changing conditions, including reallocation of labor resources. Reallocation is, however, neither instantaneous nor costless. From the point of view of analyzing the problems of workers whose jobs were permanently terminated—displaced workers—the main issues seem to be how large the reallocation costs are, whether they are borne disproportionately by a narrow segment of the work force, and what policies might be devised to reduce these costs and spread their incidence without producing side effects that could also be unduly costly.

Before discussing displaced workers, we will describe changes in employment among broad industry sectors and examine the implications of shifts in employment shares for real wage trends. Estimates of numbers of displaced workers are then discussed in the context of job changes that are always occurring in the economy. Finally, the characteristics of displaced workers are compared with those of the work force as a whole, and their experience in obtaining new jobs is analyzed.

### The Economic and Industrial Context

Recent trends in the U.S. economy indicate that a structural realignment has been taking place, a shift from goods-producing to service-producing activities. The realignment has, however, occurred primarily in employment and not in output. Real output in goods-producing industries as a share of GNP was nearly the same (about 46 percent) in 1984 as in 1973 (table 9–2). The employment share, on the other hand, declined from 39.5 percent to 31.5 percent. More rapid productivity growth (as conventionally measured) in the goods-pro-

277

## TABLE 9-1
### EMPLOYMENT, UNEMPLOYMENT RATES, AND EMPLOYMENT-POPULATION RATIO IN TEN COUNTRIES, 1960–1985

| | United States | Canada | Australia | Japan | France | Germany | Great Britain | Italy | Netherlands | Sweden |
|---|---|---|---|---|---|---|---|---|---|---|
| | Employment (millions) | | | | | | | | | |
| 1975 | 85.8 | 9.3 | 5.9 | 51.5 | 20.7 | 25.2 | 24.0 | 19.5 | 4.6 | 4.1 |
| 1980 | 99.3 | 10.7 | 6.3 | 54.6 | 21.1 | 25.7 | 24.1 | 20.4 | 5.0 | 4.2 |
| 1981 | 100.4 | 11.0 | 6.4 | 55.1 | 20.9 | 25.5 | 23.2 | 20.5 | 5.0 | 4.2 |
| 1982 | 99.5 | 10.6 | 6.4 | 55.6 | 21.0 | 25.1 | 22.8 | 20.4 | 4.9 | 4.2 |
| 1983 | 100.8 | 10.7 | 6.3 | 56.6 | 20.8 | 24.6 | 22.6 | 20.5 | 4.9 | 4.2 |
| 1984 | 105.0 | 11.0 | 6.5 | 56.9 | 20.7 | 24.6 | 23.0 | 20.4 | 4.9 | 4.2 |
| | Employment: Population Ratio (percent) | | | | | | | | | |
| 1975 | 56.1 | 56.9 | 60.1 | 61.2 | 54.3 | 52.5 | 60.3 | 46.1 | 46.6 | 64.8 |
| 1980 | 59.2 | 59.3 | 58.4 | 61.3 | 53.1 | 51.6 | 58.9 | 46.1 | 46.9 | 65.6 |
| 1981 | 59.0 | 59.9 | 58.4 | 61.2 | 52.3 | 50.7 | 55.8 | 45.9 | 46.5 | 65.1 |
| 1982 | 57.8 | 57.0 | 57.3 | 61.2 | 51.9 | 49.4 | 54.6 | 45.2 | 45.4 | 64.7 |
| 1983 | 57.9 | 56.7 | 55.4 | 61.4 | 51.3 | 48.8 | 54.2 | 44.7 | 44.8 | 64.6 |
| 1984 | 59.5 | 57.4 | 56.0 | 61.0 | 50.6 | 48.9 | 54.6 | 44.8 | 44.5 | 64.9 |

Unemployment Rate (percent)

| | | | | | | | | | | |
|---|---|---|---|---|---|---|---|---|---|---|
| 1960 | 5.5 | 6.5 | 1.6 | 1.7 | 1.6 | 1.1 | 2.0 | 3.2 | n.a. | 1.7 |
| 1965 | 4.5 | 3.6 | 1.3 | 1.2 | 1.4 | .3 | 2.0 | 3.0 | n.a. | 1.2 |
| 1970 | 4.9 | 5.7 | 1.6 | 1.2 | 2.5 | .5 | 2.0 | 2.8 | n.a. | 1.5 |
| 1975 | 8.5 | 6.9 | 4.9 | 1.9 | 4.2 | 3.4 | 4.5 | 3.0 | 5.2 | 1.6 |
| 1980 | 7.1 | 7.5 | 6.1 | 2.0 | 6.4 | 2.9 | 6.8 | 3.9 | 6.2 | 2.0 |
| 1981 | 7.6 | 7.5 | 5.8 | 2.2 | 7.5 | 4.1 | 10.4 | 4.3 | 9.3 | 2.5 |
| 1982 | 9.7 | 11.0 | 7.2 | 2.4 | 8.4 | 5.9 | 11.8 | 4.8 | 11.3 | 3.1 |
| 1983 | 9.6 | 11.9 | 10.0 | 2.7 | 8.6 | 7.5 | 12.8 | 5.3 | 14.5 | 3.5 |
| 1984 | 7.5 | 11.3 | 9.0 | 2.8 | 10.1 | 7.8 | 13.0 | 5.6 | 15.0 | 3.1 |
| 1985[a] | 7.3 | 10.6 | n.a. | 2.6 | 10.5 | 8.0 | 13.3 | 5.6 | n.a. | 3.0 |

NOTE: n.a. = not available.

a. Second quarter, 1985.

SOURCES: Joyanna Moy, "Recent Trends in Unemployment and the Labor Force, 10 Countries," *Monthly Labor Review*, August 1985, and Bureau of Labor Statistics, *Statistical Supplement to International Comparisons of Unemployment* (Bulletin 1979), September 1985.

## TABLE 9–2
### EMPLOYMENT AND OUTPUT BY INDUSTRY GROUP, 1973–1985

*Employment and Output Shares by Broad Industry Group*

|  | 1973 | 1979 | 1984 | 1985 |
|---|---|---|---|---|
| Goods-producing total |  |  |  |  |
| Output share (%) | 45.6 | 45.8 | 46.6 | 46.0 |
| Employment share (%) | 39.5 | 35.8 | 31.5 | 30.8 |
| Employment (thousands) | 24,893 | 26,461 | 24,730 | 25,010 |
|  |  |  |  |  |
| Manufacturing |  |  |  |  |
| Output share (%) | 25.9 | 24.8 | 23.9 | n.a. |
| Employment share (%) | 32.0 | 28.5 | 24.7 | 23.9 |
| Employment (thousands) | 20,154 | 21,040 | 19,412 | 19,398 |
|  |  |  |  |  |
| Service-producing |  |  |  |  |
| Output share (%) | 43.3 | 45.3 | 45.0 | 45.2 |
| Employment share (%) | 60.5 | 64.2 | 68.5 | 69.2 |
| Employment (thousands) | 38,165 | 47,416 | 53,747 | 56,250 |
|  |  |  |  |  |
| Private nonfarm employment |  |  |  |  |
| (thousands) | 63,058 | 73,876 | 78,477 | 81,260 |

*Manufacturing Employment Changes (thousands of workers)*

|  | 1973–79 | 1979–83 | 1973–85 |
|---|---|---|---|
| Durable goods | 869 | −1986 | −242 |
| Automobiles | 14 | −233 | −93 |
| Steel | −34 | −227 | −296 |
| Other durables | 889 | −1526 | 147 |
|  |  |  |  |
| Nondurable goods | 18 | −556 | −373 |
| Textiles and apparel | −259 | −282 | −584 |
| Other nondurables | 277 | −274 | 211 |

NOTES: Output shares are fractions of GNP in 1972 dollars. Output data for 1985 are for the second quarter, seasonally adjusted, and expressed at an annual rate. Employment shares are expressed as fractions of total private nonagricultural employment. Employment and employment shares are annual averages for 1973–1984. Employment data for 1985 are for June, and are seasonally adjusted in the top panel, but not in the final column of the bottom panel. n.a. = not available.

SOURCES: For output data, *Economic Report of the President*, 1985, table B-11, and *Survey of Current Business*, July 1985, tables 1.4 and 6.2. Source for employment data, *Handbook of Labor Statistics*, June 1985, tables 63 to 66, and *Employment and Earnings*, August 1985, tables B1 and B2, and Supplement to Employment and Earnings, July 1984.

ducing industries accounted for this divergence between output and employment shares.

For manufacturing, although the output share declined only slightly from 1973 to 1984, the decline in the employment share was more pronounced—32.0 to 24.7 percent. Manufacturing employment, in fact, declined in absolute numbers over that same period, by about 750,000 workers out of 20 million employed earlier. Despite the cyclical recovery, manufacturing employment remained about three-quarters of a million workers below its 1973 level in mid-1985. Cyclical changes were, of course, occurring during the period, with manufacturing employment rising to 21 million in its peak year, 1979, declining to 18 million by the beginning of 1983, and rising again by about 1.5 million workers by mid-1985.

The net reduction in manufacturing employment of three-quarters of a million workers from 1973 to 1985 was heavily concentrated in a few industries. Three broad industry sectors had net declines totaling almost 1 million workers: automobiles (100,000), steel (300,000), and textiles and apparel (600,000). These data reflect a pronounced cyclical recovery by 1985 only in the automobile industry. These developments in manufacturing stand out in strong contrast to the rise in total private nonfarm employment of more than 18 million workers over that same period.

## Implications for Wages

In view of the disproportionate concentration of job losses in manufacturing industries, many of which are well known for their high wages, questions have been raised about the implications for wages and incomes of the structural realignment taking place. Concern was frequently expressed in the media that the restructuring toward service-producing industries meant that highly paid production jobs were generally being replaced by low-paid service jobs, with the result that the overall wage level would decline, reversing the historical trend toward higher average real wages in production-level jobs.

The validity of this concern seems to be borne out by simple, superficial comparisons. For example, correlations between industry wage levels and changes in employment (weighted by industry employment shares) are generally negative. This tendency toward declining employment shares in the relatively high-wage industries is demonstrated for various periods in table 9–3. The component of changes in average real wages (column a) that can be accounted for by changes in the distribution of employment among industries is reported in column b. The thirty-cent decline in real average hourly

281

earnings (measured in 1979 dollars) from 1973 to 1979 is accounted for in part by the eight-cent decline attributed to the change in industry employment shares. That is, if industry employment shares in 1979 had instead been those that prevailed in 1973, and if industry average wages had been what they in fact were in 1979, then wages would have been eight cents higher in 1979. In this sense employment changes from 1973 to 1979 reduced overall average wages.

The share of the decline in real wages accounted for by changing employment shares between 1979 and 1984 is very similar to that in earlier years (eleven cents out of thirty-four compared with eight out of thirty, as shown in table 9–3). The effects of the recession are evident, however, when that period is divided into the two subperiods before and after 1982. Most of the recent decline in average wages attributed to changing employment shares came during the recession years when manufacturing employment declined sharply. And although real wages actually rose by three cents between 1982 and 1984, that increase occurred despite the small negative effect of changing employment shares.

TABLE 9–3
WAGE AND EMPLOYMENT CHANGES, 1964–1984

|  | Change in Average Wages (1979 dollars) (a) | Component of Wage Change Attributed to Changes in Employment Shares (b) | Component of Wage Change Attributed to Other Factors (c) |
|---|---|---|---|
| 1973–1979 | −.30 | −.08 | −.22 |
| 1979–1984 | −.34 | −.11 | −.23 |
| 1979–1982 | −.37 | −.09 | −.28 |
| 1982–1984 | .03 | −.03 | .06 |
| 1964–1973 | .83 | −.07 | .90 |
| 1973–1979 | −.24 | −.06 | −.18 |

NOTES: The data in the columns are computed as follows, with $a = b + c$:

$a = w^{-t} - w^{-t-1}$ = change in average wages in 1979 dollars
$b = \Sigma_i (e_i^t - e_i^{t-1}) w_i^t$, and
$c = \Sigma_i (w_i^t - w_i^{t-1}) e_i^{t-1}$, where $e_i$ and $w_i$ are industry employment share and industry average wages (in 1979 dollars based on the consumer price index), respectively.

Data for the four subperiods at the top of the table are based on fifty-six two-digit SIC industries for which average hourly earnings and production worker employment are available. The data on the bottom two lines are based on the forty-nine of these industries for which such data are available to 1964.

SOURCES: *Employment, Hours and Earnings*, United States 1909–1984, vols. I and II, and *Supplement to Employment and Earnings*, June 1985.

These computed effects of changes in industry employment shares should not, however, be viewed as implying a direction of causation. One possibility, for example, is that profitable production opportunities could lead to relatively high industry wages because wages are bid up in the context of expanding employment. On the other hand, high industry wages could discourage employment growth or lead to job reductions if industries are uncompetitive because of high labor costs. Relationships between industry wage levels and employment changes reflect the outcome of these and other forces.

It is clear from the last two lines in table 9–3, first, that changing employment shares have had a negative effect on overall average hourly earnings for the past two decades, as well as in earlier years for which industry data are available in less detail. Second, it is apparent that changes in overall real average hourly earnings are primarily affected by factors other than changes in industry employment shares. Real average hourly earnings increased by eighty-three cents during the period 1964–1973 and then declined by twenty-four cents by 1979, even though the effects of changing employment shares were closely comparable for both periods (seven and six cents, respectively).

The most important component of trends in real average hourly earnings has been attributable to factors other than changes in industry employment shares (reflected in column c, table 9–3). Changing trends in productivity growth have been the principal underlying influence on the difference between nominal wage increases and price increases; this difference is reflected in measures of real average hourly earnings. The effects of the changing demographic composition of the work force are also among the "other factors" influencing trends in real average hourly earnings, along with changes in the schooling and skills of workers and the capital and technology that are available to them. Finally, it is important to note that these real wage comparisons were made for wages and employment of production and nonsupervisory workers only; they do not take into account changes in the shares or wages of that part of the work force accounted for by more highly paid professional and managerial workers.

The evidence on changing patterns of industry employment confirms the impression highlighted by recent experience that shifting employment shares, taken by themselves, have reduced overall average wages compared with what might otherwise have been realized. The evidence also clearly shows that this is not a new phenomenon; this trend has been present for at least the past thirty years. Moreover, the evidence indicates that only a relatively small part of actual real wage changes can be attributed to shifts in employment shares and that over periods of several years, changes in real wages are predominantly attributable to other factors.

These data indicate that the key to real wage growth has not been shifts in employment toward industries with relatively high real wages. Efforts to protect high-wage jobs could accordingly be expected to make no significant contribution to higher average real wages, while the rigidities introduced by such efforts would inhibit the adjustments necessary to make these workers available for profitable new jobs.

## Dimensions of the Employment Adjustment Problem

How many workers are affected by permanent job loss? One widely publicized figure is that of Bluestone and Harrison. According to them, "Together, runaways, shutdowns, and permanent physical cutbacks may have cost the country as many as 38 million jobs."[1] This is demonstrably implausible as an estimate of the number of additional jobs the U.S. economy would have in the absence of the cutbacks to which they refer. If their estimate is added to the number actually employed during the recession year 1982 when their book was published, we obtain a total of about 139.2 million jobs. By adjusting the noninstitutional population over sixteen years old to exclude those over sixty-five and those between the ages of sixteen and twenty-four who are not employed or in the labor force because they are in school, we obtain a total of 137.4 million potential job holders. Thus, if 38 million is regarded as an estimate of net job losses, the implication is that the total number of jobs would exceed potential job holders by nearly 2 million workers. It is true, of course, that many over sixty-five years old can and do hold jobs, but many below sixty-five have voluntarily retired, labor force participation rates fall far short of 100 percent (especially for women), and these computations make no allowance for any unemployment, illness, or disability. Clearly, an estimate of net job losses would need to be far smaller to be realistic. Moreover, an estimate of gross job changes can hardly be regarded as a measure of "costs" to the country.

Although, apart from recessions, growing employment has meant net job gains, net losses have occurred in particular industries. The manufacturing industries as a whole had a net reduction in employment of 1.6 million from the peak in 1979 to mid-1985. Although many more individual manufacturing workers permanently lost their jobs than is indicated by the net reduction in manufacturing employment, it is instructive to compare the net change in employment with broader measures of job changes. On the basis of estimates from data on labor turnover rates and job tenure, reductions in employment on the order of 10 percent per year could be expected from normal attrition.[2] Since the actual annual rate of employment decline after 1979 was 1.33 percent, the entire decline in manufacturing employment since then could have been accommodated by attrition, with a large margin to spare, if the reduction in employment had occurred smoothly over time and evenly among industries, firms, and plants.

Gross flows of jobs on and off payrolls were, of course, much larger than the estimated attrition rates. Gross changes in jobs, even if temporary layoffs and recalls are excluded, are very large compared with changes in net employment levels. In 1981, for example, the last year for which manufacturing labor turnover data are available, new hires averaged 2 percent per month even though manufactuing employment declined by half a million workers during the year.

Neither gross job changes nor changes in net employment levels provide useful insights into the magnitude of employment adjustment problems. Assessing the policy significance of employment adjustment problems also involves more than simply estimating numbers of workers affected. Temporary layoffs, for example, have implications different from permanent separations, and the implications of a permanent job loss are different for a young and mobile worker from those for an older experienced worker. There are, in other words, economic dimensions at a more detailed microlevel that are relevant for analyzing policy significance.

One of the most important economic aspects of job loss is the magnitude of the economic loss that it may represent. This in turn depends partly on employment-related considerations and partly on personal or family circumstances. Some of the main economic considerations will be discussed briefly.

During the course of their employment, workers are making investments in skills at the same time as they are making contributions to output production. Some of these investments are general and readily transferable to other jobs. Other skills are quite specific to a particular industry, and still others are specific to a particular firm, or even an individual plant. Knowledge about operating procedures, specialized products produced, and production and marketing arrangements are examples of less transferable skills. A large share of a worker's earning capacity is typically dependent on returns to these investments in skills; the typical worker's earnings come from a portfolio of assets that is not very diversified. Consequently, the economic loss to a worker associated with permanent job separation depends on the extent to which his investments are highly specific to a particular plant or firm and on the amount of investment involved. Since the amount of investment can be expected to be strongly influenced by time spent on a job, economic losses can be expected to be larger for workers with longer job tenure. Moreover, since length of job tenure also tends to rise with age, larger economic losses are, in addition, associated with shorter time horizons for reaping returns from making new investments in job skills.

The economic loss resulting from permanent job loss also depends on other surrounding circumstances. For example, permanent job loss produces larger economic losses to workers when it is necessary to change industry, occupation, or geographic location. If a plant is closed or a firm goes out of business in an area with few alternative job opportunities and if the industry and type of work are affected by a general decline in demand, economic losses are likely to be particularly severe. Workers under these circumstances are likely to suffer losses not only in reduced earning capacity but also through reduced value of other assets, such as housing. These economic losses are mitigated somewhat, of course, by the availability of unemployment compensation and other income support programs.

In addition, the welfare consequences of permanent job loss by a worker depend on characteristics of the household, such as whether another member has a job. This is likely to be particularly important for relocation decisions, because moving to accommodate the interests of one household member could impose losses on another, employed member. Workers and their families may, of course, experience non-economic losses as well from moving if attachments to a community or to a social or ethnic group are strong.

The kinds of economic losses occasioned by permanent job separation discussed up to this point can be analyzed in the context of a set of equilibrium wages and returns produced by competitive markets. Departures from equilibrium are, of course, factors in actual observed relationships. In addition, exercise of market power by labor unions, for example, together with capital intensity and other production arrangements that developed in response to such circumstances, can give rise to a "rent" component in wages. The economic losses of workers terminated from such jobs may consequently exceed the losses that could be accounted for by factors such as the reduced value of specialized skills. While the economic losses from this source are no less real for workers affected, the difference is relevant for policy. New investment in skill development, for example, may not be sufficient to raise earnings in new jobs to levels comparable to earnings in jobs that were lost if the pay in the lost job included a substantial rent component.

The main implication of this discussion is that permanent job loss is insufficient by itself to indicate the nature and severity of the economic consequences for such displaced or dislocated workers. For individual workers, the amount of skill investment (associated with tenure on a job), the specialized character of the investments (specific to particular plants or firms, for example), and the age of the worker (influencing payoffs to new skill investments) are relevant. Characteristics of the worker's household, economic conditions in the geographic location, and demand conditions for industrial or occupational skills are also relevant. Finally, whether the worker was earning competitive returns can have an important influence on the size of the economic loss resulting from permanent job separation.

## Estimates of Displaced Workers

In a special survey conducted in January 1984, the Bureau of Labor Statistics (BLS) collected information on workers who lost their jobs during the preceding five years, along with relevant related information such as work experience on the job from which they were terminated.[3] According to this survey, 5.1 million workers with at least three years of job tenure were estimated to have been displaced over this five-year period—an average of about a million workers per year. In January 1984, an estimated 1.3 million of these displaced workers were unemployed. These estimates, of course, are quite sensitive to the important job tenure criterion, as indicated in table 9–4. Prevailing views that workers who have devoted a substantial portion of their working lives to a particular job may be especially vulnerable to losing earning power when permanently separated from their job have an economic basis, as discussed earlier, and seniority protections that reflect the reciprocal claims and responsibilities of workers and employers, respectively, lose their force in the event of plant closure.

Estimates that were developed by the Congressional Budget Office (CBO) suggest a total stock of about a million displaced workers in 1982 when a single criterion is used to define them, such as job loss from a declining industry, ten years or more of job tenure, or more than forty-five years of age. If other unemployed in declining areas are added to the estimate, the total of those directly and indirectly affected would be about twice as large. On the other hand, if more than one criterion is used to define the displaced, such as job loss in a declining industry *and* ten years or more of job tenure, only about one-quarter million workers would be estimated. These estimates are broadly consistent with the BLS special survey data, and they show the sensitivity of estimated numbers of workers involved to the specificity of definitions that are employed.

Comparison of estimates of displaced workers with data from the monthly Current Population Survey (CPS) on those unemployed because they lost their job provides another perspective. Job losers have typically accounted for about half of unemployed adults, with the job losers' share rising with unemployment during recessions. During the period from 1979 through 1983 covered by the BLS special survey, the job losers' share was unusually large in 1982 and 1983, even for a recession, when it accounted for two-thirds of the unemployed (table 9–5).

Job losers can be divided into those on temporary layoff and other job losers, with displaced workers being a subset of the latter group. According to the data in table 9–5, displaced workers may have accounted for less than one-third of other job losers in recent years. The

TABLE 9–4
ESTIMATES OF NUMBER OF DISPLACED WORKERS,
1979–1983
(millions of workers)

| | |
|---|---|
| Total | 13.9 |
| Less: Workers who lost jobs for seasonal or other miscellaneous reasons | −2.4 |
| Total "permanently" separated | 11.5 |
| Less: Job tenure of one year or less | −4.4 |
| Total with at least one year job tenure | 7.1 |
| Less: Job tenure between one and three years | −2.0 |
| Total with at least three years job tenure | 5.1 |
| Less: Job tenure between three and five years | −1.9 |
| Total with at least five years job tenure | 3.2 |
| Less: Job tenure between five and ten years | −1.7 |
| Total with at least ten years job tenure | 1.5 |

*Labor Force and Employment Status in January 1984 of Displaced Workers*

| | |
|---|---|
| Total with at least three years job tenure | 5.1 |
| Employed | 3.1 |
| Unemployed | 1.3 |
| Not in labor force | 0.7 |

NOTE: Total refers to workers twenty and older, who lost their job between January 1979 and January 1984 because of plant closing, employer going out of business, or indefinite layoff. Displaced workers are here defined as those workers with the previous characteristics who have had at least three years job tenure.

SOURCE: Paul O. Flaim and Ellen Sehgal, "Displaced Workers of 1979–83: How Well Have They Fared?" *Monthly Labor Review*, June 1985, pp. 3–16.

## TABLE 9-5
### DISPLACED WORKERS AND UNEMPLOYED ADULT JOB LOSERS, 1979-1984

| | Number of Unemployed | | | | | |
|---|---|---|---|---|---|---|
| | 1979 | 1980 | 1981 | 1982 | 1983 | 1984 |
| Total, aged 20 and older[a] | 4,435 | 5,808 | 6,347 | 8,701 | 8,888 | 7,040 |
| Job losers[a] | 2,241 | 3,477 | 3,798 | 5,808 | 5,888 | 4,150 |
| Layoff[a] | 752 | 1,369 | 1,319 | 2,016 | 1,702 | 1,107 |
| Other job losers[a] | 1,489 | 2,108 | 2,479 | 3,792 | 4,186 | 3,043 |
| Job losers as percent of total unemployed | 50.5 | 59.9 | 59.8 | 66.8 | 66.2 | 58.9 |
| Displaced Workers[a] | 500 | 619 | 833 | 1,195 | 1,206 | n.a. |
| Plant closed[a] | 344 | 351 | 407 | 531 | 550 | n.a. |
| Slack work[a] | 119 | 209 | 341 | 554 | 500 | n.a. |
| Job abolished[a] | 37 | 59 | 85 | 110 | 156 | n.a. |
| Displaced workers as percent of total job losers | 22.3 | 17.8 | 21.9 | 20.6 | 20.5 | n.a. |
| Displaced workers as percent of other job losers | 33.6 | 29.4 | 33.6 | 31.5 | 28.8 | n.a. |

NOTES: n.a. = not available. Data for displaced workers refer to individuals separated from a full-time private sector job between January 1979 and January 1984 because of plant closure or move, slack work, or the abolition of a shift or position.

a. In thousands.

SOURCE: *Employment and Earnings*, January 1980–1985, tables 12 and 13, and Bureau of Labor Statistics, displaced workers microdata file.

most important reason why displaced workers are not a dominant share of other job losers is the three-year job tenure specified in the definition (see table 9–4). The main additional factor, apparently, is that many other job losers lost their jobs for reasons other than plant closure, slack work, or abolition of their job. Still another factor complicates the comparison; numbers of job losers in principle are measures of part of the stock of unemployed at a point in time, while the displaced worker estimates are measures of the flow of workers into displaced status during those same years. Many of those displaced appear at least temporarily in the stock of job losers, but, just as in the case of the unemployed generally, there is a significant outflow from displaced and unemployed status. Although, as noted earlier, by January 1984 1.3 out of 5.1 million workers remained unemployed, this number is only slightly larger than the total displaced during 1983.

289

The information on displaced workers from the BLS survey permits a significant sharpening of estimates of numbers of workers affected, and it provides a very useful benchmark for discussion. The overall totals for displaced worker estimates, however, are influenced primarily by two features. First, the BLS estimates cover adult workers and take into account job tenure, with three years of job tenure chosen as the cutoff point. Median job tenure for the resulting displaced workers sample was 6.1 years. In view of estimates of median job tenure for all workers aged twenty-five and over of 6.9 years for men and 4.8 years for women, the three-year job tenure requirement seems a reasonable criterion.[4] Second, workers are identified as displaced solely on the basis of three kinds of circumstances surrounding their job loss, circumstances that suggest that job loss may be permanent. These criteria for identifying workers as displaced do not take into account either the probable magnitude of the economic loss involved or other relevant personal circumstances. To obtain additional insight into these factors, the characteristics of displaced workers will first be compared with those of the work force as a whole; then, how well they have fared will be compared with the experience of other workers affected by labor market adjustments.

## Demographic and Related Characteristics

It is useful to consider the extent to which displaced workers are a representative cross section of the work force. If they are predominantly older workers, for example, the choices they face and the policies that might be considered to assist them would be considerably different from those for predominantly younger workers. Similarly, the extent to which they are concentrated geographically and the degree to which the labor markets in which they typically make choices are national in scope are important.

Broad comparisons of personal characteristics are presented in table 9–6. First, males have accounted for a larger share of displaced workers in recent years than of the work force as a whole. There is a spread of about forty percentage points between males and females in their share of displaced workers compared with a spread of thirteen percentage points in their shares of employment. Comparisons by race are quite different for employment and unemployment. Black workers' share of displaced workers is somewhat larger than their employment share. Because black unemployment is disproportionately high, however, the displaced worker share is much lower than the unemployment share for black workers in contrast to the larger displaced worker share for whites.

TABLE 9–6
DEMOGRAPHIC CHARACTERISTICS OF DISPLACED WORKERS
(percent)

|  | Displaced Workers | All Employed Workers | All Unemployed Workers |
|---|---|---|---|
| Sex |  |  |  |
| Male | 69.3 | 56.6 | 59.1 |
| Female | 30.7 | 43.4 | 40.9 |
| Race |  |  |  |
| White | 86.4 | 87.9 | 75.8 |
| Black | 11.7 | 9.5 | 21.1 |
| Age |  |  |  |
| 20–24 | 6.0 | 14.5 | 26.2 |
| 25–34 | 34.6 | 30.4 | 34.6 |
| 35–44 | 23.9 | 23.2 | 18.6 |
| 45–54 | 17.9 | 16.7 | 11.7 |
| 55–64 | 14.8 | 12.0 | 7.6 |
| 65 + | 2.8 | 3.1 | 1.3 |

NOTES: Percentages for race do not total 100 because Hispanics (not separately identified in this table) may be of either race. Data for all employed and unemployed workers are 1983 averages and refer to civilians aged twenty and over. Displaced workers are individuals aged twenty and over who were separated from full-time private sector jobs between January 1979 and January 1984.
SOURCES: Bureau of Labor Statistics, *Handbook of Labor Statistics*, June 1985, tables 15 and 26, and the BLS displaced workers microdata file.

The experience of dislocated workers by age is somewhat surprising in that only workers in the lowest age category, twenty to twenty-four years old, experience less than their share. Even workers in the relatively young twenty-five to thirty-four year-old category experience more than their share of dislocation. The share for workers in the thirty-five to forty-four year-old category is only slightly larger than their employment share, and the difference in shares widens gradually until age sixty-five and older. The differences in shares by age appears to result primarily from the criterion of three years or more of job tenure; displaced workers between twenty and twenty-four account for a distinctly smaller share of dislocated workers than of employment, offset by larger shares in the rest of the age distribution. Unemployment shares for the work force as a whole fall steadily with increased age (compared with employment shares). Consequently, displaced worker shares rise markedly with age when compared with unemployment shares. Thus, older workers experience more than their share of displacement by only a small margin when compared with employment shares, but displacement is far more common among older workers than would be expected on the basis of unemployment experience by age.

In table 9–7 the incidence of displacement by occupation is compared with employment and unemployment shares in those occupations. These data confirm what is probably the common perception

TABLE 9–7
DISTRIBUTION OF DISPLACED WORKERS BY OCCUPATION
(percent)

| Occupation | Displaced Workers | All Employed Workers | All Unemployed Workers |
|---|---|---|---|
| Managerial and professional | | | |
| specialty | 14.1 | 24.5 | 8.9 |
| Executive and managerial | 8.9 | 11.2 | 4.4 |
| Professional specialty | 5.2 | 13.3 | 4.5 |
| Technical, sales, and | | | |
| administrative support | 23.1 | 32.5 | 23.6 |
| Technicians | 2.4 | 3.2 | 1.7 |
| Sales | 9.3 | 12.3 | 9.5 |
| Administrative support | 11.4 | 17.1 | 12.4 |
| Service occupations | 5.5 | 13.4 | 18.1 |
| Precision, production, craft, | | | |
| and repair | 20.8 | 12.8 | 16.4 |
| Mechanics | 5.2 | 4.3 | 3.8 |
| Construction trades | 6.3 | 4.5 | 7.9 |
| Other | 9.3 | 4.0 | 4.6 |
| Operators, fabricators, and | | | |
| laborers | 36.4 | 16.7 | 33.0 |
| Machine operators | 22.8 | 8.1 | 15.8 |
| Transport operators | 6.5 | 4.4 | 6.7 |
| Laborers | 7.1 | 4.3 | 10.6 |
| Total | 100.0 | 100.0 | 100.0 |

NOTES: Percentages may not add to 100 because of rounding. Displaced workers are persons aged twenty and older who were separated from full-time private sector jobs between January 1979 and January 1984. Data for all employed workers are 1983 averages for all employed civilians, aged sixteen and older. Data for all unemployed workers are 1983 averages for experienced workers, aged sixteen and older. Displaced and unemployed workers are classified by occupation of job lost. Private household and agricultural occupations are excluded in all cases.

SOURCES: Bureau of Labor Statistics, *Handbook of Labor Statistics*, June 1985, tables 17 and 29, and the BLS displaced workers microdata file.

that dislocation has been heavily concentrated among blue-collar workers with reasonably good job skills. That is, workers in the precision production, craft, and repair, and the operators, fabricators, and laborers categories make up a larger share of displaced workers than they do of either employment or unemployment. Within these categories, however, laborers in particular, but also construction trades workers, have larger employment shares than displaced worker shares. Machine operators and mechanics, on the other hand, make up larger shares of displaced workers than of employment or unemployment.

The incidence of dislocation by industry is consistent with that for occupations (table 9–8). Manufacturing accounts for more than 50 percent of displaced workers compared with about 25 percent of employment and about 30 percent of unemployment, and displaced workers are especially highly concentrated in durable goods manufacturing. The only other industry category with a disproportionate share of displaced workers is mining, but the numbers involved are quite small. The incidence of dislocation for construction workers also

TABLE 9–8

DISTRIBUTION OF DISPLACED WORKERS BY INDUSTRY

(percent)

| Industry | Displaced Workers | All Employed Workers | All Unemployed Workers |
|---|---|---|---|
| Mining | 3.2 | 1.3 | 2.2 |
| Construction | 8.5 | 5.3 | 12.4 |
| Manufacturing | 52.8 | 24.9 | 29.3 |
| Durable goods | 35.6 | 14.5 | 19.3 |
| Nondurable goods | 17.2 | 10.4 | 11.0 |
| Transportation | 7.1 | 6.7 | 5.2 |
| Wholesale Trade | 5.0 | 7.1 | 4.0 |
| Retail Trade | 10.6 | 20.9 | 22.9 |
| Finance | 2.0 | 7.4 | 3.4 |
| Services | 10.8 | 26.5 | 20.5 |
| Total | 100.0 | 100.0 | 100.0 |

NOTES: Percentages may not add to 100 because of rounding. Displaced workers are individuals twenty and older who were separated from private nonagricultural wage and salary jobs between January 1979 and January 1984. Data for all employed workers are 1983 averages for individuals on private nonagricultural payrolls. Data for all unemployed workers are for experienced wage and salary workers in private nonagricultural industries. Displaced and unemployed workers are classified by industry of job lost.

SOURCES: Bureau of Labor Statistics, *Handbook of Labor Statistics*, June 1985, tables 30 and 63, and Flaim and Sehgal, table 2.

exceeds their employment share, but it is small compared with their share of unemployment. Finally, the east north central census region (Illinois, Indiana, Michigan, Ohio, and Wisconsin) has a considerably larger share of displaced workers than of employment and also a slightly larger share than its share of unemployment. Although differences for other regions are not very pronounced, regional aggregates mask major differences among smaller labor market areas.

In summary, displaced workers are concentrated among males, among middle-aged and older workers compared with their normal unemployment experience, among reasonably skilled production workers, and in manufacturing—particularly durable goods manufacturing. Workers well qualified in terms of maturity, work experience, and skills are disproportionately represented among displaced workers as compared with unemployed workers as a whole. These characteristics make most displaced workers good prospects for obtaining new jobs. Geographic concentration and relatively high earnings in highly unionized industries, on the other hand, contribute to adjustment difficulties.

### Adjustment Experience of Displaced Workers

In an assessment of how displaced workers have fared, one of the most obvious questions to ask is how many are unemployed. The overall unemployment rate in January 1984 for workers displaced during the preceding five years was 25.5 percent. A major reason that this rate is so high is that making an adjustment takes time and disproportionately large numbers lost their jobs in the latter part of the period (recall table 9–5). The fraction unemployed in January 1984 declines steadily with years since displacement, from 44.6 percent for workers displaced in 1983 to 13.7 percent for those displaced in 1979.

Because the unemployment rate declined at a much slower rate after two years had elapsed since displacement, it is useful to examine what happened to employment and labor force status over the time since displacement. As shown in table 9–9, some of the decline in unemployment came as a result of leaving the labor force. A much larger share of the reduction in unemployment, however, was the result of workers obtaining new jobs. Although the fraction of these workers who remained unemployed a year or two after they were displaced is still quite high, it is important to recognize that this sample is quite different from the population as a whole from which monthly unemployment rates are obtained. All of those in the sample of displaced workers needed to obtain a new job at some time during the preceding five years. Perhaps the most closely comparable demographic group in this respect—although they differ markedly in other respects—is the twenty to twenty-four year-old age group, most of whom also at some point needed to find a job. Their unemployment rate averaged 12.5 percent for this five-year period, reaching 14.9 percent in 1982.

How long displaced workers were unemployed is another important dimension of how they fared. As shown in table 9–10, the median duration of unemployment was very significantly higher for displaced workers than for the work force as a whole. Those who obtained new jobs by January 1984, however, experienced only moderately longer unemployment duration than the unemployed as a whole, according to these data. It is important to note, though, that the two measures are not directly comparable. For the displaced workers, duration is a measure of cumulative weeks of unemployment over the entire five-year period. For the unemployed as a whole, duration is measured only for the current spell up to the time of the survey; completed spells are generally longer, and many of the unemployed experience more than one spell during a year.

Unemployment duration was quite high for those unemployed at the time of the survey, and it was extraordinarily high for those who left the labor force. Older workers left the work force to a much larger extent than younger workers, and women were much more likely than men to drop out of the labor force. For workers fifty-five to sixty-four years old, 27 percent left the labor force, but 67 percent of those over sixty-five left. Only 5 percent of men compared with 19 percent of women in the twenty-five to fifty-four year-old age group left the work force.

TABLE 9–9
EMPLOYMENT AND LABOR FORCE STATUS OF DISPLACED
WORKERS OVER TIME, 1979–1983
(percent)

|  | Year when Job Was Lost | | |
| --- | --- | --- | --- |
| Status in January 1984 | 1979-1981 | 1982 | 1983 |
| Employed | 69.3 | 62.5 | 45.6 |
| Unemployed | 15.8 | 23.8 | 44.6 |
| Not in labor force | 14.9 | 13.7 | 9.7 |

NOTES: Number may not add to 100 because of rounding. Data refer to individuals separated from full-time private sector jobs.
SOURCES: Bureau of Labor Statistics, displaced workers microdata file.

TABLE 9–10
DURATION OF UNEMPLOYMENT
(median weeks)

| | Workers Aged 25-34 | Workers Aged 35-44 | Workers Aged 45-54 |
|---|---|---|---|
| All Unemployed Workers | | | |
| 1979 | 6.1 | 6.8 | 7.5 |
| 1980 | 7.6 | 7.9 | 8.4 |
| 1981 | 7.8 | 8.5 | 8.9 |
| 1982 | 9.6 | 10.2 | 10.5 |
| 1983 | 11.9 | 13.5 | 14.8 |
| Displaced Workers | | | |
| Total | 21.9 | 22.3 | 25.8 |
| Employed | 12.5 | 15.4 | 15.3 |
| Unemployed | 33.8 | 30.9 | 32.5 |
| Not in labor force | 53.0 | 54.7 | 96.2 |

NOTES: Median duration for all unemployed workers refers to in-progress unemployment spells; that for displaced workers is cumulative weeks without work following separation to January 1984. Labor force status for displaced workers is as of January 1984.

SOURCES: For all unemployed workers, *Employment and Earnings*, January 1980–1984. For displaced workers, Bureau of Labor Statistics, displaced workers microdata file.

Measures of the duration of unemployment for the displaced worker sample are difficult to compare with conventional measures from other sources because conventional measures are not cumulated over more than a year. By restricting the displaced worker sample to those who lost their jobs during 1983, a more direct comparison can be made with data from the work experience survey, which measures total weeks of unemployment during the year. As shown in the top panel of table 9–11, duration distributions for the displaced workers and all workers experiencing unemployment are virtually identical for 1983.

The comparison in the bottom panel of table 9–11 is different in two major respects: overall unemployment data are the average for 1983, and only those workers displaced in 1983 who remained unemployed in January 1984 are included in the displaced workers sample. The principal difference evident from this comparison is that a much smaller fraction of displaced workers are in the one to four week duration category, offset by a much larger fraction in the fifteen to twenty-six week category. The main reason for this difference is un-

TABLE 9–11
DISTRIBUTION OF UNEMPLOYMENT DURATION
(percent)

| Part-Year Workers with Unemployment | Total Weeks without Work in 1983 | | | |
|---|---|---|---|---|
| | 1-4 weeks | 5-14 weeks | 15-26 weeks | 27+ weeks |
| All part-year workers | 17.8 | 32.4 | 26.3 | 23.5 |
| Displaced workers | 19.7 | 30.9 | 27.0 | 22.5 |

| Persons Unemployed in January 1984 | Duration of Current Unemployment | | | |
|---|---|---|---|---|
| | 1-4 weeks | 5-14 weeks | 15-26 weeks | 27+ weeks |
| All unemployed | 36.5 | 28.0 | 13.2 | 22.2 |
| Displaced workers | 13.8 | 28.8 | 30.2 | 27.2 |
| Plant closing | 14.6 | 27.6 | 32.8 | 25.6 |
| Slack work | 14.4 | 30.4 | 25.6 | 29.6 |
| Job abolished | 9.2 | 26.2 | 40.0 | 24.6 |

NOTES: Data for displaced workers refer to individuals separated from a full-time private sector job in 1983 who were in the labor force (top panel), or who were unemployed (bottom panel), in January 1984. Data for all part-year workers with unemployment refer to individuals who experienced at least one week of unemployment in 1983.

SOURCES: Bureau of Labor Statistics, *Handbook of Labor Statistics*, June 1985, table 47, *Employment and Earnings*, January 1985, table A-40, and the BLS displaced workers microdata file.

doubtedly the exclusion of those on short-term layoff from the displaced worker sample. For most displaced workers the reason for job loss was either plant closures or slack work. No systematic differences in the experience of workers in these categories are evident for unemployment duration, however, or for other aspects of their experience that were examined.

Moving is often viewed as a constructive response to job loss, particularly if an entire local labor market is affected by plant closure. Also, workers in some instances can be transferred by the firm to another plant if they are willing to relocate. Despite these incentives, however, the workers in the BLS survey were not a particularly mobile group. Some 10 percent moved during the first year after losing their jobs, and over 20 percent had moved by the time four or five years had passed. This can be compared with mobility for the work force as a whole; in the early 1980s almost 6 percent of the civilian labor force moved to a different county from the preceding year, and about 20 percent had moved since five years earlier. As might be expected among workers who were displaced, men made geographic moves twice as frequently as women.

Occupational mobility, on the other hand, was strikingly higher for displaced workers than for the work force as a whole. Among the displaced workers who had obtained new jobs by January 1984, just over half made a major occupational change (table 9–12). For the work force as a whole, however, only about 4 percent made a major occupational change during the preceding year. There are two major differences in the situation of displaced workers compared with all workers. First, displaced workers lost their job, making it necessary to find a new one, while most members of the work force did not face this problem. Second, for most of the displaced workers, more than a year had elapsed since they worked at their previous job. The fraction of displaced workers making a *major* occupational change is of roughly the same order of magnitude as the fraction of the work force as a whole who made a job change of some kind (in the sense that they made at least a small occupational change), but only 7.5 percent of all workers made some occupational change.

What happened to the earnings of displaced workers is an aspect of their experience that is of paramount significance. In addition to its importance for economic well-being, earnings experience provides clues about the reduction in wages that workers needed to accept to obtain new jobs. A tabulation of the BLS survey results indicates that of the 3.1 million workers reemployed in January 1984, there were 2 million who were working full time both before displacement and when surveyed and who reported earnings for both their old and their new jobs. For that group, 55 percent were earning as much or more than before they were displaced, but this comparison does not take into account the inflation that was occurring during the five-year period. The average hourly earnings index had increased by almost 36 percent from 1979 to the beginning of 1984, and it rose by about 9 percent in both 1980 and 1981.

Table 9–13 shows the ratios of earnings in new jobs compared with the old jobs in industries from which workers were displaced, with inflation since the year they were displaced taken into account by deflating on the basis of the average hourly earnings index. These constant-dollar earnings ratios show that reemployed workers were, on average, earning about 90 percent of what they earned before they were displaced. It is reasonable to suppose that those displaced workers who were able to obtain new jobs were on average in a better position to match their previous wages than those who had not yet obtained new jobs. On the other hand, conditions in the labor market were relatively unfavorable for finding jobs that paid well. Workers who were displaced were looking for new jobs during a time of recession and high unemployment.

Workers from some industries were better able than those from others to obtain new jobs with wages comparable to their previous

TABLE 9–12
OCCUPATIONAL MOBILITY RATES
(percent)

| Major Occupation Group | Percent of All Workers Changing Occupation | | Percent of Job Changers Changing Major Occupation | |
|---|---|---|---|---|
| | All changes (1) | Major changes (2) | All workers (3) | Displaced workers (4) |
| Executive and managerial | 8.1 | 4.8 | 58.9 | 57.2 |
| Professional specialty | 5.3 | 2.9 | 55.6 | 53.0 |
| Technicians and related | 6.8 | 6.1 | 89.1 | 52.1 |
| Sales occupations | 9.7 | 6.5 | 67.0 | 45.8 |
| Administrative support | 8.6 | 4.4 | 51.6 | 46.8 |
| Service occupations | 7.4 | 5.3 | 71.6 | 50.6 |
| Precision production | 6.4 | 4.3 | 66.8 | 41.9 |
| Machine operators | 8.2 | 5.3 | 64.5 | 58.9 |
| Transportation occupations | 6.9 | 5.1 | 73.4 | 41.2 |
| Handlers, helpers, and laborers | 11.8 | 10.3 | 87.3 | 77.0 |
| All occupations | 7.5 | 4.8 | 63.4 | 51.1 |

NOTES: The data in columns (1), (2), and (3) refer to all workers aged twenty-five and over who were employed in January 1982 and January 1983. The data for displaced workers in column (4) refer to individuals aged twenty and over who were permanently separated from a full-time private sector job between January 1979 and January 1984 and who were reemployed as of January 1984.

Column (1) gives the percentage of workers, classified by original major occupation, who reported an occupational change (possibly within the major occupational category) between January 1982 and January 1983. The percentage reporting a different major occupation category is given in column (2). Column (3) is the ratio of column (2) to column (1), and it gives the percentage of those workers changing occupation ("job changers") between 1982 and 1983 who also changed major occupational category.

Column (4) gives the percentage of all displaced workers, classified by major occupation in job lost, who changed their major occupation category in becoming reemployed. The mobility rates in this column differ slightly from columns (1) through (3) in that changes in occupation are over a period longer than one year.

Workers whose original major occupation group was farming, forestry, and fishing, or protective and private household service are excluded in all cases.

SOURCES: Ellen Sehgal, "Occupational Mobility and Job Tenure in 1983," *Monthly Labor Review*, October 1984, and the BLS displaced workers microdata file.

jobs. For the industries identified in table 9–13, workers displaced from the steel industry fared worst, with wages in their new jobs only 62 percent of those in their previous job. Since wages in the steel industry were 74 percent higher in 1981 and 1982 than the private nonfarm average, however, wages in new jobs of workers displaced from the steel industry compared favorably with wages of the average worker—even though the individual workers affected experienced a considerable reduction in earnings. Real wages in the new jobs of displaced steel workers were on average about 8 percent higher than wages of the average private nonfarm worker in 1984. Indeed, the only industry categories for which average real wages in new jobs fell short of the overall private nonfarm average are those for which average wages in the industry from which they were displaced were below the overall average.

TABLE 9–13

CONSTANT DOLLAR EARNINGS RATIOS BY INDUSTRY AND
YEAR DISPLACED, 1979–1983

| Industry | 1979 | 1980 | 1981 | 1982 | 1983 | 1979–83 |
|---|---|---|---|---|---|---|
| Mining | 0.70 | 0.74 | 0.86 | 0.60 | 0.89 | 0.77 |
| Construction | 1.12 | 0.76 | 0.98 | 0.93 | 0.96 | 0.94 |
| Manufacturing | 0.90 | 0.82 | 0.83 | 0.85 | 0.94 | 0.86 |
| Durable goods | 0.83 | 0.79 | 0.84 | 0.82 | 0.91 | 0.83 |
| Primary metals | 0.66 | 0.80 | 0.77 | 0.63 | 0.66 | 0.69 |
| Steel | 0.84 | 0.98 | 0.54 | 0.60 | 0.47 | 0.62 |
| Transportation equipment | 0.65 | 0.81 | 0.73 | 0.87 | 0.94 | 0.80 |
| Autos | 0.65 | 0.82 | 0.63 | 1.11 | 1.02 | 0.82 |
| Nondurable goods | 1.04 | 0.87 | 0.81 | 0.92 | 1.01 | 0.92 |
| Textiles and apparel | 1.11 | 0.89 | 0.86 | 0.83 | 0.99 | 0.92 |
| Transportation | 1.19 | 0.79 | 0.83 | 0.84 | 1.08 | 0.92 |
| Wholesale trade | 1.15 | 0.92 | 0.96 | 0.94 | 0.92 | 0.97 |
| Retail trade | 0.90 | 1.10 | 1.00 | 0.86 | 0.84 | 0.93 |
| Finance | 1.24 | 1.03 | 0.87 | 0.94 | 0.86 | 0.92 |
| Services | 0.90 | 0.85 | 0.83 | 0.96 | 1.02 | 0.93 |
| All industries | 0.96 | 0.85 | 0.86 | 0.86 | 0.95 | 0.89 |

NOTES: Earnings ratios are the ratio of weekly earnings from job held in January 1984 to weekly earnings from job lost, adjusted to January 1984 dollars using the Hourly Earnings Index. Classification by industry and by year reflects industries from which workers were displaced and date of displacement. Ratios have been calculated only for survey respondents reporting earnings in both periods, and have been weighted using BLS microdata population weights. Data pertain to individuals displaced from, and reemployed in, full-time private nonagricultural jobs.

SOURCE: Bureau of Labor Statistics, microdata file on displaced workers.

The wage experience of workers displaced from the steel industry and the decline in relative wages of workers remaining in the industry are both consistent with the presence of a considerable rent component in steelworkers' wages in recent years. The existence of a rent component is also suggested by the large increase in average hourly earnings of steelworkers compared with the average for private nonfarm workers as a whole during the 1970s. From a level about 30 percent higher than the average in 1970, steelworkers' wages rose to levels over 50 percent higher by 1975 and over 70 percent higher by 1980. After 1982, relative wages of steelworkers declined to a level about 55 percent higher than for other workers as a whole, a level similar to that for workers in the auto industry where wages were also about 30 percent above the private nonfarm average in 1970.

It is interesting to note that reemployed workers displaced from the automobile industry experienced smaller reductions in wages than steelworkers. The three main reasons for this difference appear to be that relative wages in the automobile industry were not as high as in steel (slightly over 50 percent above the private nonfarm average from 1981 through 1983), local labor markets were less isolated and perhaps less depressed for workers displaced from the automobile industry, and more of the workers displaced from the auto industry may have been reemployed in the same industry (steel industry employment continued to be weak during the recovery from recession).

The data describing how displaced workers who obtained new jobs fared in terms of real earnings are averages; some of these workers fared better, others fared worse, and, of course, still other workers had not yet obtained new full-time jobs in January 1984. As might be expected, there was considerable dispersion in how workers fared as measured by real wage ratios. About 54 percent of these workers received real wages in their new jobs that were between 75 and 125 percent of the wages in their old jobs. That workers displaced from relatively high-wage industries fared less well than other workers is also apparent in dispersion measures; about 34 percent of workers displaced from durable goods manufacturing received real wages that were 75 percent or less of the wages they received before, for example, compared with 21 percent for nondurable manufacturing industries.

Although there was considerable dispersion among individual workers, displaced workers did not, on average, apparently need to reduce their reservation wages drastically to obtain new jobs. This is consistent with the evidence that the duration of unemployment for those displaced workers who obtained new jobs was not dramatically higher than for other unemployed workers. Despite the recession and some degree of geographic concentration of permanent job losses, the

301

costs of displacement apparently did not take the form of major, widespread reductions in earnings. Instead, the main impact on economic well-being seems to have been some unemployment for most workers, extended periods of unemployment for a considerable portion of displaced workers, and eventual withdrawal from the work force for only a relatively small component.

## Conclusions

The problem of employment adjustments necessitated by permanent job loss by workers who were displaced as a result of plant closings and related cutbacks received a great deal of attention during the early 1980s. Many of the workers affected were seeking new jobs during a period of recession, unusually high unemployment, and continued sluggish employment growth in manufacturing even after recovery from the recession. Despite these circumstances, the number of workers for whom adjustment appeared to be extremely costly was apparently not large; most of the workers affected fared reasonably well, often after experiencing a period of unemployment, despite their forced departure from established jobs.

Some 5 million workers were displaced over the five-year period from 1979 through 1983 according to a special BLS survey, using the definitions they employed. The estimated number affected would be far lower, however, if more restrictive definitions were used with respect to job tenure and age. Only 1.5 million workers would be counted, for example, under a ten-year job tenure definition. Other general qualifications designed to focus on those most likely to experience serious economic loss as a result of displacement, such as an isolated or depressed local labor market, would further reduce the estimated number of displaced workers, but workers in such a more narrowly defined group could be expected to experience more severe adverse effects than those in the BLS sample. Information on personal or household characteristics, such as whether the worker displaced was a secondary worker, could be used to further refine estimates that would take into account implications for overall economic well-being.

Despite the unfavorable general labor market conditions under which displacement occurred, the great majority of these workers obtained new jobs at wages that compared reasonably well with wages in their previous job and did so after periods of unemployment that were not widely at variance with those of other workers who lost their jobs. These adjustments, moreover, were achieved without an unusual amount of geographic mobility on the part of the displaced workers themselves, although changes in occupation and industry of employment were quite important.

Some of the workers displaced were unemployed for very long periods. Many of those workers eventually dropped out of the labor force, although withdrawal from the labor force was very limited for prime-age male workers. While some of the displaced workers who remained unemployed for a long time or dropped out of the labor force may have had deficient skills, displaced workers as a whole appear to have relatively good technical skills and, by virtue of their job tenure, had demonstrated adequate general worker disciplines. Job training programs, particularly those that emphasize remedial instruction or basic skills are, consequently, not likely to be well suited to these workers' needs.

General policies to assist displaced workers or to facilitate their adjustment are particularly difficult to design in view of the diverse personal and household circumstances of the workers affected. For older workers in households in which another member is employed, for example, or for a secondary worker who was displaced, it may be optimal, not only for the worker affected but also for society as a whole, for the worker to withdraw from the work force. In other instances, it may be optimal for younger or otherwise more mobile workers to make a geographic move from a slack local labor market area that would open up the possibility of a job for an older, less mobile worker who suffered a permanent job loss. In view of such diversity in circumstances and the wide range of ongoing adjustments that indirectly affect displaced workers, the most pervasive and reliable policies to facilitate employment adjustments by displaced workers may well be those that enhance overall labor market flexibility and generally facilitate adjustment in the labor market.

Industrial plant closings and layoffs, some of which are trade related, have led to proposals for federal policies that would raise the cost to firms of making such adjustments or create special programs to assist workers affected. Policies that would raise the costs of major layoffs or plant closings could bring short-term benefits to workers directly affected. Any such benefits, however, would come at a cost to the economy as a whole. Such policies would discourage the release of workers when the value of their output fell below the cost of employing them, and these workers would accordingly not be available for jobs in which the value of their output exceeded the cost of employing them. In the longer run, new employment commitments—job creation—would be inhibited by the increased overall costs of employing new workers in an uncertain market environment.

Assistance for displaced workers is now provided primarily as a part of more general policies under the Job Training Partnership Act.[5] On the basis of the evidence in this paper, this seems appropriate. Introducing separate, specialized programs instead, with benefits that are different and contingent on the circumstances that produced displacement, would be ill advised for two reasons. First, the characteristics of workers affected by plant closings or major layoffs have not been sufficiently different from those of the work force as a whole to suggest that specialized programs should be developed. Moreover, these workers' experience in obtaining new jobs has not been radically different from that of other unemployed workers in the economy. Second, the particular workers directly affected by displacement are not necessarily those to whom special inducements for relocation or job retraining should be applied. Other workers in the same labor markets may be more mobile, for example, and skill training may be more cost effective for other workers. That is, displaced workers may well fare best as the indirect beneficiaries of adjustments that take place throughout the labor market. There are also other advantages of avoiding specialized programs with different benefit packages that are contingent on how a job loss occurred. Tracing the causes of particular jobs losses to sources such as trade, for example, is inherently difficult and arbitrary, and there is little basis in equity for distinctions that provide different benefits for workers under similar circumstances. General policies to facilitate adjustments throughout the labor market are for these reasons preferable to differentiated programs for groups without pronounced differences in claims or needs.

# Notes

1. Barry Bluestone and Bennett Harrison, *The Deindustrialization of America* (New York: Basic Books, 1982), p. 23.

2. Annual separation rates (excluding quits and layoffs) in manufacturing ranged between 8.4 and 10.8 percent over the period 1977–1981. *Monthly Labor Review*, April 1982, table 12.

3. See Paul O. Flaim and Ellen Sehgal, "Displaced Workers of 1979–83: How Well Have They Fared?" *Monthly Labor Review*, June 1985, pp. 3–16, for an overview of the survey and principal results. The BLS survey defines displaced workers as individuals with at least three years of job tenure who were premanently laid off due to a plant closing or moving, slack work, or the abolition of a shift or position. To facilitate comparison with other published sources, survey data in this paper have been further restricted (where noted) to individuals who lost full-time private sector jobs.

4. Ellen Sehgal, "Occupational Mobility and Job Tenure in 1983," *Monthly Labor Review*, October 1984, pp. 18–23.

5. Title III of the Job Training Partnership Act of 1982 provides matching funds to states for training, job search, and relocation assistance for workers affected by "mass layoffs."

# 10
# Government Policy and the Decline in U.S. Trade Competitiveness

*Sven W. Arndt*

## Summary

*Trade and competitiveness, traditionally unexciting issues, are making head-lines. The trade balance is in the red, America has become a debtor nation, and protectionist sentiment surges in Congress.*

*The public debate has thus far generated more heat than light, and many proposed solutions are bound to do more harm than good. The major cause of America's declining competitiveness, which may be measured at various levels of aggregation, is the real appreciation of the dollar in the 1980s. That appreciation is the result of macroeconomic policies and must therefore be corrected by improvements in macroeconomic policies. The trade policies being debated in the Congress cannot neutralize the adverse effects of poor macro policies. The United States cannot avoid trade deficits if it pursues policies that push national absorption ahead of national output.*

*But even if national output and absorption were brought into better balance, competitive problems would persist for some U.S. producers, quite apart from the difficulties caused by restrictive foreign trade practices. The international division of labor is changing, and the United States will have to adjust to its imperatives. U.S. manufacturing performance—measured in terms of trade balances and value added—continues to be strong in product-cycle goods (that is, in goods making intensive use of technology and human capital) while displaying weakness in Heckscher-Ohlin goods (that is, in goods of standardized design and production technologies). The share of manufac-turing employment provided by product-cycle goods is also rising.*

*If history is prologue, the United States must seek its competitive fortunes in product-cycle goods (as well as continue its strength in agricultural trade and in growing opportunities in services trade). This goal may be accomplished by maintaining and upgrading the quality of physical and human capital. Sustained efforts in this regard appear especially important to the extent that other countries are accumulating capital and skilled labor faster than the United States, thereby reducing the gap favoring the United States. As this gap narrows, the resource content of U.S. trade will change, and intra-industry trade will likely grow.*

## Introduction

This chapter examines recent developments in the U.S. competitive position from both economywide and sector-specific perspectives. At the former level, competitiveness may be measured by comparing the average of domestic prices or costs with those abroad, after allowing for changes in exchange rates; while at the disaggregated level, the price and cost comparisons are carried out with respect to sectors, industries, and products.

The two important elements determining international competitiveness are exchange rates and relative prices and costs. Since these variables are strongly influenced by macroeconomic and other government policies, shifts in those policies will alter the real exchange rate only to the extent that they affect nominal exchange rates, prices, and costs differentially. The 1980s have seen a substantial appreciation of the dollar in real terms, a significant part of that change being attributable to monetary/fiscal policies in the United States.

In addition to these more macroeconomic influences on competitiveness, gradual changes in economic structure around the globe, the spread of technology, and the emergence of new countries have brought long-run changes in comparative advantage and competitiveness, thereby mandating adjustments in the international division of labor.

Both types of change bring benefits and costs, and when the costs fall heavily on some producers while the benefits are spread more broadly among citizens, the political process may have difficulty managing the required adjustment.

## Macroeconomic Influences

In a regime of fixed exchange rates, a country's competitive position deteriorates as the average of its prices and costs rises in relation to those abroad. An increase in relative prices makes selling abroad more difficult and shifts domestic expenditures away from home-produced goods toward imports. As a result, the country's share in world exports declines while import penetration rises.

When the exchange rate is flexible, it becomes an additional element determining competitiveness. The relevant unit of comparison is the real exchange rate.[1] A rise in domestic costs or prices, for example, that is not offset by a depreciation of the home currency worsens the country's competitive position; the real exchange rate appreciates, making exports more expensive to foreigners and imports cheaper to residents. A sustained real currency appreciation leads to a deterioration of the trade balance, a decline in the country's share of world exports, and a rise in import penetration.

Nominal and real values of the U.S. dollar are displayed in figure 10-1. The upper panel of the figure shows the general decline in the trade-weighted value of the dollar in the 1970s and its steep appreciation in the early 1980s. The lower panel presents three measures of the real value of the dollar expressed in terms of relative wholesale prices, relative export unit values, and relative unit labor costs between the United States and a weighted average of her main trading partners. The dominant influence, especially in the later period, of the exchange rate in determining the U.S. international competitive position is clearly apparent from the similarity in the slopes of the curves in the two panels. Whatever may have been the differences between U.S. and foreign inflation rates, they have been swamped by the steep appreciation of the dollar since 1980.[2]

The recent deterioration in the U.S. competitive position was broadly based and affected U.S. trade with many countries and in many commodities. Figure 10-2 presents examples of the real exchange rate (here expressed in terms of relative hourly compensation) for several products and several trading partners. The general improvement in competitiveness in the second half of the 1970s and the sustained decline in the 1980s is evident throughout. These adverse developments involved more than the U.S. competitive position vis-à-vis Japan, a country that has been heavily criticized by Americans, and more than weak industries like textiles and steel.

In the 1970s U.S. monetary policy was expansionary, the rate of inflation soared, and the dollar depreciated in both nominal and real terms, as shown in figures 10-1 and 10-2. In 1979 the Federal Reserve inaugurated an anti-inflationary policy regime, and in 1981 the era of the large fiscal deficits began. This mixture of macroeconomic policies brought down the inflation rate and nominal interest rates while it raised real interest rates and launched the dollar on its sustained appreciation. As the demand for goods in the United States rose in relation to domestic output, the trade balance began a prolonged deterioration that led ultimately to a negative international investment position for the United States.

As table 10-1 shows, the deterioration of the trade balance occurred across a broad spectrum of products, confirming the pervasive nature of the disturbance. Even industries that had experienced substantial surpluses in the 1970s showed a deficit in the early 1980s. Much like the commodity composition, the country composition of the deterioration in the U.S. trade balance was broad, as figure 10-3 makes clear.

## FIGURE 10–1
### NOMINAL AND REAL EXCHANGE RATES, 1970–1985
### (1980 = 100)

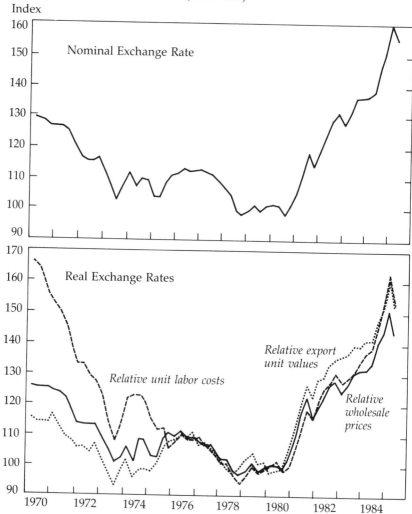

NOTES: The nominal exchange rate used was the effective exchange rate or MERM rate. This is an index combining the exchange rates between the U.S. dollar and the other major currencies with weights derived from the IMF's Multilateral Exchange Rate Model (MERM). The indicators of the real exchange rate represent the ratio of the relevant indicator for the United States relative to a geometric average of the corresponding indicators of the other industrial countries.

SOURCE: International Monetary Fund, *International Financial Statistics, Yearbook, 1985.*

## FIGURE 10-2
### REAL AND NOMINAL EXCHANGE RATES FOR
### SELECTED PRODUCTS AND COUNTRIES, 1975–1984
### (1975 = 1.00)

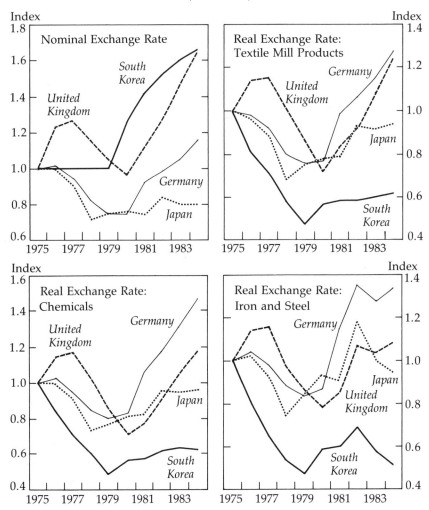

NOTES: Nominal exchange rates are measured in foreign currency per U.S. dollar. The real exchange rate, based on author's calculations, is defined as the American price level divided by the partner country's price level multiplied by the exchange rate, in this case, $(W/W^*)$ $(E)$ where $E$ is the nominal exchange rate and $W^*$ and $W$ are foreign and domestic hourly compensation respectively for that sector.

SOURCES: International Monetary Fund, *International Financial Statistics, Yearbook*, 1985, U.S. Department of Labor, Bureau of Labor Statistics, Office of Productivity and Technology, unpublished data.

TABLE 10–1
CHANGES IN U.S. TRADE BALANCES, 1973–1984
(billions of dollars)

|  | 1973–1981 | 1981–1984 |
|---|---|---|
| Agricultural goods | 16.3 | −14.8 |
| Capital goods | 31.8 | −33.5 |
| Chemicals | 8.8 | −3.4 |
| Military equipment | 2.2 | 0.3 |
| Consumer goods | −14.4 | −4.6 |
| Automotive products | −7.2 | −21.1 |
| Fuel | −65.0 | 18.4 |
| Other industrial supplies | −7.5 | −4.6 |

SOURCE: Department of Commerce, *Highlights of U.S. Export and Import Trade* (Washington, D.C.: Government Printing Office, 1985), pp. B–16, C–20.

The U.S. share of the exports of fifteen major industrial countries (excluding shipments to the United States) was virtually unchanged between 1981 and 1983, as was the U.S. share of high-tech exports.[3] At the same time, the share of total imports in U.S. expenditure on goods rose from approximately 12 percent in 1981 to 14 percent in 1984; during the period, import penetration rose from approximately 18 percent to more than 25 percent in capital goods and from approximately 12 percent to more than 17 percent in consumer durables (excluding autos).[4] Import penetration varied among commodities but was most pronounced in metal-cutting machine tools (from 26 percent in 1981 to 39 percent in 1984) and telephone and telegraph equipment (from 4 percent in 1981 to 14 percent in 1984).[5]

During the period of dollar appreciation, employment in U.S. manufacturing declined in spite of a substantial rise in employment in the nonagricultural part of the economy, suggesting that the positive effect on employment of the sustained economic recovery in the United States was more than offset by the negative influence of the dollar appreciation on output and employment in the tradable goods sectors.

Some politicians have made much of this decline in manufacturing employment, placing the blame on the trade deficit as the original cause rather than a symptom. The trade deficit and the lackluster performance of tradables manufacturing are the joint product of U.S. macroeconomic policies and the associated appreciation of the dollar. The relation between employment in an industry and the real exchange rate for that industry (expressed as relative bilateral hourly compensation in the United States and various key competitors) is

## FIGURE 10–3
## U.S. Merchandise Trade Balance
## with Selected Countries and Regions, 1970–1984

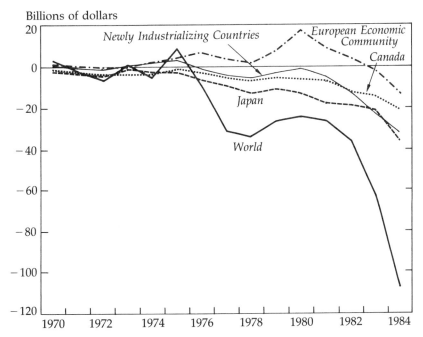

NOTES: The figures for the European Economic Community include only data for those countries that were members prior to 1985. The Newly Industrializing Countries (NICs) include Brazil, Hong Kong, Mexico, Singapore, South Korea, and Taiwan.
SOURCE: International Monetary Fund, *Direction of Trade Statistics, Yearbook*, 1985.

presented in figure 10–4. Thus employment in the iron and steel products industry began its steep decline in 1979 as the dollar began to appreciate in real terms against two of America's major competitors (Germany and Japan). Similarly, employment leveled off and then declined in chemicals and allied products as the exchange rate picture darkened. That pattern is repeated in other industries.[6]

The real exchange rate may be interpreted as the relative price between traded and nontraded goods, so that a real currency appreciation depresses the price of traded goods in relation to nontraded goods. This depression in turn decreases profitability in the former in relation to the latter and hence creates incentives for the redeployment of resources from the production of tradables to the production of nontradables.

If prices and wages are flexible and labor, capital, and other

313

FIGURE 10–4
U.S. EMPLOYMENT AND THE REAL EXCHANGE RATE, 1975–1984

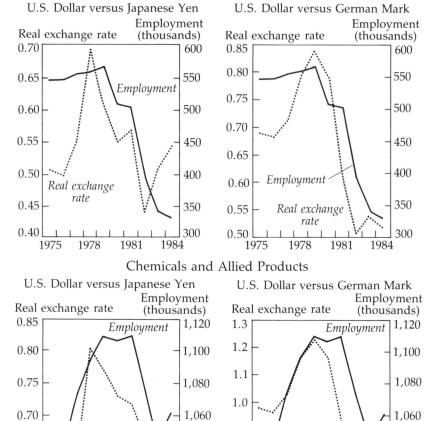

Iron and Steel Products

Chemicals and Allied Products

NOTES: Employment figures are for total U.S. employment for that sector. The definition of real exchange rate is the inverse of that in figure 10–2.

SOURCES: U.S. Department of Commerce, Office of Business Analysis, 1985 Industrial Outlook Data Computer Tape; U.S. Department of Labor, Bureau of Labor Statistics, *Employment and Earnings*, various issues; International Monetary Fund, *International Financial Statistics, Yearbook*, 1985; and U.S. Department of Labor, Bureau of Labor Statistics, Office of Productivity and Technology, unpublished data.

productive resources are mobile, the shift in the composition of output and employment required by the exchange rate change will encounter few difficulties. But if wages and prices are sticky and factories and their workers cannot be easily transferred from one use to another, then unemployment and excess capacity will be the result. That has been the situation in the United States in agriculture and manufacturing, two of the country's major tradables sectors. At the same time, the nontradables sectors, notably construction and services, have been booming.

When the tradables sector becomes depressed, it releases productive resources that must be absorbed by the nontradables sector. But if the two sectors use labor and nonlabor resources in different proportions (that is, they possess different factor intensities), then relative factor rewards must change to maintain full employment. If resources are mobile and the tradables sector is intensive in the use of capital, land, and certain kinds of labor, then land values, capital rentals, and the wages of those workers would have to fall while the wages of workers and the returns of resources used intensively in the nontradables sector rise.[7] The wage give-backs that have occurred in several tradables industries and the decline in agricultural land values are examples of such adjustment.

The economic recovery of the 1980s has been lopsided because of the dollar appreciation that has accompanied it. The growth in overall employment during the recovery may have been helped by the real appreciation as it encouraged expansion of the relatively labor-intensive nontradables sector. This raises concerns that a sustained real depreciation of the dollar will slow the growth in overall employment (and exacerbate a recession) while raising employment in the tradables sector (or reducing its rate of decline).

### Secular Shifts in Competitiveness

Besides cyclical and other macroeconomic influences, long-run shifts arising from changes in tastes, from discoveries of new products and new technologies, from the appearance of new countries on world markets, and from changes in the global supply of productive resources affect the international division of labor. These long-run shifts in competitiveness are less general than exchange rate–related disturbances, and they affect particular sectors, industries, or products.

According to traditional trade theory, a country will find its competitive strength in commodities that require large inputs of resources with which it is relatively well endowed. Such products will be exported while those intensive in the country's scarce factors will be imported.

Thus the United States, with its relatively plentiful supplies of land, skilled labor, and sophisticated capital, registers comparative advantage in products heavily using these abundant factors. Such products are important exports, while products needing large inputs of cheap, low-skilled labor, for example, are imported.

It is also to be expected that a country's exports will be dominated by products using resources of which the country has a large share of the world's total supply. Since, for example, the United States lays claim to a large share of the world supply of engineers and scientists, countries in which engineers and scientists are scarce must acquire their services indirectly through imports of the goods they produce.

Of course, product differentiation, economies of scale, and externalities complicate the picture and generate much intraindustry and interindustry trade. They have also confounded empirical tests of the propositions of traditional trade theory, but by and large that theory offers a useful analytical framework.

It has long been recognized that world economic welfare is enhanced if the global division of labor is organized according to the dictates of comparative advantage. Each country, too, tends to maximize the economic welfare attainable from a given resource endowment if those resources are deployed according to the principle of comparative advantage. The idea is simply not to produce domestically something that could be imported at lower resource cost.

This idea has lately come under mounting criticism. Whereas the traditional view saw gains in a unilateral policy of free trade, gains in production due to improved efficiency, and gains in consumption due to greater consumer purchasing power, many modern critics see in unreciprocated trade a waste of national wealth.

Others object that the traditional view is static in nature and largely irrelevant in a dynamic world, that it assumes perfect competition, and that it thus has little to offer in a world of market failure and distortions. Still others assert that it ignores political realities and distributional conflicts in democratic societies.

These are weighty concerns, both analytically and operationally, but they do not invalidate the traditional wisdom; and where they justify government intervention, trade policy is rarely the appropriate instrument of intervention.[8]

Reciprocity, for example, is unquestionably desirable for its welfare benefits, but retaliatory protection against countries with closed markets generally makes matters worse. Similarly, far from invalidating the comparative advantage principle, the presence of dynamic gains enhances its power and relevance. Where markets are imperfect and subject to distortions, government intervention is justified in principle but may be difficult to execute in practice, and the most efficient and least distorting type of intervention tends to require domestic rather than trade policies. Finally, when the political system has difficulty managing the distributional aspects of adjustment, protection is nevertheless a policy response and in general a very costly one. It is, however, preferred by politicans and their clients because it is less transparent than, say, subsidies and thus more readily undertaken without proper public debate and political discussion.[9]

Applied to the United States, the principle of comparative advantage suggests continued competitiveness in agricultural trade and in goods that are intensive in human capital, in advanced and generally R&D-intensive technologies, and in sophisticated forms of physical capital. It is often convenient but quite misleading to think of the high-tech industry as possessing comparative advantage and traditional smoke-stack industries as doomed in the high-tech sector. In practice, there are product lines (certain semiconductors, for example) that are rapidly losing competitiveness while others in the smoke-stack area (designer apparel and industrial fibers, for example) continue to show competitive strength.

In the early years following World War II, American competitiveness could be expressed on an industrywide basis. Then, as Europe rebuilt, its trade with the United States increasingly took on an interindustry and intraindustry complexion. In this instance, history is quite probably preview: the U.S. economy is likely to become still more open with manufacturing exports and imports rising and with intraindustry trade playing an increasing role vis-à-vis not only industrial but industrializing countries.

For reasons that are strongly related to its endowment, the commodity exports of the United States have shown particular strength in agricultural and product-cycle goods, while displaying weakness in Heckscher-Ohlin goods. Figures 10–5, 10–6, and 10–7 present the performance of trade balance, value added, and employment in three broad product categories. They are Ricardo goods (intensive in the use of natural resources), Heckscher-Ohlin goods (standardized in design and production technology), and product-cycle goods (making heavy use of R&D and human capital).

The loss in competitiveness brought about by the dollar appreciation is evident in all three groups in figure 10–5 as trade balances have weakened in the 1980s. On the one hand, the trade balance in Ricardo goods has been negative and on a modest secular decline (if one abstracts from the exchange rate–related changes of the 1980s). The trade balance in product-cycle goods, on the other hand, has shown a strong and rising trend (again abstracting from the macro-

317

## FIGURE 10-5
U.S. TRADE BALANCE FOR RICARDO GOODS,
PRODUCT-CYCLE GOODS, AND HECKSCHER-OHLIN GOODS, 1972–1984

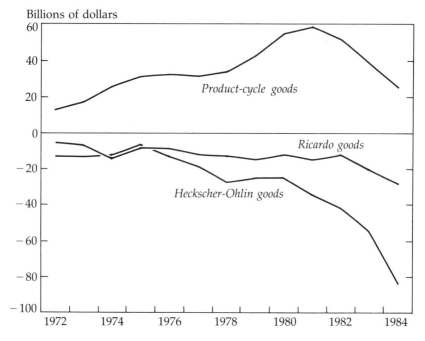

SOURCES: Author's calculations based on data from the U.S. Department of Commerce, Office of Business Analysis, 1985 Industrial Outlook Data Computer Tape, and Bureau of Census, Foreign Trade Division, Reports EA 675 and IA 275. The classification of three-digit SIC industries into Product-cycle, Ricardo, and Heckscher-Ohlin goods comes from Keith E. Maskus, "The Changing Relationship Between Basic Inputs and U.S. Foreign Trade," Competing in a Changing World Economy Project, Working Paper No. 2 (Washington, D.C.: American Enterprise Institute, August 1985).

economic distortions of the 1980s). The trade balance in Heckscher-Ohlin goods, however, has deteriorated (quite apart from the macro-economic distortions of the 1980s).[10]

Value added in relation to total manufacturing is presented in figure 10–6, which indicates the growing importance of product-cycle goods in the U.S. economy. Ricardo goods declined in importance in the 1960s but have maintained relatively stable shares since then, while the share of Heckscher-Ohlin goods was relatively stable until the mid-1970s when it began a secular decline.

Employment shares are presented in figure 10–7. The growing importance of product-cycle goods in employing Americans and the gradually declining share of Ricardo goods are clearly apparent. Until

318

FIGURE 10–6
U.S. VALUE ADDED IN RICARDO GOODS,
PRODUCT-CYCLE GOODS, AND HECKSCHER-OHLIN GOODS, 1958–1984
(percentage of manufacturing)

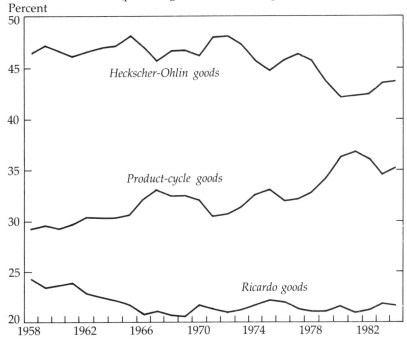

SOURCES: Author's calculations based on data from the U.S. Department of Commerce, Office of Business Analysis, 1985 Industrial Outlook Data Computer Tape, and Bureau of Economic Analysis, National Income and Wealth Division, unpublished data. See figure 10–5 for source of classification of Product-cycle, Ricardo, and Heckscher-Ohlin goods.

the mid-1970s the share of employment in Heckscher-Ohlin products was quite stable on trend, and those products continue to provide the lion's share of manufacturing employment. But in the mid-1970s the share of employment provided by Heckscher-Ohlin goods began a gradual decline.

Although the evidence must be handled with circumspection, the broad implications of the changes that have taken place are relatively unambiguous. Product-cycle goods represent strength in providing jobs and adding value in U.S. manufacturing, while Ricardo goods are gradually fading in importance. Product-cycle goods also provide strongly positive and rising trade performance. The pattern in Heckscher-Ohlin goods is more ambiguous, with the trade balance

FIGURE 10–7
U.S. Total Employment in Ricardo Goods,
Product-Cycle Goods, and Heckscher-Ohlin Goods, 1958–1984
(percentage of manufacturing)

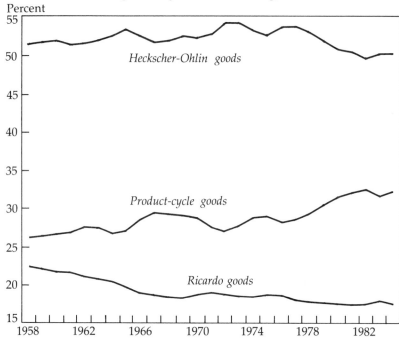

SOURCES: Author's calculations based on data from the U.S. Department of Commerce, Office of Business Analysis, 1985 Industrial Outlook Data Computer Tape, and U.S. Department of Labor, Bureau of Labor Statistics, *Employment and Earnings,* various issues. See figure 10–5 for source of classification of Product-cycle, Ricardo, and Heckscher-Ohlin goods.

negative and deteriorating, with the share of value added declining, but with employment remaining relatively stable.

The United States is most vulnerable to foreign competition in the area of Heckscher-Ohlin goods. Many commodities—running from carbon steels to textiles and apparel—that have been the mainstay of manufacturing output and employment are found in this category. They tend to be commodities with a high degree of standardization, both in design and production technology and hence easily replicable by almost anyone. Because they are produced around the world to similar specifications with similar technologies, the competitiveness of the products of various countries is determined by relative labor cost. Japan was the first to challenge the United States and Western

Europe in Heckscher-Ohlin goods; and the newly industrializing countries are repeating that challenge in a variety of Heckscher-Ohlin goods (from textiles to carbon steels to light manufactures). The United States must thus seek its fortunes in product-cycle goods to take advantage of plentiful supplies of scientists, engineers, and skilled workers. To accomplish this structural change, the quality of its capital and labor must be continually upgraded. This imperative is made more urgent by the increasingly aggressive R&D and human capital development under way in many countries, including the newly industrializing ones.

Indeed, the evidence suggests that the United States, though still relatively abundant in physical and human capital, is experiencing an erosion of its share of the world's capital. In many countries, capital formation has been faster than that in the United States, implying that the gap in capital abundance, though still favoring the United States, is narrowing. In his recent study, for example, Harry P. Bowen found that the growth rate of capital per worker in the United States was one of the lowest in a sample of thirty-four countries.[11] Ranked near the top were Korea, Japan, and many developing countries. As a result, Bowen estimated that the United States slipped from first place in 1963 to sixth place in 1975 in terms of capital per worker.

In a similar evaluation of the ratio of skilled labor to total labor, Bowen found the U.S. growth rate to be among the lowest, with many developing countries near the top in growth rates (not surprisingly, given the base from which they must start). As a result, the U.S. rank in terms of skilled to total labor slipped from second place in 1963 to seventh in 1975.

In some respects, these results are inevitable. As economic development spreads around the globe, it brings improvements in literacy rates and worker skills. Given the enormous differences between the U.S. base and that of most other countries, its share of the world stock of physical and human capital will gradually decline. And with that decline, its share in the world's trade of capital and skill-intensive goods will decrease.

Bowen's research indicates that, after rising in the 1960s, the capital and skill content of U.S. exports declined, especially in trade with developed countries. This finding suggests that many countries reduced their absorption of U.S. capital and skilled labor through trade (although they may have been large recipients of U.S. direct investment).

The long-run implication of capital and skill accumulation around the globe is that foreign competitors will be in the position to challenge the United States along a growing range of traded products, including those with increasing technical sophistication and with rising value added. In addition to the semiskilled and unskilled workers who have felt the heat of foreign competitors, America's skilled workers will face foreign competitive challenges.

Does this mean, as some have suggested, that the United States will be forced to abandon the field, to leave industrial production to others, and to specialize in services? Clearly, the evidence does not support such dire predictions. It does suggest, however, that success in trade must be sought in the application of superior physical and human capital. It suggests further that the United States will lose its customary dominance across broad ranges of products and will increasingly have to seek opportunities for specialization in particular products. Intraindustry and interindustry trade, which already plays an important role in the country's trade with Europe, will increasingly dominate U.S. trade. In many industries, the United States is likely to become an importer of products with strong Heckscher-Ohlin qualities and an exporter of product-cycle goods.

## Conclusion

Certain conclusions emerge from the foregoing analysis. Clearly, U.S. macroeconomic policies in the 1980s impaired the international competitive positions of U.S. producers of traded goods in manufacturing as well as in agriculture. From the perspective of U.S. trade, those policies were simply bad. The situation will not improve fundamentally if Congress, eager to blame others for our trade problems, resorts to protectionist policies that would only further hurt the U.S. position.

The United States has a long history of conducting its macroeconomic policies without regard for their external consequences. The lopsided macroeconomic policies of the 1980s that produced the steep dollar appreciation are only the latest example. In a highly competitive world economy such neglect is not benign; it will have to stop.

But improved policy making at the macroeconomic level will not address the secular challenges to American producers of tradable goods. In a market-oriented country like the United States, these challenges will require creative initiatives by the private sector, but the government can play a major role by setting the framework through its regulatory and other policies. The evidence suggests that America's competitive fortunes will depend on the quality of physical and human capital.

# Notes

1. The real exchange rate is the nominal price of foreign exchange multiplied by the ratio of foreign to domestic costs or prices.

2. The three relative price lines display similar patterns in the late 1970s and early 1980s compared with the substantial dispersion of movements in the early 1970s.

3. U.S. Department of Commerce, *United States Trade: Performance in 1984 and Outlook* (Washington, D.C.: Government Printing Office, June 1985), p. 121; and AEI calculations.

4. U.S. Department of Commerce, *U.S. Manufacturing at a Crossroads* (Washington, D.C.: Government Printing Office, June 1985), p. 36; and AEI calculations.

5. Ibid., p. 38.

6. These relations need to be interpreted with caution, inasmuch as the United States passed through a prolonged recession in the early 1980s. The recession and the subsequent weak recovery in the tradables sector, however, were aggravated by the dollar's real appreciation.

7. If some factors are sector specific while others are mobile, the returns to the factors specific to the tradables sector (such as agricultural land) will collapse, and the return to other factors may fluctuate before converging on their long-run values.

8. For a detailed discussion, see Sven W. Arndt and Lawrence Bouton, *Trade Policy Brief* (Washington, D.C.: American Enterprise Institute, forthcoming).

9. For a related analysis, see Jan Tumlir, *Protectionism: Trade Policy in Democratic Societies* (Washington, D.C.: American Enterprise Institute, 1985).

10. The trade balance in agricultural products had been consistently positive and rising until the 1980s, when the fortunes of U.S. farmers were smashed by the macroeconomic distortions.

11. Harry P. Bowen, "Changes in the International Distribution of Resources and Their Impact on U.S. Comparative Advantage," *Review of Economics and Statistics*, vol. 65 (August 1983), pp. 402–414.

# 11

# The World Economy: Its Performance and Prospects, with Emphasis on Trade Liberalization and Protection

*Gottfried Haberler*

**Summary**

*Section 1 sketches the overall performance of the world economy. Simon Kuznets wrote in 1975 that "peacetime product per capita in the world, developed and less developed" has grown at a rate "higher than ever observed in the past." Kuznets's optimistic diagnosis has been confirmed by later studies. The volume of world trade has grown by leaps and bounds, with slight setbacks in recession years. In the past fifteen years or so there has been a slight decline in the rate of growth of output and trade but no sharp break in the trend.*

*All this growth is in sharp contrast to what happened during the interwar period (1918–1939) and to what was widely expected in the 1930s and 1940s. Section 2 describes the intellectual climate of the 1930s and early 1940s. As a result of the Great Depression of the 1930s, the faith in economic liberalism, free enterprise, and free trade reached its lowest point in modern times. John Maynard Keynes became an outright protectionist and interventionist and took most, though by no means all, of his many followers along. Although a few years later the master returned to his early liberal beliefs, many of his followers never found their way back.*

*In his* General Theory *Keynes fatally misinterpreted the nature of the Great Depression of the 1930s: he attributed it to a basic weakness in mature capitalism, which suffers from chronic oversaving and lack of investment opportunities. Actually, the exceptional severity and length of the depression, was without doubt, due to horrendous mistakes of monetary policy. A decline in the U.S. basic money supply of about 30 percent was bound to have catastrophic consequences. Not only monetarists held this view; Joseph A. Schumpeter wrote that "avoidable" mistakes of monetary policy "turned retreat into route." Quite consistently, Keynesians predicted that the dismal experience of the 1930s would repeat itself after the war. When the expected depression again and again failed to materialize, Keynesians claimed credit for the improvement. Actually, monetarists have a better claim. Clearly the main reason no deep depression occurred in the postwar period is that the money supply did not decline sharply as it had done in the 1930s.*

*Section 3 discusses the revival of economic liberalism. Keynes's reconversion to his early liberal beliefs was an important factor. A real turning point came in 1948 with the currency reform in Germany and the simultaneous abrupt abolition of all wartime wage and price controls. This started the German "economic miracle," which was followed by similar miracles in Austria, Italy, and France—demonstrating that what Keynes called "the classical medicine" still works. Unsurprisingly, many Keynesians completely misjudged the chances and importance of the German reforms.*

*Section 4 very briefly sketches the evolution of the international monetary system from Bretton Woods, its breakdown, and the present system (or nonsystem) of managed floating up to the most recent developments: the statement of the "group of ten" industrial countries that endorsed floating (Tokyo, June 1985) and the seemingly contradictory statement of the "group of five" (the United States, Britain, Germany, Japan, and France—September 1985), which calls for coordinated official interventions in the foreign exchange market to bring down the strong dollar. Reasons are given why intervention in the foreign exchange market per se cannot achieve its purpose, a theme that is further developed in section 5.*

*The optimism of the "golden" 1950s and 1960s has given way to renewed pessimism in the 1970s and 1980s. In the 1970s it was U.S. inflation, the weak dollar, the oil shocks, and the comparatively severe stabilization recession that cast gloom. Then in 1982 the U.S. economy took off on an unexpectedly vigorous recovery that is still continuing, although it slowed down recently. Now it is the strong dollar, the large trade deficits, capital imports, and the mounting foreign debt that cause alarm. Traded-goods industries have been hurt, a situation giving rise to intense protectionist pressures. But all of these problems have not prevented the U.S. economy from adding 7.8 million jobs during the past five years. Moreover, if the protectionists were right that the strong dollar has caused a large net loss of jobs in the United States, it would follow that the weak currencies in Europe would have created many new jobs. We know the opposite has happened: Europe has lost jobs in the past few years.*

*At present the United States needs foreign capital to fill the gap between insufficient domestic saving and financing needs of productive private investment and unproductive government deficits. Reasons are given why the United States cannot continue indefinitely to borrow abroad on a large scale. The conclusion is that the government budget deficit that constitutes dissaving on a grand scale must be reduced to fill the gap when capital imports decline or stop, as they will sooner or later.*

Section 6 analyses the changing attitudes toward trade liberalization and protectionism. A protectionist explosion sharply intensified the Great Depression of the 1930s. The United States set a very bad example by imposing the skyscraper Smoot-Hawley tariff in 1930. It is, however, an exaggeration to say that Smoot-Hawley was the main cause of the depression. The dominant cause was monetary deflation as well as fixed exchange rate regimes (gold standard) that did not allow deficit countries to escape deflationary pressures by floating exchange rates.

Trade liberalization during the first thirty years after the war contributed mightily to the unprecedented prosperity. This was due largely to American initiatives working through GATT. Unfortunately, the GATT rules on non-discrimination are being increasingly set aside by all sorts of preferential tariff regimes and nontariff restrictions. The strong dollar and the trade deficits have caused intense protectionist reactions in Congress. Hundreds of bills proposing protection for individual industries have been introduced. Perhaps the most shocking example is "A Bill to Restore Balance in International Trade, to Improve the Operation of the Trade Agreements Program, and for Other Purposes," introduced by prominent members of Congress. It proposes the imposition of selective surcharges on imports from Brazil, South Korea, and Taiwan, or any country that has a bilateral surplus with the United States of 65 percent or surplus of 50 percent with the world. To aim at bilateral balance with all countries is preposterous, and when the sponsors of the bill and their academic advisers try to justify their proposal by saying that the surcharge is meant to induce the offending surplus countries to get rid of their surpluses, they miss the real nature of the problem. The United States now needs the foreign capital and the trade deficit to fill the gap between domestic saving and the capital needs. This is a macroeconomic problem that cannot be solved by protectionist measures.

Section 7 discusses the Reagan administration's attempt to revive the GATT procedure of reducing tariffs through multilateral conferences. If a "Reagan round" is to succeed, the United States will have to offer lower duties on specific goods for similar concessions from other participants. It will run into resistance from protectionists and defenders of special interests in Congress.

I discuss two extreme cases—sugar and textiles—where a reduction of import restrictions would bring enormous economic and political benefits.

Sugar has a long protectionist history, but in its present vicious form it is a legacy of the New Deal. The basic fact is that imports of sugar have been more and more restricted, so that in recent years the American users of raw sugar have had to pay three to five times the world market price. This is an enormous waste of resources both in the United States and in the tropical countries in Central America, the Caribbean, and elsewhere. Moreover this restriction has serious political consequences. For one thing, it locks Cuba *ever more firmly in the Russian orbit because the Soviets buy a large part of the Cuban sugar crop at prices above the world market price. And there is danger that they may get a foothold in some other countries.*

*Sugar, being a fairly homogenous commodity, makes protection, however inefficient, a comparatively simple administrative problem. It stands to reason that this is quite different in the textile area. The Multifibre Arrangement (MFA), which imposes quantitative restrictions on hundreds of items of clothing and apparel imported from many countries, becomes an administrative nightmare, invites evasion and fraud, and involves substantial additional cost. Sources of further information are cited as well as a few examples of fraud and evasion gleaned from news dispatches that offer a rare glimpse into that bureaucratic jungle.*

*Section 8 shows why protection does not create jobs but merely shifts them from comparatively efficient and competitive export industries to comparatively inefficient and unproductive protected industries. Finally, the question is asked why the victims of protection—export industries and consumers who have to pay higher prices—do not speak up as loudly as the beneficiaries of protection.*

## The World Economy in the Post–World War II Period

The first quarter of a century or even thirty years after World War II, there can be no doubt, was a period of almost unprecedented growth and prosperity for the whole Western world, developed and less developed. I can do no better than to quote, as I did on other occasions, the world's foremost expert on economic growth, Simon Kuznets. In his magisterial lecture, "Two Centuries of Economic Growth: Reflections on U.S. Experience," Kuznets summed up the results of the enormous amount of research that he and others, many under his guidance, have done over the years, as follows:

> Even in this recent twenty-five year period of greater strain and danger, the growth in peace-time product per capita in the United States was still at a high rate; and in the rest of the world, developed and less developed (but excepting the few countries and periods marked by internal conflicts and political breakdown), material returns have grown, per capita, at a rate higher than ever observed in the past.[1]

In his paper "Aspects of Post–World War II Growth in Less Developed Countries," Kuznets said,

> For the LDCs as a group, the United Nations has estimated annual growth rates of total and per capita GDP (gross domestic product at constant factor prices) from 1950 to 1972.

The growth rates of per capita product . . . for the twenty-two years was 2.61 percent per year. . . . Such growth rates are quite high in the long-term historical perspective of both the LDCs and the current DCs.[2]

These high growth rates are largely a recent phenomenon, the result of the post–World War II period of comparative liberalism and liberalization. Kuznets is, of course, fully aware of the dangers of using broad aggregate measures of growth for the less-developed countries (LDCs) as a group, given the great diversity among the countries in the third world. He discusses and carefully evaluates possible biases in the procedures. But after everything has been said and done, he stands by the basic soundness of his findings and is puzzled that, despite the "impressively high growth rates in the per capita product of LDCs over almost a quarter of a century," the general sentiment in the LDCs is one of dissatisfaction and gloom that "seems to ignore the growth achievements." He conjectures and gives ample reasons for the conjecture that "a rise in expectations has produced a negative reaction to economic attainments which otherwise might have elicited litanies of praise for economic 'miracles.'"[3]

As for the industrial countries, after a considerable delay it has become widely if not generally recognized that the twenty-five or thirty years since World War II have constituted a period of high prosperity. But in the six or seven years since Kuznets wrote the picture has changed again. Optimism has given way to a good deal of pessimism and gloom about the future.

The reasons for the changed outlook are not hard to find: the two oil shocks; the rising tide of inflation in the vicious form of stagflation followed by the global recessions of the late 1970s and early 1980s; the slowdown of productivity growth; the huge U.S. budget and trade deficits; the strong, "overvalued" dollar, which according to some economists is bound to collapse with disastrous consequences for the United States and the world economy; the double "debt crisis"—the threatening default of overindebted third world countries, which may push many international banks to the wall and which according to some will be overshadowed by the rapidly mounting foreign debt of the United States itself. Plenty of things to worry about!

But before analyzing some of these threatening disasters, I propose first to look at the most recent global measures on output and trade to see whether the situation has changed since the optimistic appraisal of Kuznets as updated by Kravis and Lipsey and second to sketch very briefly the evolution of the intellectual climate since World War II to put the present malaise and widespread forebodings of impending serious economic troubles, if not disasters, in historical perspective.

The latest statistics on output and the volume of world trade, both worldwide and for major groups (LDCs and DCs) and geographic regions, do not indicate a sharp break in the trend since 1980, the last year in Kravis and Lipsey's update of Kuznets's findings. The figures on world output do show a slower rate of growth in the early 1980s; but that reflects the global recession, not a sharp break in the trend. Output figures for 1984 and the projections for 1985 and 1986 indicate a rebound of the world economy from the recession (see table 11–1).

Other studies indicate that the rate of growth has slightly declined over the past twenty years.[4] That there was a decline in the rate of growth in the industrial countries since the early postwar period is not surprising. This is best brought out by considering the extreme case of West Germany. What is said about Germany applies also, though to a lesser extent, to other European countries and Japan.

When the German economy rose from the ruins of Hitler's Third Reich after the shackles of wartime controls were removed by Ludwig Erhard in 1948, the German work force, augmented by more than 10 million refugees from the East, had to work at a furious pace, literally day and night, to restore basic structures such as roads, bridges, and electric power. This restoration took quite a few years, but naturally the rapid pace was not kept up forever; to do that would not have been rational. After the standard of living approached what was regarded as normal, the workweek shortened and vacations lengthened to their normal level. Thus, up to a point, the decline in GNP growth, even per capita, does not imply a decline in the standard of living.

Policy changes that have occurred in the postwar period are an-

TABLE 11–1
WORLD OUTPUT, 1950–1986
(percent per year)

| | 1950–1980 | 1980 | 1981 | 1982 | 1983 | 1984 | 1985 | 1986 |
|---|---|---|---|---|---|---|---|---|
| World | 3.96 | 2.0 | 1.6 | 0.4 | 2.5 | 4.5 | 3.1 | 3.4 |
| Industrial countries | 3.39 | 1.3 | 1.6 | −0.2 | 2.6 | 4.9 | 2.8 | 3.1 |
| Developing countries | 4.53 | 3.6 | 2.3 | 1.5 | 1.4 | 4.4 | 3.5 | 4.1 |
| Europe | — | 1.6 | 2.5 | 2.2 | 1.3 | 3.5 | 2.9 | 3.3 |

SOURCES: See IMF, *World Economic Outlook, October 1985* (Washington, D.C.: Oxford University Press, 1985), p. 43. The figures for 1950–1980 are found in Irving Kravis and Robert Livsey, "The Diffusion of Economic Growth in the World Economy," in John W. Kendrick, ed., *International Comparisons of Productivity and Causes of the Slowdown* (Cambridge, Mass.: Ballinger, 1984), pp. 109–38.

other story. Far-reaching welfare measures, generous unemployment benefits, overregulation of industry, and failure of the European Common Market to create a real free trade area comparable to the one enjoyed by the United States have led to what is often called "Eurosclerosis." Europe has fallen behind the United States and Japan in GNP and employment growth; and unemployment is shockingly high in some European countries, for example, 17 percent in the Netherlands. All this is generally well known and need not be further discussed at this point.[5]

The upshot is that there has been no sharp break in the trend of growth. This conclusion is further confirmed by the fact that the volume of world trade has grown throughout the postwar period with brief interruptions in recession years. Thus the figures for the early 1980s reflect the global recession. But by 1984 the growth of world trade had rebounded, and projections for 1985 and 1986 point to continued high rates of growth (see below).[6]

*Growth of World Trade*
(percent per year)

| 1967-76 | 1980 | 1981 | 1982 | 1983 | 1984 | 1985 | 1986 |
|---------|------|------|------|------|------|------|------|
| 6.7 | 1.2 | 0.4 | −2.5 | 2.3 | 8.5 | 3.5 | 4.3 |

All this does not, of course, give any assurance that serious troubles will not arise in the near future. Projections often go wrong; and to declare the business cycles dead, as has been done on earlier occasions, would surely be premature. Another recession will probably occur in the next few years; however, a U.S. or even a global recession does not necessarily mark a change in the trend.

Of one thing we can be fairly sure, however: even a mild recession will be widely misinterpreted as something much more serious than it really is. Misinterpretation of cyclical and other short-run events as long-run change is, unfortunately, not a rare occurrence. Examples are the theory of the permanent dollar shortage, which flourished in the 1940s and 1950s (see below) and the widely held Prebisch-Singer theory that the terms of trade of LDCs have a secular tendency to deteriorate.

The prime example is what I called on another occasion "the fatal Keynesian misinterpretation of the Great Depression of the 1930s" as a basic weakness of capitalism, a "secular stagnation" due to chronic oversaving, lack of investment opportunities, and a slowdown of technological progress[7]. Subsequent developments have dramatically disproved this theory. Actually, the exceptional severity and length of the Great Depression was, without doubt, caused by horrendous monetary mismanagement. A contraction of the basic money supply by about 30 percent was bound to have catastropic consequences. This is not only the explanation of the monetarists but also that of Joseph A. Schumpeter who said that "avoidable" monetary mismanagement "turned retreat into rout" and of the great Keynesian and biographer of Keynes Roy F. Harrod, who flatly stated, "The monetary recipe [that is, open market operations to prevent or stop deflation] just was not tried."[8]

## The Early Postwar Period: Economic Liberalism at Its Lowest Point

We will do well to remind ourselves of the intellectual climate in the early postwar period, which shaped economic policy and colored the outlook for the future. As the legacy of the Great Depression of the 1930s, the faith in economic liberalism—in the classical sense of free enterprise, free markets, and free trade—was at the lowest point in modern times. The prestige of the two totalitarian regimes was at an all-time high. Hitler's early economic successes made a great impression, and so did Stalinist Russia's apparent immunity to the economic depression that engulfed the West and its rapid industrialization. These situations convinced many of the superiority of central planning over free markets and free enterprise. This attitude was by no means confined to Marxists and fellow travelers; it was widespread among Keynesians. At one point Keynes himself expressed great admiration for Hjalmar Schacht, Hitler's early economic wizard. Later Khrushchev's boast "we will bury you," meaning that the Soviet economy would outperform and overtake the American economy, was taken very seriously by most Soviet experts in the West. Only many years of a persistent lag of centrally planned economies behind comparable Western capitalist economies corrected these views and sharply reduced the enthusiasm for central planning. I mention a few examples. How does one explain the striking differences in the standard of living between West and East Germany, Austria and Czechoslovakia, Greece and Yugoslavia, South and North Korea, Taiwan (not to mention Hong Kong) and Mainland China?

The Great Depression had spawned the "Keynesian revolution." Keynes had shed his early liberal beliefs and had become an out-and-out protectionist—"the aberration of a noble mind," said one of his great admirers, Lord Lionel Robbins. True, when Keynes became involved in postwar reconstruction, he himself returned to his early liberal beliefs; but many of his numerous followers have continued to preach protection. Moreover, there was a confluence of Keynesian and Marxian thought. Some of Keynes's most gifted disciples became what Schumpeter called Marxo-Keynesians. The late Joan Robinson is the outstanding example.

In the 1940s the U.S. economy was confronted with the gigantic task of converting from war to peace and of finding jobs for millions of exservicemen. Contrary to what was widely expected, the transition from a war economy to a peace economy was accomplished without causing much transitional unemployment, let alone a real depression.

Few foresaw that the Western world was on the verge of a long period of prosperity and rapid growth, interrupted only by comparatively mild recessions. The numerous influential Keynesians were convinced that the dismal experience of the interwar period would repeat itself. Their picture of the economy was that of mature capitalism suffering from chronic oversaving and lack of investment opportunities, in almost constant need of resuscitation through government deficit spending. Each dip in economic activity was diagnosed as the inception of a depression requiring prompt monetary-fiscal expansion. This attitude helped to give postwar macroeconomic policy a strong inflationary bias.

Later in the 1960s, when the expected depression again and again failed to materialize, the outlook changed. Pessimism gave way to optimism and euphoria. The Keynesians claimed credit for the improvement. As a typical example, in 1967 Professor Austin Robinson wrote:

> In the year 1947–1948 we began to use in peace time the principles that Maynard Keynes had worked out for war finance. We began to plan the use of national resources. If we are looking to the credit side I think we can honestly say that the world today is a different place from what it was in the 1930s in very large measure as a result of the economic thinking that began in this Faculty in Cambridge in those exciting years of the 1930s.[9]

Similar claims were made by Keynesians about the United States. Skillful fine-tuning of the economy, it was claimed, had all but abolished the business cycle.

It has not worked out that way. The business cycle is still alive. What is true is that the cycle has become milder. Specifically, there have been no real depressions, declines in economic activity similar to the Great Depression of the 1930s or to earlier ones. This is a real achievement. But to my mind monetarists have a better case for claiming credit than the Keynesians. They argue that there has been no real depression in the post-World War II period because there has been no severe deflation—no large, sustained contraction of the money supply.

Some will say we have simply exchanged the horrors of inflation and stagflation for the horrors of deflation. Far be it from me to minimize the dangers of inflation. But I submit that until now the damage done by inflation has not been nearly so great as that of deflation in the 1930s. Although we have experienced inflationary recessions and an inflationary depression is not unthinkable, there are good reasons to believe that such a depression is unlikely to happen.[10]

## The Revival of Liberalism

In the 1940s the intellectual climate and the stance of economic policy shifted in the direction of liberalism. Keynes's reconversion to his early liberal beliefs was an important factor. A decisive turning point was the currency reform and Ludwig Erhard's simultaneous abrupt abolition of all wartime controls in West Germany. This started the German economic miracle, which was followed by similar miracles in Italy, Austria, and France. Those events proved that what Keynes called the "classical medicine"—sound finance and reliance on market forces—still works.

Most Keynesians—Thomas Balogh, Kenneth Galbraith, and Walter Heller among them—completely failed to recognize the importance of Erhard's reforms. They fumed and predicted terrible consequences, such as the Soviet zone of Germany overtaking the West. The opposite was true. The German "economic miracle" had a tremendously beneficial impact on Europe and beyond, both through the economic stimulus it provided and as a proof that sound, liberal policies still work.

Let me repeat that Keynes himself soon changed his views. In fact, one year after the publication of *The General Theory* he argued in three famous articles in *The Times* that it was time to switch policy from fighting unemployment to curbing inflation, although at that time unemployment was still a little over 10 percent and inflation was not very high by post–World War II standards. And shortly before his death he pleaded that "classical medicine" should be allowed to work. That is exactly what Erhard did.

More than thirty years later Keynesians again completely misjudged the prospects when another government followed Keynes's advice to give "classical medicine" a chance. In 1984 an article entitled

"UnKeynesian Britain," *The Economist*, a bastion of Keynesianism, put it as follows:

Britain's economy is now settling into a third year of growth that many people said could not happen. When the Thatcher government raised taxes and cut public borrowing in its 1981 budget, 364 academic economists pronounced that "present policies will deepen the depression." Shortly thereafter, recovery began. The government has gone on shrinking the public-sector borrowing requirement . . . and the economy has gone on growing. . . . Something in the British economy is defying Keynesian convention, and it is time for Keynesians to accept that.[11]

To be sure, the beneficial results of Mrs. Thatcher's policy were not nearly as spectacular as those of Erhard's dash for economic freedom. But that was not to be expected. The German economic miracle started so to speak from scratch; the economy rose from the ashes of Hitler's Third Reich. Mrs. Thatcher, on the other hand, came to power thirty-four years after World War II. The economic situation was then entirely different from what it was in 1948 when Erhard restored free markets or, for that matter, in the early 1930s when Keynes wrote *The General Theory*.

When Mrs. Thatcher came to power, inflation was deeply entrenched. It reached its high point, 21 percent per annum, a year later in 1980. To bring it down to some 5 percent without causing a prolonged decline in economic activity was quite an achievement. True, unemployment is still high, 12.5 percent. But let us not forget that Britain is not the only country in Europe that has high unemployment. In the Netherlands unemployment is above 17 percent, and even in Germany it is almost 10 percent. Considering the various handicaps—the starting point, the inflationary heritage, the miners' strike, and the Falkland war (which gave Mrs. Thatcher a political lift but was a heavy financial burden)—her economic policy must be judged an outstanding success.

## The International Monetary System in the Postwar Period

I start with some comments on the state of economic thinking on international trade during and immediately after the war. Generally speaking, it is not surprising that in a period when economic liberalism and faith in free markets and free enterprise were at their lowest point, the state of macroeconomics was not universally at its best. An example, which is truly amazing because it involved great names in economics, is the theory of the "permanent" dollar shortage that flourished in the 1940s and 1950s, especially in Britain. I cite an early statement in *The Economist* in 1943 that reflects the views widely held among British economists:

> It may be, in fact, that the [dollar] problem should not be regarded as the fruit of aberrations of policy . . . but that it should be looked upon as the result of a set of economic circumstances never contemplated by the textbooks—namely, the existence of a country which, all policy apart, needs so little from the rest of the world, while the rest of the world requires so much from it, that an equilibrium of accounts can be brought about by no means available to a free, or even a tolerably free market.[12]

The long list of well-known economists who held such views includes J. R. Hicks, D. H. Robertson, and many others.[13] Fritz Machlup dubbed the view underlying the hypothesis of the permanent dollar shortage "elasticity pessimism" because it assumes that international elasticities of demand are so low as to make balance of payments adjustment by conventional methods (including currency devaluation and floating) ineffective, or at least prohibitively expensive through a deterioration of the terms of trade. This leaves only direct controls and toleration of mass unemployment as a feasible solution.

This theory has a long history. I mention one example: the famous debate of Keynes and Bertil Ohlin in the 1920s about the German reparations. Keynes argued that since the elasticity of foreign demand for German goods was low, it would be impossible for Germany to transfer large sums as reparations. Ohlin pointed out that Keynes's analysis overlooked income effects. The transfer problem was then discussed in a huge literature. It is, I believe, fair to say that Ohlin was proved right and Keynes wrong. In fact, years ago no one less than Alfred Marshall had carefully considered the possibility of inelastic international demand for a country's products and had rejected it emphatically. In his monograph *Money, Credit and Commerce* he summarized his view as follows:

> It is practically certain that in the Ricardian example and under modern industrial conditions the total demand of each of the two countries for each other's goods is relatively elastic. And where a large and rich commercial country confronts the rest of the world, this assumption becomes absolutely certain.[14]

And again:

> Nothing approaching to this [unstable equilibrium due to

inelastic demand] has ever occurred in the real world: It is not inconceivable, but it is absolutely impossible.[15]

In view of all this it is indeed amazing that thirty years later elasticity pessimism resurfaced. Actually, ten years later, in the 1960s the chronic dollar shortage gave way to a dollar glut that again was widely regarded as stubborn and intractable.[16]

It is truly surprising that the talk about a "permanent" dollar shortage continued into the 1950s, for then the Bretton Woods system of "stable but adjustable" exchange rates had been firmly established, and a number of exchange rate changes had taken place, including the wholesale "realignment" of rates in 1949 when most European (and many non-European) currencies were devalued, ranging from 30.5 percent for pound sterling to 12.3 percent for the Belgian franc. The fact is that the protagonists of the dollar shortage strongly doubted or denied the effectiveness of devaluation.[17]

In retrospect it can hardly be doubted that for about twenty years the Bretton Woods regime worked well and greatly contributed to the remarkable performance of the world economy by providing an orderly method of changing exchange rates. The absence of this option under the gold standard in the 1930s greatly intensified the depression; it forced deficit countries to impose direct controls (import quotas and exchange controls) because they could not release the deflationary pressure by devaluation or floating. This greatly contributed to the catastrophic contraction of world trade. Bretton Woods was a great improvement over the gold standard. But it finally broke down in the 1970s because the policy of "stable but adjustable" exchange rates could not cope with the great strains and stresses caused by the world inflation that started in the late 1960s. Specifically, several dollar crises caused by bursts of inflation in the United States, especially the dollar crisis of 1971 that led to the closing of the gold window, forced floating on most reluctant policy makers. In 1978 the Second Amendment to the Articles of Agreement of the International Monetary Fund (IMF) legalized floating. It is worth mentioning that in the whole literature reviewed by T. W. Hutchison the possibility of flexible exchange rates was hardly mentioned.

Ever since then the world's monetary system, or "nonsystem" as some critics like to call it, has been one of widespread floating. All major currencies and many others float. But there are important areas of stable exchange rates: for example, the European Monetary System (EMS), a sort of regional Bretton Woods for the members of the European Community (EC) minus Britain. Equally important, many countries peg their currency to that of some other country—the deutsche mark, the yen, or some basket of currencies or special drawing rights (SDRs).

Floating has been criticized on the ground that it has produced world inflation. Actually, the opposite is true. High inflation has forced floating on reluctant policy makers. Another criticism is that floating has caused excessive volatility of exchange rates and serious, stubborn misalignments of exchange rates; the allegedly grossly over-valued dollar is the prime example. More or less radical policy conclusions are drawn from this criticism, the mildest being that the policy of "benign neglect" of the balance of payments should be abandoned and a positive balance-of-payments policy be adopted, at least in the form of vigorous interventions in the foreign exchange market.

On the other hand, the ministers and governors of the "group of ten" at their meeting in Tokyo on June 21, 1985, strongly endorsed the present system. I quote from the report of the deputies, which was accepted by the ministers and governors:

> Exchange rate flexibility has made a positive contribution to external payments adjustment and to the maintenance of an open trade and payments system in a period of massive external shocks. It can help countries, especially the larger ones, to insulate their domestic price levels from inflation abroad, and can facilitate the pursuit of sound monetary policies geared more directly to domestic conditions. Furthermore, it is questionable whether any less flexible system would have survived the strains of the past decade, while attempting to preserve it would probably have led to increased reliance on restrictions on trade and capital flows.[18]

This is a very strong endorsement, considering that the report is a negotiated document that was also signed by the French delegate, despite the fact that the French government on several occasions had recommended a return to Bretton Woods. As one would expect, the report also finds certain "weaknesses" in the operation of the present system and recommends some improvements. But the suggested changes are minor. They concern mainly "enhanced" surveillance of national policies by the IMF.[19]

Later this year, on September 22, 1985, the "group of five"—the United States, the United Kingdom, Japan, West Germany, and France—met in New York and with great fanfare issued a lengthy statement that was widely interpreted as a sharp reversal of U.S. policy of benign neglect and nonintervention in the foreign exchange market and seems to contradict the Tokyo statement of the "group of ten." The "group of five's" statement reiterates the usual pious declarations against protectionism and for noninflationary growth. On exchange rates the statement says:

> The Ministers and Governors agreed that exchange rates should play a role in adjusting external imbalances. In order to do this, exchange rates should better reflect fundamental economic conditions than has been the case. They believe that agreed policy actions must be implemented and reinforced to improve the fundamentals further, and that in view of the present and prospective changes in fundamentals, some further orderly appreciation of the main non-dollar currencies against the dollar is desirable. They stand ready to cooperate more closely to encourage this when to do so would be helpful.[20]

The administration's motive for trying to bring the strong dollar down by interventions in the exchange market is to dampen the protectionist fervor. Unfortunately, there are two interrelated reasons to doubt the effectiveness of interventions.

The first reason is that interventions in the foreign exchange markets per se cannot achieve much. True, the Federal Reserve could depress the dollar by buying foreign currencies. Since it creates the dollar, there is no limit. Actually, the Federal Reserve routinely "sterilizes" its interventions; that is to say, when it issues dollars through the foreign exchange market, it takes an equal number of dollars back through open market operations in the domestic money market. It does so because it does not want to lose control over the money supply and is afraid that nonsterilized interventions would be inflationary.

On the other side of the coin, if the German and Japanese central banks intervene to bring the dollar down by selling dollars from their reserves, they take in marks and yen. That would have a deflationary effect that they may not want and would be the opposite of what the United States urges them to do: to expand and not to contract.

All this could be spelled out in greater detail and should be slightly qualified.[21] But the bottom line is that sterilized interventions are practically ineffective and nonsterilized interventions have unacceptable inflationary side effects. Whether really intended, the policy of interventions in the foreign exchange market will not solve the dollar or trade deficit problem; that requires a stronger medicine (see below). The "group of five" report does not abrogate the report of the "group of ten," and the system of floating exchange rates of the major currencies will continue.

The second reason why a policy of internationally coordinated interventions in the foreign exchange markets cannot be expected to do much good is that it does not come to grips with the "funda-mentals," which figure so prominently in the statement of the "group of five." For the problems of the strong dollar, the U.S. capital imports, and the trade deficit, the most important "fundamental economic condition" is the huge U.S. budget deficit. I shall return to this problem below, but briefly stated it is this: contrary to the promises of supply-siders during the vigorous cyclical expansion that started in 1982 and is still alive (although it has lost some of its vigor), the U.S. economy has not generated enough savings to finance private investments and large budget deficits. This gap has been filled by capital imports from abroad, especially from Japan. Thus the capital imports and the trade deficits have been and still are an indispensable prop for U.S. pros-perity. This becomes clear if one asks the question, What would hap-pen if capital imports stopped, say, because foreign investors lost confidence in the U.S. economy? The answer is that interest rates would shoot up, government borrowing would crowd out private investment, the dollar would decline, and prices would rise.

Below I give the reason why the United States cannot continue forever to borrow heavily abroad largely for nonproductive purposes, that is, to finance government budget deficits. The question is what to do about it. The answer is that if and when capital imports decline or cease altogether, as they will sooner or later, it will be imperative that domestic savings increase to fill the gap. Since the government has no control over private savings, in practice that means that gov-ernment deficits, which constitute dissaving on a grand scale, must be reduced.

## From Optimism and Euphoria to Pessimism and Gloom

It was shown that during and immediately after the war it was not widely foreseen that the world was on the threshold of an extended period of high prosperity. Especially the numerous Keynesians ex-pected that the dismal experience of the 1930s would repeat itself. When the expected depression again and again failed to materialize, pessimism gave way to optimism. This reaction was especially strong among Keynesians who thought that Keynesian fine tuning had once and for all eliminated the business cycle. In the 1970s and 1980s the pendulum then swung again in the other direction. Once more the swing was especially pronounced among Keynesians; this was to be expected, because of the excessive promises they had made that re-mained unfulfilled.

We have seen that the latest figures on world trade and output, global as well as for major groups of countries, do not indicate a sharp break in the favorable trend since World War II described by Kuznets. Thus, the pessimism seemed to be premature. But it has been revived by the relatively severe global recession of the late 1970s and early 1980s; it is still not based on what has happened but on what may happen in the future. For one thing, the recession was relatively severe compared with earlier ones, but it was definitely not a depression. There was no decline in economic activity remotely similar to the Great Depression of the 1930s or earlier ones. Moreover, the U.S. economy has staged an unexpectedly vigorous cyclical recovery that started in November 1982. It lifted the world economy out of the doldrums of the recession, although the response of other countries, especially in Western Europe, to the American stimuli was not so vigorous as it had been in earlier recessions.[22]

On the other hand, the U.S. expansion has been increasingly marred by huge budget and trade deficits, and in the first half of 1985 it slowed down, although in the third quarter of 1985 it again picked up some speed.

Central is the problem of the strong, supposedly grossly over-valued dollar. The high-flying dollar and the large trade deficits have had a strong impact on the U.S. economy. They have helped to keep inflation in check and can be said to have moderated the expansion, thus probably prolonging its life. But to call this impact disastrous, as it is often said, not to mention the gross exaggeration that the U.S. economy is threatened with the deindustrialization and degradation to the status of a "service economy," cannot be reconciled with the basic facts: during the period of the rising dollar and mounting trade deficit, from 1980 to 1985, total employment increased by 8 million. Total employment as a percentage of the population over sixteen years of age is as high as it has ever been. True, between 1980 and 1985 employment declined in some industries, but it rose much more in others. Employment declined in twenty-three private nonagricultural industries that had 16.9 million employees in 1980, a decline of 9.6 percent, or 1.6 million. Employment rose in forty-five private non-agricultural industries that had 57.4 million employees in 1980, a rise of 16.4 percent, or 9.4 million.

It is also true that service industries have grown faster than goods-producing industries. But it is well known that this is bound to happen in a period of rising GNP per capita (rising standard of living) and service industries should not be identified with hot dog stands, pizza parlors, and the like.

Contrary to common belief, the shift of employment has not been to unskilled, low-income occupations. Between 1983 and 1985 when total employment increased by 5.5 million, or 5.3 percent, employment in managerial and professional occupations increased by 2.3 million or 10.0 percent. Employment in precision production, craft and repair occupations increased by 1.1 million, or 8.7 percent. Employment of food service workers, on the other hand, increased by only 89,000, or 1.8 percent.

Unemployment is now (September 1985) lower than any month since April 1980 (except for August 1985 when it was one-tenth of a percentage point lower). Although unemployment of workers in some industries has increased, these are few. In the past two years there has been a significant increase in unemployment only for workers from the electrical equipment industries. Some of the industries about which there has been most concern had little or no increase in unemployment. For example, unemployment of people whose last employment was in textile mills was lower in August 1985 than in any August of the previous five years. Although employment in textile mills had declined by 120,000, or 15 percent, in five years those job losers did not remain unemployed.[23]

Summarizing, we can say that the strong dollar and the large trade deficits have caused a shift in employment from traded- to nontraded-goods industries. But they have not prevented the U.S. economy from adding 7.8 million jobs in the past five years.[24] If the protectionists were right that the strong dollar has caused a net loss of millions of jobs in the United States, one would have to assume that the weak currencies in Europe have created millions of new jobs. As we know, the opposite is true. Employment in Europe has declined.

The reasons for the prolonged strength of the dollar are still being hotly debated. In an important recent paper Otmar Emminger calls it "not only the most important, but the most over-explained—and maybe least understood—economic event of our time."[25]

In my opinion there can be no doubt that the huge U.S. budget deficits are an important factor. They drive up interest rates that attract capital from abroad and thus strengthen the demand for dollars.[26] But a moment's reflection shows that the budget deficit is not the only cause of the strong dollar. The superior economic performance of the United States has a double effect on the U.S. balance of payments: by sucking in imports and reducing exports, it increases the trade deficit and by boosting returns on investments it attracts capital from abroad, thus providing automatic financing of the trade deficit.

Thus the United States has been in an almost unique position not to have to worry about financing its external trade deficits because capital from abroad has been readily available. For almost all other countries large government deficits would be poison for the exchange value of their currencies. What has made the American position unique in recent years has been the good performance of the U.S. economy especially compared with Europe. The present European weakness, often referred to as "Eurosclerosis," has been described by European and American economists as a state of inflexibility and rigidity, especially in the labor market, due mainly to excessive welfare measures, such as high minimum wages and the like, and overregulation of industry.[27] As a consequence, unemployment is now higher in Europe than in the United States,[28] and while the American economy has added 16 million jobs in the past ten years, employment has been flat in Europe.[29]

Whether Eurosclerosis is not too strong a word is debatable. The theory has been criticized, for instance, by Otmar Emminger[30] on the ground that the recent large capital flows into the United States have been largely repatriated American capital (or a decrease in U.S. capital exports) and Japanese capital; and Japan's economy can hardly be described as "sclerotic." While this surely is true, I submit that it does not contradict the Eurosclerosis argument. Why did Japanese capital go to the United States rather than to Europe? Why did American capital leave Europe? Eurosclerosis may well be the reason.

The worry about the overvalued dollar seems to give way to, or alternates with, the fear that it may decline too fast and too far; there has been much talk of an impending collapse of the dollar.

Another related cause of worry for the future of the world economy is the international debt problem. There is first the third world debt. Especially the $350 billion Latin American foreign debt seems to be coming to a boil again and is taking on political overtones. Fidel Castro's campaign for a collective Latin American default of all foreign debt seems to strike a sympathetic chord among Latins.

There is, second, the debt problem of the United States. For the first time since 1914 the United States is in the process of becoming or has already become a net foreign debtor. A rapid increase in the foreign debt and a corresponding explosion of interest payments are projected for the future.

I will try now to put the capital inflow and the external deficit in the proper macroeconomic context. It is widely recognized that budget and trade deficits reflect the fact that (contrary to what supply-siders predicted) in the current cyclical upswing the U.S. economy has not generated enough savings to finance the huge budget deficits and the large private sector investments. The capital inflow and the trade deficit have been filling the gap and, thus, have been an indispensable prop for the current prosperity. If the capital inflow fell sharply or came to a halt, say, because foreign investors lost confidence in the dollar, U.S. interest rates would go up, which would put a damper on the economy. And if the trade deficit sharply declined or disappeared—imports declining, exports rising, or both—inflation would accelerate. This would put the Federal Reserve on the spot. If it tried to keep interest rates from rising, it would court inflation; if it tried to keep prices from rising, it would create a recession.

The conclusion seems to be that the capital inflow and trade deficits are beneficial, and that there is no reason to worry. But this is not the whole story. There are at least two reasons for legitimate concern. The first is the unemployment that has been created in some export industries, which has led to intense protectionist pressure. This adjustment problem is a microeconomic problem, the solution of which requires shifts of labor that take time. It will be taken up below with the problem of rising protectionism.

But it should not be forgotten that capital inflows and trade deficits have a vital macroeconomic function at the present time, to enable the economy to maintain a high level of output and employment despite the insufficient domestic saving. This makes it clear that an attempt to eliminate or reduce the trade deficit by import restriction would have disastrous consequences.

The second reason for concern is a long-run problem. What I have in mind I can best explain by distinguishing two extreme cases. The capital from abroad can be used either to finance productive investment in plant and equipment, or it can be used to finance a government budget deficit.

The first case presents no difficulties. Productive investment will increase productivity and GNP growth, thus providing the resources to service the foreign debt without reducing real wages and the standard of living—in other words, without burdening future generations. In this case the growing interest on the foreign debt will not represent an increasing percentage of GNP.

If the capital from abroad finances budget deficits, the situation is entirely different. Budget deficits do not promote productivity and GNP growth. Loans to finance budget deficits are consumption loans. It follows that future interest payments will reduce the standard of living and will require a reduction in real wages below what they otherwise would be. In this case the interest on the foreign debt will rise as a percentage of GNP. This surely is a cause for legitimate concern. That is what those have in mind who warn that heavy borrowing from abroad cannot go on forever. A review of the facts shows beyond a doubt that a far larger part of foreign capital has been used to finance budget deficits than productive investments.

Markets, that is foreign investors, will sooner or later become aware of the growing danger and will get out of the dollar. Needless to add that other developments may have the same effect, for example acceleration of inflation or a recession, or a string of defaults of developing countries endangering U.S. banks. Such developments in other parts of the world would, however, increase investment in the American dollar.

## The New Protectionism in Historical Perspective[31]

There is general agreement, I believe, that the Great Depression of the 1930s was sharply intensified by a protectionist explosion. The United States set a bad example by imposing the skyscraper Smoot-Hawley tariff in 1930 under the Hoover administration. But it is an exaggeration to say that the Smoot-Hawley tariff was the major cause of the depression. The major cause was the monetary contraction. Under the rigid exchange rates of the gold standard the depression in the dominant U.S. economy was bound to spread to the rest of the world. Deficit countries were forced to restrict imports by quotas and exchange controls, and world trade shrank by about 50 percent in nominal terms (gold dollars) and 30 percent in real terms, the difference reflecting the steep decline in prices. Proof of all this is that many countries were able to extricate themselves from the world depression, despite the Smoot-Hawley tariff, by adopting expansionary policies and cutting the link with the dollar long before the U.S. economy emerged from the depression.[32]

It is also generally accepted that the high prosperity in the post–World War II period owes much to the liberalization of world trade that took place during the first twenty years after the war, although the main reason for the contrast between the depressed interwar period and the prosperous post–World War II period was undoubtedly the absence of depressions since the war. World trade has grown by leaps and bounds with only minor declines in recession year.

The liberalization of world trade after World War II occurred largely because of American initiative. Actually, the United States had taken the first step toward trade liberalization soon after World War I when in 1922 it adopted the unconditional most-favored-nation (MFN) principle and gave up the so-called conditional MFN principle, which until then had been the U.S. practice. Then after the protectionist interlude of Smoot-Hawley, in the midst of the Great Depression and the eclipse of economic liberalism, a tiny flame of economic liberalism was lit by the adoption of the "reciprocal trade agreement" policy in 1934. It was the work of Cordell Hull, Roosevelt's secretary of state, a convinced free trader who kept the flicker of liberalism alive during the dark days of the depression and the war. It came into full bloom much later, in the 1940s and 1950s, after the departure of its creator.

In the meantime the General Agreement on Tariffs and Trade had been set up, and in several multilateral conferences under the aegis of GATT the U.S. tariff and that of other countries were sharply reduced.

Although the GATT rules do not stipulate free trade, the MFN principle generalizes tariff concessions made in bilateral ("reciprocal") trade agreements between countries and prohibits discrimination; that is to say, import duties must be the same irrespective of the country of origin. In other words, the GATT rules prohibit preferential tariffs, in principle, with certain exceptions. The economic justification, although simple and compelling, merits spelling out because not only the general public, but also many members of Congress (judged by recent action) seem to be totally ignorant of the most elementary principles of international trade.

Any discrimination distorts trade and is costly. If country A grants preferential lower duties to country B, B's exports will rise but competing exports from a third country, C, will decline. A net increase in A's imports is a good thing on general free trade grounds. But a smaller general reduction in import duties will obviously bring this about more efficiently. Hence at best the preferential tariff reduction is merely a second best. But this is not all. Some of C's exports to A that are shut out may well find their way into B—obviously an inefficient diversion of trade. Moreover, any discriminatory, preferential tariff is administratively messy and costly, because it requires certificates of origin, rules on how much value added qualifies a commodity as originating in B, and invites evasion and cheating.

The GATT rules recognize exceptions from the strict rule of nondiscrimination. Customs unions are an obvious exception. If two or more countries wish to form a customs union—that is to say, to abolish all internal restraints of trade and adopt a common tariff around the combined area—it would not be reasonable to prevent them from doing so. The fact is, however, that a full-fledged customs union is practically impossible nowadays. Even the European Common Market falls far short of the ideal; barriers to trade between the members have not been completely removed, customs inspection at the borders is still in place, and customs officials are still busy trying to justify their existence.

Another exception is that of free trade areas (FTA). An FTA can be defined as a customs union without a common tariff, each member keeping its own tariff against outsiders. This obviously makes it impossible to abolish internal trade restrictions. Customs inspection at the border must continue with the added red tape of certificates of origin, which is a strong inducement for evasion—a very messy system indeed.

The United States, too, has recently entered the murky game in a grand way with an FTA agreement with Israel that went into effect on September 1, 1985, and provides for complete phasing out of all duties and administrative protectionism within the next ten years. A similar arrangement with Canada is under active consideration.

This comes on top of the generalized preferences that the United States has granted to all developing countries and special preferences under the Caribbean Basin Economic Recovery Act of 1984, a most confusing and messy state of affairs and an administrative nightmare. It runs counter to the principle of multilateralism and nondiscrimination underlying the GATT, which has served the world so well. It surely would be much better to have another tariff-cutting round under GATT to reduce tariffs all around and cut back the wild growth of distorting preferential arrangements. The United States has indeed been trying to revive GATT and to extend its scope from goods to services. It is to be hoped that it will succeed, despite the opposition from LDCs. But there is great danger that the administration's efforts will be undercut by the wave of protectionist frenzy that is sweeping through Congress.

It was the large trade and current account deficits and the large capital inflow that have unleased protectionist furies. Hundreds of bills have been introduced in Congress proposing protection for particular industries. One of the most dangerous, because it seems to have strong bipartisan support in the House, is the Jenkins bill, proposed by Ed Jenkins (D-Ga.).[33] It would cut U.S. imports of textiles and apparel by one-third or more. The most depressing and shocking proposal[34] has been made by Senator Lloyd Bentsen of Texas, Representative Dan Rostenkowski of Illinois, and Representative Richard A. Gephardt of Missouri to deal with the problem of the large U.S. trade deficit and rapidly rising foreign debt by imposing a 25 percent selective surcharge on imports from Japan, Brazil, South Korea, and Taiwan, or any country that has a bilateral export surplus with the United States of 65 percent or more, or an export surplus of over 50 percent with the world. Aiming at balancing trade bilaterally with each country is simply preposterous. It is like the village shoemaker trying to square his account with his tailor, carpenter, and doctor by insisting that each of them buy from him as much as he spends on their services. For example, in 1971 U.S. trade was roughly in balance—exports were $44.1 billion, imports $45.6 billion. Yet the United States had a large trade deficit with Japan and Canada, which was counterbalanced by surpluses with Europe, Latin America, and other countries.

The idea that the macroeconomic disequilibrium that manifests itself in the huge trade deficit and inflow of capital from abroad can be removed by protectionist measures is basically wrong for two reasons.

*First*, massive protectionist moves by the United States (massive they would have to be to have an appreciable effect—a high import surcharge or a number of tariffs and quotas on important commodities) would provoke swift retaliation on the part of other countries or a full-blown trade war as Smoot-Hawley did in the 1930s. In such a war there would be only losers.

*Second*, and even more important, we have seen that in the present situation the trade deficit and capital imports are an indispensable support for the U.S. economy because they fill the gap between insufficient domestic savings and the capital required to finance productive private investment and unproductive budget deficits. If that prop disappeared (for example, because foreign investors lost confidence), the dollar would decline, U.S. interest rates would rise, the trade balance would improve, but prices would rise. This would put pressure on the Federal Reserve either to hold the line against inflation and keep interest rates high, which would cause a recession, or to push down interest rates and accommodate inflation; in that case inflation would accelerate and a worse recession would occur later.

This is the true nature of the problem posed by the trade deficit and the capital inflow from abroad. It has been completely missed by the congressional proponents of the selective import surcharge and their academic supporters,[35] when they argue that the threat of the surcharge is meant to be an inducement for the offending surplus countries—Thurow compares them most inappropriately with drunken drivers who must be restrained by the threat of swift punishment—to mend their way. The Japanese export surplus cannot be reduced unless the Japanese stop exporting capital. Suppose the Japanese took the advice given to them and invested all their capital at home instead of exporting it to the United States. That would, as we have just seen, be embarrassing for the United States because the foreign capital is needed to fill the gap between insufficient savings and the capital required to finance private investment and huge government budget deficits.

The conclusion is that a selective import surcharge would be a major policy blunder. It would be counterproductive and in addition would be a clear violation of the U.S. commitment under GATT to abstain from discriminatory measures and would have all the undesirable side effects of discriminatory tariff arrangements, such as wasteful trade diversion and obnoxious red tape.[36] It is most depressing to see prominent members of Congress sponsoring this kind of policy.

While tariffs are no solution, the United States cannot go on forever borrowing abroad on a large scale, mainly for nonproductive purposes. Government deficits, unlike private investment in plant and equipment, do not yield additional output that would make it possible to service the rapidly growing foreign debt without a cut in the standard of living. Obviously this problem must be tackled at home; it cannot be shifted to the Japanese, let alone South Korea, Taiwan, and debt-ridden Brazil. What is necessary is an increase in domestic savings to take the place of foreign capital. Since in a free society the government cannot tell the private sector to save more, government profligacy must be curbed; the government budget deficit, which constitutes dissaving on a grand scale, must be reduced. What is required is not a crash program to balance the budget this year or next, nor a constitutional amendment prohibiting budget deficits from the year 1990 or 2000 on, which would merely divert attention and energies from where they are most needed. What is needed is the adoption *now* of a credible policy of reducing the budget deficit substantially over a period of, for example, three to four years, preferably by cutting expenditures, but if this is politically impossible, also by raising taxes.

### Reviving GATT, Protectionist Stumbling Blocks, and the Cases of Sugar and Textiles

If the administration succeeds in reviving the GATT procedure of reducing tariffs, it will run into fierce opposition from protectionists and defenders of special interests in Congress. To make the next tariff-slashing round—a "Reagan round," comparable to the "Kennedy round"—a success, the United States will have to make concrete proposals: it will have to designate which import duties it is willing to reduce in exchange for particular concessions by other participants in the conference. I present an example of an American offer that would not only bring large long-run benefits to the United States, but also would make a vital contribution to the economic health and political stability of many Caribbean and Central American republics.

What I have in mind is a radical change in the U.S. sugar policy of tight import controls, mainly by quotas. Sugar has a long history of protection in the United States and Europe. In its present vicious form, it is the legacy of the New Deal. According to D. Gale Johnson, in 1934

President Franklin D. Roosevelt sent a message to Congress outlining the structure of a sugar program. He said that one of the objectives was "to provide against further expansion of this necessarily expensive industry." Another objective was to keep down the price of sugar to consumers. A third objective was to retain sugar beet and sugar cane farming within our continental limits.[37]

Only the last objective was achieved. This "evil system" as Johnson calls it, has been in force ever since.

Briefly, the present situation is this. Since 1982 when the policy was reconfirmed and revised, U.S. users of raw sugar have had to pay three to five times as much as they would pay if they could buy sugar at world market prices. In May 1985, the latest figures available, the domestic price of raw sugar was more than seven times the world market price. The quotas have been decreased so that the volume of raw sugar imports has declined from a little over 5 million tons in the crop year 1978-1979 to 2.3 million in 1984-1985.[38] This implies an enormous global misallocation of resources. (The situation is even worse in the European Common Market, but I will concentrate on the American picture.) If restrictions on imports were reduced, imports of sugar would increase and factors of production (labor and capital) would shift from producing and refining sugar into other uses where the United States has a comparative advantage. U.S. GNP would rise and so would GNP in sugar-exporting countries, for example in Central America. There would be some adjustment costs, but I will concentrate on the long-run option. At this point I confine myself to saying that the U.S. economy has shown great flexibility; it is undergoing some adjustments all the time, and the adjustments can be expedited and the cost reduced by appropriate policies (retraining of workers and the like).

I will now discuss briefly the long-term options and indicate their comparative strengths and weaknesses. First, the best solution would be free trade. The United States would import sugar from the most efficient foreign producers. Thus, U.S. GNP and world GNP would be maximized. Obviously, if this ever came to pass, free trade would be approached gradually. I will address the problem of transition, including adjustment costs, later.

Second, if there is to be a certain amount of protection, there are two basic methods: an import tariff or the system of "deficiency payments." Because they minimize government interference with market forces, both are much better than the present system of direct, quantitative restrictions on trade through quotas.

Under a tariff of, for instance 50 percent ad valorem, the domestic price of sugar would be 50 percent higher than the world market price. As consumers of sugar Americans would pay a higher price, but as taxpayers they would get some relief because the difference between the domestic and the world market price would be collected by the U.S. Treasury as an import duty.

Under the system of deficiency payments the domestic price of sugar would be allowed to decline to the world market level, but domestic producers would get the same protection as under the tariff through "deficiency payments," that is, subsidies covering the difference between the world market prices and the stipulated domestic price.

Thus, it would seem that as consumers Americans would be as well off as under free trade. That is why the deficiency payments system is favored by many experts. But we should not forget three disadvantages: First, as taxpayers Americans would lose; second, compared with free trade GNP would be lower, because factors of production would not be shifted from the protected sugar industry to more productive jobs elsewhere; and, third, from the administrative point of view the deficiency payment system clearly is much more complicated and costly than a tariff.[39]

I said that the tariff and deficiency payments system are much better than the present system of direct, quantitative restriction through quotas. The reason is that quotas constitute a much more serious departure from the free market system than tariffs or deficiency payments. In the latter two systems market forces determine how much will be imported, by whom and from where; under the quota system a government bureau sets the volume of imports and by granting import licenses determines who the lucky importers will be. I call them "lucky" because quantitative controls create a large difference between the domestic price and world market price; thus importing becomes a very lucrative business. In other words, import licenses are valuable assets. It stands to reason that would-be importers try hard and spend a lot of money to obtain a slice of the quotas. In the case of sugar, the quotas are allocated to sugar exporting countries. Professor Johnson in a chapter "An Evil System"[40] vividly describes how some foreign countries have succeeded in getting a larger quota by hiring expensive lobbyists to obtain a favorable decision and how others at first failed to understand the rules of the dirty game but, after quickly learning their lesson, have joined the scramble for a slice of the loot—an unsavory system indeed!

What is the solution? To repeat, the ideal solution would be a gradual approach to free trade. Since free trade may not be possible politically, the second-best solution would be a tariff or a deficiency payment system providing about the same degree of protection as the present quota system.

If it is politically unavoidable to put a firm ceiling on the volume of imports of sugar, the best method would be to sell import licenses in a free auction market. That would be technically easy, because sugar is a homogenous commodity.[41] Like the tariff, the auction system for import licenses has the great advantage over the quota system that the price difference goes to the Treasury and not to private individuals, thus eliminating the corrupting features of the quota system. But it is still true that a tariff would be preferable because it allows market forces to determine the volume of imports in response to changes in demand and supply. This is especially important for agricultural products because of annual output changes caused by weather conditions.

It will perhaps be objected that one of the aims of the present system is to give preferential treatment to certain countries, for example, those in Central America. But that can be done much more efficiently by additional aid to enable them to buy import licenses in the free auction market.

Whichever method of protection is used, it is imperative that U.S. sugar imports be substantially increased, not only on purely economic grounds, important though they are, but also on political and national security grounds. The seriousness of the situation has recently been dramatized by a desperate attempt of ten Caribbean Basin countries to persuade the United States to save their economies and social structures from crumbling. In a letter to Secretary of State George P. Shultz they pointed out that the steady closing of the U.S. markets to imports and the decline of the price of sugar in the world market has had a devastating effect on their economies.[42] The strategic implications are ominous indeed. For one thing, the U.S. sugar policy has helped to lock Cuba ever more firmly in the Russian orbit, because the Soviets buy a large part of Cuba's sugar crop at prices substantially above the world market price. There is great danger that the Soviets may seize the opportunity to get a foothold in some other Central American or Caribbean country as well.

The sugar policy of the European Common Market is even more destructive than the U.S. policy. For one thing, natural conditions for producing sugar are less favorable in Europe than in the United States; Europe's disadvantage compared with the tropics is much greater than America's. For another thing, Europe has further increased the plight of the efficient sugar producers in the tropics by dumping sugar on the world markets.

Sugar is an extreme case. The advantages of free trade would be overwhelming. Since the U.S. disadvantage compared with the tropics is enormous, the long-run economic benefits of free or freer trade, too, would be huge. Nobody can argue, as protectionists so often do, that the sugar industry is important from the point of view of national security because it would be vital in case of war. On the contrary, protection of the sugar industry has done much damage to national security and threatens to do much more. Yet well-organized special interests have not only kept the restrictions in place but have even managed to tighten them.

Unfortunately, sugar is not the only case where special interests override the common good in both the economic and the political sense. Outstanding examples are textiles and steel. The political importance stems from the fact that U.S. protection is bound to hit less-developed countries and most embarrassingly clashes with the recent U.S. policy initiatives to provide additional international aid for those nations. This clash was dramatized by an impassioned speech by Prime Minister Lee Kuan Yew of Singapore at a joint session of the two houses of the U.S. Congress. Mr. Lee warned that

> Putting up barriers to America's markets would halt the economic advancement of the free-market-oriented developing countries. . . . Protectionist legislation would signal that the United States was willing to abandon the contest between democracy and the free market on the one hand versus communism and the controlled economy on the other.[43]

He further said the United States "has nearly won this contest for the hearts and minds of the Third World." Mr. Lee's appeal came when the House was ready to give overwhelming approval to the Jenkins bill, which provides slashing textile imports by as much as 40 percent. Lee's appeal induced the speaker of the House to postpone the vote on the textile bill. But it was passed by the House the next day, though with a smaller majority than expected.

Modern democracies, especially in large countries, are susceptible to the protectionist virus. Most congressmen are familiar with one or more firms that suffer from foreign competition. Thus it is natural that special interests unite in a common front against imports, although it should be obvious that the more general the protection, the smaller the gain of any of them.

This weakness of the democratic process is especially pronounced in agriculture. Each state of the union has an agricultural lobby, and many senators have become powerful spokesmen for some branch of agriculture—tobacco, dairy products, citrus fruits, cotton, sugar, and so on. The result is that, although the number of "farmers" has shriveled to 3.3 percent of the population,[44] public spending targeted for the agricultural sector is on the rise. Federal outlays for farm price supports have risen by over 500 percent since 1980 to a current level of $18 billion.[45] Federal outlays for the farm income stabilization program have similarly risen by 100 percent since 1980 to a current level of $7 billion. And a huge bureaucracy administers many other related programs.

Finally, a word is in order about administrative problems posed by quotas on nonhomogenous commodities such as textiles. It stands to reason that quantitative restrictions on hundreds of items of clothing and apparel as prescribed by the Multifiber Arrangement[46] lead to formidable administrative problems, invite evasion and fraud, and cause substantial additional costs. Preferential treatment accorded to developing countries compounds the complexity of the problem.

An article in *The Washington Post*, which deserves being quoted at some length, provides a rare glimpse into this bureaucratic jungle:

Last summer, a Detroit importer received a huge shipment of clothes that were described on shipping documents and labels as women's jogging suits. But U.S. Customs Service officials inspecting the cargo became suspicious when the garments appeared to be much too large for women. Moreover, the styling appeared to be more masculine than feminine. Under questioning, the importer insisted that the suits were properly labeled and that they would be sold in stores that cater to large and tall women. [An investigation found that the Japanese] manufacturer could not obtain a quota for men's jogging suits. Since he could not ship the cargo directly from Japan, he proposed to send it through Taiwan. Anxious to avoid delay, the importer asked that the manufacturer ship the suits direct but label them as women's. As a result of the investigation, the merchandise was seized and civil and criminal charges are pending. The case is one of hundreds that have been documented. [Other examples are] sleeves of a jacket imported through one American port and vests for the same garment [that] were shipped to another. This deceptive practice grew out of an attempt to avoid import quota restrictions on jackets. Asian-made products were shipped to Lebanon and relabeled there as products of that country. An investigation by Customs led to seizures of more than $5 million worth of fake Jordache jeans. Customs intercepted a shipment of more than 6,000 pairs of men's pants from Hong Kong, bearing labels showing them to be 55 percent linen. A laboratory analysis showed them to be 55 percent cotton. Cotton is under a quota; linen isn't.[47]

For every case of fraud detected, there are probably scores of others that have not been found out, and there are surely many cases of perfectly legal evasions and distortions of trade. Nobody has figured out how many "jobs" this kind of policy creates among law enforcers and law breakers.

## Protection and Employment and the Silent Victims

Unemployment, either widespread in recessions and depressions or concentrated in particular industries competing with imports, is the major cause of the clamor for protection. At present it is the latter; there is no recession unemployment now, although the rhetoric of the protectionists in Congress and elsewhere often gives the impression that the United States is in the midst of a deep recession.

Many economists on both sides of the political fence (for example, Martin Feldstein and Charles Schultze) have patiently explained why protection does not increase employment. True, it may create or save jobs in some protected industries, but more productive jobs are lost in export and in capital-intensive industries.

Protection affects export industries in different ways. The most direct way is through retaliation of other countries to U.S. protection. Even without retaliatory measures of foreign governments, foreign demand for U.S. products will decline because of the adverse effect of U.S. protection on foreign economies. This is especially obvious in the case of LDCs whose capacity to import depends largely on their ability to export to the United States. Another adverse effect on U.S. exports results from the fact that the products of the protected industries whose prices go up are often important ingredients of export industries. For example, protection of the steel industry has sharply raised steel prices. This increase has pushed up the cost of U.S. export products, making them less competitive abroad and causing the loss of many jobs. If there is no retaliation abroad, U.S. protection will push up the dollar, which again causes a loss of jobs in the export industries and in import-competing industries.[48]

The adverse impact of protection on capital-intensive (interest-sensitive) industries is a little more complicated. It stems from the fact that interest rates will be pushed up if protection succeeds in its main purpose of reducing the trade deficits. The reason is that a reduction of the trade deficit will entail an equal reduction of capital imports. As we have seen, capital imports are now a vital prop for the U.S. economy, filling the gap between insufficient domestic saving and capital requirements and holding down interest rates.

Economists often express surprise that the victims of protection, consumers who have to pay higher prices and the export industries, do not speak up, at least not so loudly, as the special interests of the protected industries and their spokesmen in Congress.

Actually, this contrast is not hard to explain. The favorable effect of protection on output and employment is highly visible because it is concentrated in the protected industries. The unfavorable consequences on the consumer are spread out more or less thinly depending on the type of product. The unfavorable effect on export industries, though compelling, is indirect and requires some economic analysis, which, though elementary, is not the forte of the general public or of the average congressman.

Quantitative restrictions on imports, which, unfortunately, have become more and more popular in recent times, often have the effect of silencing opposition to protection. If import licenses are issued to foreign exporters under a quota system, the latter become accomplices of domestic protectionists because they pocket the price differences created by the restriction. This was, for example, the case when the United States set quotas for Japanese automobiles exported to the United States. It was estimated that this policy amounted to an annual subsidy of over $2 billion a year to the Japanese exporters at the U.S. taxpayers' expense. Naturally, the foreign exporters lose all incentive to oppose the restrictions, which they otherwise would have done by bringing pressure on their government to seek a change in policy. The same may happen if the licenses are issued to well-organized domestic importers (dealers).

The same type of analysis can be usefully applied to the opposite of protection, that is, to liberalization of trade. The removal of import restrictions will initially create some unemployment in the hitherto protected industries. But there will be favorable effects elsewhere. Consumers will pay less for imported goods. Export industries will experience improvements corresponding to the adverse effects of protection analyzed above. Some costs, for example of imported steel, will be reduced, making such products more competitive abroad. Demand from abroad will increase because larger exports will enable foreign countries to buy more from the country that has liberalized trade. Another boon for the export industries will be the fact that the currency will decline in the foreign exchange market. Those changes will at least partially offset the initial deterioration of the trade balance caused by the liberalization.

Of course, the full benefits of liberalization of trade will materialize gradually as the economy adjusts to the new conditions, as factors of production, labor, and capital shift to more productive employment in export industries and elsewhere. But there are adjustment costs for the industries involved, early retirement, capital losses, as well as transitional unemployment, which are painful for the workers concerned. The U.S. economy has shown great flexibility, however. In fact, such adjustments are going on all the time throughout the economy, not only in the traded-goods sector, where they receive special attention. Fortunately, these general impressions and informed guesses have been confirmed by careful statistical studies.

One specific area where studies have been made on both the costs of protectionism and the transitional unemployment caused by liberalization of trade is U.S. textiles, an industry that is heavily protected by tariffs, quotas, and nontariff restrictions. A study by the World Bank concludes that these import restrictions save about 116,000 jobs and that the cost of permanent protection would be about $80,000 for each job.[49] This amounts to placing a $10 billion tax on U.S. consumers to subsidize a comparatively inefficient industry. This surely is job creation at an outrageously high cost.

The fact remains, however, that for the textile worker the loss of his job is a painful experience. But in a dynamic economy this is unavoidable. Unemployment benefits and retraining will mitigate the hardship and expedite the adjustment. A special study in this volume by Marvin Kosters indicates that the average duration of unemployment for displaced workers is twenty-three weeks. Furthermore, they are typically reemployed at 90 percent of their previous real wage.[50] These studies in conjunction with the fact that the U.S. economy has added about 3 million jobs in the past year should make us optimistic about the ability of the U.S. economy to shift from noncompetitive to productive industries.

In the case of trade liberalization, there is nothing corresponding to retaliation in response to protection. In other words, other countries are likely to follow the bad example of protection but are unlikely to respond to the good example of liberalization. This makes it all the more important to revive the GATT procedure of multilateral conferences to reduce tariffs all around.

# Notes

1. Richard T. Ely Lecture, *American Economic Review*, vol. 67 (February 1977), p. 14. Kuznets's findings about growth in the less-developed countries are reported at great length in his *Economic Growth of Nations: Total Output and Production Structure* (Cambridge, Mass.: Harvard University Press, 1971), chap. 1, and in his paper "Aspects of Post-World War II Growth in Less Developed Countries," in A. M. Tang, E. M. Westfield, and James E. Worley,

eds., *Evolution, Welfare, and Time in Economics: Essays in Honor of Nicholas Georgescu-Roegen* (Lexington, Mass.: Lexington Books, 1976), chap. 3. Kuznets's findings have been confirmed in an important paper by Irving Kravis and Robert Lipsey, "The Diffusion of Economic Growth in the World Economy, 1950–80," in John Kendrick, ed., *International Comparisons of Productivity and Causes of the Slowdown* (Cambridge, Mass.: Ballinger, 1984), pp. 109–52. The authors use later data, which have become available since Kuznets wrote, covering the period 1950–1980.

2. Kuznets, "Aspects of Post-World War II Growth," p. 41.

3. Ibid., p. 41.

4. See, for example, *World Economic Survey 1981–1982, Current Trends in the World Economy*, United Nations Publication E.82.II.C.1, and Edward F. Denison, *Trends in American Economic Growth, 1929–1982* (Washington, D.C.: Brookings Institution, 1985).

5. See Herbert Giersch, "Eurosclerosis" Arthur F. Burns, *My Mission in Germany*, forthcoming; Assar Londbeck, "What Is Wrong with the West European Economies (Institute for International Economic Studies, University of Stockholm), Reprint series no. 287; and Arthur F. Burns, "The Economic Sluggishness of Western Europe" (University of Dubuque, September 1984).

6. See IMF, *World Economic Outlook October 1985* (Washington, D.C.: Oxford University Press), p. 63.

7. See my paper "Liberal and Illiberal Development Policy, 'Free Trade Like Honesty Still Remains the Best Policy'," in *Pioneers in Development*, volume II, to be published by the World Bank.

8. See Joseph A. Schumpeter, "The Decade of the Twenties," *American Economic Review* (March 1946), reprinted in R. V. Clemence, ed., *Essays of Joseph A. Schumpeter* (Cambridge, Mass., 1951), p. 214. See also Roy F. Harrod, "Review of *A Monetary History of the United States 1856–1960*, by Milton Friedman and Anna Schwartz," *University of Chicago Law Review* (1964), p. 191. Harrod's overall judgment is that it "is a truly great book." p. 196.

9. E. A. G. Robinson, *Economic Planning in the United Kingdom* (Cambridge: University Press, 1967), p. 43.

10. See my paper, "The Great Depression of the 1930s—Can It Happen Again?" *The Business Cycle and Public Policy, 1920–80*, a compendium of papers submitted to the Joint Economic Committee, Congress of the United States, November 28, 1980, and American Enterprise Institute Reprint no. 118, Washington, D.C., January 1981.

11. *The Economist*, February 4, 1984, p. 13.

12. "The Dollar Problem—II" in *The Economist*, December 4, 1943, pp. 750–51. This statement was quoted in my paper "Dollar Shortage?" in Seymour E. Harris, ed., *Foreign Economic Policy for the United States* (Cambridge, Mass.: Harvard University Press, 1948), p. 436. The last part of the article in *The Economist* deserves mention because it highlights the low level of the discussion at that time: "It would be a mistake to reach a conclusion of hopelessness. There may be hitherto unrevealed factors that will help to solve the problem—for example, an inflationary rise in costs in the United States unaccompanied by any fall of the dollar or any enhancement of tariffs" (p. 751). The writer

did not realize that inflation in the United States has the same effect on the balance of payments as an appreciation of the dollar or a depreciation of sterling. For further references to the literature, see Peter Bauer and Alan A. Walters, "The State of Economics" in *The Journal of Law & Economics*, vol. 18, no. 1 (April 1975), pp. 1–23, updated in P. T. Bauer, *Equality, the Third World and Economic Delusion*, part 3, "The State of the Economy" (Cambridge, Mass.: Harvard University Press, 1981).

13. J. R. Hicks, "The Long-Run Dollar Problem" in *Essays in World Economics*, Oxford 1959. Extracts from J. R. Hicks, "Inaugural Lecture" in *Oxford Economic Papers*, Oxford 1953. D. H. Robertson, *Britain in the World Economy*, London 1954. Needless to add that their versions of the theory are much more sophisticated than the one of *The Economist*.

14. Alfred Marshall, *Money, Credit and Commerce* (London: Macmillan, 1973, 1924), p. 171.

15. Ibid., p. 354.

16. See Peter T. Bauer, "Economists and the Two Dollar Problems," *Equality, the Third World and Economic Delusion* (Cambridge, Mass.: Harvard University Press, 1981), p. 214.

17. As far as Britain is concerned, all these matters have been thoroughly discussed and evaluated with copious excerpts from, and references to, the literature by T. W. Hutchinson in *Economics and Economic Policy in Britain 1946–1966* (London: Allen and Unwin, 1968).

18. See "The Functioning of the International Monetary System," A Report to the Ministers and Governors by the Group of Deputies, Group of Ten, in *IMF Survey. Supplement on the Group of 10 Deputies' Report*, Washington, D.C., July 1985.

19. The "group of twenty-four," representing the developing countries, too, has issued a report titled, "The Functioning and Improvement of the International Monetary System." The report covers the same ground as the report of the "group of ten," which it resembles in many ways. But as one would expect, in addition it goes into the debt problem and calls for new SDR allocations and other handouts for the developing countries. The report stresses the weakness of the present system of floating exchange rates (excessive volatility) and unsurprisingly has a tendency to comment upon the perceived duties and failings of the industrial countries. It also shows a predilection for the latest gadgets such as target zones for exchange rates and the assignment of different roles to monetary and fiscal policy.

20. See the "Group of 5 Communique," *IMF Survey*, Washington, D.C., October 7, 1985, p. 297.

21. I discussed the problem at some length in my contribution "The International Monetary System in the World Recession" in William Fellner, ed., *Essays in Contemporary Economic Problems: Disinflation*, 1983-1984 Edition (Washington, D.C.: American Enterprise Institute, 1984).

22. See *International Trade 1983/84*, General Agreement on Tariffs and Trade (GATT), Geneva 1984. The reasons GATT cites for the sluggish European response are the usual ones: structural rigidities and inflexibilities due to overregulation of industries, excessive welfare and unemployment benefits,

fragmentation of the economy despite the common market. As a result unemployment in Europe is now much higher than in the United States. This has been highlighted by a recent report of the Institute for World Economics, Kiel, West Germany: *Das amerikanische Beschäftigungswunder: Was sich daraus lernen lässt?* (*The American Employment Miracle: What Can be Learned from It?*), Kiel Discussion Paper no. 109, July 1985.

23. The figures presented here on the labor force are taken from Herbert Stein, "Statement before the Subcommittee on Employment and Productivity, Labor and Human Resources Committee, United States Senate," October 22, 1985. Computations are based on the monthly *Employment and Earnings* issued by the Department of Labor, Bureau of Labor Statistics, Washington, D.C.

24. See *Employment and Earnings,* October 1985, p. 98, and *Employment and Earnings,* October 1980, p. 98, U.S. Department of Labor, Bureau of Labor Statistics, Washington, D.C.

25. See Otmar Emminger, "The Dollar's Borrowed Strength" in *Group of Thirty,* Occasional Paper no. 19, New York, April 1985, p. 3.

26. With all due respect to supply-siders. See my paper "International Issues Raised by Criticisms of the U.S. Budget Deficits" in Phillip Cagan, ed., *Contemporary Economic Problems—The Economy in Deficit* (Washington, D.C.: American Enterprise Institute, 1985).

27. See, for example, Stephen Marris, "Why Europe's Recovery Is Lagging Behind: With an Unconventional View of What Should Be Done about It," *Europe, Magazine of the European Community* (March/April 1984).

I have commented on Marris's paper and have offered additional reasons for Europe's weakness, such as its economic fragmentation—despite the so-called common market—compared with the large internal free trade area of continental size enjoyed by the United States. See my contribution to *CEP* 1985, pp. 130–32, and my book, *The Problem of Stagflation* (Washington, D.C.: American Enterprise Institute, 1985), pp. 57–60, and the literature mentioned there. See, also, Arthur F. Burns, *The Economic Sluggishness of Western Europe,* the Dunlap Distinguished American Lecture, University of Dubuque, Iowa, September 1984.

28. The only exception is Switzerland with 1 percent unemployment.

29. See *Monthly Labor Review,* August 1985, p. 65, table 9.

30. Emminger.

31. Since this was written the late Jan Tumlir's little classic, *Protectionism: Trade Policy in Democratic Societies* (Washington D.C.: American Enterprise Institute, 1985), has become available.

32. For a fuller discussion, see my papers *The World Economy, Money, and the Great Depression 1919–1939; The Great Depression of the 1930s: Can It Happen Again?;* and *The Problem of Stagflation: Reflections on the Microeconomic Theory and Policy,* all published by the American Enterprise Institute, Washington, D.C.

33. For remarks made by Mr. Jenkins in the House of Representatives, U.S. Congress, see "The Textile and Apparel Trade Enforcement Act of 1985" in *Congressional Record,* March 19, 1985. The bill, HR 1562, was later amended by the Senate to protect shoe manufacturers and copper mining also. After

being passed by both houses of Congress, the amended version was vetoed by President Reagan. An attempt to override the veto is expected in 1986.

34. See H.R. 3035, *A Bill to Restore Balance in International Trade, to Improve the Operation of the Trade Agreements Program, and for Other Purposes*, House of Representatives, Ninety-ninth Congress, 1st session.

35. See, for example, Professor Lester Thurow, "America's Plunge into the Debt Abyss," the *New York Times*, September 3, 1985.

36. All this was pointed out in a recent report of the Congressional Budget Office Staff Working Paper, *The Effects of Targeted Import Surcharges*, Congress of the United States, August 1985.

37. See D. Gale Johnson, *The Sugar Program: Large Costs and Small Benefits* (Washington, D.C.: American Enterprise Institute, 1974), p. 1.

38. *Sugar and Sweetener Outlook and Situation Yearbook*, United States Department of Agriculture, July 1985, SSRV10N2, p. 23, table 14.

39. The complexity and cost of operating a deficiency payments system depends on the structure of the industry. For example, with thousands of farmers growing sugar beets, the cost of operating a deficiency payments system must be considerable.

40. Johnson, pp. 33–40.

41. For nonhomogeneous commodities, for example automobiles or textiles, the administrative problems of quotas are formidable. To express quantities in terms of numbers of automobiles or textiles is clearly unsatisfactory. Thus the Japanese automobile exporters switched to larger, more expensive models. Value quotas are generally unattractive. There simply is no satisfactory substitute for free markets.

42. See news dispatch in the *Washington Post*, August 19, 1985. See also the article "Enslaved by Subsidies" in *The Economist*, August 10, 1985.

43. See the *Wall Street Journal*, October 10, 1985, and other newspapers.

44. See *Employment and Earnings*, Department of Labor, Bureau of Labor Statistics, Washington, D.C., October 1985, p. 28.

45. U.S. Office of Management and Budget, *The Budget of the United States Government*, annual.

46. The Multifiber Arrangement is well described in *Trade Policy Issues and Developments*, Occasional Paper no. 38, International Monetary Fund, Washington, D.C., July 1985, pp. 40–45:

> Over the past 25 years, trade in textiles and clothing has been regulated under international agreements. Following the Short-Term Arrangement Regarding International Trade in Textiles (October 1961– September 1962), and the Long-Term Arrangement Regarding International Trade in Cotton Textiles (October 1962–73), the Multifiber Arrangement (MFA) came into existence as a "temporary" derogation from normal GATT rules. The MFA's stated objectives are to achieve the expansion and progressive liberalization of world trade in textile products, while at the same time avoiding disruptive effects in individual markets and in individual lines of production in both importing and exporting countries. The original MFA (1974–78) was succeeded by MFA II (1978–81) and extended in December 1981 by

MFA III (1982–July 1986). By mid-1984, there were 42 participants in the MFA. . . . Restraints under the MFA have been applied almost exclusively to products from developing countries. A recent GATT review of operations so far under MFA III indicates that restraints were generally more extensive and more restrictive, compared with MFA II (pp. 40-41).

The pernicious effects of the MFA have been critically analyzed in considerable detail by Dean Spinanger, "Protektion im internationalen Handel mit Textilien und Beleidung—Auswirkungen des Multifaserabkommens" in *Die Weltwirtschaft*, 1985, Heft 1, Institut für Weltwirtschaft an der Universität Kiel, West Germany. See, also, Ying-Pik Choi, Hwa Soo Chung, and Nicholas Marian, *The Multi-Fibre Arrangement in Theory and Practice* (Dover, N.H.: Frances Pinter, 1985).

47. Rudolph A. Pyatt, Jr., "Hundreds of Fraud Cases Exacerbate Import Woes," *Washington Post*, October 13, 1985.

48. By cutting down U.S. imports, U.S. protection reduces the supply of dollars in the foreign exchange market; hence the dollar goes up. By cutting down U.S. exports, foreign retaliation reduces the demand for dollars; hence the dollar tends to go down. Therefore, the net outcome is indeterminate and can probably be neglected.

49. *World Development Report 1984* (New York: Oxford University Press, 1984), p. 40.

50. The study by the World Bank in *The World Development Report 1984* reaches a similar conclusion.

# CONTRIBUTORS

**Phillip Cagan**—*Editor*
Professor of economics, Columbia University; former senior staff economist for the Council of Economic Advisers. Visiting scholar with the American Enterprise Institute.

**Sven W. Arndt**
Resident scholar in International Economics and director of the International Trade Project, American Enterprise Institute; on leave from the University of California, Santa Cruz. Previously director of international monetary research, U.S. Treasury Department.

**Edgar K. Browning**
Professor of economics, Texas A & M University; former professor of economics, University of Virginia.

**Bruce L. Gardner**
Professor of economics, University of Maryland; former professor of agricultural economics, Texas A & M University.

**Gottfried Haberler**
Galen L. Stone Professor of International Trade Emeritus, Harvard University, and past president of the American Economic Association and of the International Economic Association. Resident scholar with the American Enterprise Institute.

**Rosemary Gibson Kern**
Research associate, Center for Health Policy Research, American Enterprise Institute.

**Marvin H. Kosters**
Director of Government Regulation Studies, American Enterprise Institute.

## Jack A. Meyer

Resident fellow in economics and director of Health Policy Studies, American Enterprise Institute; former assistant director of the U.S. Council on Wage and Price Stability.

## David H. Pyle

Booth Professor of Banking and Finance, School of Business Administration, University of California, Berkeley

## Joel Slemrod

Associate professor of economics, University of Minnesota; former senior economist with the Council of Economic Advisers.

## John C. Weicher

Resident fellow and first scholar named to the F. K. Weyerhaeuser Chair in Public Policy Research at the American Enterprise Institute; former deputy assistant secretary at the U.S. Department of Housing and Urban Development and past president of the American Real Estate and Urban Economics Association.

## Bruce Yandle

Professor of economics, Clemson University; former consultant with the U.S. Council on Wage and Price Stability.

## DATE DUE

| | | | |
|---|---|---|---|
| SEP 03 1986 | | | |
| DEC 0 3 1986 | | | |
| AUG 1 9 1987 | | | |
| DEC 1 4 1988 | | | |
| APR 1 2 1994 | | | |

DEMCO 38-297

Essays in Contem, Cagan, ed. (19    Phillip

Essays in Contemp ect director (19    , proj-

The Politics of Ina eds. (1986, 344    mbra,

Crisis in the Budge by David Stock Ornstein (1986,    papers rman

Protectionism: Tra $4.95)    2 pp.,

Future Markets: Tl    21.95)

Futures Markets: F    24.95)

Real Tax Reform: F    53.95)

U.S. Agricultural P 385 pp., $22.95    1985,

• Mail orders for Seventeenth Street, add 10 percent of to orders) • For info 800-424-2873 (in W out notice. • Paya    1150 dling, -epaid 1 free with-

The American Enterprise Institute invites your participation in the competition of ideas through its AEI Associates Program. This program has two objectives: (1) to extend public familiarity with contemporary issues; and (2) to increase research on these issues and disseminate the results to policy makers, the academic community, journalists, and others who help shape public policies. The areas studied by AEI include Economic Policy, Education Policy, Energy Policy, Fiscal Policy, Government Regulation, Health Policy, International Programs, Legal Policy, National Defense Studies, Political and Social Processes, and Religion, Philosophy, and Public Policy. For the $49 annual fee, Associates receive

- a subscription to *Memorandum*, the newsletter on all AEI activities
- the AEI publications catalog and all supplements
- a 30 percent discount on all AEI books
- a 40 percent discount for certain seminars on key issues
- subscriptions to any two of the following publications: *Public Opinion*, a bimonthly magazine exploring trends and implications of public opinion on social and public policy questions; *Regulation*, a bimonthly journal examining all aspects of government regulation of society; and *AEI Economist*, a monthly newsletter analyzing current economic issues and evaluating future trends (or for all three publications, send an additional $12).

*Call 202/862-6446 or write:*    AMERICAN ENTERPRISE INSTITUTE
1150 Seventeenth Street, N.W., Suite 301, Washington, D.C. 20036